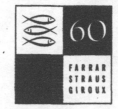

60

FARRAR
STRAUS
GIROUX

Praise for

THE ASSASSINS' GATE

"Absorbing . . . Packer provides page after page of vivid description of the haphazard, poorly planned and almost criminally executed occupation of Iraq. In reading him we see the staggering gap between abstract ideas and concrete reality."
—Fareed Zakaria, *The New York Times Book Review* (cover review)

"Packer is a rare combination: an excellent reporter, a sophisticated analyst and a fine writer . . . He has given us a remarkable history of the Iraq war, a work of keen analysis, superb reporting and deep compassion."
—Gary Kamiya, *Salon.com*

"A deftly constructed and eloquently told account of the war's origins and aftermath . . . Deeply human and maddeningly vivid."
—Daniel Kurtz-Phelan, *Los Angeles Times Book Review*

"[Packer] has succeeded in creating a book that is not only relevant but discerning and provocative. Using on-the-ground reporting and a talent for storytelling, he offers the vivid detail and balanced analysis that have made him one of the leading chroniclers of the Iraq war."
—Yonatan Lupu, *San Francisco Chronicle*

"[Packer] deftly moves among the originators and the victims of the war . . . Essential reading for anyone interested in how the United States stumbled into Mideast quicksand." —*The Boston Globe*

"[This book] is much more than an investigation of failure. It is an engrossing account of war and chaos, and it provides rich portraits of ordinary Iraqis, about whom we know so little from daily news reports." —Patrick Coolican, *The Seattle Times*

"The most complete, sweeping, and powerful account of the Iraq War yet written . . . The portrait he paints of Iraq in the year and a half after the invasion is full and vivid and utterly, utterly damning . . . Packer has done something more valuable than write the tale of his own disillusionment. He has depicted in stark colors the disillusionment of an entire nation."　　　　　　　　　—Keith Gessen, *New York*

"Packer is a storyteller, and an artful one."

—Chris Toensing, *The Nation*

"The great strength of George Packer's *The Assassins' Gate* is that it gives a fair hearing to both views. Free of cant—but not, crucially, of anger—Mr. Packer has written an account of the Iraq War that will stand alongside such narrative histories as *A Bright Shining Lie*, *Fire in the Lake* and *Hell in a Very Small Place*. As a meditation on the limits of American power, it's sobering. As a pocket history of Iraq and the United States' tangled history, it's indispensable. As an examination of the collision between arrogance and good intentions, it could scarcely be improved upon."　　　　—Tom Bissell, *The New York Observer*

"Bravura frontline reporting and laser-targeted analysis."

—*Men's Journal*

"Packer's book is written with great clarity and draws on his experience as one of *The New Yorker*'s more perceptive reporters . . . The people he writes about—Washington neoconservatives, CPA bureaucrats, and ordinary Iraqis whose lives were turned upside down by decisions made elsewhere—speak to the reader in their own voices."

—Peter Galbraith, *The New York Review of Books*

"To describe [Packer's] new book as smart and well-written (which it is) would not be saying very much . . . Snippets of the book won't convey the range of its coverage, the variety of portraiture and incident it records. Nor can it more than hint at the remarkable precision and control of the prose."　　　　　　　—Scott McLemee, *Newsday*

"The best book yet written on the Iraq war."

—Adam Kirsch, *The New York Sun*

"The richest, most unsettling synthesis of reporting and careful thinking to come out of either Washington or Baghdad about the conflict . . . A rigorous, sustained inquiry into the clashing expectations for Iraq, how the war was planned, and the staggering wreckage of Iraqi society."
—Robert Ruby, *The Baltimore Sun*

"This is the first truly great book of the Iraq war."
—*The Washington Monthly*

"George Packer, a staff writer for *The New Yorker*, blends on-the-scene reporting and thoughtful analysis in a sobering account of the unfinished war in Iraq and its impact on Americans and Iraqis. He cheers the demise of Saddam, while questioning a war with deep roots in history, but far from inevitable."
—Bob Minzesheimer, *USA Today*

"The Iraq debate has long needed someone who is both tough-minded enough, and sufficiently sensitive, to register all its complexities. In George Packer's work, this need is answered . . . Packer has a genuine instinct for what the Iraqi people have endured and are enduring, and writes with admirable empathy. His own opinions are neither suppressed nor intrusive: he clearly welcomes the end of Saddam while having serious doubts about the wisdom of the war, and he continually tests himself against experience."
—Christopher Hitchens, *Publishers Weekly*

"In the midst of a war that has raised thousands of questions, George Packer has given us a brilliant, moving, and essential book with answers. Packer, who was an up-close witness to the prewar debates and the wartime carnage, cuts past the simplistic recriminations and takes us on an unforgettable journey that begins on a trail of good intentions and winds up on a devastating trail of tears. If you want to understand how Iraq became a quagmire, and who the human beings are who suffer its consequences, you must read this book."
—Samantha Power, Pulitzer Prize–winning author of
"A Problem from Hell": *America and the Age of Genocide*

© Greg Martin

George Packer

THE ASSASSINS' GATE

George Packer is a staff writer for *The New Yorker* and the author of several books, including *Blood of the Liberals* (FSG, 2000), winner of the 2001 Robert F. Kennedy Award. He is also the editor of the anthology *The Fight Is for Democracy.* His reporting from Iraq won an Overseas Press Club award. He lives in Brooklyn.

ALSO BY GEORGE PACKER

NONFICTION

The Village of Waiting
Blood of the Liberals

FICTION

The Half Man
Central Square

AS EDITOR

The Fight Is for Democracy:
Winning the War of Ideas in America and the World

THE
ASSASSINS'
GATE

THE ASSASSINS' GATE

AMERICA IN IRAQ

■

GEORGE PACKER

FARRAR, STRAUS AND GIROUX

NEW YORK

Farrar, Straus and Giroux
18 West 18th Street, New York 10011

Portions of this work originally appeared, in different form, in The New Yorker and
The New York Times Magazine.

The Library of Congress has cataloged the hardcover edition as follows:
Packer, George, 1960–
    The assassins' gate : America in Iraq / George Packer.—1st ed.
    p.   cm.
ISBN-13: 978-0-374-29963-7 (hardcover : alk. paper)
ISBN-10: 0-374-29963-3 (hardcover : alk. paper)
1. Iraq War, 2003.   2. Insurgency—Iraq.   3. Civil war—Iraq.   4. Iraq War, 2003—
Occupied territories.   5. Americans—Iraq.   6. Iraq—Politics and government—2003–
7. United States—Politics and government—2001–   I. Title.

DS79.76.P33 2005
956.7044'3—dc22

2005011521

Paperback ISBN-13: 978-0-374-53055-6
Paperback ISBN-10: 0-374-53055-6

Designed by Abby Kagan

www.fsgbooks.com

For Laura

Dive into the sea, or stay away.
—Nizar Qabbani

CONTENTS

Contents

THE
ASSASSINS'
GATE

PROLOGUE

IN THE SHADE of a high sandstone arch, a Bradley Fighting Vehicle and a platoon of American soldiers from the First Armored Division guarded the main point of entry into the vast and heavily fortified Green Zone along the west bank of the Tigris River, where the Coalition Provisional Authority governed occupied Iraq. When I arrived in Baghdad in the summer of 2003 and first saw the arch, I mistook it for one of the city's antique gates, built during the time of the caliphs to keep out Persian invaders. The American soldiers referred to it by a name that seemed to have come straight out of the *Thousand and One Nights*. They called it the Assassins' Gate.

Early every morning, before the sun grew dangerous, crowds of Iraqis gathered at the Assassins' Gate. Some were job seekers; others were protesters carrying banners—"Please Re-open Our Factories," "We Wish to See Mr. Frawley." Demonstrators brought their causes here and sometimes turned into rioters. A man handed out copies of a table printed in English and Arabic and titled "The Names of Victims of execution of my family." Many people carried letters addressed to L. Paul Bremer III, the top civilian administrator in Iraq. With the old order overthrown, the Baath Party authorities purged, and the ministries stripped bare by looters, most Iraqis didn't know where to take their grievances and petitions, where to unload the burden of their personal histories. So, like supplicants to the caliph of ancient Baghdad, they brought them directly to the front gate of the occupation. But few Iraqis had the credentials to enter the Green Zone, and interpreters at the gate were rare. The Iraqis stood on one side of coils of concertina wire, gesturing and trying to explain why they needed to get in; on the other side stood Americans doing twelve-hour shifts of checkpoint duty in body armor, keeping them out.

One day in July, a tiny woman in a salmon-colored veil stepped out of the crowd and thrust a handwritten letter up at me. She was a schoolteacher, about thirty, with glasses and thick white face powder and an expression so exaggeratedly solemn that she might have been a mime performing grief. The letter, which was eighteen pages long, requested an audience with "Mister respectable, merciful American ambassador Pawal Bramar." It contained a great deal of detailed advice on the need to arm the Iraqi people so they could help fight against the guerrilla resistance. The teacher, who was well under five feet tall, wanted permission to carry an AK-47 and work alongside American soldiers against the beasts who were trying to restore the tyrant or bring Iranian-style oppression. She showed me the fake gun permit drawn up to illustrate her desire. She had left her position teaching English at a girls' school in the Shiite slum called Sadr City, rather than submit to the dictates of the radical Muslims who had taken charge after the overthrow of Saddam and ordered the staff to poison the girls' minds against the Americans.

"In the beginning, the Americans treat Iraqi people well," the teacher said. "But later, because Iraqis are beasts, they attack Americans and kill them, and this will affect Americans' psychology badly and so they live in more isolation from Iraqi people." She had information—it came from the most reliable source in Baghdad, she said, the children in the street—that the tyrant and his followers were cutting off the heads of Americans (this was almost a year before the first known beheading in Iraq). The stories had made her ill. She was having trouble sleeping, she said, and had all but stopped eating.

A man with a cane hobbled over from the line. His left hand, wrapped in a bandage, was missing the thumb. He explained to the teacher in Arabic that his father had been killed by a missile in the Iran-Iraq War, that he had been paralyzed in a car accident while fleeing Kuwait at the end of the Gulf War, and that at some point he had lost the piece of paper entitling him to hospital care. Now that the Americans were in charge, he felt emboldened to ask for another copy—and so he had come to the Assassins' Gate. The man, unshaven and wretched looking, began to cry. The teacher told him not to be sad, to trust in God, and to speak with the American soldiers at the checkpoint. He shuffled back into line.

"Please, sir, can you help me?" she continued. "I must work with Americans, because my psychology is demolished by Saddam Hussein. Not just me. All Iraqis. Psychological demolition."

Our conversation was brief, and it would have been briefer if my driver and translator, both of whom thought the woman completely insane, had succeeded in pulling me away at the start. Months later I saw her again: Somehow she had landed a job translating for the American soldiers who inspected IDs and searched people entering the Green Zone through another checkpoint. She had grown fat and acquired a pair of designer sunglasses.

I seldom think about Iraq without remembering the schoolteacher standing outside the Assassins' Gate, the abrupt intensity of her stare and speech, the sense that there was madness and truth in her all at once. That first summer after the Americans arrived, Iraq had the heightened, vivid, confused quality of a dream, washed in the relentless yellow sunlight. The hesitations and niceties of normal life dropped away. Something extraordinary was happening. No one knew what it was or how it would go, but it mattered more than anything and there wasn't much time.

Later on I learned that I'd been wrong about the Assassins' Gate. It wasn't ancient; Saddam built it some years ago in grandiose imitation of Baghdad's classical entrances. It wasn't even the Assassins' Gate—not to the Iraqis. The name drew blank looks from them, and then annoyance. They called it, more prosaically, *Bab al-Qasr*, the Palace Gate, because the road that passed under the arch led to Saddam's Republican Palace, a mile or so away, where the occupation authority had its headquarters. "Assassins' Gate" came from the nickname of the soldiers positioned there, who belonged to Alpha Company: A for Assassins, like "Kilroy was here." It was an American invention for an ersatz Iraqi monument, a misnomer for a mirage. Iraqis complained about the way the U.S. military renamed their highways and buildings and redrew their district lines. It reminded them that something alien and powerful had been imposed on them without their consent, and that this thing did not fit easily with the lives they'd always known, it pulled and chafed, though it had also relieved them of a terrible curse. The mesh demanded judgment and patience from both sides, and already in that first summer these were in short supply.

The name "Assassins' Gate" stuck with the Americans in Iraq, and eventually with some of the Iraqis, too. The original assassins were twelfth-century Muslim heretics; they were said to consume hashish in gardens of earthly delights before going out to kill, and they made murder such a public spectacle that it became a form of suicide as well—the assassin set upon his target at noon Friday in the mosque with a knife, knowing he too would die. Over time in Iraq, as the violence surged, and the Assassins' Gate disappeared behind watchtowers and concrete blast walls, and everything began to deteriorate, the name came to fit in a peculiarly evocative way. I imagined a foreign traveler walking under the glare of the sun through the front gate of an old walled city, believing that he was safe and welcome in this unfamiliar place, not knowing that hidden dangers awaited him just inside. At other times, it was the foreigner I saw as the assassin, taking aim from his perch high up on the arch.

The road that led America to the Assassins' Gate is long and not at all direct. The story of the Iraq War is a story of ideas about the role of the United States in the world, and of the individuals who conceived and acted on them. It has roots deep in history, yet there was nothing inevitable about the war, and the mere fact of it still sometimes astounds me. During the nearly interminable buildup to war I never found the questions about it easy to answer, and the manner in which the country argued with itself seemed wholly inadequate to the scale of what we were about to get into. I first went to Iraq, and then kept going back, because I wanted to see past the abstractions to what the war meant in people's lives. Nothing, I felt in that summer of 2003, was fixed yet. The most important struggles were the ones going on inside the minds of Iraqis and Americans alike. The war's meaning would be the sum of all the ways that all of them understood one another and the event that had thrust them together. In the end it would come down to just these encounters, millions of them, like the one at the Assassins' Gate.

1

An Unfinished War

AT THE TIME of the Gulf War, in 1991, a man going by the name Samir al-Khalil started appearing on American television news programs. The name was a pseudonym, and the man's face was always turned away from the camera, his identity further disguised by a wig. Samir al-Khalil was the author of a book about Iraq under Saddam Hussein called *Republic of Fear*. It was written during the 1980s, while Iraq was at war with Iran and hundreds of thousands of men were dying in the trenches and minefields of the two countries' long border, by poison gas and in human-wave attacks, in fighting reminiscent of the stalemate and slaughter of the First World War—except that this war was more modern, fueled in the manner of twentieth-century wars by totalitarian ideologies: in Iraq an aggressive brand of Pan-Arab nationalism, in Iran a revolutionary dictatorship of the clerics. It was a death struggle between fear and faith. More than a million men were killed or wounded in the Iran-Iraq War of 1980–88. In this country hardly anyone noticed.

Against the background of this calamity, Samir al-Khalil, who lived in Cambridge, Massachusetts, and had access to the great collection of Arab sources at Harvard's Widener Library, researched and wrote his book. *Republic of Fear* is dense and obsessive; it dissects the history and character of the dictatorship of Saddam and his Arab Baath Socialist Party in relentless detail, showing how much the regime resembled and borrowed from the European totalitarian movements, the Nazis, fascists, and communists. By the end of the book, a reader understood why its author had sought refuge behind a pseudonym and a hairpiece.

It took him three years to find a publisher. When the book finally appeared in 1989, it went predictably ignored—until August of 1990, when Saddam invaded Kuwait and put Iraq in the center of Americans' consciousness. Suddenly, *Republic of Fear* became a minor bestseller.

As the Gulf War came to a close in early March 1991, with Iraqi forces routed and in headlong retreat, Samir al-Khalil appeared in public at a Harvard forum and shed his pseudonym. His real name was Kanan Makiya. He was the son of one of Iraq's most distinguished architects and an English mother; he was a trained architect himself and had once managed his father's London firm. Makiya decided to reveal his identity because events in his country of birth were taking a disastrous turn. Shia in southern Iraq and Kurds in the north, encouraged by President George H. W. Bush's call for Iraqis to rise up against Saddam, were being slaughtered in the thousands by the remaining elite units of Saddam's army and his secret police. Iraqi helicopters were taking advantage of the cease-fire terms to massacre civilians from the air or drop suspected rebels to their deaths. At the Harvard event, Makiya urged Bush to stop the slaughter and finish the war by moving on to Baghdad and overthrowing the regime.

The first Gulf War did not turn out as Kanan Makiya had hoped. Saddam kept his grip on power, and soon Bush lost his, and Iraq slipped from most Americans' minds. But throughout the decade between the end of the first Gulf War and the morning of September 11, 2001, Iraq remained an irritant and a reminder of unfinished business. Saddam paved the lobby of an upscale hotel with a mosaic of Bush's face, so that guests had to walk over the features of the American president; apparently needing greater satisfaction, Saddam tried to have Bush killed on a visit to Kuwait. He commanded that his architects build a grand mosque, one of the largest in the world, with minarets in the shape of AK-47s, and he called it the Mother of All Battles mosque. It was as if Saddam were claiming victory after all. He had done something similar after the war with Iran, in which there was no winner, with catastrophic Iraqi miscalculations and losses. Saddam had ordered gigantic arms to be cast and smelted from models of his own, with the hands holding enormous swords that were crossed into triumphal arches over either end of the military parade ground in the center of Baghdad, about a mile from the Assassins' Gate. The helmets of dead Iranians, pocked with bullet holes, were embedded in the pavement under the arches, so that during the annual ceremonial parade Iraqi tanks would crush them and Iraqi soldiers would stomp on them.

To the world these projects seemed like preposterous delusions. But Saddam had a point: He had twice launched wars of aggression against neighboring countries, and he was still in power, Iraq's paramount ruler. Anyone who tried to overthrow him from within paid the final price. From his capital of grandiose monuments, Saddam continued to taunt and defy the superpower, the West, the United Nations, and his defiance made him a hero to young people and intellectuals across the Arab world. In 1994 he threatened a second invasion of Kuwait. His soldiers skirmished with American and British warplanes patrolling the no-fly zones that the allies had established across northern and southern Iraq in a belated move to protect the Kurds and the Shia. Over the years, not a single Iraqi missile or antiaircraft artillery round struck a single allied plane, so that you began to wonder if they hadn't been ordered to miss. Nonetheless, the engagements were reminders to a world that thought Saddam had been defeated: I'm still here. The UN sanctions on Iraq, which devastated the middle class and were estimated to have doubled the country's infant mortality rate, became a propaganda victory for Saddam in the minds of Arabs and some Europeans. The UN inspectors, who had achieved notable success in the first half of the 1990s in uncovering and dismantling Iraq's unconventional weapons programs, had to leave the country for their own safety after Saddam began to refuse them access to weapons sites and the Clinton administration responded with cruise missile attacks in December 1998; then Saddam shut the door behind the inspectors and locked it. By the end of the decade, Saddam's crushing defeat in Kuwait appeared to have become at least a moral victory—for him, if not for the Iraqi people. He had defied America and gotten away with it.

The fates of the two countries remained entangled, with brief hope, cruel disappointment, hatred born of relentless propaganda, humiliation, and ruin. All this was on the Iraqi side. On the American side, we lapsed back into our characteristic state of inattention.

After his moment in the media glare, Kanan Makiya returned to private life. He published more books, including a study of the crossed swords in Baghdad called *The Monument: Art, Vulgarity and Responsibility in Iraq*, and a passionate denunciation of the betrayal of Iraqis during the Gulf War by the Western powers and the Arab world called *Cruelty and Silence*. He even wrote a novel about seventh-century Jerusalem. It was a story of the intellectual relationships among Christians, Jews, and early Muslims at the time the al-Aqsa mosque was constructed near the Dome of the Rock—a story of relative tolerance, pluralism, and enlightenment that stood in pointed contrast to the religious ideologies of our own age. Makiya taught Middle Eastern studies at Brandeis University, and at Harvard he directed the collection and translation of a trove of official documents that had come out of northern Iraq after the Gulf War—an archive of the Anfal, the Kurdish genocide of 1987–88. He worked in a small apartment off Massachusetts Avenue that was filled with books in Arabic on Islam and the history of the region. On one wall there was a Ben Shahn poster of a characteristically existential-looking figure, and a quotation from a nineteenth-century Englishman named John Viscount Morley: "You have not converted a man because you have silenced him."

I was living in Cambridge during those years. It's not unusual to see bespectacled men walking the streets around Harvard Square with an air of disheveled preoccupation. Some are professors, some are homeless. In the mid-1990s, I began to notice among these walkers a man with a large, balding head and soft, distracted features who always seemed to be in a hurry. After perhaps a year, I figured out that this man was the Iraqi exile and author of *Republic of Fear*—Samir al-Khalil, Kanan Makiya. In a way, he was both a professor *and* homeless. I always felt a quiver of worry when I spotted him: The head bobbing along Massachusetts Avenue seemed like an easy target if there were agents of Iraqi intelligence in Cambridge.

One day I introduced myself, and after that Makiya and I would have coffee in the square a couple of times a year. He told me that after the Gulf War he and other Iraqi exiles had written a document called Charter 91, directly modeled on the Czech dissident group Charter 77, of which Vaclav Havel had been a founding member. Makiya was something I'd never encountered—an Arab dissident in the manner of Havel or Solzhenitsyn. Charter 91 was a manifesto calling for a democratic and secular Iraq—a "Republic of Tolerance." Once, when Makiya and I were talking about the relativism that had taken over liberal political philosophy, he suddenly said, in his disarmingly direct way, with his apologetic smile, "I'm a universalist." He identified with Europe's eighteenth-century Enlightenment. Human rights, he said, were an absolute that would have to be the foundation of a new Arab world—a new Iraq.

The fate of exiles is to dream and wait and decay. But Makiya wasn't decaying—he had his books, his projects. Beneath the slightly bewildered manner lay a fierce intensity and even stubbornness. Charter 91 and the Iraqi National Congress, the exiles' political organization (Makiya was a member of its assembly), seemed unlikely to create the Republic of Tolerance. The power of Saddam and the Baath Party, like the Soviet Union once, or apartheid South Africa, at that time seemed permanent, an iron lock. The miracles of 1989 and the democratic revolutions of the 1990s were not for Iraq, which belonged to an alien and frightening part of the world where governments and people routinely did terrible things and no light or air ever penetrated. I was a little embarrassed to sit with Makiya and hear his ideas. It was awkward to be confronted with this intelligence and idealism, to sympathize with his hopes, and have nothing to offer in return, not even hope. But he kept Iraq from being a complete abstraction. If not for Kanan Makiya and our irregular coffees, its future would never have crossed my mind.

DURING THE YEARS between the Gulf War and September 11, Iraq was rarely on the front page of newspapers. But another story was playing out, subtler but no less important than war: the development of certain ideas about America and its mission in the world. The Iraq War started as a war of ideas, and to understand how and why America came to be in Iraq, one has to trace their origins.

On March 8, 1992—almost a year to the day after Kanan Makiya came out of pseudonymity to urge the overthrow of Saddam's regime—*The New York Times* published selections from the draft of a document that had been leaked by an apparently dismayed official in President Bush's Pentagon. The document, forty-six pages long, was called the Defense Planning Guidance, a policy statement that outlined America's political and military strategy after the Cold War. It was written by Zalmay Khalilzad and Abram Shulsky, both of whom would become second-tier players in the Iraq War under the second President Bush. The Defense Planning Guidance was commissioned by Secretary of Defense Dick Cheney and overseen by the undersecretary for policy, Paul Wolfowitz. Its intellectual ambition confirmed Wolfowitz's reputation as a big thinker.

"Our first objective is to prevent the re-emergence of a new rival," the draft declared at the outset. The United States would preserve its preeminent power across the globe and discourage potential competitors by keeping defense spending at high levels. Those competitors were as likely to emerge in Europe as anywhere, in spite of America's longstanding alliances with the Western democracies. Germany and Japan came in for special suspicion. "Like the coalition that opposed Iraqi aggression," the authors wrote, "we should expect future coalitions to be ad hoc assemblies, often not lasting beyond the crisis being confronted." There was no mention of the United Nations or any other international organization. Instead, the document described a world of dangers and power struggles in which America had to remain the superpower, for its own security and for stability everywhere else.

The Defense Planning Guidance was one of those internal bureaucratic memoranda—like the famous NSC-68 paper of 1950 outlining an aggressive Cold War strategy—that foretell a grand historic shift. After the leak was published in *The New York Times*, President Bush at first disputed that the implications were far-reaching at all, then he ordered Pentagon officials to rewrite it. When the document was released in May, the language about preeminence was gone; the toned-down revision made reassuring noises about cooperation and alliances. The press played the story as a case of the mature, sober Defense Secretary Dick Cheney reining in the rambunctious thinking of Undersecretary Wolfowitz. In hindsight, this account seems unlikely. With its language about American dominance, ad hoc coalitions, and preemptive war to prevent threats from unconventional weapons, the Defense Planning Guidance of 1992 foreshadows with uncanny accuracy, down to the wording of key sentences, the second President Bush's National Security Strategy of 2002, which poured the foundation for what came to be called the Bush Doctrine, and its first test, the Iraq War. And this second document reflected, as much as anyone else's, the ideas of Vice President Cheney.

The DPG was a barely visible hairline fracture that over time developed into a profound break. That the leaked document was cleaned up for public presentation wasn't just a response to poor early reviews. Between its authors and the president they served lay a philosophical gulf too vast for the editing out of a few phrases to close. Bush the father belonged to the Nixon-Kissinger school of political thought. In the jargon of foreign policy, he was a "realist," which meant that he believed in preserving the balance of power between states that acted out of narrowly defined interests. For realists, the key phrase was "vital national interest." To officials of this persuasion, the fall of the Soviet Union wasn't an occasion for America to expand its military dominance across the face of the earth. It was a cause for concern, because it upset the balance of power. One realist even wrote an article titled "Why We Will Soon Miss the Cold War." The mainstream of the Republican Party was dedicated to this line of thought, and after the Cold War its leaders seemed uncertain about what course to pursue—especially once Bill Clinton defeated George Bush. With a Democrat in the White House, Republican wise men began to call for American retrenchment around the world. They disliked the new president's forays into the margins of geopolitics like Haiti and the Balkans. They especially disliked the talk of human rights and democracy as causes for expending blood and treasure abroad. To the realists, these were dangerous fantasies. What foreign regimes did to their own citizens within the privacy of their own borders was no business of the United States.

During the presidency of Bill Clinton, this view pushed the Republican Party close to its old isolationism of the years before Pearl Harbor. But throughout the 1990s, another current of thought ran alongside or beneath this mainstream, quietly at first, later gathering force.

THE IRAQ WAR will always be linked with the term "neoconservative." The connection is so tight that we've forgotten the history of the word. Neoconservatives have been around since the late sixties, when a small group of liberal intellectuals, many of them originating in the left-wing sects of the 1930s, watched the era of Vietnam, black power, and student revolution unfold. They watched in horror, and while other liberals were turning dovish or radical, they moved sharply to the right. One of them defined a neoconservative as a liberal who's been mugged by reality. The great foreign-policy concern of the first-generation neoconservatives—Senator Henry "Scoop" Jackson, Norman Podhoretz, Irving Kristol, Daniel Patrick Moynihan—was the same concern of the Truman-Acheson generation of liberals: communism. The disaster in Vietnam did not teach them the lesson that America had tragically overreached and needed to learn the limits of its power. They concluded instead that America had gone wobbly. Our unwillingness to fight, they argued, only encouraged the Soviet Union to expand, until half the globe or more would fall under communist rule. As the seventies stumbled along—the SALT talks, détente, the fall of Saigon with the humiliating evacuation off the American embassy roof, the Iranian revolution, the hostage crisis, the Soviet invasion of Afghanistan, the insurgencies in Central America—their alarm reached a dire pitch. In the pages of *Commentary* magazine, and in the statements released by their group, the Committee on the Present Danger, the neoconservatives warned that American power had grown provocatively weak. Accommodating the Soviet Empire was a sign of defeatism, not realism. The tone of these warnings was righteous and apocalyptic, laced with anger at soft-headed liberals (many of them former friends and colleagues of the neoconservatives) who'd lost their nerve in the '60s. The tone was personal and, in a sense, natural; it owed something to the left-wing version of world-historical struggle on which so many neoconservatives had nursed in their early years.

In their grim worldview, there wasn't much room for human rights outside the Soviet bloc—especially when President Carter put talk of human rights at the center of his foreign policy. This talk seemed to the neoconservatives truly dangerous, for it undermined friendly regimes (Nicaragua, South Africa, Iran) whose behavior we might not like (they were corrupt, they tortured and killed their own citizens) but whose survival was essential for the resistance to communism. In 1979, one of the neoconservatives, Jeane Kirkpatrick, published an essay in *Commentary*, "Dictatorships and Double Standards," arguing that the tendency of human-rights do-gooders to undermine America's friends and leave the way open to our enemies turned both grand strategy and morality on their heads. Our friends might be nasty, but our enemies were worse; the difference between them was the difference between benign and malignant cancer. It was America's mission to prevent authoritarian friends from becoming totalitarian enemies, which by their essence locked whole populations in eternal prisons that could never be opened from the inside. The essay caught Reagan's eye and the following year won Kirkpatrick an appointment as UN ambassador under the newly elected president.

IN REAGAN the neoconservatives found their champion. His election and his administration's policies, which were partly inspired by the ideas of men like Podhoretz and Kristol, showed the neoconservatives that ideas could lead to power, and that power required ideas. This was not a lesson that came naturally. Their earlier lives in left-wing sects in the 1930s and '40s had been studies in political futility, all the more intense for their impotence, carried on as if New York was St. Petersburg and Toledo Kiev, and America itself on the verge of its own dialectical orgasm of revolution. But these fights at least taught the participants to take themselves and their ideas very seriously, to treat intellectual combat as an extension of the political and even the weaponized kind. In 1980, the long training of their younger years paid off.

To the neoconservatives' ideas about American power Reagan added a quality of his own: a benign disposition. This wasn't a mere quirk of temperament. Reagan's character, his comfort with the plain American idiom of optimism, gave the confrontational worldview a smiling face that suggested something higher than grim combat. American power, Reagan said, was a force for good in the world—this at a time when respectable opinion, in America and elsewhere, was still riveted by the memory of napalm igniting the jungles of South Vietnam. In 1976, Reagan won a fight at the Republican convention against the establishment forces of President Ford and his cold-blooded secretary of state, Henry Kissinger, to put a "morality in foreign policy" plank in the party's platform. To large numbers of Americans, including Republicans, morality in foreign policy meant minding our own business. At best it meant speaking up for dissidents in the Soviet Union or Chile. Reagan meant something far grander: confronting and defeating communism all over the world. And though he lost the nomination battle to Ford in 1976, he won the war for his party's soul.

In 1981, the first year of Reagan's presidency, Elliott Abrams, who was Reagan's aggressive assistant secretary of state for Latin America and, later, human rights, wrote a memo arguing that the administration shouldn't simply oppose communism; it should also promote democracy, in communist and noncommunist countries alike. The memo contradicted the harsher view expressed two years before by Jeane Kirkpatrick in the magazine edited by Abrams's father-in-law, Norman Podhoretz. Out of personal inclination as well as strategic calculation, Reagan in his rhetoric embraced the idea of promoting democracy. In 1982, speaking before the British parliament at Westminster, he presented a vision of democracy expanding across the globe. The words inspired a new generation of young officials orbiting around Reagan's sun.

One of them was Robert Kagan. The son of a Yale professor of Greek history, Kagan is about the same age as I, but we learned the opposite lesson from the historical moment of our early years: After Vietnam, I (and everyone I knew) feared American overreach; Kagan (and the new generation of conservatives) feared American drift. "When I was in college in the late seventies, I remember all of us thinking that those hippie antiwar guys who came before us were a little ridiculous," Kagan said when we met in Washington in early 2004. "That somehow wasn't the way to be. I came of age really after Vietnam. The seventies were my formative experience in the broadest sense, because then it was all—at least as far as I saw—American weakness, leading to these catastrophes: Iran, Afghanistan, Nicaragua. Just the weakness and the embarrassment of Jimmy Carter."

So in his twenties Kagan became a soldier in the Reagan revolution. He first wrote speeches for Secretary of State George Shultz, then helped to develop Nicaragua policy under Elliott Abrams. But in the small proxy fights of the late Cold War, the choice was between two kinds of armed ugliness. The Nicaraguan contras made unconvincing founding fathers; and when the Salvadoran military agreed to hold an election in 1983, the Reagan administration played a double game—midwifing the democratic process and ensuring victory for our man in San Salvador, José Napoleon Duarte. Despite his close involvement in the Nicaragua policy, Kagan emerged unscathed from the Iran-contra scandal that tainted Abrams with a perjury conviction (he was later pardoned by the first President Bush). In practice, morality in foreign policy looked less inspiring than the shining city on the hill. The Reagan administration's policy on Iraq was no different from Henry Kissinger's: to support the Baathist regime in the name of the national interest, even when the regime was committing genocide against the Kurds.

Still, the idea and the language took hold in the minds of younger thinkers like Kagan: Anticommunism was only half a worldview; the other half was democratic idealism, a faith in the transformational power of American values. At the end of the decade, after Reagan left office, communism collapsed in Europe; the following year, in 1990, the Nicaraguan Sandinistas lost power in a democratic election; and in 1991, Kagan watched the demise of the Soviet Union up close in Moscow, where his wife was stationed as a diplomat. All of this confirmed for the Reaganites that history was on their side. But the Cold

War was over, and most of them no longer knew how to think about America and the world, and the neoconservatives started to drift.

A few years later, in the relative silence and obscurity of the Clinton era, Kagan began to publish a series of articles that outlined a vision for post–Cold War foreign policy. They appeared in *Commentary*, the house organ of neoconservatism. But by the mid-1990s the tone and some of the content had changed. Kagan, the ideological son of Reagan, was shaped by the experience in Nicaragua (which, in his book *A Twilight Struggle*, he described as a great success for Reagan's foreign policy) and the fall of communism—not by Vietnam. He was a man of the '80s, not the '60s; his tone was affirmation, not warning. In our conversation, Kagan brushed aside the term "neoconservative," and when I asked whether he ever wondered if he was a liberal, he shot back, "I *am* a liberal. In foreign policy I'm a liberal. The conservative tradition in foreign policy is the minimalist, realist tradition." The liberal tradition, in Kagan's genealogy, has upheld an activist foreign policy that reflects American ideals as well as interests, and it runs from Hamilton through John Quincy Adams, Lincoln (the Civil War was a pivotal case, as the Union embraced a liberal "foreign policy" toward slavery in the South), Theodore Roosevelt, Wilson, FDR, Truman, Kennedy, and ultimately to Reagan.

The real target of Kagan's *Commentary* articles, published between 1994 and 1997, was the Republican Party. He regarded with dismay the party's turn away from activism in foreign policy after the end of the Soviet Union. One by one, he watched his idealistic comrades from the Reagan years drop their former commitment to global democracy under the pressure of partisan politics or changed world circumstances or their own shifting views—until the only one left standing to support, for example, the invasion of Haiti on behalf of its elected government, was Robert Kagan. Everywhere he looked, both in the administration of the first Bush and in the congressional opposition to Bill Clinton, Republicans were in tired retreat. Interventions in messy little wars like Bosnia's would lead to quagmire, warned such foreign-policy titans as Senator John McCain, sounding like a liberal Democrat still recovering from the trauma of Vietnam (rather than a war hero for whom the trauma was not at all figurative). Without Reagan and the Soviet Union to focus its mind, the party had wandered back into cautious realism. Its wise men warned about "imperial over-stretch" and invoked that indispensable phrase from the Nixon-Kissinger years, "vital national interest." So much for morality in foreign policy. If Yugoslavs and Rwandans were determined to slaughter one another, if Somalia was plunging into chaos while its people starved, these unhappy events were probably outside our power to remedy and certainly outside our concern.

Against this timidity Kagan launched a powerful analytical attack. The end of the Cold War, he argued, was precisely the moment not to withdraw but to extend. America shouldn't mourn the loss of a balance of power but instead use its unrivaled power all around the world to pursue its interests and its values—which almost always go together. No corner of the earth is too distant or obscure to be allowed to fester dangerously or be deprived of the benevolent effects of American hegemony, namely democracy and a stable peace. Seeking to revive the spirit of Reagan, Kagan reached farther back to Theodore Roosevelt and "the idea that the American people should take a hand in shaping mankind's destiny, that playing such a role accords honor, and that the right to such honor must be earned." For Kagan, the extension of democracy around the world was as much about America's national destiny as it was about doing good things for unhappy people in foreign countries. The values might be universal, but only one country could secure them. Kagan was expressing a kind of nationalism, not so different in ambition from the British nationalism of Kipling's white man's burden (without the racial baggage), the French *mission civilisatrice* (without the religious baggage), and the antique *Pax Romana* (without an actual empire).

This strain of national messianism is as alien to the hard-boiled realism of Nixon, Kissinger, and the first Bush as it is to the Wilsonian utopianism of liberals who believe in international law. Though they supported many of the same interventions in the nineties, Kagan dismissed these liberals as "a shrinking camp of internationalists with nothing but airy 'humanitarianism' on their side." Unlike them, he was a nationalist, and he had no faith ·that the Clinton administration would carry out the call to greatness. "The present generation of Democratic leaders simply does not have the stomach for world leadership," Kagan wrote. The only hope lay in the Republicans. His mission was to purge the party of realism and restore the higher aims of the great ex-president who was disappearing into the sunset of senescence out on the coast.

One of Kagan's articles mentioned the original draft of the Defense Planning Guidance—"unfortunately rejected," he lamented. The areas of convergence between the internal Pentagon memo and the journal articles are obvious: Top Republican officials and neoconservative foreign-policy thinkers were sketching similarly large plans for the party and the country. But there are differences, perhaps not so obvious at the time, but ones that would prove critical a few years later, when these plans and ideas became the foreign policy of the second President Bush and laid the groundwork for a second war with Iraq. Though the DPG acknowledged that the Cold War was over, it was a document of Cold Warriors—the hard-liners of the 1970s who rejected accommodation with the Soviet Union. Paul Wolfowitz had been a member of the famous Team B, the group of outside experts that was appointed in 1976 by CIA director George Bush to review intelligence on the Soviet Union, and that came to far more dire conclusions about Soviet capabilities and intentions than the pro-détente officials of the Nixon and Ford administrations. The DPG, written in 1992 under Wolfowitz's guidance (though he claims not to have read the draft before it was leaked), was very much a continuation of the neoconservative thinking that had spawned the Committee on the Present Danger. The skies were always ominous, threats always loomed on the horizon; even though the Soviet Union was no more, the sunlit vistas of the Reagan years had gone dark again. To officials like Wolfowitz, it was always 1979. And what were the new threats? They were everyone and everywhere: European allies, Arab dictatorships, Muslim terrorists, resurgent Russians, Chinese and North Korean communists, weapons proliferators. And what was the remedy? American power, everywhere—but not in the cause of democratic values. The DPG duly advocated "the spread of democratic forms of government and open economic systems," but only as a gesture. When it came to the Middle East, "our overall objective is to remain the predominant outside power in the region and preserve U.S. and Western access to the region's oil. We also seek to deter further aggression in the region, foster regional stability, protect U.S. nationals and property, and safeguard our access to international air and seaways." This is the language of realism, not Reaganism. It's the balance of power without a balance. "With regard to Pakistan," the document continued, "a constructive U.S.-Pakistani military relationship will be an important element in our strategy to promote stable security conditions in Southwest Asia and Central Asia." The possibility that continued access to oil and good relations with Muslim dictators might ultimately be the cause of instability or worse didn't occur to the DPG's authors. The prospect of democracy in this dangerous region was never mentioned.

Here, Kagan and the Pentagon hard-liners parted ways. Kagan saw no daylight between security, stability, and democracy. One of his *Commentary* articles took direct aim at the indulgence Jeane Kirkpatrick had extended to right-wing dictatorships in the same magazine a decade and a half earlier. What good was an international order if it didn't bring freedom?

There was another difference between Kagan and the Pentagon hard-liners. They had no use for international alliances and institutions if these got in the way of America's freedom to act. Kagan, though no lover of the UN, didn't make a point of rejecting internationalism; at times, sounding like a Truman-era Democrat, he even invoked it as an important source of American influence.

In 1996, Kagan and his friend William Kristol, by then editor of Rupert Murdoch's new magazine *The Weekly Standard*, published an essay in *Foreign Affairs* called "Toward a Neo-Reaganite Foreign Policy." It was a consolidation of the *Commentary* articles into a stirring manifesto, with Kristol, Dan Quayle's former chief of staff and a shrewd Republican operative, adding the publicist's touch to Kagan's more analytical style. It's hard to think of a less auspicious moment for a foreign-policy manifesto than the summer of 1996. The Internet and the stock market bubble were expanding fast. The presidential race was a snooze. The Republican candidate Robert Dole was trying to claim, as Kagan and Kristol wrote, "that there really are differences in foreign policy between him and the president, appearances to the contrary notwith-standing." In 1996, as far as most Americans were concerned, the rest of the world disappeared.

Yet here were Kagan and Kristol summoning America to "benevo-lent global hegemony." They had the advantage over their neoconser-vative fathers of having already seen a small, determined grouplet, writing combative articles in obscure journals, influence power in Washington. There was no reason to think it couldn't happen again, with discipline and persistence and perhaps a bit of luck. The first goal was for their ideas to take over—or take back—the Republican Party. Then, in a few years, the nation. After that, the world. This is the les-son that the American right has fully absorbed and put into practice ever since the 1960s: Ideas matter. The focused efforts of a handful of organized ideologues can win the political war when the opposition is confused and the country distracted. But they have to be willing to fight, and often lose, obscure battles over years and even decades.

The next year, in 1997, Kagan and Kristol helped found the Project for the New American Century, or PNAC, a pressure group of lead-ing foreign-policy conservatives in the spirit of the Committee on the Present Danger. It included Donald Rumsfeld, Wolfowitz, Abrams, Richard Perle, William Bennett, and James Woolsey; more than half of the founding members would go on to assume high positions in the administration of George W. Bush. On January 26, 1998, PNAC put itself on the map in the form of an open letter to President Clinton urging him to make a change of regime in Iraq the nation's policy. "The current policy, which depends for its success upon the steadfastness of our coalition partners and upon the cooperation of Saddam Hus-sein, is dangerously inadequate," the letter's signers wrote, not hesi-tating to embarrass the president. After its publication, Rumsfeld, Wolfowitz, Perle, and one or two other signers went to the White House to discuss Iraq with Sandy Berger, Clinton's national security adviser, and came away "appalled at the feebleness of the Clinton ad-ministration," Perle said. The letter hadn't specified exactly how Sad-dam and the Baath Party were to be overthrown; the signers disagreed about the means. But within a few months the Republican Congress overwhelmingly passed, and the Democratic president (besieged by the Monica Lewinsky affair) reluctantly signed, the Iraq Liberation Act. Regime change in Iraq became official American policy.

WHY DID IRAQ become the leading cause of the hawks? It had received no special attention in the Defense Planning Guidance; it was barely mentioned in the writings of Kagan and Kristol. A year after the letter to Clinton, in 1999, Kosovo replaced Iraq as the overriding concern of PNAC. Still, by 1998 Saddam was beginning to slip out of the constraints imposed on him after the Gulf War and get away with it. Economic sanctions were breaking down, and some European countries, especially Iraq's leading trading partners, France and Russia, were making noises about lifting them altogether. UN weapons inspectors were withdrawn from Iraq for security reasons after Saddam refused to continue cooperating with them; then he denied them reentry. Saddam was increasingly, in foreign-policy jargon, "out of his box"—apparently free to pursue the unconventional weapons that had been his long-standing desire.

Perhaps the most important name on the PNAC letter was Paul Wolfowitz. Iraq had been on Wolfowitz's mind since the late 1970s, when he was a midlevel official in the Carter Pentagon and was instructed by Secretary of Defense Harold Brown to direct what would become a prophetic project, called the Limited Contingency Study. Wolfowitz set about to review threats to American interests outside Europe, and he ended up focusing on Persian Gulf oil—in particular, on the possibility of an invasion by Iraq to seize the oil fields of Kuwait or Saudi Arabia. Wolfowitz's thinking took him well beyond conventional Cold War analysis, and it was received without enthusiasm at the Pentagon, where the study was shelved. The Iranian revolution in 1979, and the Iran-Iraq War that followed, turned American policy in the Gulf toward Iraq even as Saddam Hussein consolidated total power and exercised it with extraordinary brutality on his own population as well as on the Iranian enemy. There's no reason to think that Wolfowitz, serving in several different capacities under Reagan and Bush in the 1980s, dissented from the tilt to Iraq. The concern of the Limited Contingency Study had been strategic threats to Persian Gulf oil, not the nature of Arab totalitarianism.

But Wolfowitz was cut from finer cloth than Donald Rumsfeld, who on a diplomatic errand in 1983 famously shook Saddam's hand, or Dick Cheney, who spent the decade in Congress opposing human-rights legislation, or George H. W. Bush, who looked the other way when the Chinese army crushed a popular movement in Tiananmen Square. Wolfowitz was raised on ideals in the household of Jack Wolfowitz, a Cornell mathematics professor whose family had fled anti-Semitism in Poland in 1920; several family members who had stayed behind eventually perished under the Nazis. Paul Wolfowitz grew up reading Orwell, John Hersey's *Hiroshima*, and his father's library of books on war and the Holocaust. The atmosphere in the Wolfowitz home was morally serious, academically ambitious, and, politically, devoted to the midcentury liberalism that worshipped the memory of Roosevelt and supported Truman's anticommunism.

When Wolfowitz entered Cornell in the early 1960s, where he lived in an intellectual pressure cooker called Telluride House, he fell into the orbit of Professor Allan Bloom, for whom politics raised and answered the deepest questions about the purpose and value of human life, and whose late-night conversations at the house became legendary. In Saul Bellow's fictionalized homage to Bloom, *Ravelstein*, published in 2000, Wolfowitz appears thinly disguised as Philip Gorman, a high government official who likes to phone his former teacher Bloom/Ravelstein with the latest inside dope from the councils of government, always careful to keep state secrets to himself. Ravelstein has his own classified information—the higher truths of the human soul that date back to the Greeks. "It was essential to fit up-to-the-minute decisions in the Gulf War made by obviously limited pols like Bush and Baker into a true-as-possible picture of the forces at work, into the political history of civilization. When Ravelstein said that young Gorman had a grasp of great politics, something like this was what he had in mind."

But at Cornell, Wolfowitz kept some distance from Bloom's magnetic pull; he was already politic enough to recognize that Bloom was a divisive figure. Throughout his career, Wolfowitz has had a talent for charming powerful people and becoming a protégé without also becoming a threat. He was always a good boy, the kind on whom adults fasten their dreams, with a yeshiva student's purity about him, though his education was entirely secular. He organized a journey with friends to join the March on Washington in 1963, but when antiwar protest came to Cornell in Wolfowitz's last semester in 1965, he and two others formed the Committee for Critical Support of the U.S. in Vietnam and held up signs at a tiny counterprotest. (Wolfowitz, like nearly every other architect of the Iraq War, avoided military service in Vietnam, in his case through student deferments. Dick Cheney, who received five deferments, later explained, "I had other priorities in the sixties than military service." John Bolton, who, like George W. Bush, joined the National Guard, was more straightforward: "I confess I had no desire to die in a Southeast Asian rice paddy.") "There's a certain public-spirited prudery about him," one of Wolfowitz's Telluride housemates, who would also go on to a career in neoconservative politics, said. "Paul is sort of the good citizen." When Allan Bloom died of AIDS in 1989 and a colleague at the Pentagon called Wolfowitz with condolences, the undersecretary of defense for policy stayed on the phone for forty-five minutes talking about what it meant to live an upright and purposeful life, as his old professor had.

His one act of defiance was to pursue graduate studies in political science at Chicago, where Bloom's master Leo Strauss was teaching, rather than in biophysical chemistry at MIT, as Wolfowitz's father wanted. The decision set the course of his adult life. But after Wolfowitz left academia for government, and as he moved upward from job to job under Presidents Nixon, Ford, Carter, Reagan, and Bush, he never allowed his intellectual or moral passions to get too far out ahead of professional prudence. In the first two decades of his career, Wolfowitz was known as a technical and theoretical wizard with decidedly hard-line views, but not as a crusading ideologue. In the mid-1980s, when Ferdinand Marcos was clinging to power in Manila after stealing an election, and the Reagan administration was debating what to do, the *New York Times* reporter Leslie Gelb interviewed all the key officials, including Wolfowitz, then the assistant secretary of state for

East Asia. Gelb wrote that there was an emerging consensus in the administration that Marcos had to go. As soon as the article appeared, Wolfowitz called to complain that he had said no such thing. While they were still talking, Gelb checked his notes and realized that Wolfowitz was right: He had walked up to the line but carefully avoided crossing it. Reagan himself was still hesitating, and if there was a consensus among others, Wolfowitz wasn't yet prepared to be named as part of it. But a few years later, by which time the wisdom of forcing Marcos out had become a given, Gelb came across an article in *The Washington Post* that identified Wolfowitz as the force behind Marcos's ouster. By then Wolfowitz was happy to take credit.

Democracy and human rights might have been the stuff of his moral education, but they didn't play a central role in his early career in government. A sort of turning point might have come in the last days of the Gulf War in 1991. The decision to end the war before the Iraqi Republican Guard divisions were destroyed, and to allow Saddam's helicopters to fly after the cease-fire, led directly to the massacres of tens of thousands of Shia and Kurds who had risen up against the regime. Wolfowitz, the undersecretary of defense for policy under Cheney, was appalled and argued strenuously that the United States should resume operations to stop the helicopter attacks. But Cheney, along with everyone else at the top of the administration, didn't want to undermine General Norman Schwarzkopf's field authority, or risk the breakup of Iraq; Saddam was gone from Kuwait, and that had been the objective. According to James Mann's excellent group biography *Rise of the Vulcans*, a Pentagon official told Cheney, "You know, we could change the government and put in a democracy." Cheney answered that the Saudis would object. So the Iraqi intifada was allowed to be crushed.

Richard Perle told me that, at the end of the Gulf War, Wolfowitz "wanted to finish Saddam's regime, and not only did he want to finish it, he believed that there was a strong basis for doing so." There's no evidence that Wolfowitz at the time argued or even held the view that the United States should have overthrown Saddam; what's clear is that he wanted to give Iraqis themselves the chance to do it. But in the years that followed the defeat of President Bush, when Wolfowitz was finally out of government and serving as dean of the Johns Hopkins

School of Advanced International Studies, he kept returning to the unfinished business in Iraq, as if the terrible events that followed the cease-fire wouldn't leave him alone. At a private meeting on Capitol Hill, he flatly contradicted the former secretary of state, James Baker (and, incidentally, the future vice president, Dick Cheney), who was claiming that the Saudis had argued at the time against supporting the intifada for fear that Iran would gain a foothold in Iraq. "I was on those trips, and it's nonsense," Wolfowitz insisted—but he acknowledged, in the title of one essay, that "Victory Came Too Easily," that the United States had squandered the chance to help Iraqis free themselves of the dictator. These writings had the fitful, inconclusive quality of a divided mind: Wolfowitz wanted to get rid of Saddam, but he still accepted the rationale for not having done so in 1991. He never came around to the position that the American-led coalition should have seized Baghdad and occupied Iraq. The obvious question would have been: What then? It's a question that Wolfowitz never managed to answer.

By 1997, he was arguing that the Clinton administration's policy of containment was doomed to fail, while sanctions continued to inflict pain on ordinary Iraqis and Saddam was once more becoming a threat. At the end of that year, Wolfowitz and Zalmay Khalilzad coauthored a piece in *The Weekly Standard* called "Overthrow Him." Regime change in favor of a democratic Iraq had become Wolfowitz's official position, and the following month, in the PNAC letter, it was embraced by the leading foreign-policy neoconservatives, for whom the appetite to finish off Saddam was scarcely stronger than the desire to cudgel the Clinton administration. Most of them soon moved on to other concerns, but for Wolfowitz, Iraq was now an obsession, and he never stopped writing and talking about it.

The other significant name on the PNAC letter was Richard Perle. He was as abrasive, incautious, and self-indulgent as his old friend was prudent and industrious. (For all of his French-baiting, Perle has a house in southern France and a living room in Chevy Chase full of French cookbooks.) Perle and Wolfowitz had known each other since the summer of 1969, when they interned together in Washington at the modestly named Committee to Maintain a Prudent Defense Policy, under the guidance of two giants of the Cold War, Dean Acheson and Paul Nitze. The two young grad students did research and wrote memos for sympathetic congressmen in defense of the antiballistic missile system, which brought Perle to the attention of Senator Henry "Scoop" Jackson, the Democrat from Washington who was the favorite hawk of the early neoconservatives until Reagan began to ascend in 1976. Perle joined Jackson's staff and never returned to grad school. Through the 1970s he specialized in finding intellectual talent and connecting it to Washington power on behalf of hard-line Cold War policies. One evening, he heard the Princeton professor Bernard Lewis give a brilliant talk on the Middle East; the next day Perle mentioned Lewis to Jackson, and before long the professor was introduced to the world of policy makers and became an adviser on Middle East issues to Jackson as well as Daniel Patrick Moynihan, who was then ambassador to the UN. Perle also recruited two young unknowns named Douglas Feith and Elliott Abrams to come work for Senators Jackson and Moynihan. When I half jokingly suggested that the Iraq War began in Scoop Jackson's office, Perle said, "There's an element of that." Richard Perle was its impresario, with one degree of separation from everyone who mattered. More than anyone, he personified the neoconservative insurgent, absolutely certain of himself and his ideas, always drawing new cadres into the cause, staging frequent guerrilla ambushes on the establishment, preparing to seize ultimate power.

The most important contact Perle made came after Jackson's death, when he went to work at the Reagan Pentagon and earned a reputation for clinging to decidedly dour views of the Soviet Union's intentions even as it was palpably weakening and opening up under Gorbachev. (Perle even wrote a novel in which a top arms-control official saves an American president from giving away the whole nuclear arsenal in negotiations with the Soviets—as Perle claimed to have done with Reagan at Reykjavik.) In 1985, at an event in Washington, Albert Wohlstetter—the hawkish Cold War defense theorist, whose daughter Perle had dated in high school in Los Angeles, who had mentored Paul Wolfowitz at Chicago, and who had brought Perle and Wolfowitz together in Washington in the summer of 1969—introduced Perle to an Iraqi exile with a doctorate in theoretical mathematics from Chicago named Ahmad Chalabi.

By the time of the PNAC letter in January 1998, Perle knew exactly how Saddam could be overthrown: Put Ahmad Chalabi at the head of an army of Iraqi insurgents and back him with American military power and cash.

IN 1996, some of the people in Perle's circle had begun to think about what it would mean for Saddam Hussein to be removed from the Middle East scene. They concluded that it would be very good for Israel. Perle chaired a study group of eight pro-Likud Americans, including Douglas Feith, who had worked under Perle in the Reagan administration, and David Wurmser, who was the author of the paper produced under the group's auspices (Perle lent his own name without ever reading it). Afterward, the group was pleased enough with its work to send the paper to the newly elected Israeli prime minister, Benjamin Netanyahu. "A Clean Break: A New Strategy for Securing the Realm" called for Israel to free itself from both socialist economic policies and the burdens of the Israeli-Palestinian peace process. Instead of retreating from occupied lands in exchange for dubious promises of peace, Wurmser wrote, Israel should take the fight to the Palestinians and their Arab backers and create a realignment of forces in the Middle East that would guarantee Israel's security. Iraq played a central, if utterly fanciful, role in this scenario. The paper dreamed of restoring the Hashemite family of Jordan (deposed from the Iraqi throne in 1958, the year of the republican coup and Chalabi's departure) to rule in Baghdad. The monarchy, in turn, despite being Sunni Muslim, would win over Iraq's Shia because "the Shia venerate foremost the Prophet's family, the direct descendant of which—and in whose veins the blood of the Prophet flows—is King Hussein." With Shiite support, the newly enthroned Hashemites "could use their influence over Najaf to help Israel wean the south Lebanese Shia away from Hezbollah, Iran, and Syria." Then the Palestinians, isolated and alone, would have to accept Israeli demands. Thus, a kingdom invented by T. E. Lawrence and other British officials after World War I to sustain colonial rule and defuse the problem of Arab nationalism resurfaced in 1996 as the quasi-mystical key that would unlock almost every stubborn problem of the contemporary Middle East—the Israeli-Palestinian conflict, the jihadi terrorism and resistance of Hezbollah, America's reliance on oil from Wahhabist Saudi Arabia, and the secular Baathist tyranny of Saddam Hussein.

Wurmser elaborated the theory in his 1999 book *Tyranny's Ally: America's Failure to Defeat Saddam Hussein*, published by the American Enterprise Institute, the right-wing think tank where he was a scholar. The overthrow of Saddam would destabilize both Syria and Iran, isolate Hamas, Islamic Jihad, and Hezbollah, and realign the entire Middle East so that—though this was never spelled out, as if the author feared making himself too clear—Israel would no longer need to negotiate with the Palestinians over the occupied territories. *Tyranny's Ally*, with an introduction by Richard Perle and acknowledgments to Perle, Chalabi, Feith, Lewis, and several other intellectuals of the Iraq War, is a strange and revealing book. It reads as if a graduate student were feverishly trying to apply the half-digested concepts he'd learned in a class with Leo Strauss to subject matter he'd learned in a class with Bernard Lewis. There's an undercurrent of deep distrust of the modern world: Modernity gave us totalitarianism, therefore modernity must be undone. Wurmser wanted to return Iraq to traditional values, especially to Shiite religious tradition (about which he knew almost nothing). "The root of the violence is a century-old radical attack on the Arab world's traditional elite," he wrote. "Proponents of the secular ideology assumed the prerogative to shape and reshape mankind according to their concept of perfection." Dostoyevsky's antirevolutionary novel *Demons* is invoked; the political ideas of Wurmser and a few other proponents of American intervention in the Middle East were closer to Dostoyevsky's religious authoritarianism than to John Stuart Mill's secular liberalism. They advocated democracy, but at bottom they were anti-Enlightenment.

A few weeks before the start of the Iraq War, a State Department official described for me what he called the "everybody move over one theory": Israel would annex the occupied territories, the Palestinians would get Jordan, and the Jordanian Hashemites would be restored to the throne of Iraq. By then, several of the paper's signers, including Feith, Perle, and Wurmser, occupied key policy positions in the administration of George W. Bush, where they were shaping the imminent war to overthrow Saddam.

Does this mean that a pro-Likud cabal insinuated its way into the high councils of the U.S. government and took hold of the apparatus of American foreign policy to serve Israeli interests (as some critics of the war have charged, rather than addressing its merits head on)? Is neoconservative another word for Jewish (as some advocates of the war have complained, rather than addressing their critics head on)? For Feith and Wurmser, the security of Israel was probably the prime mover. But for others, such as Wolfowitz, Iraq stood for different things—an unfinished war, Arab tyranny, weapons proliferation, a strategic threat to oil, American weakness, Democratic fecklessness—and regime change there became the foreign-policy jackpot. A leading Israeli journalist, Ari Shavit, answered the conspiracy theory this way: Jews are drawn to ideas. The idea of realigning the Middle East by overthrowing Saddam Hussein was first proposed by a group of Jewish policy makers and intellectuals who were close to the Likud. And when the second President Bush looked around for a way to think about the uncharted era that began on September 11, 2001, there was one already available.

MOST AMERICAN LIBERALS opposed the Gulf War in 1991. The prospect of a ground assault by half a million troops (even if this was desert and not jungle) touched the extremely sensitive place where America's last land war remained as a muscle memory. And this anxiety played no small part in the "no" votes on the war resolution cast by two young Democratic senators who were veterans of that last war, Bob Kerrey and John Kerry. Vietnam turned most Democrats born after World War II—including me—dovish. Still, the footage of grateful Kuwaitis waving at columns of American troops streaming through the liberated capital knocked something ajar in my worldview. American soldiers were the heroes. In northern Iraq, after the Kurdish uprising, militiamen known as *peshmerga* drove around with pictures of George H. W. Bush taped to their windshields. This was something new.

The decade that followed the Gulf War scrambled everything and turned many of the old truths on their heads. The combination of the Cold War's end, the outbreak of genocidal wars and ethnic conflicts in Europe and Africa, and a Democratic presidency made it possible for liberals to contemplate and even advocate the use of American force for the first time since the Kennedy years. There was more than a little one-eyed partisanship in this thinking, but there was also idealism, for it drew on a powerful idea that came out of one of the twentieth century's greatest movements, the movement for human rights. The idea was that governments should not be allowed to abuse their own citizens on a massive scale; that sovereignty did not excuse rape, torture, murder, and genocide; that it was the world's interest and obligation to end these crimes. This new kind of war became known as humanitarian intervention, and in this country its advocates acquired the name liberal interventionists or, in shorthand, liberal hawks.

Most liberals' preferred institution for doing the intervening was the United Nations. By 1994, Bosnia and Rwanda, scenes of the decade's two genocides, had shown that the UN wasn't up to the task—its efforts in both places only seemed to perpetuate the slaughter and put innocent civilians at greater risk. Though Franklin Roosevelt envisioned the UN as an antifascist organization, it was founded as a body of sovereign nations; its ultimate function was to resolve disputes between them and preserve the status quo. With Libya taking its turn as chair of the Human Rights Commission, the UN was hardly the ideal instrument for stopping atrocities. Nor was it given the necessary push by the powers that sat on the Security Council, especially the United States. The UN and the Western powers passed responsibility for these tragedies back and forth, like a holding-company scheme. But for many citizens, including many American liberals, the unstopped bleeding in these distant places demanded a response, and if it wasn't going to come from the UN or the European countries, it would have to come from the superpower.

Without a Soviet Union or a Cold War, these interventions didn't carry the odor of "vital strategic interest." The very thing that disqualified Bosnia, Rwanda, Haiti, and Kosovo from meriting American force in the eyes of conservatives ("We don't have a dog in that fight," Secretary of State James Baker said of Bosnia) made force more thinkable to liberals. The rare Republican supporters of intervention (including Paul Wolfowitz), who saw national interest and the spread of human rights as inextricable, attacked liberals for their utopian dreams. "Airy humanitarianism" sneered Kagan. The fact that some liberals and conservatives supported the same military policies in the nineties didn't mean that they had started from the same place; nor, a few years later, would they end up together.

The Republican Party—again, partly out of strategic principle and partly out of naked partisanship—did everything it could to tie Clinton's hands and prevent the American military from being used to fight distant, obscure wars or provide security in the inevitably messy aftermaths. Few terms were more reviled by Republicans than "nation building." As Kagan, one of the rare dissenters, observed in 1995, "In a few short years, America had passed through a looking glass into an upside-down world where (some) liberal Democrats were calling for U.S. military action abroad while conservative Republicans warned of swamps, sand traps, neocolonialism, and 'another Vietnam.' The result was a timid and uncertain Democratic President whose few half-hearted gestures toward internationalist leadership were attacked and constrained by a Republican opposition in Congress."

For lifelong doves, the first sip of this drink called humanitarian intervention carried a special thrill. All the drama, the intense heat of argument, was generated in the decision whether or not to go to war. In this moment one's moral credentials were on the line. It was a kind of existential choice, a statement of values, all the more potent for being politically unorthodox and sometimes even brave. None of this made the decisions any less serious or sincere, but the more mundane questions of what would happen later tended to dissolve in a mist of high purpose. And because liberal hawks responded to humanitarian crises, they were less likely to think strategically about the shape of the world in ten or twenty years; the long-range answers they offered, such as international criminal courts, UN resolutions, and regional intervention forces, seemed like noble wishes rather than practical answers. Over and over, they had to fall back on the solution with which they felt least comfortable—American power.

Among the causes of the liberal hawks of the nineties, Iraq never made the list. Iraq had been a humanitarian crisis in 1988, when Saddam committed genocide against the Kurds at the end of the Iran-Iraq War, and again in 1991, when Saddam massacred the Shia and Kurds who had risen up at the end of the Gulf War. Apart from Kanan Makiya and a few other lonely voices, no one was calling for armed intervention to overthrow the Baathist regime back then. The idea hadn't yet taken hold. Of course, one could argue, every day under Saddam's rule in Iraq was a humanitarian crisis. Human Rights Watch and other organizations meticulously documented the Baath Party's vast crimes. But without the eyes of the media, without reports of mass graves, and with the fear that war in Iraq would produce large-scale casualties, a dictator who had far more blood on his hands than Slobodan Milošević managed to avoid the relentless opprobrium of the interventionists of the nineties. Perhaps the Arab world was somehow beyond the reach of human rights in a way that Bosnia and Kosovo were not. Perhaps the fact that the United States had strategic interests in the region (oil), and that the issue of Iraq involved unconventional weapons as well as mass murder, made the question of war more complicated for "airy humanitarians." In any event, the Clinton years ended with no sense that the achievement in the Balkans should be followed up in Mesopotamia, or anywhere else. The liberal hawks had always been a minority, even among Democrats.

The small, inconclusive wars of the nineties raised but failed to answer the essential questions of the post–Cold War world: What do human rights have to do with national security? What should the United States do about threats that the world insists on ignoring? Is it necessary for war to have the sanction of an international body? What are the limits of sovereignty? Can democracy be brought by force? Whose responsibility does a defeated country become after a war? Most of all: What role should America's preeminent power play in shaping the answers? These questions hung in the air unanswered by the time the century turned. Soon the new administration in Washington would bring them all into focus, over Iraq.

BY 2000, the lame-duck President Clinton showed no sign of wanting to deal once and for all with a defiant Iraq. The Iraq Liberation Act was on the books but had never been in Clinton's heart. Iraq became the neoconservatives' leading cause because the Clinton policy of sanctions and occasional missile attacks seemed to be failing, but for a larger reason, too: They saw Iraq as the test case for their ideas about American power and world leadership. Iraq represented the worst failure of the nineties and the first opportunity of the new American century. In the middle of the 2000 presidential campaign, Kagan and Kristol published a warning shot in the form of an essay collection pointedly, and perhaps nostalgically, called *Present Dangers*. It was a book-length exposition of the themes of their earlier articles, and the contributors included many of the leading figures in what was becoming a critical mass of hawkish foreign-policy opinion. Richard Perle's essay dripped scorn, claiming that Clinton's December 1998 bombing of Iraqi installations, widely ridiculed as a "wag the dog" distraction in the middle of impeachment hearings, "had no lasting effect" (an assertion that was refuted after the invasion by the Iraq Survey Group, which found that the missile strikes had helped to finish off what was left of Saddam's chemical weapons facilities). Without mentioning his friend Ahmad Chalabi by name, Perle proposed the Iraqi National Congress, or INC, led by Chalabi, as the crowbar with which America could pry Iraq free from Saddam's grip. Finally, Perle broke the last taboo and broached the possibility of a U.S. military role: "As a last resort . . . we should build up our own ground forces in the region so that we have the capacity to protect and assist the anti-Saddam forces in the northern and southern parts of Iraq."

Paul Wolfowitz's essay was far more judicious, an on-the-other-hand attempt to apply principles learned during the Cold War to the new world, with its many new dangers. Though this ex-Democrat was as contemptuous of the Democrats as the book's other essayists, Wolfowitz seemed in no mood to assert America's benevolent hegemony across the globe. He even glanced back worriedly at the trauma that had made so many liberals into pacifists. "We cannot ignore the uncomfortable fact that economic and social circumstances may better prepare some countries for democracy than others," wrote Wolfowitz, who had served a stint as a widely admired ambassador to Indonesia (most of the other neoconservatives had spent their entire careers in Washington). "Oddly, we seem to have forgotten what Vietnam should have taught us about the limitations of the military as an instrument of 'nation-building.' Promoting democracy requires attention to specific circumstances and to the limitations of U.S. leverage. Both because of what the United States is, and because of what is possible, we cannot engage either in promoting democracy or in nation-building as an exercise of will. We must proceed by interaction and indirection, not imposition. In this respect, post–World War II experiences with Germany and Japan offer misleading guides to what is possible now, even in a period of American primacy."

Thus Paul Wolfowitz in the year 2000—sounding like a prudent expert at the Carnegie Endowment for International Peace—the same man who within a few years would acquire the epithet "Wolfowitz of Arabia" after unlearning in Iraq everything quoted above. There are no pure ideas and straight lines in the history of great events. When policy makers change their views, "Usually it's because circumstances change," Kagan told me, "or they got insulted by somebody in power." In Wolfowitz's case, he might have been angling for a job in the administration of the leading Republican presidential candidate, George W. Bush, whom he served as a foreign-policy adviser during the campaign and who made it clear that crusades to transform the world after America's image were not going to be his thing. Bush's guide to the world could be found in a *Foreign Affairs* article—not Kagan's and Kristol's from 1996 but an essay in the January 2000 issue by the provost of Stanford University, Condoleezza Rice, which called for a return to the great-power realism of Nixon, Kissinger, and Bush's father.

But after the disputed election, when the younger Bush's national-security team began to take shape, one found sprinkled throughout the government the names of neoconservatives who knew one another from years in and out of power, and whose ideas for the post–Cold War world had come into focus during the nineties: Wolfowitz, Feith, Wurmser, Shulsky, Stephen Cambone, and others at the Pentagon; Wolfowitz's former aide I. Lewis "Scooter" Libby, John Hannah, and William J. Luti in Vice President Cheney's office; Stephen Hadley, Elliott Abrams, and Zalmay Khalilzad on the National Security Council; John Bolton at State; Perle, Kenneth Adelman, and R. James Woolsey on the advisory Defense Policy Board. Their patrons were Cheney and the new secretary of defense, Donald Rumsfeld. Rumsfeld was a hard-edged old Cold Warrior, an aggressive nationalist. Cheney, Rumsfeld's protégé, colleague, and pal through several administrations, came from the same stock.

Many of these officials had served at the middle levels under Reagan, embracing his hawkish idealism. The fall of communism and the emergence of the United States as the world's only superpower had given them a sense of historical victory. Then they had spent the nineties watching the first Bush administration return to narrow realism and the Clinton administration founder from crisis to crisis, squandering Reagan's triumph. They had made their long march through the think tanks and policy journals, honing their ideas and perfecting their attacks. Now they were coming back to power as insurgents, scornful of the entrenched bureaucracy, the more cautious moderates in their own party (including the new secretary of state, Colin Powell), and the tired, defeated Democrats. They were supremely confident; all they needed was a mission.

I asked Robert Kagan how his ideas had traveled from the pages of *Commentary* to the foreign-policy apparatus of the Bush administration. He waved me off. It didn't work that way, he said. "September 11 is the turning point. Not anything else. This is not what Bush was on September 10."

The ideas of the neoconservatives had nothing to do with it?

Kagan sighed. "Here's what I'm willing to say. Did we keep alive a certain way of looking at American foreign policy at a time when it was pretty unpopular? Yes. I think probably you need to have people do that so that you have something to come back to. And, in a way, then you have a ready-made approach to the world."

2

FEVERED MINDS

IN THE SPRING of 2002, I met Kanan Makiya for one of our irregular coffees in a Harvard Square basement café. By then I'd moved from Cambridge to New York, where on the morning of September 11, 2001, I rushed down Fifth Avenue against the current of ash-covered men and women who were streaming uptown from the place where the World Trade Center towers had been, and crossed the Brooklyn Bridge in an exodus of red-faced workers as smoke and dust poured into the sky.

Six months and one war in Afghanistan later, Makiya was talking about another war, this one in Iraq. It would be the war he had called for, to no avail, back in 1991—a war to overthrow Saddam Hussein.

As early as January 2001, at the new administration's first national security meeting, officials floated plans to the freshly sworn-in president for the removal of Saddam, in accord with the largely symbolic Iraq Liberation Act of 1998 (though this would emerge only three years later, in an insider's account by Bush's first, short-lived treasury secretary, Paul O'Neill). In April, at the administration's first meeting on terrorism, Richard Clarke, the leading counterterrorism official of three administrations, found that Bush's new appointees, especially Deputy Secretary of Defense Paul Wolfowitz, were far more interested in the threat from states like Iraq than from the stateless and shadowy band of global jihadis called al-Qaeda. "I just don't understand why we are beginning by talking about this one man bin Laden," Clarke later quoted Wolfowitz as saying.. "You give bin Laden too much credit. He could not do all these things like the 1993 attack on New York, not without a state sponsor." Wolfowitz meant Iraq. Having fought and—as they saw it—won the Cold War with their hard-line policies, officials like him who had come back to power still viewed the world of dangers in terms of heavily militarized enemy states. The 1990s hadn't changed their thinking. To them, those were lost years: Under Clinton there had been far too much focus on globalization and international institutions and "soft," borderless threats like poverty and ethnic conflict.

Then came September 11. Within minutes of fleeing his office at the devastated Pentagon, Wolfowitz told aides that he suspected Iraqi involvement in the attacks. A little past two in the afternoon, while the air in lower Manhattan and along the Potomac was still full of acrid smoke, assistants to Defense Secretary Donald Rumsfeld took notes as their boss held forth in the National Military Command Center: "best info fast. Judge whether good enough hit S.H. at same time. Not only UBL [Usama bin Laden]. Go massive. Sweep it all up. Things related and not." That same afternoon, one of Bush's speechwriters, David Frum, having been evacuated from the White House and taken shelter in the offices of the American Enterprise Institute, got on the phone with Richard Perle, Washington's most assiduous proponent of regime change in Iraq. "Whatever else the President says," Perle urged from his vacation home in the south of France, "he must make clear that he's holding responsible not just terrorists but whoever harbors those terrorists." That night, in a televised address from the White House, Bush followed Perle's advice to the word and then expanded on it: The rest of the world was either with America or with the terrorists. The day after the attacks, according to Richard Clarke, Bush ordered his counterterrorism team to find out whether there could be any connection to Iraq. "See if Saddam did this. See if he's linked in any way."

"But, Mr. President, al-Qaeda did this," Clarke replied.

"I know, I know, but . . . see if Saddam was involved. Just look. I want to know any shred."

Three days later, in a crisis meeting at Camp David, Wolfowitz kept returning to Iraq as the most important target for the initial American response, until the president finally shut him up. Afghanistan would be first, but the idea of Iraq was in play, and Bush was not unreceptive—after all, Wolfowitz had been given plenty of air time, much to the frustration of Secretary of State Colin Powell. On September 17, six days after the attacks, Bush told his war council, "I believe Iraq was involved."

"Until I'm persuaded otherwise, this is what I think," Robert Kagan said. "Paul may have brought it up, but Bush from the beginning was thinking about Iraq. I think that Bush had Iraq on the brain. Paul, who is a deputy secretary of defense who does not get along with his secretary of defense and whose alone time with the president is probably minimal, fighting giants like Powell, who was much stronger than he was? I think it had to be the president. This is what the president wanted to do."

Richard Perle, Wolfowitz's friend for more than three decades, agreed. Until September 11, he said, proponents of regime change in Iraq were losing the argument within the administration. "Nine-eleven had a profound effect on the president's thinking. It wasn't the arguments or the positions held by me, or Paul, or anyone else before that. The world began on nine-eleven. There's no intellectual history." But there was already in place across the top levels of the national-security bureaucracy a group of people with a definite intellectual history, who could give the president's new impulses a strategy, a doctrine, a worldview. Perle, like Kagan, cautioned against making too much of papers published in obscure foreign-policy journals. What mattered was who held positions of power. "The people are important, and the ideas are important in connection with the people," Perle told me one winter afternoon in the living room of his large house just outside Washington. "But the ideas themselves—let's put it this way: If Bush had staffed his administration with a group of people selected by Brent Scowcroft and Jim Baker, which might well have happened, then it could have been different, because they would not have carried into it the ideas that the people who wound up in important positions brought to it. The ideas are only important as they reside in the minds of people who were involved directly in the decision process."

Bush's two key appointments were Cheney and Rumsfeld. Neither man brought particularly original thinking to the discussion of America's role in the world after September 11; their influence lay in position and force of character. Rumsfeld, Gerald Ford's defense secretary, had been a businessman for almost a quarter century; his most passionate interest on returning to government was missile defense and, more broadly, the transformation of the military into a high-tech fighting force. He was an unmatched bureaucratic infighter, but if he had any well-considered foreign-policy views, he kept them to himself. During the Afghanistan War that followed September 11, he became the administration's most visible face, handling the press with great panache, and when the Taliban fell more quickly and easily than the experts predicted, Rumsfeld became the strategic genius no one dared to doubt. But the aftermath of that war provided a clue to the administration's thinking about postwar Iraq: The American commitment to securing and rebuilding Afghanistan was so thin that the government of Hamid Karzai controlled little of the country outside Kabul. Senator Joseph Biden, the Democrat from Delaware who chaired the Foreign Relations Committee in 2002, told me in December 2003, "My bet from day one—I hope I am wrong—has been that the dominant element of this administration was going to be the neorealists, Cheney and Rumsfeld, who no more are committed to nation building than this table is committed to go home with me in my back pocket. And so I look at Afghanistan as a template. That's the canvas on which you paint Iraq's future." No one at the top level of the administration was less interested in the future of Iraq than Donald Rumsfeld. Yet he would demand and receive control over the postwar, and he would entrust it to his more ideologically fervent aides, in whom he placed the same incurious confidence that the president placed in Rumsfeld.

The administration's great mystery was Cheney. With the possible exception of Rumsfeld, no one had a darker, more Hobbesian vision of international affairs. But he had a talent for keeping his thoughts to himself, and as George H. W. Bush's secretary of defense he seemed, publicly at least, to hold the same moderate Republican views as his boss. Unlike Wolfowitz, he never doubted the wisdom of how the Gulf War ended. Kenneth Adelman, Cheney's old colleague and friend, who had introduced him and Rumsfeld to Wolfowitz in 1981, said, "Cheney didn't reconsider leaving Saddam in place in '91. It bothered Paul, not Dick." Adelman added that Cheney wasn't particularly engaged in foreign-policy debates in the nineties. Cheney sharply criticized the interventions of the Clinton years, but otherwise he was occupied running the oil-services giant Halliburton in Dallas, where, for obviously mercenary reasons, he advocated lifting sanctions on Iran. His name didn't even appear on the PNAC letter.

When Cheney came back to power as vice president, Iraq was nowhere near the top of his agenda in the first months of 2001, and spreading democracy around the world didn't make the list. But September 11 confirmed Cheney in his essential instinct about the nature of the world. His speeches after the terror attacks conveyed almost a sense of relief that here finally was a global enemy on the scale of communism. The Defense Planning Guidance of 1992, written by former Cheney aides who were all back in the new Bush administration, had laid the framework for a post–September 11 foreign policy a decade earlier. Cheney now emerged from his self-created obscurity as its godfather and the hardest of hard-liners on Iraq. Though he never let the nation in on his change of mind, he had reversed his own position on the end of the Gulf War. Richard Perle said of Cheney, "Nine-eleven was a turning point with respect to tolerating the risk of leaving Saddam unmolested. And how far behind that this caboose of democratization was placed on the train, I'm not sure." Once Cheney had Saddam and Iraq in his sights, he never blinked.

Like Rumsfeld, Cheney surrounded himself with ideologues for aides. Unlike Rumsfeld, after September 11 he took a serious interest in what they thought. He invited intellectuals to the White House to talk about the future of the Arab-Muslim world. He showed a relish for grand strategy (without ever abandoning his disdain for the messy details of postwar reconstructions in which Clinton had gotten bogged down). Still, his role in shaping policy remained elusive to almost everyone who encountered him. "I've never seen anything like it," said a senior official who had occasional dealings with Cheney and his staff. "He comes to meetings, sits there, never says a word, or asks one or two really good questions—you never knew where they were standing, you never knew what their viewpoint was, except occasionally when you would rub them wrong on something like Taiwan. But most often they disguised it marvelously well. And then twenty-four hours later, forty-eight hours later, ninety-six hours later, you thought a decision had been made—and all of a sudden policy was being implemented 180 degrees opposite that decision."

Until Biden's invitations to the White House stopped coming in the buildup to war with Iraq, the chairman of the Senate Foreign Relations Committee would meet with the president in the Oval Office, and Bush would listen and nod, seeming convinced by Biden's arguments for more troops in Afghanistan or more money to secure Russian nuclear material, while Cheney sat mute and motionless, "like a big bullfrog on a log." Suddenly, the vice president would open his mouth and croak, "No, Mr. President, that's not right." Soon the meeting would end, and Biden would realize that his arguments had gone nowhere. "I underestimated Cheney's power," Biden admitted. His power came not just from the dependence of a new president on his far more experienced number two, but on Cheney's character. He had what Leslie Gelb, the former president of the Council on Foreign Relations, called "great presence at table. Cheney is shrewd, a quick thinker, a good arguer, the best I've ever seen. So much better than the Democrats." Compared with Democrats, Gelb said, Cheney and the other top Bush officials "are far more ruthless. They scare the shit out of Democrats and the foreign-policy establishment, the same way the Committee on the Present Danger did in the late 1970s—by talking about threats." Cheney's ruthlessness made him a formidable partisan. He didn't just want to win; he wanted to destroy the opposition as well.

If Cheney and Rumsfeld were the bureaucratic heavyweights, the leading intellect of the post–September 11 policy was Wolfowitz. In the weeks after the terror attacks, there was a surprising convergence between the former oilman president, whose favorite philosopher was Jesus and who could mock his own submediocre academic record because it didn't matter when your last name was Bush, and his brilliant deputy secretary of defense, a secular Jew with a Cornell BA in mathematics and a Chicago PhD in political science, whose influences were Albert Wohlstetter, Leo Strauss, and Allan Bloom. Bush and Wolfowitz—both of them now free of the stifling authority of Bush's father—saw the world in the same way. They believed in the existence of evil, and they had messianic notions of what America should do about it. Bush once said of Saddam, "He tried to kill my dad," but on Iraq it was Bush himself who seized the chance to cast off the Oedipal burden and prove that he was his own man, better able than his father to deal with an old enemy.

In January 2002, at his first State of the Union address, Bush set down a rhetorical marker for the coming year: Iraq, he declared, belonged to an "axis of evil." In February, he ordered General Tommy Franks of the Central Command to begin shifting forces from Afghanistan to the Gulf. In March, he interrupted a meeting between his national security adviser, Condoleezza Rice, and three senators: "Fuck Saddam," the president said. "We're taking him out." By the early spring of 2002, a full year before the invasion, the administration was inexorably set on a course of war.

Throughout the spring, Richard Haass, the director of policy planning in the State Department, began to hear more and more "bureaucratic chatter" about a war, but he didn't take it too seriously until, in June, he went to see Condoleezza Rice at the White House for their regular meeting on key foreign-policy issues. When they came to Iraq, Haass began to give the State Department's reasons for misgivings about a war. "Save your breath," Rice interrupted. "The president has already made up his mind." This was news to Haass. Everyone at the top level of the administration could recite the arguments on either side by heart; the question was how to weigh them. Now the policy had been set without the weighing ever taking place. "It was an accretion, a tipping point," Haass said. "A decision was not made—a decision happened, and you can't say when or how."

When we met for coffee, Makiya didn't know this yet. But there was talk in the air. He had just spoken at a conference at Brandeis University on the Islamic world and the West after September 11. At the conference, Makiya raised the possibility of regime change in Iraq, only to be told by the other participants that the subject was out of bounds. The consensus among "progressive" intellectuals was also set: War with Iraq was unspeakable. "They wouldn't let me talk about it," Makiya said in his mild, nervous way. This bewildered rather than angered him. He seemed slightly breathless, as if he were suppressing excitement. Something was happening. The lonely dream he'd pursued for so many years in Cambridge was suddenly converging with history. Such chances did not occur often in life, and Makiya was determined to make the most of this one. He was already in touch with members of the administration, in the vice president's office and the Pentagon. They were receptive to his talk about democracy in Iraq.

"There's a kind of relationship between the United States and Iraq that's become incestuous, incestuous," Makiya said to me once during that decisive year 2002. "For eleven years it's grown. A country of 250 million, the only superpower in the world, and this tin-pot little dictatorship by comparison (Iraq is no Germany), this nothing little country by contrast, is essentially at the center of world politics. It's totally disproportionate. It's completely bizarre. And they're locked in this embrace that the first Gulf War created, and therefore it becomes natural for Iraqis now to see in the resolution of this incestuous relationship a future."

WHY DID THE UNITED STATES invade Iraq? It still isn't possible to be sure—and this remains the most remarkable thing about the Iraq War. Richard Haass said that he will go to his grave not knowing the answer. It was something that some people wanted to do. Before the invasion, Americans argued not just about whether a war should happen, but for what reasons it should happen—what the real motives of the Bush administration were and should be. Since the invasion, we have continued to argue, and we will go on arguing for years to come. Iraq is the *Rashomon* of wars.

The answer has something to do with September 11. But what, exactly?

The debate over Iraq began with the wounds of the terror attacks still open. Through the winter of 2002 into spring, while the blasted graveyard of city blocks downtown was cleared by excavation crews working twenty-four hours a day, I took part in endless conversations about how the world had and hadn't changed. After years of trivial, bitterly partisan politics, September 11 had reopened large questions in a way that was both confusing and liberating. A natural response would be to fall back into familiar postures, and many people in America did this. But extraordinary times called for new thinking. Searching for a compass through the era just begun, I was drawn to people who thought boldly.

One of them was the writer Paul Berman, who was working out a theory about what was now being called the war on terrorism. Some of his thinking took place aloud in the midnight hour over food and drink at a bistro in the Brooklyn neighborhood where we both lived. Berman, in his early fifties, lived alone in a walk-up apartment that was strewn with back issues of the *Anarcho-Syndicalist Review* and volumes of French literature and philosophy in the original. He lived above a Palestinian grocery store half a block from Atlantic Avenue, where there was an established Middle Eastern community, with Syrian antiques shops and Yemeni restaurants and bookstores that carried Arabic literature, including the works of some of the great Muslim thinkers of the twentieth century. After September 11, Berman explored the neighborhood bookstores and began to read the works of Sayyid Qutb, the leader of the Egyptian Muslim Brotherhood who was hanged by Nasser in 1966. Qutb's writings about Islam, the West, and global jihad inspired other Islamist thinkers, such as the Palestinian Abdullah Azzam, who in turn inspired Osama bin Laden. (In the late eighties the U.S. headquarters of al-Qaeda's predecessor organization, the Afghan Service Bureau, occupied a storefront at 566 Atlantic Avenue, next to a Moroccan textile shop; until they closed down after September 11, there were also radical mosques on Atlantic Avenue that followed the blind Egyptian sheikh Omar Abdel-Rahman, spiritual leader of the worldwide jihad, who was convicted in 1995 of plotting to bomb New York's bridges and tunnels.)

Qutb's ideas confirmed the theory that Berman had begun to develop, which was this: The young Arab men who had steered those four airplanes to apocalyptic death were not products of an alien world. They weren't driven by Muslim tradition, or Third World poverty, or the clash of civilizations, or Western imperialism. They were modern, and the ideology that held them and millions of others across the Islamic world in its ecstatic grip had been produced by the modern world—in fact, by the West. It was the same nihilistic fantasy of revolutionary power and mass slaughter that, in the last century, drove Germans and Italians and Spaniards and Russians (and millions of others across the world) to similar acts of apocalyptic death. This ideology had a name: totalitarianism. Its great explainers were Orwell, Camus, Koestler, Arendt, Solzhenitsyn. In Europe its feverish mood had long since broken by 1989, but in the Islamic world, where modernity failed successive generations, the sickness had been spreading. Berman was saying that the Islamist movement is one that Westerners should be able to recognize—except when they are so blinded by a wishful belief in rationality that only an event on the scale of September 11 alerts them to its existence. Even then, for some, the urge not to see remains overpowering.

Totalitarianism is a revolt against liberalism. And the answer to it is liberalism—liberal ideas (Berman never ceased to talk about the war of ideas) but also liberalism armed, liberalism without the dream of paradise. Berman was a member of the generation of 1968, and he still spoke fondly of his comrades in the tiny anarcho-syndicalist movement. But by 1989 he had made his peace with liberalism, and his politics had grown close to that of certain liberals during the early Cold War—that is, antitotalitarian and prodemocratic. In the decade after the revolutions of 1989, the clarity of this politics faded a bit. The humanitarian disasters in Africa, the skirmishes in the no-fly zones over northern and southern Iraq—these were hard to understand in terms of the Hegelian movement of history toward human freedom. Even the wars of Serb fascism felt like aftershocks, radiating outward from the last place in Europe that hadn't received the news. After September 11, Berman (and others, among liberals and leftists as well as on the right) found his way back into the twentieth century, the age of ideology and the tremendous intellectual excitement it stirred up. Suddenly all the books of modern history and politics crammed into Berman's apartment sprang back to life on their shelves or in their stacks on the floor—along with new ones, by the likes of Sayyid Qutb.

Berman set about his project with a fierce and solitary intensity. There must have been weeks on end when he never emerged from his apartment. He called it "war duty"—after all, New York had become a front line. Berman believed strenuously that it was the job of intellectuals to explain and mend the rent that had just been made in the fabric of our world. For him, the answer lay in literature and philosophy as much as politics, let alone policy. One night, upon leaving his post long enough to share a late meal at the bistro, he announced, "I've found a master text!" It was Camus' *The Rebel*, subtitled *An Essay on Man in Revolt*. Nihilistic terror was nothing new; the hijackers went back to the French Revolution. "Here, murder and suicide are two sides of the same system," Camus wrote, giving Berman an epigraph. His conversation those nights had the quality of annoying and yet undeniably thrilling excess under the pressure of a justifiable obsession. He almost visibly trembled with his discoveries, though the work was hard, even discouraging, and Berman was personally given to grim self-assessment. He would order his cheeseburger and red wine (the waitresses all knew him) and, drumming a finger on the table to a rhythm only he could hear (he played jazz viola), or wagging the same finger in the air for emphasis, he would begin an account of Victor Hugo's plays and the bombings of the late nineteenth-century Russian nihilists, which on the inexorable curve of Berman's thinking would lead us forward to the most recent suicide attacks in Jerusalem and bin Laden's latest communiqué from the mountains of the Hindu Kush. I listened, occasionally asking a skeptical question, admiring the dedication of his project (who else was really trying to figure this stuff out?), mostly sympathizing—but also worrying about Berman's tendency toward sweeping, distinction-erasing intellectual moves. What, for example, did his theory have to do with Iraq?

It wasn't hard to see that the Arab Baath Socialist Party in Baghdad was totalitarian. Makiya had shown this in his *Republic of Fear*. The regime held power through a cult of leader worship, pervasive terror created by endless acts of astonishing violence against its own citizens, overlapping and ubiquitous security agencies, continuous wars of aggression, and a climate of conspiratorial thinking and paranoia toward the Zionist and imperialist enemies. Saddam seemed to have modeled his regime on Orwell's *1984*, right down to Big Brother's mustache. His hero was Stalin, whom Saddam, more than any other of the world's dictators, resembled. The founder of the Baath Party in Damascus in the early 1940s, Michel Aflaq (whose tomb is in Baghdad), was deeply influenced by Nazi ideology. But Baathism—like its European progenitors—was nominally secular. It was hostile to Islamist regimes and ideologies. It was also visibly in decay. The days of its ability to move masses of people to frenzies of hatred and violence were over. Then why go to war with Iraq in order to fight al-Qaeda?

Berman answered: because Baathism was one of the "Muslim totalitarianisms," the other being Islamism. The terror war was not just a police action or a military campaign. Like the war against fascism and the Cold War, it was an ideological war, a "mental war." Victory required that millions of people across the Muslim world give up murderous political ideas. It would be a long, hard, complicated business. But the overthrow of Saddam and the establishment of an Iraqi democracy as a beachhead in the Middle East would show that the United States was on the side of liberal-minded Arabs like Kanan Makiya and against the totalitarians and their ideas. Regime change would show that we, too, were capable of fighting for an idea—the idea of freedom. The willingness of liberal democracy to defend itself and fight for its principles is always in doubt. Alexis de Tocqueville worried about it; Hitler and Mussolini scoffed at it; so, more recently, did bin Laden. But the greatest affirmation of this willingness was made by Lincoln at Gettysburg, where he vowed that a nation (and not only his own—any nation) "conceived in liberty and dedicated to the proposition that all men are created equal" could long endure.

This was not the kind of thinking that gets one invited to join the Council on Foreign Relations. Berman wasn't particularly interested in military strategy or policy issues. The answers to September 11 were just as likely to be found in Dostoyevsky and Camus as at the Brookings Institution or in the pages of Foreign Affairs. He was responding viscerally to the event (our late-night talks kept coming back to the scale of destruction just across the East River, shocking evidence of the Islamists' ambition) and also at an extremely high altitude of abstraction, where details become specks.

THE YEAR AND A HALF BETWEEN the terror attacks and the invasion of Iraq was crowded with large, aggressive ideas. Like the liberal revolutions of 1848, or the Bolshevik surge of 1917, or the utopian spring of 1968, September 11 gave political intellectuals plenty of work. Throughout 2002, as the Bush administration pursued its course of inevitable confrontation with Saddam, at the same time, outside the walls of power, there rose a clamor of arguments about the coming war, the nature of the enemy, the role of America in the world. Ideas burned hot across an astonishing assortment of minds.

Some of these minds were granted access to the highest offices of government. Bernard Lewis, the eminent British-born professor emeritus of Middle Eastern studies at Princeton, who had first been introduced to official Washington in the early 1970s by Richard Perle, became the administration hawks' chief guide to the Arab world, along with Fouad Ajami, a suave Lebanese-born scholar at the Johns Hopkins School of Advanced International Studies, where his friend Paul Wolfowitz was dean during the nineties. In 2002, Lewis and Ajami were summoned to meet with Dick Cheney. They told the vice president what everyone else could read in books such as Lewis's *What Went Wrong?* and Ajami's *The Dream Palace of the Arabs.* The once-great Arab and Muslim world is a sick man, afflicted with corrupt dictatorships, repressed populations, extreme ideologies, paranoid conspiracy theories, cultural and economic backwardness. For decades, even centuries, this civilization has steadily fallen behind as the West and the rest of the world progressed into modernity. This decay is a source of humiliation and rage to millions of Arabs and non-Arab Muslims. In recent years, the sickness has produced a threat that ranges far beyond the region. American power has helped to keep the Arab world in decline by supporting sclerotic tyrannies; only an American break with its own history in the region can reverse it. The Arabs cannot pull themselves out of their historic rut. They need to be jolted out by some foreign-born shock. The overthrow of the Iraqi regime would provide one.

"Above and beyond toppling the regime of Saddam Hussein and dismantling its deadly weapons," Ajami wrote in early 2003, "the driving motivation of a new American endeavor in Iraq and in neighboring Arab lands should be modernizing the Arab world." The inevitable outcry from Arabs should be discounted as "the 'road rage' of a thwarted Arab world— the congenital condition of a culture yet to take full responsibility for

its self-inflicted wounds." Ajami, whose prose employs the archaic ca-
dences and vocabulary of a nostalgist, was proposing an American project as grand as the British colonial mission in the Middle East: "the
spearheading of a reformist project that seeks to modernize and transform the Arab landscape. Iraq would be the starting point, and beyond
Iraq lies an Arab political and economic tradition and a culture whose
agonies and failures have been on cruel display."

Ajami and Lewis were experts, area specialists. They were joined in
championing the coming war with Iraq by a motley crew of general-
ists—writers, journalists, professors, activists. There was, to begin,
Robert Kagan. He and William Kristol had supported John McCain as
the candidate of "national greatness" during the 2000 Republican primary; George W. Bush's call for "humility" and narrowly defined interests in foreign policy represented everything Kagan had argued against
during the nineties. But after September 11, President Bush began to
sound like a neoconservative, and *The Weekly Standard* became his most
influential journalistic champion, enjoying the same privileged relationship that the early *New Republic* had with Woodrow Wilson when
he brought America into the First World War. Writing in January 2002,
Kagan and Kristol urged military intervention in Iraq as part of America's
reassertion of global leadership: "The failure of the United States to take
risks, and to take responsibility, in the 1990s, paved the way to September 11." Nothing short of the survival of "liberal civilization" itself
depended on American action in Iraq. In the summer of 2002, Kagan
wrote a long essay called "Americans Are from Mars, Europeans Are
from Venus" that quickly broke out of the obscure pages of *Policy Review* and became the subject of intense debate on both sides of the Atlantic (it was subsequently published as a book, *Of Paradise and Power*).
Having laid much of the intellectual groundwork in the nineties for the
administration's assertive foreign policy, Kagan now described a new
era in which America and Europe have parted ways. Europe, weakened by the wars of the twentieth century, seeks cooperation and
peace through multilateral institutions such as the European Union and
the UN. America, at the zenith of world leadership, is strong enough
to face alone the beasts in the jungle outside the civilized camp of the
West. America will use power because it can, and it should not expect

Europe to go along. Venus, Mars; Kant, Hobbes; paradise, power: Europe and America no longer live in the same world, as they did under the Cold War alliance, and everyone would be better off admitting it. Kagan's essay was a philosophical brief for unilateralism.

There was the American Enterprise Institute, a Washington think tank whose tentacles extended deep into the administration. At seminars and in papers, AEI's resident fellows began to incubate grand theories of an unrivaled and unapologetic American empire, more powerful than any in history, which would spread democracy by force, securing national interests by exporting national values, beginning in Iraq. "You have to start somewhere!" exclaimed Danielle Pletka, a vice president of AEI and former aide to Senator Jesse Helms. "There are always a million excuses not to do something like this." Pletka wrote the prowar testimony that Reagan's secretary of defense, Caspar Weinberger, gave to Congress in August 2002, including these words: "People say there will be chaos. I disagree, but I must confess frankly that even chaos would be better than Saddam."

There was Victor Davis Hanson, a struggling raisin farmer in California's Central Valley and prolific classics professor at Fresno State University. Hanson's scholarly writing on ancient Greece theorized that Athens became the greatest military power of the Mediterranean because its soldiers were yeoman farmers and citizens: They fought as freemen for a republic, not as slaves for a tyrant; they fought with reason rather than superstition, which gave them superiority on the battlefield. This marriage of democratic ideology with annihilating force became the key to the success of Western civilization over the following centuries, unto the American imperium, with our democratizing mission and massive firepower. In the months after September 11, in the pages of the conservative magazine *National Review*, Hanson's interpretation of preclassical Athens made him a fierce advocate of the use of overwhelming U.S. force almost anywhere in the world we might have enemies. His writings caught the attention of Vice President Cheney and won the gloomy farmer-professor with the taste for warmongering rhetoric a dinner invitation to the White House.

There was nothing unusual about a classicist dining with the Bush administration. A number of neoconservatives—Wolfowitz was the most prominent, but there were many others in policy-making positions under Bush and, earlier, Reagan—had been students of Leo Strauss, or of his disciple, Allan Bloom. Strauss emigrated from Germany in the early thirties and ended up at the University of Chicago, teaching Plato, Xenophon, Maimonides, Machiavelli, Spinoza, and Nietzsche to two decades of enthralled young Americans. Strauss's intellectual project was to call into question the complacent materialism and secularism of the modern West and to send his students back for deeper wisdom to close readings of classical political works, starting with the Greeks. His pedagogical intensity and disenchantment with what he saw as the relativism, even nihilism, of liberal thought turned several generations of students, already disposed by the upheavals of the sixties and seventies to a sort of cultural pessimism, into members of the Strauss cult.

I ran into it as a freshman at Yale in the late seventies. In the classrooms of young Straussian professors, with their awkward social manners and pale cryptic smiles, one had the sense of a secret body of understanding to which only a select few would be admitted. They taught the classics in translations by their own (Bloom's version of Plato's *Republic*, for instance) because the correct wording of key ideas revealed hidden meanings—the art of concealment that was the subject of Strauss's 1952 book *Persecution and the Art of Writing*. The classical thinkers wrote in an esoteric vein, Strauss argued, on different levels—an untrammeled inquiry into truth available to the wisest readers, a more careful and responsible discourse for the broad public—because philosophy is dangerous to authority and, ultimately, to the philosopher himself, as Socrates found out. Strauss wanted to rescue philosophy from the comfortable mediocrity of the Enlightenment. He reopened questions about truth, politics, and the soul that seemed to have been settled by rational science long before the twentieth century. In this country, Strauss's zealous followers seized and distorted his teachings, ironing out every irony in pursuing their rigidly virtuous and peculiarly American crusade against the malaise of the modern world, which was nowhere more corrupt than in the university itself. At Yale, these disciples—almost exclusively male—wore bow ties and joined clubs with aristocratic-sounding names and generally cultivated an air of special knowledge and "excellence."

In 1981, one of the Yale Straussians, Charles Fairbanks, was hired by Wolfowitz to work on the Reagan State Department's policy planning staff. Over the next two decades, as they and the American university found each other increasingly uncongenial, Straussians and their influence shifted to Washington and spread throughout the archipelago of conservative publications, advocacy groups, think tanks, and foundations. With the congressional Republican ascendancy and the election of George W. Bush, Straussianism (and, more broadly, neoconservatism) became the unlikely intellectual spinal cord of the party in power. A European-produced, deliberately elitist, twilit view of the modern world was somehow wedded to the sunny all-American politics of triumphal capitalism, cultural piety, and flag-waving nationalism, under the most anti-intellectual president since at least Warren G. Harding. America is Sodom, and America is the light of the world—the last hope for the ancient idea of natural right. Mark Lilla, a professor in the University of Chicago's Committee on Social Thought, where Strauss once taught, observed, "How these eschatological and apocalyptic ideas about America can exist in the same breast, without some effort at reconciliation, remains a mystery to every outsider who glances at a neo-conservative magazine today. They appeal, though, to political Straussians, whose hearts beat arhythmically to both Sousa and Wagner." Neoconservative events in Washington took on the aspect of a carnival freak show, where, Lilla went on dryly, among "older New York intellectuals, professors in exile from politically correct universities, economic visionaries, Teddy Roosevelt enthusiasts, home-schooling advocates, evangelical Protestants, Latin-mass Catholics, Likudniks, and personalities from shock radio," there were always Straussians standing around who "will explain to you the logical connection between ancient philosophy and the latest press release from the American Enterprise Institute. It would take a comic genius, an American Aristophanes, to capture the strangeness of this little world."

Interviewed by a journalist a month after the fall of Baghdad, Strauss's former student Paul Wolfowitz scoffed at the notion of a Straussian connection to the Iraq War. "It's a product of fevered minds," he said. "I mean, I took two terrific courses from Leo Strauss as a graduate student. The idea that this has anything to do with U.S. foreign policy is just laughable."

Much abused by his disciples and their critics alike, Leo Strauss, who was born in 1899 and died in 1973, can't be held responsible for the invasion of Iraq. The neoconservatives don't meet secretly after hours in the Pentagon's E-ring or the offices of the Foundation for the Defense of Democracies to pore over heavily underlined copies of *Natural Right and History* looking for guidance on overthrowing Saddam. There is no Straussian conspiracy. "People in Washington don't read books," Richard Perle said.

But the neoconservatives, whether inside government or outside, do possess shared mental habits, with far-reaching consequences in the real world. These fevered minds are united in boldness and certainty. Surrounded by their invertebrate enemies in the deep decay of American institutions—the universities, the media, the bureaucracies, the courts—they cradle a truth that no one else has the courage or vision to see. They conceive of themselves as insurgents, warring against an exhausted liberal establishment that doesn't have the moral clarity to defend itself, let alone the country—that has no principles left to defend. They are the vanguard of democracy.

BUT ISN'T A "VANGUARD" historically associated with the left? Isn't it the core leadership of a revolution?

In fact, the advocates of war—many of them—vaguely resembled the vanguardists of earlier struggles. Daniel Cohn-Bendit, who was known as Dany the Red in May 1968 when he was a youthful leader of the student revolution in Paris and has since become a member of the European parliament, debated Richard Perle a few weeks before the invasion. Dany the Red told the Prince of Darkness, "Your government has been behaving like the Bolsheviks in the Russian Revolution. You want to change the whole world!" It's possible to imagine that Perle enjoyed the comparison. An apocalyptic cast of mind, and the desire of a small group in possession of a big idea to push history in a dramatically new direction, belongs exclusively to neither the left nor the right. Often, it's a characteristic of individuals who migrate from one flock to the other without pausing to graze on tasteless facts under the dull sky of moderation. The original neoconservatives had once been leftists themselves—not ordinary Adlai Stevenson, John F. Kennedy liberals, but Trotskyists, Lovestoneites, Schachtmanites, and other exotica of the hothouse world of New York intellectuals in the 1930s and '40s. Christopher Hitchens, the British polemicist, told me, "That crowd, the neocon group, somewhere in their cortex is the name of Leon Trotsky. If I were to say 'Kronstadt' to Trent Lott, I don't think I'd get a whole hell of a lot for my trouble," Hitchens said, referring to the 1921 mutiny of Russian sailors that was put down by Trotsky's forces. "But if I were to say 'Kronstadt' to Paul Wolfowitz, I think he would more than know what I was talking about."

Perhaps this explains why several of the most prominent Iraq hawks came from the left. Most prominent of all was Hitchens himself. After the terror attacks, he broke with comrades such as Noam Chomsky and Edward Said, jettisoned his long-standing column at *The Nation* magazine, became a vocal Bush supporter, and heartily girded himself for battle with what he called "Islamo-fascism."

Hitchens could be as gracious and thoughtful in private as he was scathingly contemptuous in public and in print. When I sat down with him for lunch near his apartment in Washington in late 2002—an expensive, all-afternoon business—he seemed to have rediscovered his youth in the New Left. The Iraqi National Congress of Ahmad Chalabi had taken the place of the revolutionary socialist movement, and Hitchens relished the coming war. "I feel much more like I used to in the sixties," he said, "working with revolutionaries. That's what I'm doing, I'm helping a very desperate underground. That reminds me of my better days quite poignantly. Waving a banner with Saddam Hussein's slogans on it, namely, 'No War on Iraq,' which confuses Iraq with Saddam, which is what he wants—that's not revolutionary politics to me."

An American-led overthrow of Saddam would be "revolution from above"—a phrase coined by none other than Leon Trotsky, to describe Stalin's concentration of power in the hands of the Communist Central Committee. Trotsky meant it ironically; I was fairly certain that Hitchens did not. All the rhetorical firepower he had once directed at the conservative foreign-policy establishment he now turned on Islamists and antiwar leftists. He brandished his disdain for religion like a gun, especially toward the belligerent faith of the jihadis. "You want to be a martyr?" Hitchens blustered. "I'm here to help."

This militant secularist now found himself brother-in-arms with evangelical Christians and Orthodox Jews, on behalf of liberal democracy in the Arab-Muslim world. Having spent most of his life attacking American foreign policy, Hitchens had come to the conclusion that "after the dust settles, the only revolution left standing is the American one. Americanization is the most revolutionary force in the world. There's almost no country where adopting the Americans wouldn't be the most radical thing they could do. I've always been a Paine-ite." Hitchens looked forward to drinking champagne in Baghdad with his Iraqi comrades by Valentine's Day 2003.

Believers on both the right and left were proposing one of the most audacious turns in the history of American foreign policy: to establish, by force of arms, "a beachhead of Arab democracy in the Middle East," as Paul Berman called it. To put an American political and military stamp, with a friendly government and permanent bases, in the heart of the region where al-Qaeda drew most of its recruits. To bring the ballot box and the public-affairs program to decaying sunbaked cities and tribal deserts. (How banal the ultimate goal of all this ardor!) The whole appeal of the idea lay in its audacity. It would, with one violent push, shove history out of a deep hole. By a chain reaction, a reverse domino effect, war in Iraq would weaken the Middle East's dictatorships and undermine its murderous ideologies and begin to spread the balm of liberal democracy. The road to Jerusalem, Riyadh, Damascus, and Tehran went through Baghdad. To persist with caution toward the sick, dangerous status quo of the Middle East would be contemptible, almost unbearable. Who wouldn't choose amputation over gangrene? With will and imagination, America could strike one great blow at terrorism, tyranny, underdevelopment, and the region's hardest, saddest problem.

Ideas as big as this attract strange bedfellows. The pairings both for and against grew so weirdly promiscuous that it was less useful to think in terms of left and right than of interventionists and anti-interventionists, or revolutionaries and realists. Old-fashioned realists from the Republican establishment found themselves on the same side of the debate as anti-imperialist leftists and far-right isolationists, while liberal veterans of humanitarian war became uneasy allies of administration hawks. Brent Scowcroft was tangled up with Gore Vidal and Pat Buchanan; Michael Ignatieff woke up next to Paul Wolfowitz. Berman wondered whether he and the believers in the administration even wanted the same thing. "I'm not sure we're speaking the same language because I don't know how to judge the language of the neoconservatives," he said one night at his apartment. "If the language is sincere, and there is an idealism among the neocons that echoes and reflects in some way the language of the liberal interventionists of the nineties, well, that would be a good thing. It's true that neoconservatism had a left-wing origin, and were it to turn out to be the case—which I'm extremely skeptical about—that some of the neocons would return to their earliest intellectual roots, that would be excellent." But if this warplane ever took off, "liberal interventionists of the nineties" would not be at the controls. So the administration's intentions mattered greatly. "It's extremely hard to judge what the people in the administration really do think," Berman said. "On what points are they sincere? On what points are they hypocritical? They haven't allowed us to be able to tell."

But the administration's sincerity wasn't even the biggest question. There was also the question of its knowledge and judgment. The prowar lobby's supreme impatience with things as they are disturbed even some supporters. If the war against radical Islamism must ultimately also be a war for liberalism, the West's own history should be taken as cautionary. Liberalism didn't suddenly appear "one scorching July day in France in 1789," Leon Wieseltier, the literary editor of the prowar New Republic, told me. It was a "violent rupture" after centuries of conflict within Western theocracy and autocracy. Liberalism is, by definition, difficult and destabilizing. It shouldn't be undertaken with missionary zeal. The attempt to bring it to the theocratic and autocratic Middle East from outside, by force, on the simple faith that people everywhere long to be free, end of story—this was a profoundly unliberal idea. "If there's one thing that liberalism has no time for, it's an eschatological view," Wieseltier said. "Liberalism is an essentially anti-eschatological view of the world. And now that various people have woken up to the rough political and philosophical realities of most of the world, the idea that the United States must send its troops everywhere to fix the world once and for all is stupid. They want a final answer. They want it over. And there is no final answer. There's slow, steady, fitful progress toward a more decent and democratic world." Nonetheless, Wieseltier supported a war, on the only grounds the administration gave for waging it: the threat from Saddam's arsenal of unconventional weapons and his history of using them.

THROUGHOUT 2002, those officials who were actually charged with making policy on Iraq were not talking about liberal civilization or revolution from above. It wasn't at all clear that Bush's inner circle shared the dreams and visions of war intellectuals outside government. The basis for war—the casus belli—was clearly and narrowly defined by the Bush administration, beginning with the president's own warning in his State of the Union address: "The United States of America will not permit the world's most dangerous regimes to threaten us with the world's most destructive weapons." If there was to be war, the reasons would be syllogistic, not eschatological: Saddam has had and still seeks weapons of mass destruction; he has used them on his own citizens in the past; he might now give them to al-Qaeda or another terrorist group; terrorists want to destroy the United States. Therefore, the United States must disarm or overthrow Saddam.

The president's "axis of evil" speech, coming just weeks after the fall of the Taliban in Afghanistan, signaled the next stage in the war on terrorism and the basis for further action. The speech dramatically expanded the theater of the war, but it did so on relatively narrow grounds. As Wolfowitz told an interviewer after the fall of Baghdad, WMD was the least common denominator: "The truth is that for reasons that have a lot to do with the U.S. government bureaucracy, we settled on the one issue that everyone could agree on, which was weapons of mass destruction." Wolfowitz suggested that he himself had bigger ideas—a realignment of American power and influence in the Middle East, away from theocratic Saudi Arabia (home to so many of the 9/11 hijackers), and toward a democratic Iraq, as the beginning of an effort to cleanse the whole region of murderous regimes and ideologies. This would have been a much broader case for war than WMD and closer to the arguments of influential people outside the administration, such as Bernard Lewis, Fouad Ajami, and Robert Kagan. Resting on a complex and abstract theory, it would also have been much harder to sell to the public.

Throughout the year, WMD remained the administration's rationale for a war it had in all likelihood decided upon as early as November 2001. (There was a recurring locution that expressed the diplomatic doublespeak of the prewar period and that officials continued to use up to the very brink of invasion, as if the administration were being dragged against its will into hostilities with Iraq that it was doing everything possible to avoid: "If or when war becomes necessary . . .") Having settled on WMD as the cause for war—if or when there was to be a war—the administration was stuck with the limits of its own argument. In July 2002, Sir Richard Dearlove, Britian's head of foreign intelligence, reported back to Tony Blair and his top officials about meetings in Washington. According to a secret memo made public in May 2005, Sir Richard told his colleagues: "Military action was now seen as inevitable. Bush wanted to remove Saddam, through military action, justified by the conjunction of terrorism and WMD. But the intelligence and facts were being fixed around the policy. The NSC had no patience with the UN route, and no enthusiasm for publishing material on the Iraqi regime's record. There was little discussion in Washington of the aftermath after military action."

So when, in the late summer and fall of 2002, a high-profile campaign to convince the American public of the need for a preemptive war against Iraq began, the rhetoric had the quality of protesting too much. Just a year earlier, Iraq had been viewed as an outlaw state that was beginning to slip free of international constraints and might present a threat to the region or, more remotely, the United States in five years or so. Now, suddenly, there wasn't a day to be lost. In late August, Dick Cheney surprised Colin Powell and other Iraq skeptics when he declared before the Veterans of Foreign Wars that the Saddam Hussein regime without a doubt possessed stockpiles of chemical and biological weapons and had "reconstituted" its nuclear weapons program.

Within a year, Saddam could possess a nuke—and Cheney wasn't shy about suggesting that the Iraqi dictator might well hand one over to al-Qaeda.

It didn't matter that there was no strong evidence to back up the doomsday prognosis. A possible medium- to long-term threat had become a "grave and gathering danger." Condoleezza Rice came up with an ominous metaphor, and Bush used it in a warlike speech in Cincinnati in October: the smoking gun in the shape of a mushroom cloud. The campaign of persuasion proceeded by rhetorical hyperbole, by the deliberate slanting of ambiguous facts in one direction, and by a wink-and-nod suggestion that the administration knew more than it could reveal. Conflicting and inconclusive intelligence about Saddam's weapons programs was selected and highlighted for the worst-case analysis favored by the White House. A shipment of aluminum tubes that experts in the Department of Energy doubted could be used as centrifuges for enriching uranium were, Condoleezza Rice asserted in a television interview, suitable for nothing else. Documents recording the sale of yellowcake uranium from Niger to Iraq kept being cited by top officials, including the president, long after they had been discredited as fraudulent. A group of civilians at the Pentagon under the direction of Douglas Feith and William Luti was culling through raw data on Saddam's possible ties to al-Qaeda in order to produce the desired result that the established intelligence community, including the Pentagon's own Defense Intelligence Agency, would not provide. Outside the government, war advocates like Perle, Kristol, and Kagan warned that time was running out. It was as if the administration were working around the clock to head off a nuclear Pearl Harbor and simultaneously prove that it was about to happen. One didn't need special expertise in the fields of intelligence or proliferation to smell something wrong. The administration had boxed itself in by deciding to go to war before it knew exactly why.

Even as Bush and his war cabinet made their particular case on Iraq, they laid out a far-reaching grand strategy for the use of American power in the world. The president began to articulate it in a series of speeches to the military academies. Rice codified it in a document prepared under her supervision and titled "The National Security

Strategy of the United States of America." The first draft, written by Richard Haass, was too long and mild for Rice's taste, and she turned over the revision to Philip Zelikow, a University of Virginia professor who had been her colleague on the NSC under the first President Bush. Zelikow produced a short, eloquent statement of principles with a new passage on preemptive war, which, when the document was released in September, was immediately taken as a justification for war with Iraq. It was as if that earlier and almost forgotten bureaucratic document, the Defense Planning Guidance of 1992, drafted near the end of the administration of the first President Bush, had been put in a deep freeze for safekeeping during the long exile of the Clinton years, to be restored to life a decade later after September 11 in the second Bush presidency by some of the same players who had written, directed, and approved the original. The new document announced a new Bush Doctrine. This doctrine promised "a distinctly American internationalism that reflects the union of our values and our national interests." It would seek to promote "a balance of power that favors human freedom." Bush and his national security adviser Rice seemed to be splitting the difference between the realism of Bush's father and *his* national security adviser, Rice's mentor Brent Scowcroft, and the idealism of the neoconservatives who were now ascendant. But in fact, the new document's high-flown language and, even more, its substance marked a decisive break with the foreign-policy establishment. The "balance of power" was out; in the new era, the old Cold War policies of containment and deterrence no longer applied. Rogue states and global terrorists could not be deterred. America, preeminent and without rivals, would ensure the peace in part by preempting threats to peace. It would do so within the existing international framework if possible but with ad hoc "coalitions of the willing" if necessary, or even alone. American might did not make America right; America was right by virtue of being America. But American might would uphold the right across the globe. And this is where the new post–September 11 strategy differed from the old post–Cold War strategy of the Defense Planning Guidance: After the terror attacks, the world's superpower could no longer be neutral toward the politics practiced inside other countries, where "stability" might actually be a dangerously advanced form of decay. America would now actively promote freedom around the world. "Freedom" was the key word of the 2002 document, whose opening lines are these: "The great struggles of the twentieth century between liberty and totalitarianism ended with a decisive victory for the forces of freedom—and a single sustainable model for national success: freedom, democracy, and free enterprise."

In its long struggle for the soul of the Republican Party and American foreign policy, neoconservatism had finally triumphed. The first chance to test the creed was coming up fast, in Iraq.

The worm in the apple, the seed of future trouble, is easier to see in retrospect. The leading figures of the Bush war cabinet had all worked at high levels in at least one previous administration; some of them had served in three or four. No Democratic contemporary could claim anything like their experience. Counting his years in Congress, Dick Cheney had been an influential insider under every Republican president since Nixon. Except for the Clinton years, Paul Wolfowitz's career in government extended through every administration from Nixon to the second Bush. George W. Bush's foreign-policy advisers were vastly experienced, they were aggressively self-confident, and they were peculiarly unsuited to deal with the consequences of the Bush Doctrine.

They entered government in the aftermath of the trauma in Vietnam, and they were forged as Cold War hawks. They devoted their careers to restoring American military power and its projection around the world. Through the three decades of their public lives, the only thing America had to fear was its own return to weakness. But after the Cold War ended, they sat out the debates of the 1990s about humanitarian war, international standards, nation building, democracy promotion. They had little to say about the new, borderless security threats—failed states, ethnic conflict, poverty, "loose nukes" in postcommunist Russia, and global terrorism. Clinton's foreign policy was feckless; once they got back into power, they told themselves, they would do everything differently. Cheney, the hardest of hard-liners, expressed contemptuous disapproval of every intervention of the decade. Rumsfeld hadn't formed a new idea since opposing arms control as Gerald Ford's secretary of defense. Powell and Rice were deep skeptics of open-ended military commitments on behalf of "soft" ideals. Bush himself came into office with no curiosity about the world, only a suspicion that his predecessor had entangled America in far too many obscure places of no importance to national interests. Wolfowitz alone among them supported the interventions in Bosnia and Kosovo, but his worldview left even him unprepared to deal with or even to acknowledge a stateless organization with an ideology of global jihad. When September 11 forced the imagination to grapple with something radically new, the president's foreign-policy advisers reached for what they had always known. The threat, as they saw it, lay in well-armed enemy states. The answer, as ever, was military power and the will to use it.

3

EXILES

IN APRIL 2002, with the Pentagon already deep into planning for a war, the State Department realized that it had better start thinking about a postwar. The department's Bureau of Near Eastern Affairs recruited Iraqi exiles with expertise in various fields and organized them into seventeen committees that would draft reports on subjects of importance for administering Iraq after Saddam—technical reports on topics like electricity, health, transitional justice, and policing. Among those Iraqis whom State invited to participate in its Future of Iraq Project was Kanan Makiya. But Makiya declined.

He had been publicly advocating the overthrow of Saddam ever since shedding his pseudonym at the end of the Gulf War in March 1991, but Makiya distrusted the State Department's whole approach to the question. In his view, the department's officials, and especially the Arabists at the Bureau of Near Eastern Affairs, were bulwarks of the Middle Eastern status quo—the kind of bureaucrats who had always favored leaving Saddam in charge of Iraq for the sake of "stability." They were compromised by their accommodation with the Sunni Arab dictators of the Middle East, Makiya thought, and disbelievers in the possibility of Arab democracy. In the sinister new light of September 11, they were part of the problem. Now that regime change in Iraq was not just official American policy but the focus of intense pressure and planning in Washington, Makiya worried that State—and the ideologically sympathetic CIA—would try to guide the policy toward "a Musharraf-like figure, a reformist-minded, Western-orientated, military-type figure," in the mold of the Pakistani general who had seized power in 1999. In other words, a friendly strongman—not democracy. Makiya wanted no part of that kind of regime change. He particularly distrusted the "facilitator" of the Future of Iraq Project, a bureau official named Thomas Warrick. At a meeting in Detroit, Makiya heard Warrick singing the praises of an Iraqi ex-general who had compared democracy to a well-functioning army.

"Some people are talking about democratic change," Makiya told me late that year, referring to the neoconservatives at the Pentagon and the vice president's office, who ardently supported Makiya's friend Ahmad Chalabi, the State Department's bête noire. "But they're only some people, and there are other people who think that's all a pile of garbage, that that's nonsense. They really are out there. They're in the State Department and they're in the CIA today. They are very powerful players."

The Future of Iraq Project's various workshops began to meet in July. In early August, Makiya took his family camping outside Washington, D.C. At some point he found time to venture from the campsite to the capital, where he met with State Department officials, including the head of the Iraq desk at Near Eastern Affairs, a veteran foreign service officer named Ryan Crocker. Makiya found that the rhetoric had changed; the officials were now talking about democracy in Iraq. Would Makiya reconsider?

He decided to call their bluff. "I was trying to hoist them on their own petard," he explained later, "and get something out of this that I could then use to pin the U.S. government with." Makiya agreed to join the project's Democratic Principles Working Group, and he suggested putting the group's final report up for consideration at a planned conference of the Iraqi opposition in exile. The Americans readily agreed. There were thirty-two Iraqis on the committee, most of them sent as representatives of the various exile political parties and groupings. "Some of them were political hacks," Makiya said, adding that this suited the State Department, which wanted an inoffensive document that would make no hard choices and offend no one. "I hated writing this in committee. I'm not a politician really. I'm going to do these things, say these things that other people think don't get said, and let it be, let the chips fall where they are. That's what the Iraqis who support me like me for, and that's in my nature, that's what all my books in one sense or another are about. I'm not going to stop doing that. But it'll never make me a politician truly, for this very reason."

Makiya wasn't particularly interested in the opinions of most of the committee's other members; the word "inclusive" got on his nerves. As one of the State Department's American advisers on the project put it, in bland officialspeak, "Makiya did not pay heed to standard protocols for working in committee." Instead, he and two close friends and colleagues—Rend Rahim, director of the Washington-based Iraq Foundation, and Salem Chalabi, a London lawyer and nephew of the Iraqi National Congress chairman—essentially left the others out and took over the writing of the report, all the while fending off pressure from the State Department to produce something politically neutral. The small group labored through the fall to draft a detailed blueprint for Iraq's transformation from totalitarianism to democracy. Makiya wasn't after the kind of document that could be produced by committee.

"It's the architect in me," he said, nursing a cold over Japanese tea in Cambridge in early December. A decade earlier, Makiya had confessed, "Architects are such megalomaniacs."

IT WAS ALSO THE EX-TROTSKYIST in him. For somewhere in the cortex of Kanan Makiya—not deeply buried, either—was the name of Leon Trotsky, and alongside it the Trotskyist idea of an intellectual vanguard leading from the front, forcing history to move in the desired direction. Makiya left Baghdad in 1967 to attend the Massachusetts Institute of Technology, and in the summer after his freshman year the most extreme faction of the Arab Baath Socialist Party, with an ideology that demanded the total dissolution of individual identity into the collective "Arabness" of the state, an ideology that the Baathists themselves described as a form of love, came to power in a coup—probably the least noticed and soonest forgotten of 1968's many utopian events. Public hangings of suspected Zionist spies soon followed before gigantic throngs in Baghdad's Liberation Square, and Iraq fell under the spell of fear that would continue for thirty-five years, during which Makiya never returned to his native country.

He joined left-wing exile politics at the most quixotic point along the spectrum—as a revolutionary socialist from the Middle East. The Six-Day War and the Palestinian cause galvanized him, as it did a whole generation of young Arabs, and for a time Makiya was a member of the Popular Democratic Front for the Liberation of Palestine. But according to his and his comrades' Marxist analysis, the conflict was in essence a class struggle. Ultimately, the workers in Israeli factories and kibbutzim would join hands with the oppressed Arab masses to throw off the yokes of imperialism, feudalism, and capitalism. In Middle Eastern politics this was something of a minority view, and it meant that Makiya pursued a tributary separate from the great wave of Arab nationalism that surged in the 1960s. (As for political Islam, the wave that came next when the nationalist regimes showed themselves to be impotent and corrupt, it had no appeal whatsoever for the resolutely secular and atheist Makiya.) Nonetheless, he and his Iranian-born wife, Afsaneh, threw themselves into the intense world of exile politics, first in Cambridge, later in London, as militant critics of the Western powers, especially the United States.

They followed events in their home region from afar, through the 1970s and '80s: as the Palestinian liberation movement turned to terrorism, as Lebanon degenerated into a civil war in which all the factions resembled one another in their barbarism, as the revolution in Iran fell under the control of theocratic mullahs who imposed a reign of terror, as Iraq and Iran plunged into a seemingly endless war that consumed the lives of an entire generation in both countries. And at some point along the way, Makiya's thinking changed.

"I could no longer blame it on the United States," he said. "This was probably the seismic shift in my consciousness. It wasn't the abstract abandonment of Marxism on the basis of some general principles. No. It was a felt experience—watching and seeing the Lebanese civil war, which had nothing to do with Marxist categories. Watching and seeing the Iranian revolution—again, Marxist categories were defeated. Watching and seeing the Iraq-Iran War. It wasn't the United States, it was Iraqis and Iranians who were bleeding themselves to death. The fact that there were people out there selling them guns was certainly deplorable, but I'm not going to turn my priorities upside down and refuse to see who's responsible. So it was this sense that the malaise was principally in my world, and not principally in the United States, that was the seismic shift in my politics."

The shift would have large implications. If the malaise was principally in his part of the world, then all the isms of collective salvation—Marxism, nationalism, Baathism, Islamism—now looked like various roads to hell. The region had tried to leap from the Middle Ages right over the eighteenth century to modern, mostly imported dogmas, without enduring that profound rupture when legitimacy is separated from both might and faith, and the rights of the individual are enshrined as the basis of government. What the Middle East needed was an Enlightenment. In 1984, in a letter to a leftist friend, Makiya asked, "Could it be possible that a Marx today in a Middle Eastern political context is far less of a revolutionary than, say, a Voltaire?" Living a fairly marginal existence in New York and Cambridge, auditing classes at local universities, reading for the first time the works of Arendt, Hobbes, and Locke in libraries, and working hard on the manuscript of *Republic of Fear*, Makiya became a liberal.

As an Iraqi involved in politics, Makiya was something rare in the Arab world. There were plenty of liberation fighters; there were very few dissidents. The Arab sense of victimization at the hands of the imperialist and Zionist foreign enemy left little breathing room for an Egyptian Solzhenitsyn or a Syrian Havel to emerge (let alone survive). Without denying the justice of the Palestinian cause, Makiya began to feel that Arabs shouldn't regard it as the key to solving regional problems—Palestine no longer came first, either in time or in moral urgency. The crucial issue was no longer national liberation but democracy based on rights and, more profoundly, the value of life. Long after the end of colonialism, though, the stance of the democratic dissident—the critic of homegrown dictatorship—still looked in many Arab circles suspiciously like apostasy, especially when it was carried to its logical conclusion, as Makiya did at the end of the Gulf War, when he came forward and called on America to overthrow the tyrant in Baghdad.

By 1991, Makiya had come all the way around to the view that America's sins in the Middle East—and in his mind there were many—were sins of omission, not commission. Far from being an omnipotent puppet master, the United States was ineffectual in the region. The fall of the shah, the Iranian hostage crisis, the botched rescue attempt, the massive bombing at the marine base in Beirut followed by a hasty withdrawal from Lebanon, the kidnapping crisis, the silence that greeted Saddam's gassing of the Kurds: One display of American fecklessness after another prepared Saddam to believe that he could invade Kuwait with impunity. The United States was a force for ill in the region not because of what it was doing but what it was failing to do. Makiya had originally called on Arabs themselves to repel Saddam's aggression (the only other Arab willing to push this line, though for very different reasons, was a Saudi construction tycoon named Osama bin Laden), but the task was left to the armies of the Western powers. With the defeated Iraqi army in humiliating retreat back across the border along the "Highway of Death," with Iraq's Kurdish and Shiite populations rising up to throw off Baathist rule, America was in a position to erase its shameful record in the region. But the Gulf War ended with a treaty that not only left Saddam where he was but allowed his helicopters to mow down thousands of Iraqis who'd had a glimpse of hope. For Makiya, there was no greater sin of omission.

After the war, he traveled through the Kurdish region of northern Iraq to hunt down official Baathist records of the Anfal, the genocide of the Kurds in the late 1980s, and to film a BBC documentary called *Saddam's Killing Fields*. In Kurdistan and later in London, Iraqis and Kuwaitis sought out Makiya to tell their stories of the genocide, the occupation, and the bloody repression of the uprisings. If he had simply collected them in his next book and called it *Cruelty*, he wouldn't have become a lightning rod of controversy. But his anger at the Arab intelligentsia's complacency in the face of Saddam's crimes was burning too high, and *Cruelty and Silence*, which came out in 1993, was not a cool meditation but a cri de coeur. Makiya sought to strip away the

Arab world's apologetics and push the reader's face down into the stinking truth. Imagery of the foul smells produced by human cruelty pervades the testimony of witnesses. "There can be no more romance and no more false heroics in the Arab world," Makiya wrote. "There is only the legacy of pain which must be grappled with by a new language and in a new style."

Cruelty and Silence was a provocation. One of the intellectuals arraigned by Makiya was Edward Said, the Palestinian-born professor of literature at Columbia University, author of the groundbreaking study *Orientalism*, which taught a whole generation of younger Arab intellectuals to see their world as the victim of age-old Western cultural imperialism. Said, who in his wearily elegant literary critic's prose had dismissed *Republic of Fear* as anti-Arab, who blamed the Gulf War on Western cultural imperialism, who (Makiya pointed out) had expressed doubt that Saddam's regime really gassed the Kurds. Said— the preeminent Arab intellectual in the West, a culture hero to Arabs and Western leftists alike—won no deference from the younger, little-known Iraqi. Makiya's own prose style, simple and intense, amounted to a rebuke: It said that Said's language and ideas were part of the moral wreckage of the region. This was more than an intergenerational quarrel between two Arab writers in exile. The larger contest was between two kinds of politics, two interpretations of the role of the intellectual and the source of Arab defeat.

Said's supporters in the academic world heaped abuse on *Cruelty and Silence*. Makiya, whose nature provided him with one skin too few, seemed to withdraw from the fray for the rest of the 1990s and devoted himself, in his book-filled Cambridge flat, to his historical novel. The name of Edward Said grew ever more illustrious, while Kanan Makiya slipped back into obscurity. But a decade after the Gulf War, when Makiya suddenly emerged as a highly visible supporter of a new Iraq war, one that would finish what the first had left undone, Said turned on him with fury, as if the argument had never stopped churning beneath the surface.

Writing in the Cairo weekly *al-Ahram*, Said swept aside Makiya's views about the democratic and federal shape of a future Iraq. Instead, he wanted to know "who he is and from what background he emerges." Said answered his own question: Makiya was a vain, posturing, compassionless man, living "between countries and cultures and with no visible commitment to anyone (except his own upwardly mobile career)," eager to serve his masters in the U.S. government (where Said imagined Makiya occupying a desk at the State Department) just as Makiya's father, the architect Mohamed Makiya, had once worked for Saddam. (This was true, for a period in the early 1980s, and it had caused a breach between Kanan and his father that took years to heal. That Makiya had indirectly benefited through his share of his father's firm's profits was also true; Makiya had used those profits to write *Republic of Fear*. That Makiya himself had worked for Saddam, as Said charged more than once, was false.) Said once wrote approvingly of the Arab tendency to ask of any speaker, *"Min warrah?"*—Who's behind him? Look behind Kanan Makiya and you found Richard Perle, Paul Wolfowitz, Donald Rumsfeld. That was enough for Said.

So there was a quality of conspiratorial thinking in Said's attack, as well as a remarkable stream of ad hominem invective. But the donnish superiority that was Said's habitual tone kept cracking as if under pressure. The possibility that none other than Kanan Makiya might be "the voice and the example of the future of Iraq," while history bypassed Edward Said, and his own cause, the Palestinian cause, turned to rubble, was so ludicrous that it seemed to induce a kind of panic.

The essay sent the world of Arab exile politics into an uproar. I spoke with Makiya shortly after it came out. He was trying for intellectual detachment. "Said is expressing an ideology that was dominant in Arab political culture, that I was a part of in the post-'67 period, the view that the Palestinian question came first," Makiya said. "But you look at it from an Iraqi point of view, he'll tell you: 'Have you got a million dead? How many people died in your second intifada? One thousand five hundred?'" He returned to Said. "I think he's cut a tragic figure, really. His politics is in a deep sense—and this is probably what he's deep-down angry at—it's what we called in Arab politics, in common parlance, rejectionist politics. You reject, you reject, you reject. You don't ever work to make it better." Still, I could tell that Makiya was hurt and a little stunned by the nastiness of Said's attack. His own polemical style was sharp but clean, aimed at the idea rather than the man. He tended to take people at face value, not to look for hidden agendas or irrational motives. He expected to be approached in the same way, and because his feelings were too sensitive for his own good, the tumultuous history into which he now threw himself made him vulnerable. There was more than a little naïveté in Makiya—a worrying trait, given the project he was about to sign on for.

FOR, AFTER ALL, who *was* behind him?

The arc of history had taken Makiya from radical leftist politics to liberalism, to a belief that human rights, not nationalism or socialism, was the supreme cause and, in his home region, the truly revolutionary one. By political affiliation, he identified with the liberal wing of the Democratic Party. But as an Iraqi living at the start of the twenty-first century, his cause made him the ally of American neoconservatives. A few of them had the name of Leon Trotsky somewhere in their cortex, but most were likelier to cite Ronald Reagan as their inspiration. The fit was imperfect. The neoconservatives saw American power in almost messianic terms—they were nationalists—while Makiya was interested only in what American power could achieve in Iraq on behalf of liberal ideals.

In the later months of 2002, he made frequent trips to Washington, where he met with Paul Wolfowitz and other civilians at the Pentagon, and then the hawkish top officials of the vice president's staff, and then Cheney himself and Condoleezza Rice at the White House. In these meetings, Makiya and the American officials were courting each other and sussing each other out. The Americans wanted the imprimatur of Iraq's leading intellectual on their war, and they wanted to know what Makiya thought American soldiers would find in Iraq. Makiya wanted to know whether the administration was committed to his vision—a democratic vision for Iraq. The neoconservatives at the Pentagon and the vice president's office said exactly what Makiya wanted to hear. Unlike the career bureaucrats in the State Department, they seemed to feel passionately that the Middle East, starting with Iraq, could be transformed by democracy. They had their reasons for wanting to believe this, reasons that Makiya didn't entirely share, but the area of overlap was what mattered to him.

"If it is the right thing being done by the wrong people, I would still work with it," Makiya said when I asked whether his newfound allies worried him at all. "That could very well end up being the case. But politics is far more complicated. I've seen so many really good people do such terrible things. It's very hard to judge any longer." He rejected the way of thinking that pitted a "Wolfowitz school" against a "Clinton administration school" and passed judgment accordingly. "I suppose one way in which I've abandoned ideological politics is I prefer for people to think of me as a moralist more. You have to have moral criteria, constructed in such a general way that you shouldn't be able to say the wrong people, the right people. It's not that easy anymore."

The test Makiya set was whether those in power were willing to do this moral thing: overthrow Saddam, establish democracy. And the Bush administration, led by its neoconservatives, seemed to be serious about both. For a man with Makiya's history, this was the promise of deliverance, and he didn't ask himself whether these Americans, or any Americans, were capable of achieving his goals. He didn't pause to worry that the damage their policy was doing to the Atlantic alliance and the UN, the arrogant posture of leading administration figures, the questionable claims about WMD and terrorist connections, Rumsfeld's ideas about military transformation, the history and ideology of Bush's war cabinet—that all of this might actually contribute to the undoing of his dream. Makiya couldn't afford to regard these matters as anything but peripheral to the main chance.

Along the way, he was generating plenty of ill will. In the interagency battles between Defense and State, even as he continued working on the State Department's Future of Iraq Project, Makiya sided quite publicly with the Pentagon. His monomaniacal style in the Democratic Principles Working Group bruised the feelings of more than a few of his fellow Iraqi exiles. And he made the fateful choice of linking his reputation with the most controversial exile of them all.

Ahmad Chalabi, the scion of a wealthy and politically powerful Shiite family, had left Baghdad as a teenager in 1958 after the nationalist coup that overthrew the monarchy. He was educated in England

and in the United States, where he earned a doctorate in theoretical mathematics at the University of Chicago. But Chalabi made his first fortune and reputation in Jordan, as a banker with close ties to the royal family. He wore English-cut suits and silk ties and was known for his wide-ranging intellect, until he became better known for financial scandal. In 1989, Chalabi's Petra Bank collapsed, ruining numerous families in Iraq, and he fled Amman to London just ahead of an arrest warrant. When Makiya met him in Salahuddin, Iraqi Kurdistan, in October 1992, at an organizational meeting of the new Iraqi National Congress, Chalabi had recently been convicted in absentia by a Jordanian military tribunal on charges that included embezzlement, theft, and forgery, and sentenced to twenty-two years at hard labor. Chalabi claimed that the charges were politically motivated due to his opposition to the Saddam regime, from which Jordan was getting cheap oil. Jordanian officials have always insisted that Chalabi was a crook. At the very least, he was a careless manager given to self-dealing and sloppy record keeping—practices he kept up as the INC's chairman once the CIA, which played a central role in creating the organization after the Gulf War, began financing the INC with tens of millions of dollars. The agency also helped to transform Ahmad Chalabi from disgraced banker into opposition leader. Within a few months of his April 1992 conviction, he was already climbing his way to the top of Iraqi exile politics.

The shady past didn't interest Makiya. He was drawn instead to Chalabi's mind. They were seatmates on a flight once in 1994, and when Chalabi got up to use the lavatory, Makiya glanced at the book he'd been reading: a thick tome on the reconstruction of Germany after World War II. It was the beginning of a long mutual attraction. In Chalabi, Makiya saw a brilliant palace politician, a product of the monarchy when Iraq had a parliament and educated, secular men led the country. Makiya admitted that Chalabi had no practical experience of democratic politics. His rise to the top of the INC had nothing to do with elections. "His biggest failing is he operates like one of these nineteenth-century, T. E. Lawrence–type figures, behind the scenes—cloakroom, big-power politics. Mass politics mean nothing to him." Nonetheless, Makiya convinced himself that Chalabi shared his liberal democratic beliefs. He also believed that the INC, unlike the established parties, which were founded years ago in the image of the Baath Party, "is porous, it's open, it doesn't work as a clandestine organization. It could never conspire." Makiya saw in Chalabi a man of the future, a leader of independent-minded Iraqis who had already freed themselves from the region's failed ideologies. "He's not got a shred of Arab nationalist politics in him," Makiya told me. "He doesn't think like an Arab or a Shiite or a religious person. He's the most likely of all those capable of leading Iraq to go in a democratic direction."

The INC in its early days was an umbrella organization of Iraqi dissidents that included communists, monarchists, Islamists, Kurds, ex-Baathists, ex–military officers, and assorted liberals—including Kanan Makiya—in an uneasy and often unruly cohabitation. Chalabi maneuvered his way into the chairmanship of the INC and eventually set up its headquarters in the fashionable London neighborhood of Knightsbridge. But with the INC's botched coup attempts and bloody setbacks of the mid-1990s, Chalabi and his Washington benefactors turned on one another. From that point on, CIA and State regarded Chalabi with unconcealed suspicion and disdain. The agency began to look for other white knights, and it peeled the Kurdish, Shiite, and ex-military parties away from the INC's leadership.

Noah Feldman, a law professor who served as a constitutional adviser to the occupation authority in Iraq, called Chalabi "the Jay Gatsby of the Iraq War." After 1996, Chalabi set about to reinvent himself again. Out of favor with the Clinton administration, he abandoned his doomed efforts to overthrow Saddam from Iraqi Kurdistan and established a new base of operations, in Washington, with a new plan. Assisted by his young American representative, Francis Brooke—an evangelical Christian and PR man who had first met Chalabi in London while on the CIA's payroll—Chalabi began to court the Republican right. His Virgil through Washington's purgatory was Richard Perle, who introduced Chalabi to a network of backers at such institutions as the American Enterprise Institute, the Project for the New American Century, and the Gingrich Congress. Chalabi also ingratiated himself with Dick Cheney, who was running the Halliburton Corporation, with Paul Wolfowitz, who saw in Chalabi a like-minded intellectual, and with congressional conservatives like Trent Lott, Jesse Helms, and Newt Gingrich. These Republicans were all too happy to turn Clinton's failures in Iraq against the president.

And here was an Iraqi who was saying all the right things. In June 1997, Chalabi told an audience at the Jewish Institute for National Security Affairs—the group that had sponsored the conference from which the "Clean Break" strategy paper issued—that the INC could overthrow Saddam with modest American help and establish a democratic state with friendly ties to Israel. The INC also seemed to produce an inexhaustible supply of defectors with top-secret information about Saddam's efforts to rebuild his unconventional weapons programs and his terrorist training camps. When Congress passed and a politically weakened Clinton was forced to sign the Iraq Liberation Act, the INC became the beneficiary of millions of more dollars in government funding. Chalabi played the partisan wars of the late Clinton years in Washington perfectly, and he made himself the favorite Iraqi of the Republicans who were about to come back to power.

So when the new Bush administration got serious about regime change; not in principle and through the dubious cadres of Iraqi exile groups but with the full might of the American military, it was natural that Kanan Makiya and Ahmad Chalabi should turn to each other. "Ahmad needed a thinker, a liberal democratic thinker. He found Kanan," a friend of both men told me. "Kanan needed a strong man committed to his ideas of liberal democracy, and he couldn't find anyone but Chalabi." Makiya inherited Chalabi's old wars with agencies of the U.S. government—the State Department, the CIA—and made them his own; but unlike Chalabi, Makiya wasn't a born politician, and he handled his new role without the necessary smoothness and legerdemain. Feisal Istrabadi, a tough-talking Chicago lawyer whose family had lived near the Chalabis in Baghdad before 1958, first met Makiya at an opposition gathering in June 2002. "Kanan said to me that Iraq has one democrat—Ahmad Chalabi," said Istrabadi, who would become Iraq's deputy ambassador to the UN in the interim government of Prime Minister Iyad Allawi. "My response was, 'If there's only one democrat, so much for democracy in Iraq.' He was a religious zealot of Ahmad's, and he promoted the neocons' view, the Defense

Department's view, that the Future of Iraq Project was going to weaken Ahmad. He opposed the project because a wider net weakened Ahmad—he used those words."

That same month of June, Douglas Feith, the undersecretary of defense for policy, who would oversee planning for postwar Iraq, invited Istrabadi to the Pentagon. Feith had one question: Whom did Istrabadi support in the Iraqi opposition? "I knew the answer he wanted," Istrabadi told me, "but I said, 'I support the principles of the INC.'" That wasn't good enough. Within a month, the civilians at the Pentagon who had been courting Istrabadi dropped him, and by the end of the year their hostility was undisguised. In the meantime, Makiya had changed his mind and joined the Democratic Principles Working Group. Istrabadi, who was also a member, soon realized that Makiya, as head of the coordinating committee, wanted to take control of writing the report. Some members dropped out; others were pushed aside. The feuds within the U.S. government spilled over into the group. In England for the first formal session, Istrabadi was startled one evening to find Tom Warrick of the State Department and Samantha Ravich from Cheney's office standing on the sidewalk outside a fancy London restaurant, screaming at each other. "That was the first time I realized how deeply personal the fight between the neocons and those who knew what they were talking about was."

Makiya wasn't interested in keeping everyone happy and arriving at a consensus that would ensure no spoilers would be left out. He was more concerned with the democratic product than the democratic process of the Democratic Principles Working Group. Dissenting views were relegated to footnotes or appended at the end of the report. In one appendix, a political economist named Isam al-Khafaji emphasized the irony in Makiya's method:

A FINAL COMMENT regards the exaggerated self-admiration and quotes of certain declarations, or acts—no matter how trivial—that one member of the coordinating committee has written or done. THIS, ALONG SIDE THE PATRIMONIAL ROLE OF THE DOCUMENT WHICH DECIDED TO REJECT WHAT DOES NOT FIT WITH ITS POINTS OF VIEW, SEND AN ALARMING SIG-

NAL TO ALL OF US ABOUT OUR DEMOCRATIC PRETEN-
SIONS WHILE WE ARE STILL IN EXILE!!!!

"Kanan," said Feisal Istrabadi, "wants to be the bride at every wedding and the corpse at every funeral."

Yet the "Report on the Transition to Democracy in Iraq" is a visionary document. It could never have been written by a committee:
There's something in it to offend everyone, for Makiya didn't shy away
from the implications of his own ideas. In discussing federalism, the
sine qua non of Kurdish participation in a future Iraqi state, he argued
that regions based on Arab and Kurdish identity would lead to a
patchwork nation of second-class citizens; to guarantee absolute
equality, federalism should be geographic, not ethnic—and a federal
Iraq would no longer be an officially Arab Iraq. On the relation between mosque and state in overwhelmingly Islamic Iraq, Makiya
wrote that a separation of the two "will have assisted in realizing the
creative and spiritual potential present in religious faith when it is not
shackled to the ebb and flow of politics." This non-Arab, secular country should be demilitarized, along Japanese lines, so that Iraq would
never again be an aggressor nation, and debaathified, along German
lines, in order to root out the totalitarian ideology from the state and
the society. There should be war-crimes trials, a truth and reconciliation commission, and a human-rights commission. A liberal constitution, with protections for individual and minority-group rights, should
be written in advance of elections, or else democracy would produce a
tyranny of the majority. Finally, since no opposition politics existed inside Saddam's Iraq, the nucleus of the first post-Saddam government
should be formed at the opposition conference scheduled for the end
of 2002 in London. It should be prepared to take authority over the
first piece of Iraq liberated by American and allied troops (this provisional government should eventually double its numbers within Iraq).
Thousands of exiles should be trained as a security force to impose law
and order after the fall of the regime.

Makiya hadn't lived in Iraq for thirty-five years, the years of Saddam. In the report on democracy, he was trying to think his way out

of all that blood-drenched history. As exiles dream and languish, they give in to grandiosity or despair, sink in their own insignificance and then rebel against it. The trouble with the Iraqi émigrés, Condoleezza Rice told Makiya's close colleague Rend Rahim in late November, is that "they're like the London Poles"—the ineffectual Polish government in exile during World War II. In the nostrils of hardheaded American officials, these Iraqis carried an odor of inauthenticity; they had no business setting up provisional governments; the real Iraqis were inside the country. Makiya rejected this scheme, and when others accused him of refusing to accept Iraq's realities, he bridled. "I don't want to accept them, as they are," Makiya told me. "They are political realities, after all. There are other realities." Philosophically, Makiya was a universalist. He was ready to believe that Iraqis inside Iraq were hungry for new realities, and that they were the same ones he himself believed in, if only leadership would show the way. Other Arab countries were mired in anti-Western ideologies, but the disastrous years of Baath Party rule had created what might be called Iraqi exceptionalism. When he met Rice at the White House, Makiya tried to sum up half a lifetime of thinking. The political consciousness of Iraqis had diverged from that of their Arab neighbors in very important ways, he told her. While the Arab and Muslim worlds criticized the United States for interfering in internal Iraqi affairs, Iraqis criticized the United States for not interfering enough. For these reasons, he said, "A new kind of politics is imaginable in Iraq." Iraq was uniquely suited to become the first liberal Arab country. The report on the transition to democracy was Makiya's attempt to will the outcome.

"The document is just paper at the end of the day," he told me one snowy evening at his Cambridge apartment in late 2002. "One of the less grandiose impulses behind it was this: There's a world of people out there deeply, deeply skeptical whether or not this country can make it to democracy. And I know deep down that they have good reason to be skeptical. I'm not really as rosy, I'm not as naïve, as sometimes I appear on this question. But it seems to me, for history's sake, important to have a group of Iraqis turn out a decent document that can be taken seriously, that will be picked up and remembered and churned over and used as some kind of a test, some kind of a yardstick against which to measure the progress of things afterward. And it was, after all, produced by Iraqis—so that Iraqis can lift their heads up a bit and go out there in the world and say, 'We meant it. It wasn't all a word game. Some of us tried to give it a shot.'"

IN LATE NOVEMBER, Makiya was invited to appear on a panel at New York University. Everyone else on the panel—academic experts, liberal journalists, a British former diplomat—opposed a war in Iraq. Professor Michael Walzer, a political theorist who had written the book *Just and Unjust Wars*, explained in his soft, hesitant way that a war in Iraq wouldn't qualify as just. There was no imminent threat to merit preemption. There was no humanitarian crisis to warrant intervention. The time to overthrow Saddam was in 1988, when Kurdish villages were being gassed, or in 1991, when Iraqis were rising up against the regime, or even in 1998, when Saddam defied the world and threw out UN weapons inspectors. But now, with a new round of inspections just beginning, and diplomacy ongoing at the UN, and the allied no-fly zone protecting the Kurds in the north, what was the just cause for war? "There is no mass murder now," Walzer said. "That's the box we're in." The administration in Washington was contemplating a preventive, not a preemptive war, Walzer argued, and there's no basis in just-war theory for such wars of choice. Containment was still working—even if the Iraqi people were among those being contained. Walzer, a passionate supporter of the Balkan interventions in the 1990s, with no illusions about the nature of the regime in Baghdad, seemed unhappy with his own conclusion. But there it was. One by one, the others agreed. The crowded auditorium settled into a comfortable consensus.

Makiya was the last to speak. In a charcoal jacket and gray shirt open at the collar, he leaned forward with an apologetic smile and said, "I'm afraid I'm going to strike a discordant note." The discussion, he said, had been a selfishly American one. The other panelists had failed to take into account the Iraqi people themselves, who would pay the highest price in the event of a war, and whose organized opposition

groups overwhelmingly wanted one. He described the opposition conference planned for early December in London, and then he turned to
the division within the Bush administration. Mistrust was now so
great that the Pentagon and vice president's office had sent representatives to sit in on State's Future of Iraq Project meetings. "The
strongest support for democrats and independents comes from these
hawks," he said. "We have the support of those arch-warmongers Paul
Wolfowitz, Secretary Rumsfeld, and the vice president's office. The
reasonable Colin Powell is utterly uninterested in this and wants to
have nothing to do with us." Makiya called Powell "an appeaser."

Having upended his audience's settled categories, Makiya went on
to describe the vision of democracy drawn in his report. "This is radical stuff in the Arab world," Makiya said. "This is dynamite stuff." He
was coming to the end, his voice growing stronger, and there was a
sudden ungrounded energy in the room. He had everyone's attention.
"The Iraqi opposition is something new in Arab politics. It can be encouraged or it can be crushed just like that. But think about what
you're doing if you do crush it. I rest my moral case on the following:
If there is a sliver of a chance of what I just said happening, a five to
ten percent chance, you have a moral obligation, I say, to do it."

The room exploded in applause. The other panelists looked startled. Against the reasonable arguments of these reasonable people,
Makiya was offering something more attractive—the face of hope,
however slender.

"It's very hard to respond," Walzer said.

It was hard because a man like Walzer didn't want to stand in the
way of a dream like Makiya's. He didn't want to be on the other side of
a great moral question. "I would not join an antiwar movement that
strengthened the hand of Saddam," Walzer told me later, and when I
asked whether there could be an antiwar movement that didn't, he admitted, "It's very hard to think of what form it could take."

In fact, by the winter of 2002–2003, with the excruciatingly long
buildup and the ritual dance of diplomacy at the UN, there was an actual antiwar movement, in the United States and around the world,
and it was growing very fast. It embraced the full spectrum of opposition, from the banners of extremist groups that proclaimed "No Blood

for Oil" to the moderate calls for weapons inspections and international law of the far larger Internet-based organization Moveon.org. The message, though, like that of most protest movements, was a simple one: Stop the war. All the difficult questions raised by the prospect of a war in Iraq were erased by these three words. For the antiwar movement, morality lined up entirely on its side.

I met the most appealing face of the movement that winter in a bright yellow room two floors above the traffic of West Fifty-seventh Street in Manhattan—a room so small that its occupant burned himself on the heat pipe when he turned over in bed and could commute to his office without touching the floor. Eli Pariser, twenty-two, tall, bearded, was spending long hours every day at his desk hunched over a laptop, plotting strategy on behalf of Moveon.org and directing the electronic traffic of an instantaneous movement that was partly assembled in his computer. In three months it had gathered the numbers that took three years to build during Vietnam.

Pariser's divorced parents, who had raised him in rural Maine, were veterans of the sixties. Pariser was something else: a self-described patriot, unfailingly polite and thoughtful, with a copy of the Constitution on his bookshelf, who worried about the effect of a war on America's reputation in the world. He seemed to exist so that the rest of the country couldn't dismiss the antiwar movement as a fringe phenomenon of graying pacifists and young nihilists. Pariser told me, "I just don't know that it makes sense for us to risk everything that we're risking both in terms of international stature and in terms of the lives of our military people for a vague idea that people think it could be better without this guy."

There was a case to be made for this nuanced view, and it moved millions of Americans. But the first thing to notice was its essential conservatism. Containment preserved the status quo along with a notion of American virtue. Pariser descended on his father's side from Zionist Jews who helped found Tel Aviv, and on his mother's from Polish socialists. But the aggressive antifascism that once characterized young people on the left had given way, in the wake of Vietnam and the green movement, to a softer, more cautious worldview that often amounted in practice to isolationism. The antifascist wars of our own time—in Bosnia and Kosovo—never strongly registered with Pariser's generation of activists. When I asked whether the desires of Iraqis themselves should be taken into account, he said, "I don't think that first and foremost this is about them as much as it's about us and how we act in the world."

This was more honest than much of what I heard on the morning of February 15, 2003, at the massive antiwar rally held near the United Nations. It was a frigid day in New York, but hundreds of thousands of people braved the cold (millions more came out worldwide), filling First Avenue from Fifty-first to Seventy-second Street. Behind the makeshift stage, Pariser made a point of introducing himself to Dennis Kucinich, the elfin, jug-eared Democratic congressman from Cleveland who was hinting that he might launch an antiwar campaign for president. Kucinich, who had followed Pariser's rise, declared, "Eli has proven we're in a new era of grass-roots activism. The basis for human unity is not just electronic—the human unity precedes the electronic, and then is furthered by it. Eli represents 'the advancing tide' which Emerson said 'creates for itself a condition of its own. And the question and the answer are one.'"

The spirit of Emerson was on First Avenue. There is a very old American type of protester—Emerson's friend Thoreau, for example, or John Brown, whom they both admired, or more recently the Berrigan brothers—who sees politics as an expression of personal morality and for whom strategic thinking is a kind of sin. Once the basic question of conscience has been answered, these moralists don't take much interest in the details or the consequences. In Thoreau's words, "They attend no caucus, they make no compromise, they use no policy." This spirit has its evangelical strain as well—it belonged to President Bush as much as to his antiwar opponents, who mirrored each other in viewing the world through a lens of moral polarity. So the prospect that the antiwar movement might strengthen Saddam's hand didn't matter. I asked Leslie Cagan, the founder of the group that had organized the rally, whether a speaker who wanted to make explicitly pro-Saddam remarks would be kept off the stage. "We try not to edit people," she said.

When Eli Pariser had his ninety seconds onstage, wearing a suit and tie, he was almost literally bouncing on his toes in the arctic air, unable not to smile. "For each person who's here, there are a hundred who weren't able to make it," he announced to the cheering throng up First Avenue. "I know—I get e-mail from them. They're ordinary, patriotic, mainstream Americans." Most of the other speakers were more strident, and at times the event took on the tone of a solidarity rally with the Iraqi people, lumped together with the Palestinians, as if their interests were the same. A young woman from Def Poetry Jam shouted, "We send our love to poets in Iraq and Palestine. Stay safe!" The notion that there was neither safety in Iraq nor, strictly speaking, poets—that the Iraqi people, while not welcoming the threat of bombs, might be realistic enough to accept a war as their only hope of liberation from tyranny—was literally unthinkable. Richie Havens sang "Freedom," just like at Woodstock, but I couldn't help wondering: for whom? The protesters saw themselves as defending Iraqis from the terrible fate that the United States was preparing to inflict on them. Why would Iraqis want war? The movement's assumptions were based on moral innocence—on an inability to imagine the horror in which Iraqis lived, and a desire for all good things to go together, for total vindication. War is evil; therefore, the prevention of war must be good.

That winter, Americans lived in a nearly unbearable pause. Everyone knew deep down that war was coming. But the great powers were enacting an artificial drama to try to avoid war, and in the seemingly eternal interim a kind of rhetorical hysteria thrived on all sides. Anyone who raised perfectly legitimate questions about the war became a "cheese-eating surrender monkey," whole nations of Europe were branded with the shame of appeasement, and in the congressional cafeteria French fries were renamed Freedom fries. War fever induced a surge of testosterone in lifelong noncombatants who had suddenly discovered their inner Churchill. Meanwhile, President Bush's implacable certitudes drove his opponents to paint him as one of history's monsters of aggression, deluded by Zionists and intoxicated with oil lust. Politicians and movie stars traveled to Baghdad and got taken in by the Baathist propaganda machine. A few of them stayed on as human shields, doing their best to keep a true monster of aggression in power over his silenced countrymen.

In the midst of this din, it was hard to think clearly. Many people allowed historical analogies to do their thinking for them. In the end it came down to two. Leon Wieseltier of *The New Republic* told me, "I've always thought that people in our generation, maybe in the last fifty years in America, have operated with two primal scenes: one was the Second World War, one was the Vietnam War. And you can almost divide the camps on the use of American force between those whose model of its application was the Second World War and those whose model for its application was Vietnam." For Wieseltier, the primal scene was World War II, because his parents had survived it in Europe. "The Second World War still makes me cry. People for whom Vietnam is their primal scene—and there are lots of them—I expect very little from them in the way of understanding. It's sort of the isolationism of the wounded or of the traumatized."

But World War II and Vietnam were not reliable guides to Iraq. The invocation of Munich and appeasement by one side, or Tonkin Gulf and deception by the other, seemed like ways to shut off debate rather than engage it. My most heated and confounding arguments over the war occurred when there was no one else around. I would run down the many compelling reasons why a war would be unwise, only to find at the end that Saddam was still in power, tormenting his people and defying the world. The administration's war was not my war—it was rushed, dishonest, unforgivably partisan, and destructive of alliances—but objecting to the authors and their methods didn't seem reason enough to stand in the way. One doesn't get one's choice of wars. To give my position a label, I belonged to the tiny, insignificant camp of ambivalently prowar liberals, who supported a war by about the same margin that the voting public had supported Al Gore. This position descended from the interventions of the last decade in Haiti, Bosnia, and Kosovo. The Iraq War was about something other than human rights and democracy, but it could bring similar benefits. I wanted Iraqis to be let out of prison; I wanted to see a homicidal dictator removed from power before he committed mass murder again; I wanted to see if an open society stood a chance of taking root in the heart of the Arab world. More than anyone else, Kanan Makiya guided my thinking, and I always found it easier to imagine a happy outcome when I was within earshot of him.

BEFORE THE WAR, at least three million Iraqis lived in exile, and in the second week of December 2002 most of them seemed to turn up at the London Hilton Metropole. It was a garish new hotel on an anonymous stretch of Edgware Road, not far from Paddington Station. The shiny elevators and corridors were jammed with the hundreds of mullahs, monarchists, ex-officers, party bosses, businessmen, intellectuals, and schemers who comprised Iraq's opposition in exile. In their turbans and robes, their kaffiyehs or business suits, they huddled in conspiratorial-looking groups, bathed in camera lights, clutching cell phones to ears. It struck me how many of them looked nothing like Kanan Makiya's liberal-minded independents. Some resembled beefy apparatchiks from the old Soviet republics of Central Asia. Others, solemn, bearded Shiite clerics, brought to mind the words "fatwa" and "stoning." Of the very few women, some were concealed within full *hijab*s.

Sprinkled among them, palely lurking, were the Americans. There were the discreet emissaries of various government agencies, and the less discreet personalities of the regime change community in Washington. There was Francis Brooke, Chalabi's smugly smiling PR man. There was Randy Scheuneman, formerly a staff aide to Trent Lott, now of the Committee to Liberate Iraq, and Danielle Pletka, formerly on the staff of Jesse Helms's Foreign Relations Committee, now vice president of the American Enterprise Institute. There was Laurie Mylroie, a short, blockish freelance scholar, peddling copies of her book that claimed to prove an Iraqi connection to the 1993 World Trade Center bombing, which featured a blurb from Paul Wolfowitz. There was a slight, laconic young man in a business suit, named Charles Forrest, who hovered against a wall with an air of possessing some burning secret knowledge. Charles Forrest worked for a government-funded organization in Washington that was preparing a legal case against Saddam Hussein, but his career path through various government and business jobs in the Middle East sounded like the cover story of a spy. "People suddenly see this whole region as a threat to us. The whole thing is inflamed and it's endangering us," Charles Forrest exclaimed. "The time has come. The whole thing's got to change." There was Senator Sam Brownback, a Christian conservative from Kansas, holding an impromptu press conference with the party leaders of the opposition, whom he compared to Jefferson, Adams, and Franklin. "Democracy is difficult, but ultimately it is the only form of government that allows people to progress," Senator Brownback declared. "Destiny has called upon these leaders to take on the heavy burden of rebirthing a nation." These Americans moved through the throng of Iraqi exiles with the glowing and watchful fervor of missionaries among the converted.

A new movie had just been released of Graham Greene's novel about a young American in Saigon with a shelf of books on democracy and a head full of dangerously innocent ideas, working undercover to create a "Third Force" that would transform Vietnam in America's image. *The Quiet American* had been ready for distribution just after September 11, but Miramax's fears that the movie might be thought unpatriotic delayed the release for more than a year. As it turned out, the timing couldn't have been better. I was wary of Greene's anti-Americanism, which was a form of British snobbery, his jaded postures, his love of fallen Catholics in opium dens—the whole Baudelaire-in-Saigon bit. Yet back in 1955 he had seen that America's capacity for mistakes and crimes was proportionate to its innocence and self-righteousness. It was impossible not to think of these new zealots as the latest generation of quiet Americans.

At the London Hilton Metropole, Kanan Makiya was an anomalous sight, looking rumpled in shirtsleeves, baggy corduroys, and all-weather shoes, his face as always clean shaven. The politicos from the Kurdish, Shiite, and ex-military parties complained that Makiya's casual appearance lacked respect. The rumored contents of his report, not yet distributed to the conferees or even completely translated into Arabic, troubled them as well. Worst of all was the bluntness with which Makiya kept talking about the need to move beyond the "old politics" of the ethnic parties.

He wanted the conference to vote up or down on his report, and he feared that some of the parties with heavier numbers—especially the Shiite hard-liners—would present their own hastily drafted proposals to head off his. He had spent the days before the conference trying to convince Condoleezza Rice and her envoy to the Iraqi opposition, Zalmay Khalilzad, that the traditional parties were overrepresented, and that the independent professionals of the INC, whose diversity and ideas were closer to those of Iraqis inside the country, should have their numbers increased. He sent a list of forty or fifty new names to Khalilzad. "We independents . . . are a noisy, fractious and difficult lot," he wrote in his cover letter. "But we are solid on the question of the core values that we want to see in Iraq, which are in the end values we have learned from the West. A quarter of a century of my work on Iraq has been devoted to spreading such values among Arabs."

Khalilzad, the defense intellectual and longtime Wolfowitz aide who had drafted the controversial Defense Planning Guidance in 1992, was in London to make sure the fractious Iraqi opposition presented a unified face to the world. The administration's own policy on postwar Iraq was far from clear, but Khalilzad let the Iraqis know that no government-in-exile or "transitional authority" was going to be chosen in London. Yet here was Makiya, with powerful backers at the Pentagon and the vice president's office, refusing to play the game, insisting that he and his friends and fellow independents were the true face of Iraq, that the traditional parties "will unquestionably become the greatest single obstacle to the kind of economic and political renaissance of Iraq that I know the U.S. government wants to see happen." Makiya and the INC had somehow convinced themselves that they would have no greater enemies in liberated Iraq than State Department bureaucrats and Kurdish and Shiite politicos.

There was furious behind-the-scenes maneuvering. "Who is Kanan Makiya to propose these names?" an official with the ex-military party demanded. Chalabi was flying in from Tehran after cutting a deal with the Kurdish and Shiite parties to form a provisional government in spite of the Americans. Then the Sunni delegates revolted over their scant numbers. Khalilzad, an Afghan-American who understood the bazaar nature of regional politics, brokered the horse trading: Sunnis and independents were added, watering down the Shiite numbers. Makiya was racing to get his 329-page report (dissenting appendixes and all) translated and printed, at a cost to the U.S. government of at least twenty thousand dollars. On the phone he and Tom Warrick, his old nemesis at the State Department, haggled over the price. "I can promise you," Makiya said with a sigh, "no one is trying to make money off this."

As a politician, Makiya was his own worst enemy. He brought to the fray the earnest, intense style that made his writing so powerful, and he left even his friends shaking their heads. Perhaps he was out of his depth in the dangerous waters of Iraqi politics; he was a writer, he thought for himself, he had never worried about coalitions and deals. But over the course of 2002 he had eased himself down into the stream and then plunged headfirst and been swept along. He tried to bring this passage of history under his control, but as Randolph Bourne wrote of the American intellectuals who went to war in Europe in 1917 with the highest humanitarian motives, "If it is a question of controlling war, it is difficult to see how the child on the back of a mad elephant is to be any more effective in stopping the beast than is the child who tries to stop him from the ground." Makiya was arrogant, he was idealistic, he was reckless, he was courageous. What else could he have done?

One afternoon, he and his friend Sam Chalabi met in Bloomsbury, not far from Makiya's parents' flat, across the street from the British Museum at a café next to the Oriental bookshop run by an elderly English widow where Makiya had loved to browse when he was young. Together they surveyed the damage. Chalabi, whose cranial dome and willfully mysterious cool left no doubt whose nephew he was, had been Makiya's closest collaborator on the document, but over cappuccino he told Makiya that his outspokenness was hurting their cause. The Kurdish parties were vehemently opposed to the proposal for nonethnic federalism, which would mean the end of their decade-long experiment in self-rule. They had fought hard to gain recognition and coequal status with the Arabs, and they were not going to relinquish it without a fight. The views of the Shiite party on the section dealing with religion and the state had not been solicited. The Sunnis were unhappiest of all. There had been a lack of inclusiveness.

Makiya nodded. "I've begun to hate the word 'inclusive' here," he said. "I know it's going to mean the lowest common denominator. Nothing will be said that means anything." He was sweating, the lines deepening in his forehead. I had never seen him so high-strung—he looked exhausted. His cell phone, a new acquisition, was bedeviling him. The months of work, the pressure of his will, the storm that always swirled around him, seemed to be placing him under an intolerable strain.

"They see you as an interloper imposing something on them. Let's emphasize the parts of the document the others can get behind," Chalabi, a mergers and acquisitions lawyer, said. "Human rights, transitional justice."

"They want to come out of this as one big happy family. They want to show unity and support for the Americans. I want to win something concrete." Makiya wanted the opposition to commit itself to a set of principles and force the Americans' hand before the shooting started and the logic of war took its course. "But I'm afraid we're fighting a losing battle."

"I don't want to give up, or withdraw the document," Chalabi insisted. "But you have to play it more like a game."

Makiya looked helplessly at Chalabi, distress etched across his face. "I guess so."

Chalabi urged him to lower his profile. Makiya relented.

That evening, I went to the offices of the INC in fashionable Knightsbridge. Upstairs, a group of smartly dressed young staffers hovered around a fleshy, balding man in an armchair who was answering e-mails while listening to Albinoni's *Adagio in G Minor* on CD. It was Ahmad Chalabi, wearing a brown, pin-striped, double-breasted suit and a yellow silk tie done in a Windsor knot. He glanced up and greeted me with the magisterial smile that was his eternal public expression. There was no time to talk; he had just flown in from Tehran and had business that would last into the night.

I went along for a short drive with Chalabi, Makiya, and a few others. At one point Chalabi took a call on his cell phone: He was discussing Jalal Talabani, one of the two Kurdish leaders. "He's a Marxist, a Groucho Marxist," Chalabi said with a chuckle. "'You don't like my principles? I have some others.'"

Nabil al-Musawi, Chalabi's right-hand man, turned to me. He was a tall, good-looking former pizzeria manager in a turtleneck and blazer, with a carefully trimmed goatee. "The independents are the leading edge between the politics of the past and the politics of the future. By the politics of the past I mean not just the traditional parties but the State

Department, with their cynical thinking that these Arabs can't have democracy, they need someone strong to control them." By now I had the argument down cold, but it was striking to spend an hour in Chalabi's inner circle and feel the breezy certainty, the sense of an elite group riding a giant wave of history into a future that belonged to them.

The world of the London Iraqis could have been created by Conrad: the coffee-shop owner who was founder-president of the Iraq-Israel Friendship Committee, banned in both countries; the newspaper editor who kept pictures of himself with Saddam from the old days and had plans to start a paper called *Babylon Times* when he returned to Baghdad; the underemployed journalists who worked out of briefcases; the strategy sessions over hummus and kebab in dingy outer London cafeterias, and the nostalgia-drenched conversations in living rooms over late-night chai; the bitter intrigues among men who knew one another too well. Far from their original habitat, they had grown to look more alike than they knew. They had been waiting half their lives for this tremendous event to take place. It was up to the Americans.

Mustafa al-Kadhimi arrived in London in 1999 with nothing except a carved Ottoman window shutter from his family's house in an old Baghdad neighborhood. When I met him he was thirty-four, but his lean, slightly ravaged face and gray-flecked hair made him appear a decade older. "I have a tragic story," Mustafa told me matter-of-factly. He was born into a family of wealthy Shiite merchants, but the Baathists confiscated the house, then the businesses, and eventually began arresting Mustafa's brothers, who, like thousands of Shia, had joined the Khomeini-inspired Dawa Party in the early eighties. Mustafa himself flirted with the Dawa, and when his three best friends were arrested and killed, Mustafa fled Baghdad through the north. It was 1988, and the Anfal was at its height. A family of Kurdish refugees from a destroyed village entrusted their five-year-old daughter to Mustafa's care, but on his way to the Turkish border an Iraqi Air Force helicopter flew low overhead and startled the horse on which Mustafa and the girl were riding. She fell off and died in his arms— "a picture I cannot get out of my head."

The girl's family had gone to Tehran, where Mustafa found them and broke the terrible news. The year he spent in theocratic Iran showed him "the true face of Islamist ideology." It reminded him of nothing so much as the regime in his own country; he was even jailed for forty days after publishing a newspaper article deemed blasphemous. After 1989, Mustafa began a decade of wandering. He went from Iran to Syria, to Lebanon, and eventually to the Greek islands, where he worked as a waiter at a resort. One day in the mid-1990s, the guest was none other than George H. W. Bush. Serving the ex-president's table, Mustafa summoned enough courage to lean forward and ask why the American government had left Saddam in power to slaughter rebellious Iraqis after the Gulf War in 1991. When I met him, he was still waiting for the answer. In London, Mustafa became a hotel porter, but soon he fell into the INC circle and met Kanan Makiya, whose books transformed his mind and completed his evolution into a liberal democrat.

I never quite learned how Mustafa made a living (his wife was expecting their first child). He had connections at Radio Free Europe and at the INC weekly paper; his business card read "Iraq Future Affairs Institute." Two months earlier in Damascus, a cab driver recognized his accent and said, "Congratulations. The Americans are coming to help you. Let's hope they come to help us afterward." This, Mustafa assured me, was the true opinion of the Arab street, not the vitriol shown in the Arab media. "The problem with Arabs is we live on our history," he said. "And the history is a big lie." Mustafa was ashamed of his English, but he had an epigrammatic way with language. As far as he was concerned, the next president of Iraq should be either a woman or a man without a mustache. Exile had cost him almost everything. His mother, whom he hadn't seen since 1988, died in Baghdad just a few months before the start of the war that would have reunited them. Mustafa was one of those fugitives from dictatorship whose whole life hangs in suspension until the regime's fall. He spent a full day driving me around Iraqi London, insisting on paying for everything. When we said goodbye, he warmly kissed my cheeks and promised that we would meet again soon, in Baghdad. It was impossible not to wish it so.

IN THE GRAND BALLROOM of the London Hilton Metropole, Makiya was sitting at a long table next to Ahmad Chalabi and a few other opposition figures before a throng of journalists. Conspicuous by their absence were the leaders of the ethnic parties. Makiya had promised to say nothing, to let the others speak, to let the document speak for itself, and for a while he kept his word. But when reporters began lobbing questions in his direction, he described what was in the report and, as usual, he grew intense. "It carries forward a completely new idea that doesn't exist anywhere in the Arab-Muslim world. This is something tremendous, this is something unbelievable. We're talking above all of an idea of democracy that isn't only majority rule, an idea of democracy that is about minority rights and group rights and above all individual human rights."

Murmuring spread among the press corps, a ripple of excitement. Who was this guy? He sounded nothing like the parade of speakers who had been droning on throughout the weekend.

"This is a fighting document, by the way," Makiya said. "We intend to fight for it on the floor of the conference."

When the session broke up, the journalists flocked around Makiya. Into the ballroom rushed Hoshyar Zebari, a leader of one of the Kurdish parties, red faced and furious, telling anyone who would listen that Makiya's document had no authority at the conference.

Later, I asked Zebari what he thought of Makiya's ideas about federalism, about the ethnic parties, about old and new politics. Zebari (who would become the very capable foreign minister of the new Iraqi government, the first Kurd to hold the office in Iraq's history) was a bear of a man with a thick black mustache. He smiled through his answer, but he kept thumping me in the chest as he spoke. "We are rooted in the country, we are the ones who have suffered," he said. "What Kanan Makiya has done, I appreciate his intellectual work, but it's just an intellectual exercise."

"Makiya is trying to give it teeth," I suggested.

"He's the only one," said an American in a blue suit, hovering around the conversation. He was David L. Phillips, an official from the Council on Foreign Relations, who had consulted with the State Department on the Future of Iraq Project. "The report is not a political document—it's not a blueprint. If it becomes one, it will be divisive." Phillips sharply criticized Makiya for hijacking the writing of the report and then lobbying so hard for its provisions. The ideas were too lofty, too far ahead of their time, to stand a chance of being realized soon. "Iraqis aren't quite ready for the new politics. The tribal structures, the ethnic groupings—they matter to Iraqis. They're important. This isn't a Brandeis laboratory."

The London conference ended with expressions of unity and support for that vague thing called democracy in Iraq. But no provisional government was formed, and the report of the Democratic Principles Working Group, printed and distributed, with hundreds of pages of appendixes and dissents, was never officially discussed. Back in Washington, officials thanked the group for its advice and shelved the report that the State Department had solicited. Makiya had called their bluff, and now they were calling his.

The movement toward war kept rolling forward, with or without democratic principles. Makiya had antagonized a sizable part of the Iraqi opposition, but he still had strong backers in Washington. On January 10, 2003, Makiya, Rend Rahim, and a doctor from a prominent Sunni family in Tikrit named Hatem Mukhlis were ushered into the Oval Office for a meeting with the president, Cheney, Rice, and Khalilzad. Bush asked them for their personal stories, but the exiles also spent a good portion of the time explaining to Bush that there were two kinds of Arabs in Iraq, Sunnis and Shia. The very notion of an Iraqi opposition appeared to be new to him. Bush struck Mukhlis as unfocused on the key policy questions of the future of the Iraqi army, debaathification, and an interim government. "But we saw in his eyes that we were going to war." Cheney kept his thoughts to himself; he seemed on edge. It was clear that the administration still hadn't settled on a postwar plan.

Makiya tried to push one into existence. With Rahim, he urged the president to announce a provisional government of Iraqi exiles before the war. "The Iraqis on the inside have been brainwashed," he said, "and a government in exile would be prepared to take over when there's change." Makiya told the president that his actions would transform the image of America in the Arab world, that war could be a force for progress, for democracy. "People will greet the troops with sweets and flowers," he said.

Mukhlis agreed, but he added, "If you don't win their hearts at the start, if they don't get benefits, after two months you could see Mogadishu in Baghdad." Mukhlis gave the president other warnings: A government of exiles would not be accepted by Iraqis inside the country, and dissolving the Iraqi army would change the complexion of American forces there, from the liberators Bush said he intended them to be into occupiers. Bush asked whether Iraqis hated Israelis, and again Makiya and Mukhlis, who had been schoolmates at Baghdad's elite Jesuit high school in the mid-1960s, gave contradictory views: Makiya said that Iraqis were too focused on their own oppression; Mukhlis insisted that they were brought up and educated in school to be anti-Zionists. Makiya and Mukhlis also disagreed about the nature of Iraqi society. It was still strongly tribal, Mukhlis said; Makiya argued that over the past fifty or seventy-five years Iraqis had become engineers, doctors, capable citizens of a modern state. No one in the room pursued the obvious contradiction between this optimism and Makiya's vision of a nation of the brainwashed.

Both Iraqis left the meeting convinced that Bush saw things as they did. "I thought Bush understood where I was coming from," Mukhlis later said. "At that time I was absolutely certain Iraq was going to be paradise."

Makiya emerged from the White House and declared himself "deeply reassured" by the president's dedication to Iraqi democracy.

Two months later, in mid-March, Vice President Cheney appeared on *Meet the Press* and told the country that American troops would be greeted as liberators in Iraq.

"If your analysis is not correct," Tim Russert pressed him, "and we're not treated as liberators, but as conquerors, and the Iraqis begin to resist, particularly in Baghdad, do you think the American people are prepared for a long, costly, and bloody battle with significant American casualties?"

Cheney wasn't worried. "Well, I don't think it's likely to unfold that way, Tim," the vice president said in his low-key, soothing way, "because I really do believe that we will be greeted as liberators. I've talked with a lot of Iraqis in the last several months myself, had them to the White House. The president and I have met with them, various groups and individuals, people who have devoted their lives from the outside to trying to change things inside Iraq. And like Kanan Makiya, who's a professor at Brandeis but an Iraqi, he's written great books about the subject, knows the country intimately, and is a part of the democratic opposition and resistance. The read we get on the people of Iraq is there is no question but what they want to get rid of Saddam Hussein and they will welcome as liberators the United States when we come to do that."

Upon hearing these words, Feisal Istrabadi, the Chicago lawyer, felt his heart sink. "I knew nobody who spent four decades in exile knew what was going on in Iraq. I didn't and Kanan didn't. The only difference was I was a hell of a lot more cautious. He always made promises he knew he could not keep." Makiya knew that "sweets and flowers" were unlikely to be the response, Istrabadi said. "But he also knew Bush didn't know any better. He wanted Bush to go in. We all did."

About one thing Cheney was right: Makiya had written great books on the subject. In *Republic of Fear* and *Cruelty and Silence* he had stared unflinchingly at totalitarian Iraq and the consequences of Baathist terror, the human wreckage it produced, the sight and smell of it. After the Gulf War, when he and other dissidents drafted Charter 91 outlining principles of tolerance for a new Iraq, Makiya received a severe letter from an old friend that he was honest and brave enough to reprint in *Cruelty and Silence*: "I think—and please allow me to tell you this—that the ideas of the Charter issue from an ivory tower which has elevated itself so high up into the sky that we who are standing down below can hardly see or hear where they are coming from. You see, our society today has become like *1984*. There is no one who remembers or who even dares to remember the meaning of words like 'freedom,' 'democracy,' 'brotherhood,' or 'humanity.' They no longer know what 'human rights' are. I mean, what does this have to do with them! . . . Their only preoccupation is to survive and to live, like sheep."

Makiya knew all this, and when, in late January, he crossed the snowy mountains along the border between Iran and Iraqi Kurdistan with a small group that included Ahmad Chalabi, and met old com-

rades in the Kurdish town of Salahuddin, and a man he didn't know
threatened his life one night over a perceived slight, Makiya sent an
e-mail to a few friends describing the incident. "This is the human raw
material that you want to build democracy for," he wrote. "Every day in
the last five weeks of my travels I have come across such damaged and
wounded people, people who breathe nationalism, sectarianism, without knowing that they are doing so, and people who are deeply chau-
vinistic and suspicious toward their fellow Iraqis. These are the facts
of life for the next generation in this poor, unhappy and ravaged land.
Don't even think of coming back to it after liberation if you are not prepared to deal with such facts."

Reading these words, I was reminded of the voice that I first heard
before I ever met Makiya—the fearless voice of his books. As a writer,
Makiya knew what Iraq had become. But now he was also playing a
central part in a great historical drama, an event on such a vast and
audacious scale that no one could imagine the full extent of the consequences. He had become a politician, and he wrote in his e-mail
from Kurdistan, "Politics is the harshest judge in the world that there
is, infinitely harsher than the God of the Old Testament or the Allah of
the Quran." What he had been able only to dream about throughout
his life was suddenly within reach. There would be no second chance,
and his own future was uncertain, for Makiya had been diagnosed
with the same form of leukemia that killed Edward Said. So he made
himself forget what he knew long enough to say a few words to the
president of the United States that will some day feature prominently
in his obituary.

The sound of the first bombs falling on Baghdad was, to Makiya, a
joyful noise. Three weeks later, on April 9, he sat with the president in
the White House and watched the statue of Saddam Hussein fall to
the ground in Baghdad's Firdos Square, and he wept.

And after that, the trouble began.

4

SPECIAL PLANS

IN THE SUMMER of 2003, a young American from Rochester, New York, named Andrew P. N. Erdmann was working for the Coalition Provisional Authority in an office on the second floor of the Republican Palace, on the west bank of the Tigris River in central Baghdad. The sign on the office door said "Ministry of Higher Education and Scientific Research." Erdmann, a thirty-six-year-old State Department employee with a doctorate in history from Harvard, was the Iraqi ministry's senior adviser—in effect, the acting minister.

Drew Erdmann was a rangy, broad-shouldered former rower with a strong chin, short sandy hair, and a bushy mustache, which (until it disappeared at some point over the summer) turned his face into a British colonial official's circa 1925. He was getting just a few hours of sleep a night, in a cramped shared trailer on the grounds behind the palace. When he woke up every morning before six, without an alarm, Erdmann's first thought was: Saigon—shit. His roommate, an Englishman named Philip, would say, "How are you doing this morning, Dr. Erdmann?" And Erdmann would reply, "Another day in paradise." The anxiety of all that needed to be done in the day ahead was already racing through him.

When I met him in mid-July, Erdmann was still seething from a meeting earlier that day in which he had tried not to humiliate a university president who asked what "operating budget" meant in the middle of the fifth or sixth discussion of the subject. Two weeks before, a twenty-two-year-old soldier from Erdmann's security detail, Specialist Jeffrey Wershow, had been shot in the head at point-blank range on the campus of Baghdad University while waiting for him to come out of another meeting. Erdmann had helped evacuate the dying soldier.

Erdmann's features and oarsman's physique, together with the double-barreled middle initials, prepared me for a terse, anglophilic bureaucrat. Instead, lying on his cot in the trailer and fiddling with a Swiss army knife, feet propped on an army duffel bag, his desk littered with water bottles and empty packets of Meals Ready to Eat and unread books on the Middle East, Erdmann brooded. He spoke in long reflective sentences that were frequently interrupted by second thoughts and qualifications, then settled into a faster, more explosive rhythm when recounting something that angered or amused him. By his own account he was short-tempered and close to nervous exhaustion.

The ministry that was his responsibility, like almost every other government building, had been looted down to the wiring and pipes; even the urinals had been unbolted from the bathroom walls. The top ministry officials, along with the presidents of Iraq's universities, were all prominent Baath Party members and had been sacked; one of them, the notorious president of Baghdad University and a doctor, was soon afterward shot dead in his office while writing a prescription. University classrooms and libraries across the city and across the country were trashed and plundered, thousands of books and computers stolen, windows lifted from window frames, desks left lying in twisted heaps amid the dust and broken glass. Erdmann was trying to see the interrupted academic year to its close, and students were sitting for exams in ovenlike classrooms without air conditioners, fans, or steady electric light.

The Iraqi state had collapsed, and there was nothing to take its place.

I wanted to know how the study of history had prepared Drew Erdmann for the job that he was trying to do in Baghdad. What were the historical analogies that he was carrying in his head? The British in colonial Iraq? The Americans in occupied Germany? Erdmann flashed a self-mocking grin. "I'm a historical cipher. I can't think historically," he said. "There've been times when I don't even know what I did forty-eight hours before. I try—it's like a test for myself. Can I remember what I did the day before? I eventually can, but it takes effort. But I think that's not a good situation. You should be able to remember what you did in the last twenty-four hours."

One of Erdmann's favorite books, which he was trying to find time to reread in Baghdad, was the French historian Marc Bloch's *Strange Defeat*, a firsthand account of the French collapse before the Nazi blitzkrieg in the spring of 1940. Bloch served in the French army in both world wars and then joined the resistance before his capture, torture, and execution by the Nazis. In talking about his own work in Iraq, more than once Erdmann cited a passage from *Strange Defeat* that was marked in his old paperback copy. "The ABC of our profession," Bloch wrote, "is to avoid these large abstract terms in order to try to discover behind them the only concrete realities, which are human beings."

The deadly chaos that followed the American invasion of Iraq is a story of abstract terms and concrete realities. Between them lies a distance even greater than the eight thousand miles from Washington to Baghdad, yet the ideas of the war's architects produced consequences as tangible as gutted offices and homemade bombs. Those consequences must be understood above all in the lives of human beings, Iraqis and Americans, thrown together by the fierce history of a war.

BEFORE GOING TO IRAQ, Drew Erdmann had done a lot of relevant historical thinking. The quotation from *Strange Defeat* served as the epigraph of his Harvard dissertation, which was titled "Americans' Search for 'Victory' in the Twentieth Century." It examined the way the concept of securing political ends by military means changed over the course of the century in the minds of Americans. The gap between military and political in the transition from war to peace was a recurring problem throughout the century, and bridging it became the object of increasingly self-conscious effort. The creation of institutions like the Army War College, the National Security Council, and the State Department's policy planning staff showed that, at high levels of government and the military, there was a growing realization that the aftermath of war is a complex process and just as crucial to ultimate victory as battlefield success. "The language that we live with today of 'exit strategy,'" Erdmann said, "which is already cliché, the focus on the 'end game,' another cliché—that's recent, and that's part of this historical evolution."

His thesis ended with the reaction against Vietnam and the rise of the Powell Doctrine of "decisive force." But this latest concept, Erdmann wrote, is not a once-and-for-all solution to the problem of achieving victory any more than the twentieth century's earlier concepts had been (as interventions in the Balkans showed even as he was writing). The learning process throughout the century was fitful and halting. He wrote, "Americans—leaders and citizens alike—have thus been usually ill-equipped to conceive of the ramifications of the use of force when the next crisis arrives, as it surely does in this tragic world."

The thesis was exploratory and inconclusive; it showed a keen interest in the models and values that shaped Americans' thinking about war and peace. It was not the kind of dissertation written to land a job. Erdmann always called it "a failure."

He received his PhD in 2000 and promptly abandoned an academic career. His interests were out of favor in the field. And there was something self-punishing and obsessive in his character. A life spent analyzing military history would be insufficient; he was the sort of academic who had to know how he would do under fire. In his copy of *Strange Defeat* there was another marked passage to which he drew my attention: "The real trouble with us professors was that we were absorbed in our day-to-day tasks. Most of us can say with some justice that we were good workmen. Is it equally true to say that we were good citizens?"

In early 2001, Erdmann was about to fly to Kosovo and take the first job he could find—"Anything. Load bags of grain. That's how far away I wanted to get from academia"—when a call came from Richard N. Haass, who had just been named director of policy planning at the State Department by Colin Powell. Haass had once taught with Erdmann's thesis adviser, Ernest May, and Erdmann's name had been passed along by Philip Zelikow, the University of Virginia professor who had been Rice's colleague in the first Bush presidency. By June,

Erdmann was in Washington, working in an office he had already re-searched extensively for his thesis. At Harvard he had been an Eisen-hower specialist, and he entered government in the old-fashioned spirit of a political independent. "This is a little too grandiose," he said, "but there is a previous tradition in foreign-policy circles of being more nonpartisan, serving the national interest."

On September 11, 2001, Erdmann was in his office at the State De-partment writing a draft of a policy document on America's role in the world, and in fact was in the middle of a sentence on the threat of ter-rorism, when the phone rang: It was his wife, with the news of the World Trade Center attacks. The effect on Erdmann's life was dra-matic—not just in the greatly raised stakes and intensity of doing government work (he was assigned the counterterrorism portfolio at policy planning), but in his sense that what he was doing could make a difference. "It confirmed the wisdom of my decision to leave the world of academia."

In the summer of 2002, when war with Iraq became the adminis-tration's unannounced policy, Haass directed Erdmann to write an analysis of postwar reconstructions in the twentieth century. In fifteen single-spaced, classified pages—epic length for a State Department memo—Erdmann applied the ideas in his dissertation to a series of case studies from the two world wars through more recent conflicts such as Bosnia and Kosovo. One of his fundamental conclusions was that long-term success depended on international support. In the short run, he explained when we met in Baghdad, "the foundation of everything is security," which partly depended on having sufficient numbers of troops. "That was the concern of the project, and my con-cern—were we prepared to do what it took in the postwar phase? Not exactly rocket science."

That fall, Powell circulated the memo to Cheney, Rumsfeld, and Rice. "It may have been irrelevant," Erdmann said. "Maybe it wasn't read."

THE REAL ACTION was elsewhere. In September, around the time that Erdmann's memo was making the pro-forma rounds in Washington, across the river at the Pentagon, the Office of Near East and South Asia's Northern Gulf Directorate was setting up an annex in empty offices one floor above its regular location on the fourth floor. The extra space would accommodate and also separate the overflow of people who were being brought in to work on planning for Iraq. The new unit was called the Office of Special Plans. It was overseen by Douglas Feith, the Pentagon's undersecretary for policy, and his deputy William Luti. Feith, a Washington lawyer, had been out of government for almost two decades; in 1983 he had been fired by Reagan's national security adviser William Clark and was then brought over to the Pentagon by Richard Perle. Feith's political activities and writings were largely devoted to bolstering the hard-line policies of the Likud Party. He owed his important new job to his friend and former boss Perle, who had turned it down himself and then recommended this relatively unknown man to Rumsfeld. "All right, I'm taking Feith," Rumsfeld told Perle, "and he'd better be as good as you say." So it was Douglas Feith who assumed the administration's crucial position on postwar Iraq. After the invasion, he would claim that Special Plans' enigmatic name was necessary: "At the time, calling it Iraqi Planning Office might have undercut our diplomatic efforts." This lawyerly reasoning didn't explain why the State Department's Future of Iraq Project was taking place in full public view with no adverse consequences—why the postwar planning effort couldn't be seen as a credible threat that strengthened the administration's hand at the UN.

But for the Office of Special Plans, secrecy was not only convenient, it was necessary. One could even say that it was metaphysically necessary. The man brought in by Feith and Luti to direct the operation was Abram Shulsky, a former Perle aide and consultant at the Pentagon's in-house think tank, the Office of Net Assessment. Shulsky, Wolfowitz's housemate at Cornell and Chicago, had coauthored a short essay in 1999 called "Leo Strauss and the World of Intelligence (By Which We Do Not Mean Nous)." Shulsky believed that the writings of his old professor Leo Strauss could be useful antidotes to the narrow-mindedness of the American intelligence community. Rather than relying on statistics and social science, which are based on universal categories, intelligence analysts should turn back to the giants of political philosophy, such as Thucydides, who understood that the nature of regimes differs profoundly. ("Regime," translated by Strauss from the Greek *politeia*, suggested the character of a society's ideals and its leaders; perhaps it's not an accident that the rubric of the administration's Iraq policy became "regime change.") Tyrannies cannot be understood in the image of democracies, and the tendency of established analysts to try (known as "mirror-imaging") guarantees that they will fail to grasp the essential nature of an Ayatollah Khomeini when he comes along. Tyrants rely on deception, which makes the work of the analyst harder but also more philosophically interesting, and which brings to mind the relevance of Strauss's idea of esoteric or hidden writing in the great political texts: "Strauss's view certainly alerts one to the possibility that political life may be closely linked to deception," Shulsky wrote. "Indeed, it suggests that deception is the norm in political life, and the hope, to say nothing of the expectation, of establishing a politics that can dispense with it is the exception."

It isn't such a long step from this insight to the creation of an office that conceals its work behind a deliberately obscure name like "Special Plans." There's mirror-imaging of a different kind going on here—not the mistake of seeing your enemy as a reflection of yourself, but the mistake of trying to see your enemy as he sees himself until you begin to reflect him. "When you look long into an abyss," wrote Nietzsche, the bête noire of the Straussians, "the abyss also looks into you." Something like this had already happened in Feith's office before Special Plans was set up, in a predecessor unit, the Counter-Terrorism Evaluation Group. The idea for the unit was Wolfowitz's, and it went all the way back to 1976 and Team B, the group of CIA-appointed outside experts, including Wolfowitz, that had come to much more alarmist conclusions about the Soviets than the intelligence agencies. This time, the purpose was to gather intelligence on weapons of mass destruction, terrorism, and their possible nexus in Iraq. The operation was led by David Wurmser, author of *Tyranny's Ally* and the "Clean Break" strategy paper from which it emerged. Together with his partner, F. Michael Maloof, who had served under Perle in the Reagan Defense Department (all roads from Special Plans led back to Perle), Wurmser collected raw data, much of it from defectors provided by the Iraqi National Congress, in order to prove an assumption: that Saddam had ties to al-Qaeda and was likely to hand off WMD to terrorists. Wurmser and Maloof were working deductively, not inductively: The premise was true; facts would be found to confirm it. All the better that much of the data was doubted or even dismissed by the CIA, the Defense Intelligence Agency, the State Department's Bureau of Intelligence and Research, and the Energy Department. In the eyes of the Pentagon civilians, the methods of the intelligence agencies were deeply suspect, and mainstream analysts had a long record of failure in the Middle East. A new method was urgently needed, starting with the higher insights of political philosophy rather than evidence from the fallen world of social science.

By the time Feith and Luti set up the Office of Special Plans, Wurmser had already moved on to work for John Bolton, undersecretary of state for arms control and international security, the lone high-level neoconservative in the State Department. (Wurmser would end up in the vice president's office, suggesting that in the Bush administration lateral movement could be more important than the vertical kind.) Maloof would eventually have his security clearance revoked. But the work of their disbanded intelligence unit was absorbed into Special Plans, as bullet points on policy papers and PowerPoint slides, and then piped by Luti and Shulsky directly to the White House, where the neoconservatives had allies in Cheney's chief of staff, I. Lewis "Scooter" Libby, and Rice's NSC director for the Middle East, Elliott Abrams. Just as the new methods of analyzing intelligence evaded the cumbersome old requirements of vetting, this configuration of like-minded officials dispersed on key islands across the national-security archipelago allowed the intelligence "product" and its effect on policy to circumvent the normal interagency process, in which the unconverted would have been among the participants and might have raised objections. It was an efficient way of working if you knew what you wanted to achieve.

It's difficult to say exactly what, all through that fall and winter, the Office of Special Plans planned. Luti would later claim the existence of hundreds of pages of documents, but they were never released. Luti, a former Navy captain, Newt Gingrich aide, and Cheney adviser, was a passionate supporter of war with Iraq and a man of occasionally manic temperament who could drive himself to public tears in his zeal about the subject. Once, in office conversation, he called retired General Anthony Zinni, the former head of Central Command and Bush's envoy to the Middle East, a traitor for expressing doubts about an Iraq war. Luti was known among colleagues as "Über-Luti." Under his and the gentler, professorial Shulsky's leadership, the office's main purpose was to manage information and control policy. Shulsky directed the writing of Iraq, WMD, and terrorism memos according to strictly supervised talking points.

To think through the politics of postwar Iraq, Special Plans recruited Middle East experts. One of them was Michael Rubin, a young Iran scholar at the American Enterprise Institute who had lectured at universities in Jerusalem and Iraqi Kurdistan. Another was Harold Rhode, a protégé of the Princeton professor Bernard Lewis, who like Shulsky was brought over from the Pentagon's in-house think tank. Rhode and Rubin were extremely close to Chalabi and the Iraqi National Congress, and when one INC member visited the Pentagon, he found Rhode in an office wallpapered with quotations from the hadith, the sayings attributed to Mohamed and compiled a hundred years after his death. Rhode was musing that one way to transform the Middle East would be for Iran to change the Farsi alphabet to Roman, as Atatürk had done with Turkish. "But how are you going to do it, Harold?" the Iraqi asked. "It's a concept," Rhode replied.

Rhode had begun his study of Islam with Sunnism, he told an Iraqi friend, but he soon decided that it had no intellectual substance, no room for original thinking. Then he met Fouad Ajami and other Arab Shia, and as he began to read in Shiite theology and jurisprudence, Rhode found a religion for intellectuals, like Judaism. He also subscribed to the idea, advanced in Wurmser's book, of restoring the Hashemite kingdom in Iraq, with King Hussein's brother Prince Hassan on the throne and Chalabi as prime minister, which would effectively return Iraq to its pre-1958 government, with a Shiite at the top. Shiite power was the key to the whole neoconservative vision for Iraq. Rhode even once compared Chalabi to the Prophet: "At first people doubted him, but they came to realize the wisdom of his ways."

The convergence of ideas, interests, and affections between certain American Jews and Iraqi Shia was one of the more curious subplots of the Iraq War. An administration official once put the obvious question directly to an Iraqi friend: "Do you ever wonder why a religious Jew who's American would want to help the Shia in Iraq?" He answered his own question with a story. He and his wife had difficulty conceiving a child, and he approached his rabbi to ask if advanced fertility treatments fell within the rules of Orthodox Judaism. The rabbi gave his blessing. But the official wanted to know his reasoning, and the rabbi explained it. When the official went to the Middle East during the Iraq War, he found a Shiite cleric and put the same question to him. Not only did the official get the same answer; the theological reasoning was exactly the same, too. Eureka! The experience clinched his belief that the Shia and the Jews, oppressed minorities in the region, could do business, and that traditional Iraqi Shiism (as opposed to the theocratic, totalitarian kind that had taken Iran captive) could lead the way to reorienting the Arab world toward America and Israel.

This thinking ran high up the policy chain at the Pentagon. Douglas Feith once told Kanan Makiya, "You Shia in Iraq have a historical opportunity. Do whatever you can—but don't speak about it." Not speaking about it fit the Shiite concept of *taqiya*—dissembling in defense of the faith, the sanctioned lying to outsiders that allowed a persecuted religious sect to survive. *Taqiya* also explained the decoy name and hidden work of the Office of Special Plans, home of that other persecuted sect newly arrived in power, the neoconservatives.

Their indulgence toward Iraqi Shiism did not extend to the whole Arab and Muslim world, which the Pentagon's thinkers saw more in terms of sickness than opportunity. Harold Rhode would report with satisfaction that some of his Muslim friends had grown so ashamed of what was being preached in the name of their faith that they hesitated to take their children to the mosque. A government official who had frequent dealings with Feith, Rhode, and the others came up with an analogy for their attitude toward Islam: "The same way evangelicals in the South wrestle with homosexuals, they feel about Muslims—people to be saved, if only they would do things on our terms. Hate the sin, love the sinner."

Among these ideological speculators, Ahmad Chalabi was a master politician, and he became their North Star in the project of transforming Iraq. "They thought that Ahmad's loyalty was to the ideal of the group," an associate of Chalabi said. "They were young, bookish, not politically savvy. Ahmad fooled them easily."

BUT WHAT ABOUT THE MASSIVE TASK of planning for postwar Iraq? The State Department's Future of Iraq Project was toiling away, and an interagency working group was meeting regularly under the auspices of the National Security Council; but there was still no postwar policy. How long would the United States stay in Iraq? Would the country be under American military occupation or international supervision? When would a new Iraqi government be set up, and how, and who would run it? The press speculated, but no one really knew, because the Bush administration couldn't make up its mind. Rice and Stephen Hadley, the national security adviser and her deputy, allowed the questions to remain open while diplomacy at the UN broke down, troops poured into the Middle East, and the momentum toward war built irreversibly.

In 1997, President Clinton had signed an obscure document called Presidential Decision Directive 56, which created an interagency planning group for "managing complex contingency operations." PDD 56 amounted to an admission that the peacekeeping operations of the 1990s had not gone well, that extensive training and early planning were necessary, and that these efforts needed to be coordinated at a high level, that of the number-two official in the key departments and agencies. After President Bush took office with an undisguised disdain for peacekeeping, his first national security directive, signed on February 13, 2001, abolished Clinton's system of interagency working groups and downgraded the "contingency operations" group to a bureaucratic level where it was bound to languish—and it did.

In early 2003, a Marine major on the NSC staff drafted a memo that analyzed force levels and population size in previous peacekeeping operations. If Kosovo were used as a model, half a million troops would be required to secure Iraq. Rice saw the memo (it isn't clear if she showed it to Bush), but it had no effect on the planning. State and Defense were at odds about every issue of the postwar, from the role of exiles in an interim government to the role of Americans in providing security. "This was the most important thing that did not occur in Iraq and did in Kosovo," said a Pentagon official with experience in both operations. "NSC didn't force the departments to reconcile a known disagreement that was very deep between the two agencies. They kind of papered over the differences instead of dealing with them." Looking back on the prewar period, Richard Haass located a failure in Rice's function as the national security adviser. "The N.S.A. is not just an honest broker but an honest balancer. Part of the job is to introduce arguments maybe not held by people around the table. What if there are better arguments not represented?" Rice, in charge of coordinating policy, proved more skillful at seconding the president than obliging him to consider the range of arguments and resolve them in a coherent way. At his meeting with the Iraqi exiles in early January, when the problems of postwar Iraq came up, Bush turned to Rice and said, "A humanitarian army is going to follow our army into Iraq, right?" Right, Rice affirmed, but she glanced down in a way that suggested she knew how inadequate the answer was.

In October 2002, Leslie Gelb, the president of the Council on Foreign Relations, had approached Rice and Hadley with an offer of help. The council and two other think tanks, the Heritage Foundation and the Center for Strategic and International Studies, would form a consortium that would gather a panel of experts to provide facts and options for the postwar. Their work would be politically palatable, coming from across the ideological spectrum, not insisting on a single plan that would corner the administration. "This is just what we need," Rice said. "We'll be too busy to do it ourselves." But she didn't want the involvement of Heritage, which had been critical of the idea of an Iraq war. "Do AEI."

Chris DeMuth, president of the American Enterprise Institute, where the administration's neoconservatives drew their support and many of their personnel, neither consented nor refused when Gelb broached the possibility. On November 15, the representatives of the think tanks met with Rice and Hadley in Rice's office at the White

House. John Hamre of CSIS went in expecting to pitch the idea to Rice, but the meeting was odd from the start: Rice seemed attentive only to DeMuth, and it was as if the White House was trying to sell something to the American Enterprise Institute rather than the other way around. When Gelb, on speakerphone from New York, began to describe his concept, DeMuth cut him off. "Wait a minute. What's all this planning and thinking about postwar Iraq?" He turned to Rice. "This is nation building, and you said you were against that. In the campaign you said it, the president has said it. Does he know you're doing this? Does Karl Rove know?"

Without AEI, Rice couldn't sign on. Two weeks later, Hadley called Gelb to tell him what Gelb already knew: "We're not going to go ahead with it." Gelb later explained, "They thought all those things would get in the way of going to war."

From the beginning of the Bush administration, Rice seemed outmatched by the vastly more experienced men who were now her bureaucratic peers. She had served as a midlevel staff official and Soviet expert on George H. W. Bush's National Security Council, after which she took the number two job at Stanford. It was a thin résumé indeed compared with Cheney's, Rumsfeld's, and Powell's, and during her first two years as national security adviser nothing suggested that she was becoming their equal. On issue after issue—Iran, North Korea, above all Iraq—policy decisions were either never made or never argued out before they were made. Her only achievements seemed to be her closeness to the president and her controlled, brittle, relentless defense of him. At the State Department, which lost so many of those early battles, there was a sense that Cheney and Rumsfeld were simply rolling Rice. Richard Armitage, Powell's deputy, began to call her office "dysfunctional." One senior administration official had trouble squaring the near-brilliant woman he knew Rice to be with her seemingly feckless performance in office. "She brings all the right ingredients," he said. "The work ethic, the sublimated whatever it is that turns into a drive for power, whether it's a sublimated sexual drive or whatever—she's got it. The Romans would say 'ambition.' She's dexterous when it comes to manipulating people and getting what she wants. So it's difficult for me to see her as an inept administrator."

Over time, this official began to wonder if the appearance of weakness was misleading. By the end of the first term, when Rice was appointed to replace Powell as secretary of state, the official was entertaining a far different account of her work as national security adviser. In this version, Rice knew exactly what she was doing by failing to reach decisions through the interagency process and instead allowing Cheney and Rumsfeld to do end runs around it. "Either she was complicitous with the president and the vice president, and to a certain degree with the secretary of defense, or she was using the secretary of defense and the secretary of state to further what were in fact the vice president's and the president's goals." In other words, Rice wasn't letting her boss down; she was doing his will in a particularly agile way. "How better to get your decisions made in ways that they will be easily implemented, rather than difficultly implemented, than to have an alternative NSC in which the national security adviser for the statutory NSC is complicit? And to pull the wool over your secretary of state's eyes?"

Eventually, not just the Council on Foreign Relations and the Center for Strategic and International Studies, but a who's who of foreign policy and military think tanks—the Rand Corporation, the Army War College, the United States Institute of Peace, the National Defense University's Institute for National Strategic Studies—produced reports that were striking for their unanimity of opinion. Security and reconstruction in postwar Iraq would require large numbers of troops for an extended period, and international cooperation would be essential. This had been Drew Erdmann's conclusion as well. "It's just common sense," said Ray Salvatore Jennings of the U.S. Institute of Peace, the author of two separate reports. But none of the forecasts penetrated the Pentagon or the Oval Office.

Thomas E. White, secretary of the Army until he was fired after the invasion, later said, "With DOD the first issue was, we've got to control this thing—so everyone else was suspect. And the second thing was, we had the mind-set that this would be a relatively straightforward, manageable task, because this would be a war of liberation and therefore the reconstruction would be short-lived."

Where it mattered and could have made a difference, the advice of experts was unwelcome. At the Pentagon, officials in the Office of

Stability and Peace Operations—the former Office of Peacekeeping, which was a dirty word in the Rumsfeld Pentagon—were systematically excluded from planning meetings on Iraq, and their memos went ignored. With one reconstruction task already in trouble in Afghanistan and another looming in Iraq, the Pentagon nonetheless had plans to close its Peacekeeping Institute in Carlisle, Pennsylvania. In mid-February 2003, Rumsfeld gave a speech in New York titled "Beyond Nation Building." The postwar reconstructions of the 1990s had bred a culture of dependency, he said, and Iraq would follow a new model—the minimalist approach of the United States in Afghanistan. The experience of peacekeeping specialists in Haiti, the Balkans, and East Timor was an actual liability in the eyes of the Iraq planners. "The senior leadership at the Pentagon was very worried about the realities of the postconflict phase being known," a Defense official said, "because if you are Feith or if you are Wolfowitz, your primary concern is to achieve the war." This official and his colleagues, whose careers had been devoted to preparing for such contingencies, spent the months leading up to the war in a state of steadily deepening demoralization. But none of them was willing to speak up loud enough inside or outside the five-sided building to get Rumsfeld's attention. The one who did showed the others the price they would pay.

In February, General Eric K. Shinseki, the Army chief of staff, appeared before the Senate Armed Services Committee and was asked about troop requirements. He did his best not to answer the question directly, for he must have understood the consequences. Finally, Shinseki said that, based on his experience of peacekeeping in the Balkans, postwar Iraq would require "something on the order of several hundred thousand soldiers." This estimate prompted Paul Wolfowitz to get on the phone with White, the Army secretary. "He was agitated that we in the Army didn't get it," White said. "He didn't give arguments or reasons. Their view was almost theological in nature—that it was going to go the way they said it was going to go." A few days later, Wolfowitz appeared before the House Budget Committee and pronounced General Shinseki's estimate "wildly off the mark." The deputy secretary explained, "It's hard to conceive that it would take more forces to provide stability in post-Saddam Iraq than it would take to conduct the war itself and to secure the surrender of Saddam's security forces and his army. Hard to imagine."

Paul Wolfowitz was the intellectual architect of the war. He made the case for war with more passion and eloquence than anyone else in the administration, often speaking publicly about the nature of Baathist tyranny and the stifled talents of the Iraqi people that were just waiting to be set free. Listening to him, you sometimes felt that he had dozens of close Iraqi friends and perhaps even a few distant cousins in Baghdad and Basra. He once told an interviewer who asked whether democracy in Iraq might lead to Islamist rule, "Look, fifty percent of the Arab world are women. Most of those women do not want to live in a theocratic state. The other fifty percent are men. I know a lot of them. I don't think they want to live in a theocratic state." This, too, it seemed, was hard to imagine.

More than Perle, Feith, and the neoconservatives in his department—certainly more than Rumsfeld and Cheney—Wolfowitz cared. For him Iraq was personal. He didn't seem driven by other agendas: Military transformation and shoring up the Likud Party and screwing the Democrats were not his obsessions. He wasn't a religious ideologue possessed by eschatological visions of remaking biblical lands. He was the closest thing to a liberal in the group. He had been pursuing this white whale for years, and he had everything to lose if Iraq went wrong. Why, then, did he find it all so hard to imagine?

Whether he agreed with the war plan or not, Wolfowitz was not about to go up against his hugely powerful boss on the subject Rumsfeld jealously owned. Wolfowitz was a true believer, but he was also a bureaucratic survivor of many administrations, and when it mattered he was more than capable of bowing to political reality. In the late 1990s, when regime change in Iraq became his signature issue, Wolfowitz lined up behind the flimsy idea of overthrowing Saddam with a few thousand followers of Ahmad Chalabi, because he understood that the public had no interest in committing large numbers of American troops to the cause. And now that America was about to go to war and finish the job that Wolfowitz had long felt had been left incomplete in 1991, he accepted the terms: light force, little commitment in the postwar. He told the public again and again that the reconstruction would be cheap, that it could be paid for by Iraqi oil revenues. He said this in the face of expert advice from oil company executives who knew the state of Iraq's neglected oil facilities. The White House's estimates of cost were absurdly low: By April, the Office of Management and Budget had asked Congress for only $2.5 billion for postwar reconstruction. When Bush's economic adviser Lawrence Lindsay candidly predicted that the war could cost as much as $200 billion—a figure that would turn out to be low—the administration's only public dissenter besides General Shinseki was quickly reprimanded and eventually fired. The administration systematically kept forecasts of the war's true cost from the public and, by the insidious effects of airtight groupthink, from itself. This would be historic transformation on the cheap. Wolfowitz as much as anyone else was responsible.

Like Kanan Makiya, Wolfowitz believed in the ability of Iraq's people to transform their society. And, like Makiya, he believed this in spite of everything he knew about the Middle East. When he was appointed assistant secretary of state for East Asia in 1982, leaving behind Middle East policy for Asia was "like walking out of some oppressive, stuffy room into sunlight and fresh air," he said. "I felt that I was going from a part of the world where people only know how to create problems to a part of the world where people solve problems." Twenty years later, he was now a tireless booster of the new Iraq. He had no trouble imagining its promise, and at planning meetings he spoke about Iraq after Saddam as if it would be like Poland after the fall of communism—like "Eastern Europe with Arabs," said one official. His ardent desire for the war led him to accept compromises that were bound to put its gains in jeopardy. Eventually, the deals one makes with others turn into deals made with oneself.

Once, in mid-2002, Wolfowitz visited Kabul just after a disastrous incident in which an American AC-130 gunship had bombed four Afghan villages, killing forty civilians, including members of a wedding party. The fragile new government of Hamid Karzai was enraged, and the U.S. embassy had sent its Pashtun-speaking political officer to drink tea with the survivors, attend a funeral, and apologize. No one doubted that innocent lives had been lost; the only uncertainty was whether celebratory gunfire or perhaps even anti-aircraft fire from guerrillas in the area had provoked the attack. But when Wolfowitz met with embassy officials, he began to grill the political officer: "Why do you assume there was a wedding party? How do you know?" Maybe, Wolfowitz said, the Taliban had disguised themselves as revelers—that was his hunch about the incident. "We shouldn't be so passive in apologizing. We should be more confident." The officials listened in silence, appalled. Later, one of them told me, "It was almost like he was creating this alternate reality." With Wolfowitz, self-righteousness had a dangerous habit of overwhelming inconvenient facts. A government official who worked with him on Iraq said, "Paul Wolfowitz, for all his good qualities, has an unfortunate ability to delude himself because he believes so passionately in things."

So it was Wolfowitz who ended the one serious public discussion of the fundamentals of the war plan before it had even begun. There would not be another. His message to Shinseki was a message to everyone in and out of uniform at the Pentagon: The cost of dissent was humiliation and professional suicide. An Air Force officer involved in the war planning later said, "After seeing Wolfowitz chew down a four-star, I don't think anyone was going to raise their head up and make a stink about it." Less than a month before the start of the war, Wolfowitz had helped to kick the props out from under his own grand project.

The warning from Shinseki, and from the experts and dissenters at the Department of Defense, the State Department, the CIA, the NSC, Congress, and the think tanks, was "hard to imagine" only where it was ideologically suspect and politically inconvenient. It went against the whole thrust of Rumsfeld's Defense Department, in which the overriding goal was military transformation: to continue the post–Cold War drawdown of active-duty divisions and focus strategy and spending on Special Forces, air power, and advanced weapons systems. Peacekeeping—never fully embraced by Clinton and openly dismissed by Bush in the 2000 campaign—became a discredited relic of an earlier era. "The type of operation a stability operation is—troop presence, police presence, these mundane activities—that's not high-tech, exotic, 'we're going to have satellites and Predators and hunt these guys down in the back roads of Yemen,'" Thomas White said. "This is boots on the ground and it is very untransformational." Afghanistan, with stunningly precise air power and small numbers of Special Forces working on the ground with local militias, was the brilliant new model for warfare. In planning for Iraq throughout 2002, Rumsfeld obliged General Tommy Franks of Central Command to whittle his invasion force down from an original half million (the maximum number in the war plan of Franks's predecessor, Anthony Zinni, which Rumsfeld called "old and stale") to around 160,000. It was partly done by picking out units from their normal command structure and interfering with the military's standard deployment schedules in order to preserve an element of disguise during the buildup and continue sending troops into the theater after the invasion. If Franks hadn't offered some resistance, the number would have dropped well below 100,000. But again and again, the secretary with the overpowering will got his way.

It wasn't the job of the uniformed services simply to salute their civilian leaders and march off to war. Franks, who was known to rule by fear, and his staff also had an obligation to the men and women under their command. Yet they never seemed to ask themselves what would happen if Rumsfeld was wrong—what might happen to their troops once they were in Iraq, without the necessary forces and protection, if things did not go according to plan. Plan A was that the Iraqi government would be quickly decapitated, security would be turned over to remnants of the Iraqi police and army, international troops would soon arrive, and most American forces would leave within a few months. There was no Plan B. Many of the officers at Central Command and the Joint Staff had concluded that Rumsfeld, however much they despised working for him because of his high-handed arrogance, must know what he was doing. His reputation was at its height, inside the administration and with the public. He was dazzling at press briefings and relentless at staff meetings. To the Air Force war planner, a major in the reserve named Glade Taylor, Rumsfeld's triumph in Afghanistan discredited the Army, which had predicted that huge numbers of troops would be needed there. Shinseki sounded like a throwback to the Cold War. This was the future: Iraq would be won with shock and awe. One day, a crusty Army colonel who had served with the military police in Bosnia and Kosovo pulled Taylor aside and said, "Major, you're deluding yourself." In the Balkans, the colonel had seen incomprehensible numbers of factions vying for power in the postwar vacuum. The same could happen in Iraq; the country could disintegrate.

General Anthony Zinni, who preceded Franks at Centcom, had anticipated just that. The allied bombing of Iraqi targets in December 1998 had rattled the regime in Baghdad, and Arab leaders had warned privately of a power vacuum if Saddam fell. Zinni, realizing that the responsibility for a postwar would fall on the military, began to work on a plan for Iraq's reconstruction to go along with his war plan. "Desert Crossing" covered the protection of infrastructure, the sealing of borders, humanitarian crises, politics, economy, even social issues like the role of women. "It should be seamless with the military plan," Zinni told me. "In 2000 I left it with General Franks. It was not complete, but it was far along." In the weeks before the invasion of Iraq, Zinni, by then retired, sensed that the Bush administration was unprepared for what awaited it after the fall of the regime, especially given the troop numbers he was hearing about. Shortly before the war, he called Centcom and said, "You know, you guys ought to dust off Desert Crossing, take a hard look at that." The deputy commander asked, "Desert Crossing? What's that? Never heard of it." At the Pentagon, Zinni learned, Desert Crossing had been dismissed because its assumptions were "too negative," almost as if, he thought, it was tainted for having been drafted when Clinton was in office, though the military was supposed to be nonpartisan. Franks made one effort to get Zinni's advice before the Iraq War began. He was stopped by someone higher up.

The military term for postwar operations in Iraq was Phase IV. Planning for Phase I (the buildup of troops in the region), Phase II (initial, mostly covert operations), and Phase III (main air and ground assaults) went on for the better part of a year. Iraq was a war of choice, and few wars have given war leaders more time to get ready. But for months, postwar matters appearing at the bottom of progress reports from Central Command to the Pentagon remained "open items," still to be answered. By March 2003, the planning for Phase IV was barely under way. "There's a real problem with the idea of Phase IV, doctrinally," a retired Army Special Forces lieutenant colonel named Kalev Sepp told me. "The idea that the conclusion of Phase III is the point of victory, that's the intellectual failure of the design of the four phases." Phase IV should be seen as the objective of a war, he said, not the aftermath. "But what Phase IV became over the years for American military planners was that's when you put everything back in the sea, air, and land containers and ship it back to Fort Stewart, Georgia." This was war without politics, the opposite of Clausewitz's famous dictum. Franks always insisted that he was determined not to make the same mistake as General William Westmoreland in Vietnam: Franks would tell the civilians to stay the hell out of military matters, and he would keep out of their business. When an officer at a Centcom meeting raised the question of Phase IV planning, Franks said, "Mr. Wolfowitz is taking care of that." His approach to war was that of a professional engineer. As a result, Franks had no strategic vision of what it would take to win in Iraq.

Major Taylor got the impression that Franks and his planners at Central Command didn't even think of the postwar as their responsibility. "The amount of pressure we would get from Centcom on Phase IV wasn't enough, frankly. The attitude was: 'Don't worry about that—that's ORHA. ORHA will take care of that.' But what is ORHA?"

ON JANUARY 20, 2003, President Bush signed National Security Presidential Directive No. 24. He signed it without hearing the strenuous objections of his State Department, and yet it would prove to be one of the fateful decisions of the Iraq War. NSPD 24—drafted at the Office of Special Plans—gave control over postwar Iraq to the Department of Defense, and it established a unit within the Pentagon that would administer Iraq immediately after the fall of the regime. The unit was called the Office of Reconstruction and Humanitarian Assistance.

In the history of American bureaucracy, ORHA was a new kind of organization. It drew its personnel from various agencies of the government, including the Departments of State, Treasury, Defense, and Commerce, and from among private citizens. It was also "expeditionary"—the team would travel to the region, and eventually to Iraq after the war. For an indeterminate period of time it would function as the administration of Iraq but under the operational command of the ground force, ultimately reporting to Rumsfeld.

To lead ORHA, Rumsfeld and Feith chose a retired lieutenant general named Jay Garner. Given the Pentagon's agenda, Garner was a logical choice. At the end of the Gulf War in 1991, he had run Operation Provide Comfort, the first humanitarian intervention of the post–Cold War era, which saved thousands of Kurdish lives in the snowy mountains along the Turkish border. Since his retirement, he had also been a successful Crystal City defense contractor, a member of Rumsfeld's commission on missile defense in the late nineties, and a favorite of the Jewish Institute of National Security Affairs, the group that had sponsored the writing of the "Clean Break" strategy paper. So from Defense's point of view Garner had the right experience and was connected to the right people. "He'll be my man in Iraq," Rumsfeld told Franks.

Garner was from Florida, short and compact, a laid-back, shirt-sleeves kind of guy who knew everyone's name and insisted on being called Jay. He led by instinct, preferring what one of his subordinates called "line-of-sight tasking": An idea would pop into his head and he would give it to the first person he saw. He surrounded himself with a tight group of other retired senior military, some of whom were also his fishing buddies. They called one another "bubba"; others called them the "Space Cowboys," after the Clint Eastwood movie about a group of astronauts brought out of retirement for one last mission.

If one thought of postwar Iraq as a limited humanitarian operation, as opposed to an open-ended political-military undertaking more vast and complex than anything the United States government had attempted since the end of World War II, Garner had the right stuff. He was not a sophisticated thinker; he knew little about the region beyond his experience with the Kurds. While military and civilian officials were learning from the messy aftermaths of the interventions of the late 1990s, he was earning money in the private sector. It made sense for an agency that had just been granted postwar control over a country in which it had no intention of doing serious political and economic reconstruction to appoint a man like Garner to oversee it.

He had seven weeks to get ready. "That's what it takes to get a computer connection at the Pentagon," a Defense Department official said.

In early February, ORHA moved into office space on the fourth floor of the Pentagon's B ring. This put it one floor below the Office of Special Plans, yet between these two postwar planning agencies within the Pentagon there was hardly any communications traffic at all. "OSP had as little to do with us as possible," said Army Colonel Paul Hughes, Garner's chief of planning. "It was a pain in the ass just to get them to open the door up there." One day, Abe Shulsky and Michael Rubin brought down a PowerPoint slide that sketched in the most general terms Iraq's future governing structures. "That's all the interest they took in ORHA," Hughes said. When Hughes suggested to Garner that they draft a political-military plan—an exhaustive document of the kind detailed in Clinton's defunct PDD 56, which would have empowered ORHA to establish its assumptions, mission, objectives, priorities, and end state, then submit the whole thing to the other departments for approval—Feith stopped the idea cold. This was way above ORHA's pay grade. There would be no political-military plan, no detailed documents at all. Everything important remained unwritten.

Garner broke his operation down into three "pillars": humanitarian assistance, reconstruction, and civil administration. His experience in northern Iraq led him to focus on the most urgent business, the potential for a humanitarian disaster: displaced populations, starvation, outbreaks of disease, large numbers of prisoners of war, and above all, chemical weapons attacks. The UN was warning of the possibility of half a million deaths. And if any of these nightmares had come to pass, outsiders would perhaps now know all about ORHA's thorough preparations for them.

On February 21 and 22, the hundred or so officials of ORHA gathered at the National Defense University in Washington to go over their plans. In ORHA's military parlance, Garner called it a "rock drill"—a vetting of everything done and known to date. The rock drill struck some participants as ominous.

"I got the sense that the humanitarian stuff was pretty well in place, but the rest of it was flying blind here," one of them later said. "A lot of it was after hearing from Jay Garner: 'We don't have any resources to do this and we've got a plan and the plan's going to cost three billion dollars—we have thirty-seven thousand.' Or: 'Now we're working on building up the civilian administration, that's our job—all we've really thought about is oil.'" The danger of looting was discussed, but the planning officers sent over from Centcom had been instructed not to respond to such "postconflict" issues, in part because the invasion force lacked enough troops to address them. Plans for running the Iraqi ministries were rudimentary—ORHA had almost no information at all. The chief of the civil administration team had changed twice: David Kay, who would later lead the search for weapons of mass destruction in Iraq, replaced the first leader for two days and then quit without telling Garner why. He was replaced, at Douglas Feith's insistence, by Feith's former law partner, Michael Mobbs, who had written the Defense Department's legal policy that exempted prisoners at Guantánamo from the Geneva Conventions and declared certain American citizens to be enemy combatants without constitutional rights. Mobbs, a political appointee, made the decision to award Halliburton, Cheney's old company, a secret, seven-billion-dollar, no-bid contract to restore Iraqi oil fields after clearing it with Cheney's chief of staff, Scooter Libby. Until Kay quit, oil was supposed to be Mobbs's only responsibility in ORHA. He was a reticent man—everyone thought him nice enough—but he was a Feith guy with absolutely no relevant experience for the task ahead in Baghdad. One officer on Garner's staff concluded that Mobbs couldn't have led a platoon. He joined ORHA just before the rock drill and then immediately afterward flew to Iraqi Kurdistan to meet Chalabi and the rest of the opposition, essentially abandoning his duties before he ever assumed them. In the end, civil administration would turn out to be the pillar that mattered most.

During the rock drill, a professor from the Marine Corps' School of Advanced Warfighting named Gordon W. Rudd, who had been detailed to Garner's team as a historian, noticed a man sitting four rows below him in the auditorium at NDU. The man kept interjecting comments during other people's presentations. "At first he annoyed me," Rudd said. "Then I realized he was better informed than we were. He had worked the topics, while the guy on stage was a rookie." The man "seemed frustrated that he had more than anyone else but he wasn't in charge."

It was Tom Warrick, the prickly coordinator of the State Department's Future of Iraq Project, and his frustrations had just begun. Garner was so impressed with him at the rock drill that he asked Warrick on the spot to join ORHA and go to Iraq. About a week later, in early March, after Warrick had moved his files from the State Department over to a desk at the Pentagon, Rumsfeld pulled Garner aside at the end of a meeting in the secretary's office. Shuffling through some papers on his desk, Rumsfeld picked one up, glanced at it, and said, "Jay, do you have two people in your organization named Warrick and O'Sullivan?" Meghan O'Sullivan was a thirty-three-year-old sanctions specialist in the State Department's policy planning office. "I've got to ask you to take them off the team." When Garner started to object that they were too valuable to lose, Rumsfeld cut him off. "I've gotten this from such a high level I can't turn it down." Later, Garner learned that the order had come from Cheney, who despised Warrick and disliked some things that O'Sullivan—a protégée of the ideologically moderate Richard Haass, and therefore suspect—had written.

Garner assured Warrick and O'Sullivan that he would get them back onto ORHA. He tried to go through Hadley, Rice's deputy, but Hadley turned him down: "Too hard." Colin Powell was livid on behalf of the two employees from his department, and he protested to the White House and the Pentagon, confiding to Garner, "I told Rumsfeld, 'I can take prisoners, too.' What I should have done was taken everybody from the State Department off your team, but that wouldn't have served any purpose. We want you to be successful." The impasse embodied Powell's dilemma over the entire war, in which he almost always ended up the team player on the losing end. Garner continued to plead with Rumsfeld, and just a few days before deployment to Kuwait, Rumsfeld told him, "Take the female back. Nobody'll know that." Meghan O'Sullivan was allowed to return to ORHA.

Tom Warrick, who had done as much thinking about postwar Iraq as any American official, became a casualty of the interagency war and didn't get to Baghdad for a year. The Pentagon held up for weeks the appointments of other senior State Department officials of questionable ideology and long experience in the Middle East—not openly, but simply by failing to clear them. "We underestimated who we were playing with," said Ambassador Barbara Bodine, an Arabist in the foreign service who joined ORHA in early March. "It took a while to realize they were playing a different game with different rules, and we were set up to lose." The reports of the Future of Iraq Project were archived. Months later, in Baghdad, I met an Iraqi-American lawyer named Sermid al-Sarraf, who had served on the transitional justice working group. He was carrying a copy of its 250-page report, trying to interest occupation officials. No one seemed to have seen it.

The Pentagon even replaced the State Department's team of Iraqi exiles with its own, absorbing some from the project, excluding others, and recruiting new ones from a group that was invited to hear Wolfowitz speak in Dearborn, Michigan, in late February. Tom Warrick had been cultivating a relationship with the Iraqis in Michigan for at least a year, but he was pointedly not invited to the meeting with Wolfowitz. Warrick warned "his" Iraqis not to work with the Pentagon, helping to seal his own fate. The exiles were assembled under Wolfowitz's supervision as the Iraqi Reconstruction and Development Council and set up in cubicles spread out across two floors of an office building near the Pentagon, behind tight security. Signs on the cubicles said "Ministry of Defense," "Ministry of Interior." They had a little more than a month to organize the civil infrastructure of a transitional government in Baghdad. The group included a number of competent Iraqis, many of whom would go on to work with the occupation. But they were tasked to reinvent the wheel.

Barbara Bodine had originally been asked by Richard Armitage to join ORHA as the head of civil administration. By the time she reached the Pentagon, Feith had already installed Mobbs in that position; barely two weeks before deployment, Bodine was given the open slot of administrator for Baghdad and central Iraq. When she and Wolfowitz sat down with a map of Iraq to determine which provinces would come under the central region, Wolfowitz began musing about redrawing the provincial boundaries altogether. It was as if Iraq were a blank slate, to be remade in the image of its liberators. Wolfowitz was unconsciously slipping into the role that he always insisted the administration didn't want—that of an arrogant colonial power. He could imagine Iraqi suffering, and he could imagine Iraqi potential, but he couldn't imagine Iraqi resentment. Bodine wondered if a man as intelligent as Paul Wolfowitz might not have heard of Sykes-Picot, the secret 1916 agreement that had divided up the Ottoman Empire into British and French zones of control. She suggested that for a Western power to redraw Iraq's lines once again wouldn't be a good idea. "Look at the road network," she told Wolfowitz. "This is the pattern that has evolved over centuries. This is how the Iraqis see themselves."

If Wolfowitz was edging toward grandiosity on the eve of war, his boss remained indifferent to the point of negligence. When Bodine briefed Rumsfeld on the administration of Iraq after the fall of the regime, she emphasized the need to pay civil servants immediately in order to head off chaos or resistance. Rumsfeld saw no hurry—the Iraqis could wait a couple of weeks, or even a couple of months. More important was the fact that American taxpayers shouldn't have to foot the bill. As for the possibility of disorder in the cities, the secretary of defense suggested that this could be used to persuade the countries of old Europe to chip in troops.

By mid-February, it was becoming clear to people paying attention that the administration wasn't remotely prepared for dealing with postwar Iraq. A few of those people were in Congress. On February 11, Feith and his counterpart at State, Undersecretary for Political Affairs Marc Grossman, appeared at a hearing of the Senate Foreign Relations Committee and tried to present a united front. Their testimony reads like a pair of schoolboys trying to fake their way through a teacher's questions about a joint homework project they had been cobbling together and fighting about fifteen minutes before class. "There was no unanimity," a senior State Department official later said. "Whenever Marc goes to testify it's to show that the State Department can show up. We need someone with staying power and the ability not to conflict too drastically with the fellow on your right." Grossman was scrambling to make the teacher happy; the fellow on his right was trying to outsmart the teacher. Under exasperated prodding by Senators Joseph Biden of Delaware and Paul Sarbanes of Maryland, Grossman put a two-year figure on a strong American overseer role in Iraq, outlined a three-stage process to Iraqi self-rule, and left most of the details to future briefings that never happened. As for Feith, whose

Office of Special Plans had been in charge of postwar planning since the previous September, the uncertainties of war put the whole subject in the realm of the unknowable. His answers took on the gnomic quality of a Zen master's sayings: Iraq will belong to the Iraqis. America has a commitment to stay and a commitment to leave. We will stay as long as it takes but not a day longer.

> SEN. CHAFEE: Do you have a plan, either an exit strategy or some kind of planning if this turns into a debacle . . . ?
> FEITH: The short answer is, yes. We are planning for worst-case eventualities, and what I'd like to assure the committee is that every one of the—
> SEN. CHAFEE: When will you share those plans with us?
>
> SEN. DODD: Tell me why you think the nation-building here and holding this together is something that can be achieved in, using your response to Senator Feingold, two years.
> FEITH: First of all, Senator, the two years was my esteemed colleague, Undersecretary Grossman's, answer.
> SEN. DODD: All right.
> FEITH: And I don't think I want to venture into the prediction business.

Feith later insisted that there had never been an intention to transfer power to Ahmad Chalabi. "The idea that we had a rigid plan for the political transition is a mistake," he told me. "We developed concepts, policy guidelines—for example, organize as much authority as possible in Iraqi hands. That is a policy guideline. But as for specific names and timetables and rules, nobody here presumed to dictate that, because you can't possibly know that. That's like trying to tell a local commander in advance of the battle exactly how many people to put where as the fighting proceeds. Nobody can work with a plan that rigid. Nobody here in Washington is micromanaging."

Just two or three days before leaving for Kuwait, Jay Garner held his first and only press conference. When a reporter asked whether he would hand power over to Chalabi and the INC, Garner replied, "I don't intend to empower the INC. I don't have a candidate. The best man will rise."

That night, he received several agitated calls from Feith. Garner found him so difficult to work with, simultaneously overbearing and mentally scattered, that he had taken to sending his deputy, a retired lieutenant general named Ron Adams, to deal with the undersecretary. On the phone Feith lamented, "You've damaged the INC, you've caused Ahmad embarrassment."

Garner snapped, "Hey, goddamnit, then what you need to do, Doug, is have a little press conference in the morning and say, 'We're firing Garner because he embarrassed Ahmad Chalabi.'"

"We can't do that."

"Then get off my ass."

Wolfowitz, in his smoother way, urged Garner to be nicer to the INC. Garner was forbidden to speak to the press again, and when he complained about the embargo to Rumsfeld, he learned that the order had come from the White House. The word was that ORHA's chief was "politically tune-deaf" and needed to be kept under control.

BY EARLY MARCH, Condoleezza Rice had given up on the Office of Special Plans. The Pentagon civilians turned out to be more skillful at arguing and winning policy fights than at actually doing anything. Their idea of training six thousand Iraqi followers of Ahmad Chalabi at a military base in Hungary to fight alongside the U.S. invasion force fizzled out when the Iraqis failed to materialize; at the end of training, the Free Iraqi Forces consisted of seventy men. Having seized the bureaucratic turf of postwar Iraq, the officials under Wolfowitz and Feith managed to pull together just one policy briefing, on oil. Mobbs's presentation was so long and unfocused—forty-eight slides instead of the usual five or six—that Rice decided to push Special Plans aside and hand the postwar policy issues to an official at her own agency named Frank Miller.

On March 10 and 12—barely a week before the start of the war—Miller briefed the national security deputies, the principals, and finally the president on dozens of postwar items. Debaathification would disqualify from government service the top 1 percent of Baath Party members; the Iraqi army would be reduced but not disbanded and employed to do public works projects; an interim government would be set up according to a timeline, with some ministries such as defense kept under American supervision longer than others. Everyone up to the president approved these eleventh-hour decisions. And yet, somehow, they would never matter in Iraq. They seemed to exist so that, in case anyone ever asked, someone could say, "Yes, the president was briefed and he signed off."

Garner, who was about to head out to the Middle East with his ORHA team, wanted as little instruction as possible; he had his own ideas. He found Miller, Elliott Abrams, and the White House staff "at best disruptive. They were a pain in the ass. Whatever we were doing, they were trying to achieve the opposite. From my side of it, they were determined to make sure it failed. That's a strong statement, but they did everything they could to cause us problems." Meanwhile, over at the Pentagon, Feith was planning on sending out his ideological appointees, Rhode and Rubin, to keep tabs on ORHA in Kuwait and give Chalabi a head start in Baghdad. Rumsfeld's spokesman, Larry Di Rita, would accompany Garner everywhere he went. Even as it prepared to take over a foreign country, the administration remained hopelessly at war with itself. No one in charge was asking the most basic question: what will we do if it all goes wrong?

ON MARCH 16, three days before the first bombs fell on Baghdad, 169 ORHA members flew from Washington to Kuwait. Among them was Drew Erdmann.

Though he had left academia behind, Erdmann's reasons for going to Iraq were, in a sense, professional. "My analysis was that we really are at a defining turning point in history. I had a particular historical perspective. I felt that this was a defining event which, good or bad, would have an impact for the next decade. If it went bad, the consequences would be worse than Vietnam. And second—this was not exactly rocket science—the postwar phase was going to be the most important. So that's the syllogism: postwar, defining turning point, and you have an offer to participate."

In Erdmann's view, Saddam was becoming an increasing threat as containment eroded with the expulsion of inspectors and the weakening of sanctions. This was the "realist" argument for war, but Erdmann, like most people, didn't think entirely in the categories of international relations theory. He also believed in American exceptionalism—the idea that America's role in world affairs was something higher than mere power politics, that from the founding of the republic American liberty was inextricably bound up with human liberty (this was the subject of one of his dissertation chapters). He differed from the neoconservatives less in what he thought than how he thought. His idealism was tempered by a historian's natural attraction to facts and a sense of the fallibility and occasional folly of American behavior in the world.

He had to convince both his boss, Richard Haass, and his wife, who didn't see the need for a war, to let him go to Iraq. "I knew if I didn't, I'd always regret it. And my wife did, too—she knew that my regret would be corrosive."

Erdmann asked to join the civil administration team, led by Feith's ex–law partner Mobbs. By the time they reached the beachfront villas at the Hilton Hotel south of Kuwait City, where ORHA set up headquarters, the operation was in disarray. Upon arrival, Garner and his inner circle disappeared without a word into their own villa, and the other ORHA members didn't see their leaders for two days. Among the fishing buddies and Space Cowboys there was tremendous élan, but it never traveled outside their group. Everybody liked Jay, but nobody understood the mission. Mobbs, looking as if he were dressed for West Palm Beach, was frozen out of the retired generals' deliberations, and his sporadic meetings with his own civil administration team never produced any decisions. Garner had almost no contact with the team at all. Gordon Rudd, the military historian, was worried enough to speak to him about it. "We're not putting enough attention on civil administration," Rudd said. "Gordon, that can wait," Garner replied.

"We've got to focus on humanitarian assistance." At the time, Rudd thought, the choice made sense: Save lives first, then reform Iraq.

But in the humanitarian assistance pillar, led by a peacekeeping expert named George Ward, things weren't much better. Meghan O'Sullivan found herself tasked with spending the day as an extra body in a car to fulfill security requirements. She was kept out of meetings where larger policy questions, the kind that had been her bread and butter at State, were discussed; she and her colleagues couldn't even get phones. O'Sullivan was an attractive, fair, slender redhead from Massachusetts whose light self-mockery could be misleading, since she was also ambitious and cool under pressure and had a knack for landing professionally on her feet (it would happen again after she got to Baghdad). She had written a book on "smart sanctions" as a fellow at the Brookings Institution before joining the State Department—which, in the eyes of the neoconservatives, made her soft on Iraq. Iraq had been one of America's biggest foreign-policy problems her whole adult life: What Europe had meant to a previous generation, Iraq and the Middle East meant to hers. O'Sullivan's reasons for supporting the war were essentially the same as Erdmann's, her colleague from policy planning. As far back as September, she had told Richard Haass during a walk on the Mall that, if there was a war, she wanted to go to Iraq afterward. By the early spring of 2003, after advocating the administration position at conferences in Europe and being repeatedly hammered, after months of almost unbearable pressure, she had also reached the point of simply thinking: Let's just do it, for God's sake! Now the war had started, and she was seventy miles away in Kuwait and desperate to get to Iraq.

One day early in the war, O'Sullivan saw a Silkworm missile fly overhead and realized that if she were back at policy planning in the State Department she would have her hands on all sorts of classified intelligence about what was happening just to the north; as it was, she knew nothing beyond what she saw on CNN. She started waking up in the middle of the night with an unfamiliar emotion that she couldn't at first identify but that seemed to be consuming her physically. It was regret. She lay awake second-guessing the decision that had brought her to Kuwait.

Even Barbara Bodine, a senior member of the team, was cut out of the loop. Bodine had served in the Baghdad embassy in the 1980s and been held hostage in the embassy in Kuwait for several months after the Iraqi invasion in 1990. Her tenure as ambassador to Yemen under Clinton was controversial: After the bombing of the USS *Cole* at Aden in 2000, she and the FBI's chief investigator, John O'Neill, clashed over his team's comportment in the country, and eventually she barred his reentry. O'Neill quit government service in disgust and took a job as chief of security at the World Trade Center, where he died on September 11. Among the senior people in Kuwait, Bodine was one of the few nonmilitary and the only woman, and she found herself slowly disappearing from the circle of leaders like the Cheshire Cat. Just to keep in touch with the State Department, she had to go around Garner and the Pentagon and have communications gear flown in from Washington to the embassy in Kuwait City. In furtive conversations she urged her colleagues at State whose appointments were being blocked by Feith's office to fly in under embassy country clearance. And she spent hours counseling and consoling tearful young men and women who had left interesting jobs in Washington to languish in Kuwait on what felt like a terrible five-week holiday at the beach, amid the stress of frequent gas-attack alerts, the close quarters, the humiliations of menial work and intellectual idleness, the information blackout, and the confusion of not knowing what they would do once they got to Baghdad. No planning documents were distributed to the team; there weren't even org charts of the Iraqi ministries. In the end, ORHA produced a single, elegantly written twenty-five-page paper called "A Unified Mission Plan for Post-Hostilities Iraq." It was never sent back to Washington for approval, so its only real function was historical. The document began, "History will judge the war against Iraq not by the brilliance of its military execution, but by the effectiveness of the post-hostilities activities." The top of the title page read "Initial Working Draft," and it was dated April 16, 2003—three days before the first members flew up to Baghdad, which had fallen a week earlier. "That wasn't a plan," Bodine said. "It was an outline that never saw the light of day. The 'plan' was to be out of Iraq by the end of August."

Garner was talking about putting in ninety days in Iraq and then heading home. This struck O'Sullivan, Erdmann, and others as not even remotely realistic. At dinner in the Hilton restaurant with two Senate staffers who had flown in from Washington, Garner laid out his timetable: reconstruct utilities, stand up ministries, appoint an interim government, write and ratify a constitution, hold elections. By August, Iraq would have a sovereign, functioning government in place. There was a stunned silence. Someone at the table said, "Which August?"

Garner was carrying out his instructions from Defense as he understood them, but they were vague and sparse. The makeup of an interim government remained unknown; Garner knew that if he floated any names, one agency or another of the bitterly divided administration would shoot them down. The only subject on which Garner thought he had everyone's sign-off was the Iraqi army: He had briefed the president, Rice, Rumsfeld, Wolfowitz, and Feith, and they all agreed with his plan to keep it intact and pay salaries. There were daily video teleconferences in Kuwait with the Pentagon, and at Garner's side the whole time, shadowing him, was Rumsfeld's spokesman, Larry Di Rita.

The night Di Rita flew into Kuwait in early April, he was briefed by ORHA's senior officials, and when the deputy leader of the reconstruction pillar, Chris Milligan of USAID, spoke about the need to show early benefits to the Iraqi people, Di Rita slammed his fist down on the table. "We don't owe the people of Iraq anything," he said. "We're giving them their freedom. That's enough." A few days later, by which time ORHA officials realized that Di Rita had the full confidence of Rumsfeld, the secretary's spokesman stood up at a meeting of about fifty people in the Hilton conference room. The State Department messed up Bosnia and Kosovo, he told his audience (which included many foreign service officers), and the Pentagon wasn't going to let that happen in Iraq. "We're going to stand up an interim Iraqi government, hand power over to them, and get out of there in three to four months," Di Rita announced. "All but twenty-five thousand soldiers will be out by the beginning of September." To Paul Hughes, Garner's planning chief, "It sounded like they were going to package up five pounds of shit in a nice foil wrapper and hand it off and say, 'Good luck.' It might look nice, but it would still be a package of shit."

Other Pentagon officials, including Harold Rhode from the Office of Special Plans, joined ORHA in Kuwait, but no one could figure out what they were doing; they seemed to exist in a parallel universe. Rhode stayed in a villa with members of the Iraqi National Congress, where he and Salem Chalabi punched out memos back to Wolfowitz and Cheney. Rhode was pushing for the swift formation of an Iraqi interim government led by Chalabi and the INC. Other ORHA members began to think of the Defense officials among them as commissars, sent to Kuwait to keep an eye on the team. Chatting at dinner, people would suddenly glance over a shoulder to see who might be listening. One of them finally said, "Isn't this the kind of regime we're supposed to be getting rid of?"

Drew Erdmann began to feel so unguided that he looked around for tasks to assign himself. Together with a few colleagues, he drew up a list of sixteen key sites around Baghdad that the military should secure and protect upon the fall of the city. For help they consulted a Lonely Planet guidebook. At the top of the list was the Central Bank. Number two was the National Museum. "Symbolic importance," Erdmann explained.

The rest were ministries, with the Ministry of Oil last. On March 26, the list went to the military at Camp Doha, an hour away near the Iraq border. Franks had put ORHA under the operational control of his war-fighting commanders on the ground there, rather than taking direct responsibility for the postwar himself, with the higher authority of Centcom. "I don't want to get into the business of managing bus schedules," Franks told Garner.

The distance between ORHA and Camp Doha replicated in Kuwait during the war the lack of joint planning for Phase IV between the Pentagon and Centcom during the prewar—even as the Third Infantry Division and First Marine Expeditionary Force were chewing up hundreds of miles of desert on their way to the Iraqi capital, leaving in their path liberated but unsecured territory. The military-police and civil-affairs units were far behind and extremely thin on the ground. On the second day of the war, a young contractor with USAID named Albert Cevallos was standing with a group of civil-affairs officers at the Iraq-Kuwait border, when one of the officers turned to him and asked, "Albert, what's the plan for policing?"

Cevallos's job was in the field of human rights. "I thought you knew the plan," he said.

"No, we thought you knew."

"Haven't you talked to ORHA?"

"No, no one talked to us."

Cevallos wanted to run away. He later remembered the incident as "a Laurel and Hardy routine. What happened to the plans? This is like the million-dollar question that I can't figure out. There was planning—I know there was. I saw it, I took part in it. It was a failure either to accept those plans or to communicate it down to where it mattered, on the ground."

A few weeks later, as Baghdad fell and intense looting got under way, Erdmann and the others went to Camp Doha to find out what had happened to their list of sites. They met with a young British lieutenant colonel, sitting on a stool in desert camouflage, who said, "Well, you know, I just yesterday became aware of this big stack of stuff that you ORHA guys had done." The officer held his hand up a few inches from his face. "You must understand. We've been focused like *this* on fighting the war. Now we can begin looking at what you sent." The list had fallen somewhere into the bureaucratic gap between ORHA and the military, and now it was too late—Erdmann was watching the sites being looted and burned on television. "This is, in a microcosm, how the gears, or the communication network, the rhythms, were just not right," he said. "And I don't know if it's because we weren't taken seriously."

In Washington, a government official took his concerns about the looting over to the Pentagon. He told Feith's deputy, William Luti, that the administration needed to learn the Arabic for curfew: *mamnua al-tajawwul*, "it is forbidden to go out." Luti didn't seem alarmed; the generals in the field knew what they were doing, he said.

THE FALL of the statue of Saddam in Baghdad's Firdos Square on April 9 was received by many Americans as the sudden and dramatic end of a lightning war. The liberation of Iraq had come faster, with fewer casualties and less destruction, than anyone, even the optimists, had imagined possible. None of the disasters that ORHA had prepared for—refugees, chemical weapons, burning oil fields, massive civilian casualties—came to pass, thanks in part to the astonishing speed of the invasion and of the regime's collapse. In many cities, Iraqis celebrated in the streets and embraced American soldiers. Some even threw the flowers that Kanan Makiya had predicted.

There was celebration in Washington, too—an outburst of triumphalism and gloating that was as much partisan as patriotic and looked not at all like the simple joyful kiss of a sailor and a nurse in Times Square on VJ Day. On April 13, Dick and Lynne Cheney threw a dinner party at the vice president's residence with their friends Ken and Carol Adelman, Paul Wolfowitz, and Scooter Libby. Adelman had predicted in print that Iraq would be a "cakewalk," and the small group toasted the president and savored the victory over the naysayers (the press, Brent Scowcroft, above all Colin Powell) as much as over the Baathist regime. The leading neoconservative publication, *The Weekly Standard*, declared that the weakness of the Clinton years was over and the world had been made new. "The battles of Afghanistan and Iraq have been won decisively and honorably," wrote the editor of the *Standard*, William Kristol. "But these are only two battles." And his colleague David Brooks, quoting Orwell, warned, "Now that the war in Iraq is over, we'll find out how many people around the world are capable of facing unpleasant facts." Brooks meant the Arabs, the Europeans, and the Bush haters, none of them able to accept the American liberation of a Muslim country. Neither writer noticed, let alone faced, the unpleasant facts unfolding on the ground in Iraq even as they declared victory in Washington. From the Pentagon, flush with the success of his war plan, Rumsfeld regarded the rising chaos in Baghdad with equanimity. "Stuff happens," the official in charge of postwar Iraq said, "and it's untidy, and freedom's untidy, and free people are free to make mistakes and commit crimes and do bad things."

Rumsfeld's words, which soon became notorious, implied a whole political philosophy. The defense secretary looked upon anarchy and saw the early stages of democracy. In his view and that of others in the administration, but above all the president, freedom was the absence of constraint. Freedom existed in divinely endowed human nature, not in man-made institutions and laws. Remove a thirty-five-year-old tyranny and democracy will grow in its place, because people everywhere want to be free. There was no contingency for psychological demolition. What had been left out of the planning were the Iraqis themselves.

For Rumsfeld, this view was a matter of convenience more than anything else, since nothing in his career suggested that he had given the subject any thought. For others, including those working under him at the Pentagon, it was something like an article of faith, and when their critics used the word "theology"—as they often did—to describe the neoconservative approach to spreading democracy in the region, they weren't completely wrong. This faith defied both history and the live evidence on CNN. It led directly to the gutting and burning of all the key institutions of the Iraqi state.

General Franks's innovative strategy used enough troops to take the country but nowhere near enough to secure it. Even so, a concerted effort could have stopped the most egregious looters and warned off others with a show of force. It never happened. In vain, employees of the museum begged the leader of a nearby tank platoon to park one tank at the museum entrance and scare off the pillagers who were making free with the country's antiquities. Soldiers without orders to intervene stood by while men and boys hauled computers, copiers, desks, staplers, carpets, and eventually wiring and pipes out of the ministries and other government buildings and took them away in trucks, cars, donkey carts, rickshaws, and on their own backs. In the war log of an infantry captain, the days leading up to the fall of Baghdad are crowded with incident. But immediately after April 9, the entries turn brief to the point of minimalism: "Nothing significant to report, stayed at airport all day doing maintenance and recovery operations." It was as if the sole objective had been the fall of the city. An administration official who had served in Vietnam used the phrase "commanders' intent"—the mind-set instilled down the chain to soldiers on the ground: "All of a sudden they got there—and there was no intent. There were no rules of engagement. Everything was for the battle. And commanders sat around and didn't do anything about it." Meanwhile, the destruction being visited upon the city and its leading institutions by Baghdadis themselves was far outstripping the damage from bombing and firefights. Afterward, some Iraqis insisted that they had seen soldiers not just permitting but encouraging and helping looters, as if the mayhem were joyous celebration of the fall of the regime. This was the secretary of defense's view. Only the Ministry of Oil was protected.

Martial law was not declared; a curfew was not immediately imposed. No one told Iraqis to stay at home or to go to work. Later, Douglas Feith would insist to me that, technically, the American military asserted its authority early on. "When the Saddam government fell, it was going to be necessary to issue a first proclamation," Feith said. "But there had been an Iraqi history that whenever there was a coup, somebody issued Proclamation No. 1. So we decided that we didn't want that, which is why it was renamed 'Freedom Message.'" Feith pointed out that the Freedom Message even announced the creation of the Coalition Provisional Authority, which most people assume began with the arrival of Paul Bremer in May. But this was just the kind of lawyerly cleverness that had once led Tommy Franks to conclude that Feith was "the fucking stupidest guy on the face of the earth." If anyone in Iraq actually received a copy and read the statement issued on April 16 from Centcom in Qatar by the man who was in charge—General Franks himself—it had no discernible effect in the streets of Baghdad. The implications weren't lost on Iraqis, including potential adversaries. "We're incompetent, as far as they're concerned," said Noah Feldman, the New York University law professor who went to Baghdad as a constitutional adviser to the Coalition Provisional Authority. "The key to it all was the looting. That was when it was clear that there was no order. There's an Arab proverb: Better forty years of dictatorship than one day of anarchy." He added, "That also told them they could fight against us and we were not a serious force."

When Saddam suddenly ordered the release of tens of thousands of prisoners from Abu Ghraib and other jails in October 2002, the surge of inmates from within the walls and family members from without overwhelmed prison guards and crushed a number of people to death at the very moment of freedom. Reporters who ventured into the bowels of the prison were struck by the appalling smells of long human confinement. Six months later, when the American invasion finally broke the seal on Saddam's Iraq, the surge was just as intense, and the smell of decades of repression just as pungent. Seeing that no one would stop them, more and more Iraqis made mistakes and did bad things, until the civil disorder turned into rampant violence, much of it perpetrated by criminal gangs of those same freed prisoners: carjackings, kidnappings, rapes, murders, score settling of all kinds, and, soon enough, sporadic attacks on American troops. Iraqis still refer to the spoils of looting by the name Saddam gave to this war—*al-hawasim*, the decisive one.

Eventually, CPA officials did a rough calculation of the economic cost of the looting in those early weeks. The figure they came up with was $12 billion, canceling out the projected revenues of Iraq for the first year after the war. The gutted buildings, the lost equipment, the destroyed records, the damaged infrastructure, would continue to haunt almost every aspect of the reconstruction. But the physical damage was less catastrophic than those effects which couldn't be quantified. Iraqis' first experience of freedom was chaos and violence; the arrival of the Americans brought an end to the certainty of political terror and at the same time unleashed new, less certain fears.

THE DISORDER kept Garner and ORHA stuck in Kuwait for two weeks. Garner wasn't able to secure Franks's clearance to fly to Baghdad until April 21; most of the others drove up òn April 23 in a convoy of several hundred Chevy Suburbans, past blown-out tanks, past heaps of empty MRE bags, past crowds of Iraqis, some waving, some giving unfriendly stares, some busy looting, straight into the rush-hour traffic of southern Baghdad. They moved into the vast Republican Palace on the west bank of the Tigris because it was in better shape after the fighting than any other suitable government building—though even the palace at first lacked water, electricity, working phones, and even window glass. Everything was coated in half an inch of fine yellow silt, and across the floors were footprints of the soldiers who had taken the palace two weeks before. There was rotten meat in the kitchen, and half the toilets were clogged with human waste. Next to the parking lot, American firepower had turned Iraqi army foxholes into fifty-eight shallow graves. One of Drew Erdmann's first ideas was to install window screens to keep out the bugs.

The scale of the looting in Baghdad left Garner stunned. In Kurdistan in 1991, the looting had been relatively light (though in the south it had been extensive and violent). But after spending just twenty-four hours in Baghdad, Garner flew north to Kurdish territory, where he knew the people and the terrain, and was acclaimed as a hero. He was still fighting the last war. He met with the two Kurdish leaders, Massoud Barzani and Jalal Talabani, to discuss the political handoff. The Kurds and the other opposition leaders who had been in exile—including Chalabi—would form a leadership group in Baghdad, along with a few "internals," Iraqis from inside the country. The exiles had been trying to agree on a ruling structure ever since the London conference. "And what I assumed at the time, rightly or wrongly, was this was just an extension of those talks and all the work that had gone on," Garner told me when I visited his business offices near the Pentagon in the fall of 2003. Once there were Iraqi faces on the American presence, the Americans could slough off responsibility without giving up power. Gordon Rudd, the military historian, called Garner "a world-class informal leader," and Garner described his moves in Iraq as if the political component had been left to his intuition. I asked if these were his instructions from the Pentagon. "I never got a call from anybody saying, 'Don't do that,'" Garner said. "You follow me?"

But Chalabi short-circuited the plan. According to a prominent Iraqi politician who was close to the negotiations, the INC chairman, along with the late Shiite leader Mohamed Baqr al-Hakim, who was killed in an August 2003 car bombing outside the holy shrine in Najaf, resisted expanding their ranks beyond the original circle. This would have been closer to the State Department's idea of a broad-based interim government. "If the group of five became twenty-five or became fifty, their influence will diminish. They wanted basically to control who will be there," the politician said. "The exiles—they made a big mistake, thinking that because they have the Americans on their side, they thought that they can ride an American tank into Baghdad, they can gain legitimacy. It just doesn't work that way. It would have been a colossal mistake to push them on the Iraqi people. They would have been immediately identified as nothing but surrogates of the United States."

The Pentagon was still trying. Without informing the White House or military commanders, it had flown Chalabi and seven hundred follow-ers—with American uniforms and weapons—from northern Iraq down to the desert outside Nasiriya. The idea was to give Chalabi a head start in the race to power. He and his followers found their way to Baghdad, installed themselves at the exclusive Hunting Club in up-scale Mansour (where Chalabi was soon joined by Harold Rhode), and began commandeering choice property. One of Uday Hussein's Ferraris ended up parked outside the house occupied by Chalabi's good-looking young aide, Nabil al-Musawi. After things went wrong in Iraq, Chalabi, Makiya, and their allies in the administration would blame the failure to stop the looting and bring order to Baghdad on the State Department, which, they charged, had held up the plans to train six thousand Iraqi exiles. This has far more merit as an alibi than an ar-gument. The Iraqi army and police had vanished. "The state disap-peared," Erdmann said. "Either the people melted away or the institutions were melted down by them." This was exactly what the INC had advised would not happen, and the resulting security vac-uum was far too vast for a few thousand half-trained Iraqi exiles, many of them strangers to their own country of years or decades, to fill. Those who had been flown in with Chalabi did more to join the loot-ing than to stop it. Gordon Rudd warned Garner that the Free Iraqi Forces were beginning to look like a "warlord group." Garner, whose opinion of Chalabi was sinking rapidly, said, "Gordon, I don't like that word." The exiles' countrymen did not receive them as the natural rulers of free Iraq. The neoconservative answer to every hard question about postwar Iraq, the ingenious escape clause drawn up at the American Enterprise Institute, *The Wall Street Journal*, and the Office of Special Plans, fell apart in Baghdad while the toasts were still being drunk in Washington.

One afternoon, Barbara Bodine, who was nominally in charge of Baghdad, drove through the wrecked city with Lieutenant General Dave McKiernan, commander of ground forces in Iraq, past a check-point manned by Chalabi's militia, to a house in a well-off neighbor-hood. The CIA, trying to head off the Pentagon's plan for an imminent handoff of power to the exiles, had organized a meeting for Bodine and McKiernan with fifteen or twenty local businessmen, academics, and judges. One by one, the Baghdadis told their stories of lives lived inside Iraq under Saddam. Then one of them came to the point: "Would you Americans please impose martial law? There is anarchy out there. We don't want authoritarianism, but we need authority." As if to underscore the urgency of the plea, while the meeting was going on, with the escort of the leading American civilian and military authorities in Baghdad parked outside, several of Chalabi's militiamen came over and carjacked the host's car, with the driver inside.

The troops standing around while Baghdad was sacked were under McKiernan's command. He had instructed his senior officers that war fighting should not be distracted by postwar planning, and had amended the instruction only on April 19. But the incident in Baghdad finally brought home to McKiernan the gravity of the situation. The next day, he wrote a brief order declaring the coalition to be the "military authority" in Iraq. Bodine relayed the order to the State Department and was stunned to learn that it was the first assertion of legal responsibility under the Geneva Conventions. The administration's rhetoric of liberation had become a cover for abdicating its obligations to the Iraqis and was creating conditions that were bound to threaten the troops themselves. But McKiernan's order was never backed up by Rumsfeld in Washington or by Franks in Qatar. It became one of the noble failures of those irretrievable early days.

General Franks and his commanders wanted to get out of Iraq as quickly as possible. Rumsfeld suspended the deployment of the First Cavalry Division into Iraq and gave an order for accelerated withdrawal of troops in mid-April. As late as early May the Pentagon was anticipating a force level below thirty thousand in country by the end of summer, on the assumption that countries that had sat out the war would begin contributing troops. Everything was going to be turned over to ORHA—a skeletal, disorganized, impecunious crew of fewer than two hundred unarmed civilians wandering around in the dust and dark of the Republican Palace searching for colleagues because they didn't have phones to call one another. ORHA was going to get Rumsfeld and Franks out of Iraq. The thought in Washington and Qatar was: Over to you, Jay. The abysmal coordination now took on the most concrete and disabling forms. There were never enough military escorts to provide security so that ORHA members could leave the palace and go out into the city in search of Iraqis with whom they could work. Though telephone service was down all over the country, the military officer in charge of communications saw no reason why Iraqi university presidents should be given satellite phones. There were nowhere near enough translators to go around. Timothy Carney, a career foreign-service officer who was called out of retirement by Wolfowitz to work in Baghdad, said that the military simply didn't understand or care what ORHA was supposed to do. "It was as if these guys didn't have a clue what Jay Garner was on about. There was no priority given to the essential aspects of the mission."

With hardly any solid information, Erdmann and the others in civil administration tried to find the highest-ranking officials from the old regime still left standing—if only to fire them. A few stalwart Iraqis would show up at work, hoping that someone from ORHA would stop by. The continued functioning of the state depended almost on random meetings around the city—where firefights were not uncommon—between Iraqi bureaucrats and newly arrived foreigners. Erdmann recalled these encounters as something out of a *Star Trek* episode. "Welcome. Take me to your leader," the Iraqis would say. "I represent the Grand Galactic Federation. The Federation of Planets. We are not implementing the prime directive here." "Who are you?" the Americans would call out, and the translator would repeat it (Erdmann cupped his hands around his mouth to make a ghostly echo): *"Who are you?"* "And what is your position?" The Iraqis would announce their position, and the Americans would look at one another. "What the hell office is that?"

Back in Washington, Mitchell Daniels, the director of the Office of Management and Budget, and his assistant Robin Cleveland were determined to keep ORHA on a lean diet so that the administration's rosy financial predictions for Iraqi reconstruction could be kept. As a result, the ministerial teams in Baghdad initially had just twenty-five thousand dollars to resurrect the devastated Iraqi administration. Even this wasn't cash—the funds required grant applications that took several weeks for approval. Erdmann longed for the fistfuls of dollars with which Special Forces in Afghanistan had jump-started projects and won cooperation in the crucial early days, before that window shut. "Postconflict reconstruction, you need to have the ability to deliver the resources right away," he said. "People in a desperate situation need help. Boy, that's a blindingly obvious insight. The next thing is that if you're not giving them help, they're going to go somewhere else."

GARNER RETURNED from Kurdistan still trying to carry out the Pentagon plan. On April 28, he stood up in his open-neck polo shirt before a meeting of 350 Iraqis at the Baghdad Convention Center, which was littered with broken glass and debris. There was no agenda. Kanan Makiya, back in the city of his birth for the first time in thirty-five years, read a paper on the need for a liberal constitution to protect individual rights. When he finished, a tribal sheikh stood up and said, "I have no running water, no electricity, no security—and you are talking about a constitution?" Another sheikh asked Garner, "Who's in charge of our politics?"

"You're in charge," Garner answered. There was an audible gasp in the room. Noah Feldman, the constitutional adviser, realized later, "They were losing faith in us by the second." Iraqis, for whom any sign of individual initiative could have been fatal under Saddam, were waiting to be told what would come next, and no one told them. An old man in a Shiite neighborhood approached Feldman and asked who was running Iraq. No one seemed to know.

But the disturbing news was beginning to filter back to Washington. On May 6, President Bush announced that the former diplomat and counterterrorism expert L. Paul (Jerry) Bremer III would replace Jay Garner in Baghdad. (Rumsfeld had informed a surprised and hurt Garner, on April 24, that he was a lame duck.) The Pentagon would always maintain that the changeover had been planned from the beginning. But the original idea had been for a civilian to come later on and with a lower profile, as a kind of super ambassador to what would be the interim government. As it was, Bremer told me, "I had ten days to get ready to come here." As a hard-liner he was acceptable to Rumsfeld, and his selection represented a brief truce in the war between Defense and State. Though it marked a sudden turn toward a more rational policy, no one in the administration has ever explained the decision that led to Garner's hasty departure. Barbara Bodine, who was fired by Rumsfeld just before Bremer's arrival, concluded that there was only one person in the world with the knowledge, access, and influence to point out to Bush that Iraq was hemorrhaging and it needed to be stopped: Tony Blair.

On May 10, Garner flew to Qatar to brief Bremer. When Garner mentioned that there would be a meeting with the Iraqi leadership group in several days, Bremer looked at his predecessor and said, "That probably isn't going to happen." Garner found Bremer cold, if hardworking, and imagined that Bremer considered him to be out of his depth, the man who had screwed things up in Iraq. The period of their overlap in Baghdad promised to be excruciating, and Garner was determined to keep it as short as possible.

On May 12, Bremer arrived in Baghdad wearing a dark suit. He was referred to as "Ambassador Bremer." Three weeks later, Jay Garner, whose fishing buddies had begun to grumble that they'd been set up by the neoconservatives back in Washington, quietly went home. He was taken by Rumsfeld to the White House for a farewell conversation with the president. Garner had written up a two-page memo for Bush and Rumsfeld, dated May 27, that portrayed Iraq as a country well on the road to stability and just a few weeks away from full reconstruction. This good news made it all the easier for Bush to thank Garner graciously for the work he had done. Garner, in turn, assured the president that he had chosen a wonderful successor in Bremer. "I didn't choose him," Bush said. "Rumsfeld chose him." This was news to Garner, whom Rumsfeld had once called his man in Iraq.

The conversation lasted forty-five minutes, with Cheney and Rice sitting in for the second half, and yet the president did not take the chance to ask Garner what it was really like in Iraq, to find out what problems lay ahead in the weeks and months to come. When Garner had come back from northern Iraq in 1991, after Operation Provide Comfort, he had answered questions for four or five days. This time, no one—neither Bush, Cheney, Rumsfeld, nor Rice—seemed to give a damn what he had to say.

"You want to do Iran for the next one?" the president joshed as the meeting came to an end.

"No, sir, me and the boys are holding out for Cuba."

Bush laughed and promised Garner and the boys Cuba. And that was it: Garner shook hands with the president, then with the vice president, who had said nothing the whole time, and he caught Cheney's wicked little smile on his way out. Garner left with the impression that Bush knew only what Cheney let into his office. It was early June 2003, and anyone listening to the conversation between the officials who had greatest responsibility for Iraq could only conclude that Operation Iraqi Freedom was a triumph.

In Baghdad, ORHA was dissolved into the Coalition Provisional Authority, and Bremer, with the status of a presidential envoy, the legal imprimatur of a UN Security Council resolution, and the command authority that Garner never had, let it be known that he was in control. The Iraqi army was promptly abolished, all members of the top four levels of the Baath Party were expelled from government service, Chalabi's militia was disarmed, and the formation of an interim government was stopped cold. There was even talk of shooting looters, though it didn't happen. The Pentagon extended indefinitely the deployment of battle-weary divisions. What had been conceived as a swift liberation became a prolonged occupation.

LOOKING BACK, Drew Erdmann was impatient with any facile condemnation of the planning. Citing his hero Marc Bloch, he insisted on the actual circumstances in which the planners had to work. When I mentioned a four-hundred-page manual that the U.S. military produced for the occupation of Germany, he shot back that, given the available lead time, a fairer comparison with Iraq would be the wartime occupation of French North Africa, which was so beset with problems that it nearly cost General Eisenhower his job. In the case of Iraq, any planning at all was a delicate matter: The administration had to prepare for the effects of a war it was still claiming it wanted to avoid. "How much diplomacy would there have been at the UN if people had said, 'The president is pulling people out of the Departments of Agriculture and Commerce to take over the whole Iraqi state'? That's the political logic that works against advance planning."

But the administration's failures in the weeks following the fall of Baghdad, which set Iraq's course after Saddam and continue to haunt the American effort today, were not entirely the result of constraints and mistakes. In a sense they were deliberate. If there was never a coherent postwar plan, it was because the people in Washington who mattered never intended to stay in Iraq. "Rummy and Wolfowitz and Feith did not believe the U.S. would need to run postconflict Iraq," said a Defense Department official. "Their plan was to turn it over to these exiles very quickly and let them deal with the messes that came up. Garner was a fall guy for a bad strategy. He was doing exactly what Rummy wanted him to do. It was the strategy that failed."

The chief beneficiaries of the failed strategy were those Iraqis who had no interest in allowing a new society, under American guidance, to emerge from the ruins of Saddam's Iraq. Seemingly defeated, they were already beginning to regroup. An Army major named Isaiah Wilson III, a historian of Operation Iraqi Freedom in a study group formed by General Shinseki, later wrote in an unpublished paper that when Army commanders realized in late May that they would have to stay on in Iraq and looked around for a postwar plan, the response "was silence. There was no Phase-IV plan." General Franks, the man responsible for this failure, went on leave in May and retired over the summer to go on the lecture circuit, write his memoirs, and collect a Presidential Medal of Freedom, leaving behind the tens of thousands of soldiers he had led into Iraq to continue fighting a war that was far from won. Major Wilson's paper went on, "In the two-to-three months of ambiguous transition, U.S. forces slowly lost the momentum and the initiative they had gained over an off-balanced enemy. During this calm before the next storm, the U.S. Army had had its eyes turned toward the ports, while Former Regime Loyalists (FRL) and budding insurgents had their eyes turned toward the people. The United States, its Army, and its coalition of the willing have been playing catch-up ever since."

And yet the faith of the authors in their own strategy remained unshakable. In the fall of 2003, Dick Cheney approached his longtime colleague Colin Powell, stuck a finger in his chest, and said, "If you hadn't opposed the INC and Chalabi, we wouldn't be in this mess."

But Cheney didn't believe that the postwar planning would matter in the end, anyway. Like the president, Cheney maintained an almost mystical confidence in American military power and an utter incuriosity about the details of its human consequences. "He thought Bush had figured out how to focus on what was essential and important, where to spend his time," Bob Woodward wrote in his book *Plan of Attack*. "The president didn't waste time on trivia. Over the nearly 16 months leading up to war, he had zeroed in on the military plan."

As for the postwar plan, there was no need to worry. The president had already been told what he wanted to hear—by his vice president and national security adviser, by his secretary of defense and his secretary's deputies, by Kanan Makiya and other exiles, by his ardent supporters in the think tanks and the press, by his own faith in the universal human desire for freedom. And so the American people never had a chance to consider the real difficulties and costs of regime change in Iraq.

5

PSYCHOLOGICAL DEMOLITION

AMONG THE LOOTERS who followed on the heels of the Americans, some broke open the locked gates of the al-Rashad long-term psychiatric hospital on the eastern edge of Baghdad. Besides stealing the antidepressants and antipsychotics of some previous generation, the antique electroshock boxes, and the sewing machines from occupational therapy, the looters liberated about six hundred of the hospital's one thousand chronic schizophrenics and other hard-core, burnt-out cases. Wandering out into the terrifying freedom of chaotic Baghdad, some of the patients were raped and a few were killed. Two hundred or so eventually found their way back or were returned by family members, American soldiers, and the remnants of the Iraqi police. The hospital stood across the road from the barbed wire and perimeter wall of an American military camp, next to a man-made lake in a bleak, half-empty stretch of the city. On the day I visited, the landscape looked grainy and ominous, with windblown dust clouds blocking out the sun.

Dr. Baher Butti, the hospital's chief psychiatrist, was a small, balding, nebbishy man of forty-three, with a pinched face and an insignificant mustache. He gave me a tour of the facility and grounds, which had the penal aspect of an insane asylum from a 1940s B movie. The patients swarmed and drew close: gaunt, half-naked men with shaved heads, tapping me on the shoulder, calling in English, "Mister, good morning, how are you, I love you, good-bye"; unveiled women shouting hellos with wild smiles, or sitting immodestly on the floor and smoking, staring into space. The fall of the regime had induced a kind of post-traumatic stress disorder, Dr. Butti said—not just here, but all over the country. It was not a new syndrome for Iraqis. They had been suffering from it for twenty or thirty years. "My own condition has deteriorated," Dr. Butti confided. "Before, you knew where the danger was and you went in the other direction. Now the danger is all around you."

Under the old regime, Dr. Butti had sometimes worked for two or three dollars a month, not unusual for the downwardly mobile middle class in the years of sanctions. He had a wife and two children; he was a Christian by origin but the son of a communist and thoroughly secular. He feared the rising danger of Islamic fundamentalism. Until the arrival of the Americans, he had been a Baathist. "No, I did not commit crimes," he said when I started to tiptoe up to the subject.

Dr. Butti keenly felt his professional isolation from the modern world and had made it his goal to practice what he knew of the talking cure and group therapy in a country where psychological care wasn't always distinguishable from the methods of the security police. He felt that, in order to understand the mental situation of Iraqis after decades of tyranny, war, and now occupation, I needed to meet his patients. Several days a week he treated people in crisis at the Ibn Rushd Teaching Psychiatric Hospital, a clean and austere oasis on the east side of the Tigris, in central Baghdad.

Dr. Butti drove me across the city in his little 1982 Nissan, a battered metal box with leprous rust patches and a cracked windshield. Baghdad was teeming with abused cars and minibuses and orange-and-white taxis years past their expiration date, driven by underweight, fatigued, prematurely gray men who hung out their windows to escape the intolerable heat of the car for the exhaust and noise and barely more tolerable heat of the street.

In the first room at Ibn Rushd, an old man was lying on his side, moaning to someone named Ahmad that looters were trying to get in. He had been an employee of the Ministry of Agriculture. In the next room—nearly bare, painted green, and badly in need of cleaning, like the first room—a young man was sitting cross-legged on the bed as if waiting for our arrival. He was bearded and handsome, with dilated blue eyes and a polite smile. His name was Ibrahim, and he believed himself to be the prophet of the same name. He had been admitted two days ago after trying to stab his cousin. "My cousin said something that made me feel there was hot water pouring over me," Ibrahim told me calmly, tracing his finger on the bedsheet. What his cousin had said was that Ibrahim should defend Muslim honor and land by killing Americans. "I should have answered that the Americans won't take our land, but I didn't. It's a false challenge—it's not only Muslims who know about honor and land, everyone does. The whole world is my land. Not just Iraq. The whole world."

Ibrahim's father, standing next to the bed, said that his son's deterioration had begun as a teenager during the first Gulf War, when he was left alone at home during allied bombing. In 1996, Ibrahim tried to run against Saddam for president; he made it halfway to the palace before his father caught up with him and saved his life by dragging him home. Ibrahim's condition had worn out the whole family. Four days before the start of the recent war, his delusions had flared up again and he'd been hospitalized until the fall of Baghdad. Ibrahim believed in one world government, led by the Americans. They had demonstrated their fairness by protecting the Jews, he said, seeming happier the more he talked. They had earned the right to be the world's policeman and rule with justice. This was a minority view in Iraq; I never heard it outside the Ibn Rushd Teaching Psychiatric Hospital.

In the general ward, a wary-looking middle-aged man with rotten teeth sat smoking on a bed. He was Nabil Rahim, a Shiite follower of the martyred Ayatollah Mohamed Baqr al-Sadr, the uncle of Moqtada al-Sadr and founder of the Islamist Dawa Party. In 1980, after being forced to watch his sister gang-raped and killed by interrogators, Sadr had nails hammered into his skull. "It's no use now," Rahim said, "Mohamed al-Sadr is gone, his knowledge is gone. I want to live, that's all. I want to live."

Wherever he went, Rahim saw people whispering about him—the security police, he believed. "It's a common delusion here," Dr. Butti remarked. To make his point, the patient showed me a cigarette burn on his right shoulder. The Americans were less dangerous for him than Saddam's police, he said, but in the end they were no better, because they had come to steal the oil.

The line between justifiable paranoia and outright delusion wasn't easy to draw in Iraq. Dr. Butti himself was having trouble making up his mind about the Americans. In the turbulent weeks following the fall of the regime he didn't know which way to turn, fearing for his own safety and distrusting equally Iraq's new political groups and the Americans' ability to create a decent society. The looting had been a terrible blow to their natural allies in the middle class. Now, people like him were hesitant to stick their necks out. "Is it that we are paralyzed," he asked, "or that the American administration is paralyzing the situation so they can come up with their own ideas?" Dr. Butti once attended a meeting with occupation officials on the subject of forming local NGOs and concluded that, to get funding, he needed to be a fundamentalist. "I felt miserable, because those people are leading us, are ruling us, but they are just bureaucrats," he said as we sat in his spartan office at Ibn Rushd. "Bremer sees it as a job, not making history." Nonetheless, Dr. Butti had sent letters to Bremer and other American officials with ideas about the development of social science in the new Iraq and a vague request to be absolved of his onetime membership in the Baath Party (his rank was too low for him to be officially debaathified). He had received no response.

With a few old classmates from Baghdad's Jesuit high school, Dr. Butti was setting up an NGO called the Baghdad Rehabilitation and Development Group. One of its proposals was the construction of the Gilgamesh Center for Creative Thinking. In the prospectus, Dr. Butti wrote with perhaps a bit of self-criticism:

> A great number of Iraqi people are suffering a great deal because of the severed communication with the civilized world, they suffer from lacking the ability to communicate with the others, they have lost the hope in the future, they suspect anything foreign, they are not sufficient in their professional performance, they don't feel enough responsibility towards the society, they lack the power to experience

freedom, they don't comprehend the correct performance of democracy, they cannot deal with group working . . . etc. Rebuilding what the war has destroyed is a simple effort if compared with the task of rebuilding the distorted human person.

The Gilgamesh Center for Creative Thinking would be a place where Iraqis could learn such skills as "logical and rational thinking," "how to dialogue and discuss with others," and "secrets of the successful negotiation." It was hard to think of a better idea for the reconstruction of Iraq, but Dr. Butti was having trouble finding money.

From Ibn Rushd he drove me to his private club, the once-exclusive and now rather shabby Alwiyah, where we could still get a beer (fundamentalists were firebombing the liquor shops on Saadoon Street), and then on to the home of a classmate from the Jesuit high school. On the way, our conversation kept turning to the past. Dr. Butti had joined the Baath Party, like at least a million other Iraqis, for professional advancement. Yet he believed that its ideology wasn't wholly mistaken. Dr. Butti was astonished I didn't know that the two blue lines on the Israeli flag represent the Nile and the Euphrates, the borders of Greater Israel, or that the pyramid and eye on the back of an American dollar bill were Zionist symbols, or that a photograph of an American tank positioned next to the ancient Babylon gate indicated Zionist revenge for the Babylonian captivity. His view was basically that of a communist who quit the party only after Khrushchev denounced Stalin: Until around 1980, he thought, the Baathists had been a force for progress, with some good ideas about the Arab nation. The revolution had simply gone wrong, he said. "Like *Animal Farm*."

I asked about the seventeen Iraqis, thirteen of them Jewish, who had been hanged before hundreds of thousands of people in Liberation Square in 1969, after the Baathist takeover. Wasn't the revolution rotten from the start?

"They were spies," Dr. Butti said, the way he said everything, with a sort of verbal shrug and a pained smile, as if it was an unhappy fact that he could do nothing about. "Any patriotic system would have done the same."

The hanging incident filled several pages near the beginning of

Republic of Fear. In Makiya's account, it was as chilling an omen as Kristallnacht. I'd taken it as an article of faith that any Iraqi who welcomed change would agree: This was one of the fixed ideas I had brought with me to Iraq. Yet here was Dr. Baher Butti, an educated professional, from Iraq's most pro-Western minority, well aware of the psychic damage done by Saddam, hungry for contact with the Americans—still insisting that those thirteen Jews had been spies. We were stopped in traffic, and I glanced over at him. He met my look and the smile flickered under his mustache. I was about to argue, then thought better of it. That Makiya's version was true didn't matter. I had been in Iraq about three weeks and had already begun to realize that most of my ideas about the place were going to be of no use.

IRAQ WAS RESTLESS and convulsive, as if liberation had introduced a virus into the organism and a fever was burning through the country. Day and night the background noise was gunfire, and it grew especially intense after the ten o'clock curfew, when no one who cared about his safety went outside. Now and then the walls shook with a grenade or mortar round. The only force of order was the American military, but convoys of Humvees rattled through the city streets at speeds that had more to do with force protection than policing. Guerrilla attacks on soldiers were already occurring at a rate of twenty per day in Baghdad alone.

When I arrived in mid-July, summer was going full blast. The temperature usually passed 120° by midafternoon, and on some days it reached 130°. Sticking your head out the window of a moving car felt like turning a blow-dryer directly on your own face, or standing behind a jet engine at takeoff. If there was no shade to be found, simply being outside for more than ten minutes in the blinding yellow light made you start to weaken, and if you tried to keep going through the day, a moment came around three o'clock when a wave of woozy inebriation swept over you and you felt that you might faint. Relief came only hours after dark, but even at night the heat was oppressive enough that Iraqi families slept out on their roofs, unless gunfire and helicopter patrols made it too loud or too dangerous. A soldier once said that his deployment in the Iraqi desert was like being in the middle of a loaf of baking bread, thrown this way and that as the dough rose, with no idea what was happening or where he was. To me, the Iraqi heat had the quality of a malevolent and inescapable tyranny, turning everyone stupid and passive.

The electricity was on barely half the time in postwar Baghdad, and the hours of operation from neighborhood to neighborhood were unpredictable. Iraqis who didn't own a generator stayed up most of the night fanning their small children; in the morning they looked exhausted. The telephone exchange had been badly damaged by bombing and looting, so there were scarcely any working phones in the city and carrying out the simplest business, such as arranging a meeting, took enormous effort (in August a Bahraini company managed to put up enough transmission towers for rudimentary cell phone service, which didn't exist under Saddam, but it was unlicensed and lasted only a single day before the occupation authority, which had its own internal MCI network, shut it down). There were also shortages of fuel and liquefied petroleum gas, and the lines outside filling stations of those who couldn't pay black market prices stretched a mile or more. The streets were choked with angry drivers, each one a president of the republic unto himself. The stoplights no longer worked, the traffic cops had abandoned their posts, and the network of arteries was clotted with American military roadblocks and the sealing off of the vast Green Zone, which fouled up all the normal patterns. In addition, with the borders wide open, a million cars were pouring into the country from Jordan and Kuwait, most of them illegally. There was nothing and no one to control traffic, so each driver made up his own rules, racing along streets and roundabouts the wrong way, taking shortcuts over curbs and across highway dividers. Every intersection was either a dangerous game of chicken or a dense knot of hundreds of vehicles. In the middle of a traffic jam a driver would grow desperate enough to get out and direct the cars around him, and the knot would start to come loose a few inches at a time. The noise of honking was incessant. In this bedlam I was never able to get oriented to the layout of the city, partly because I never drove and partly because the postwar grid was irrational. The Iraqis themselves were disoriented.

One of the first things that struck me in Iraq was the look of the faces. I noticed it as soon as I crossed the border driving in from Jordan and saw a group of men hanging around the first filling station: Compared with the Jordanians on the other side, who after all were brother Arabs and probably members of the same border tribe, the Iraqis looked poor and beaten down. Their cheeks, covered with gray stubble, were leathery and hollow, their eyes downcast and at the same time quick and watchful in the way of people used to anticipating dangers and seizing furtive chances. They reminded me of the faces in postwar Italian neorealist movies, with the roles played by ordinary men and women wandering through the rubble of bombed cities in search of work. Even the frayed, long-outmoded jackets the Iraqi men wore and the eternal cigarette butts dangling from their lips looked the same. As a rule, Iraqi men always turned out to be at least a decade younger than my first guess, and this became a sort of bleak joke. I once rode in a taxi—the usual wheezing orange-and-white metal oven—and the driver asked my age. When I told him, he said, "Forty-two? Forty-two?" He drew the number with his finger on the dashboard, thinking he must have misunderstood my English. "Forty-two?" He pointed at the digital clock on the dash, which read 5:41. "This forty-one. You, forty-two?" Finally accepting it, he said in wonder, "You are beautiful." I knew what was coming next. "Me, forty-three," he said. It was my turn to be shocked—I'd figured him for at least sixty. I told him that he was beautiful too, but he wasn't having any of it. He pointed at the grizzled beard and mass of wrinkles on his face. "Iraq no good."

Another time, I met an old man who was trying to make his living by selling straw fans outside a restaurant. Though he was still in his fifties, he had only one tooth left. "Saddam was a dog," he slurred. "He took ten years of my life." The man had gone to prison for refusing to go fight in the war with Iran. "Under Saddam if I were talking to you like this, the Mukhabarat would come at once and pick me up." He laughed, dancing from foot to foot, and the tooth came into view. "I feel young again. Thanks forever to the Americans and British. You can make us whole human beings again." In the first summer of the occupation it was still possible to hear such things.

Baghdad was a crumbling, sun-blasted city. It was hard to tell how much of the squalor was recent and how much came from habitual neglect. Almost nothing in the capital looked new or well maintained. The garbage piled thick along the roads never seemed to get picked up, and some residents told me that, with no functioning sanitation system, only those who paid off the trucks now enjoyed service. You could identify the looted buildings at a distance by their hollow windows and fire-blackened outer walls. These far outnumbered the structures that had been bombed during the war, such as the palaces and party buildings in the Green Zone, or the telecommunications building a little north along the river, or the high-rise on the eastern bank that Iraqis called the "Turkish restaurant" and that had housed Uday's militia. The bombing had done its work relatively cleanly: The missile often plunged directly down the core, causing the roof and multiple stories to implode like a building demolished deliberately with munitions. These war wrecks, together with the bullet-pocked facades along avenues in western Baghdad, added to the city's general appearance of collapse, but the damage done by looting looked more sinister and contagious—the difference between a deep bruise and septicemia. There was rubble everywhere, and green ponds of sewage filled the streets in the poor, Shiite eastern and southern districts, and coils of concertina wire wound around important buildings or American checkpoints, and fourteen-foot blast walls were starting to arrive on flatbed trucks from Iran or Turkey and rise up in sections along the main thoroughfares of the Green Zone. A coat of summer dust lay on everything; by the end of the day my shoes were always the monochrome ocher of Baghdad. The city seemed to have become ugly by design. Only the Tigris still had a sluggish sort of majesty. The river was a couple of hundred yards wide, and each bank was lined with a stone wall slanted downward at a shallow angle, and every hundred feet or so a flight of steps cut the wall, running from the street down into the water. Not all of the palm and eucalyptus trees had been cut back, and as the sun set behind the shallow turquoise dome of the Republican Palace in the Green Zone and the heat died a little, it was possible to feel the picturesque romance of the river. But swimming was forbidden, and a number of Iraqi boys who didn't know or care about the new rules had to be scared out of the water by warning shots from American soldiers. A few swimmers who ignored them were killed.

In the first days, I kept finding myself drawn to the Baghdad Zoo. It was in the middle of Zawra Park, a rectangle of tired eucalyptus trees and parched grass that ran opposite 14th of July Street from the Rashid Hotel and the Baghdad Convention Center, the two structures in the Green Zone to which Iraqis still had some access. At the other end of the park from the zoo was the Unknown Soldier monument, a hideous overgrown flying saucer in concrete, and next to it the parade ground, with the gigantic crossed swords at either end and Saddam's viewing stand in between. This part of the city was imposing, vast, and deserted. It had been the same under Saddam—these were his palaces, his monuments, and ordinary Iraqis generally stayed clear unless they had official business—but the zoo had been a popular place for families to come and picnic in the evening or on Friday.

Now it was empty, except for the company of Army engineers that was undertaking a modest reconstruction project, and the Iraqi employees, and the animals. I visited the zoo several times, and the experience was always upsetting. It was the one place in Iraq where the old regime seemed still to exist. The cages looked like prison cells. In one, a blind bear that had mutilated its own chest sprawled in a catatonic heap. In the next cage, dogs and puppies lay panting beside bowls of dirty water. "Spp Fox—dog. Origin: UK" said the placard. The puppies wagged their tails when I approached the bars, but the adults had long since stopped knowing that they were dogs. They were in the zoo, I was told, because dogs had been favorites of Saddam, though some were fed to the lions when food supplies ran out during the war.

The animal population had been dramatically reduced by war, from 650 before the invasion to only thirteen. Monkeys, birds, lizards, and the ostrich were gone; the creatures that remained had survived the firefights when the city fell and were too dangerous or worthless to loot. The soldiers from the Third Infantry Division who had occupied the zoo in April found a baboon loose on the grounds; it proved harmless to them, but when one of the zookeepers, who had been hiding in his office, was brought out the animal flew into a rage and attacked him, so that the soldiers had to shoot the baboon to save the Baathist. A few months later, a group of soldiers, drinking after hours, were fooling around near the cage of a Bengal tiger, when the hand of one soldier started to disappear into the tiger's mouth. His buddy shot the animal dead.

A South African named Brendan Wittington-Jones, from a conservation group called Thula-Thula Zululand, was collaborating on the renovation with a sweating, harassed captain from the engineer company. Both men were frustrated with the zoo's Iraqi staff, who, in the absence of familiar authority, were terrified of making any decision. The one responsible and competent Iraqi had been fired because he was a Baathist. So the foreigners were taking the lead. "The military's got to get a win, something that's big and visible," Wittington-Jones said. "The park is like a big green lung in the middle of Baghdad—it's the only green area. It would be good for PR, and give the kids something to do." The occupation authority spent one hundred thousand dollars on the initial renovation, and the zoo reopened to the public in late July, with great fanfare, though it had received only a face-lift—the cages still looked like animal prisons. On a subsequent visit I found the place nearly abandoned. Its location in the heart of the Green Zone, surrounded by American checkpoints, was too intimidating for most families, and its hours of opening, ten to six, put in place for security reasons, were almost intolerably hot. The Baghdad Zoo combined the cruelty and injustice of the old regime with some of the stupidity and carelessness of the new.

PHYSICALLY, the city appeared to be stricken, or dying, or convalescing from a life-threatening illness. But in the very first hours, beneath the decrepit surface of things, I was aware of Baghdad's intensity. It came from the constant fear of violence, but even more from the sense of a momentous experiment going on every minute of every day: Iraqis and Americans thrust together into something uncertain and new. I remember driving across the Jordanian border at sunrise and seeing the first American soldier at the first checkpoint on the Iraqi side, and being stupefied that all the abstract arguments over the idea of a war had actually led to *this*—this soldier wearing camouflage in the red desert of western Iraq, leaning against his vehicle, saying, "Looks like it's getting to be a nice day. What part of the country you from?"

Before leaving for Iraq, I'd had dinner at the usual Brooklyn bistro with Paul Berman. He kept comparing the situation in post-totalitarian Baghdad to Prague in 1989. I kept insisting that Iraq was vastly different: under military occupation, far more violent, its people more traumatized, living in a much worse neighborhood. Yet one reason I wanted to go was to see the political and cultural flowering post-Saddam Iraq might produce. I expected young people to be joining political parties, attending public lectures, staging poetry readings and film festivals. I expected to see exciting things.

The Hiwar Gallery was a bohemian oasis, next to the Turkish embassy, in the otherwise die-hard Baathist district of Adhamiya in northern Baghdad. It opened after the Gulf War, and because its owner, a gimp-legged sculptor and bon vivant named Qasim al-Sabti, had paid off the secret police with grilled fish and whiskey, the gallery and its tight coterie of artists had been left alone by the authorities. "There was government pressure on the theaters and writers," the owner told me, "but about the plastic arts there was no pressure because contemporary art is a high language. The Baathists didn't understand it. They only understood realism. So we played free in our island here."

The paintings on exhibit were mostly abstract and meditative, the art of internal exile. In the outdoor café, where actresses and poets and painters sat drinking tea, I asked a professor of architecture from Baghdad University where in town I could see a play or movie. Nowhere, he answered. "You need security before you can take the next step." Security, electricity, and minimal confidence in the future. "Saddam spoiled the way of thinking. Now you see nothing in Baghdad. It's all spoiled, and what you see is a mess which doesn't represent anything because it's not the natural way for Iraqis to live."

I remarked that liberated Iraq didn't seem a very happy place.

"No one can bring you happiness immediately like this," the professor said. He had an air of melancholy refinement. "It doesn't come from God. Have you heard the Iraqi songs? They're very sad. Why? Because it's been like this for a long, long time. Even if you are talking about love and nice women and beautiful things, you look at it as very sad. But effective: You touch others."

The professor asked me what the Americans planned for Iraq. I told him in all honesty that I didn't know.

"I think you need to spend years to understand Iraqis," he said, suddenly growing animated. For example, Iraq was half urban, half bedouin. The urban personality was on display all around us. The bedouin personality came from the deep past, and it was the one causing problems for America. The bedouin personality explained why Iraqis shouted: In the desert, they had to shout to be heard. "You have spent lots of efforts during those crucial years—on what? When you come in you are not understanding the people. I don't know why. Everyone is asking the question. Military, it's easy—you have complicated, sophisticated forces. But what will be after? This is the question. They have to have a plan." He seemed genuinely bewildered by what he'd seen since the fall of the regime. "Anyone who wants to live in Iraq must understand Iraqis. He must change himself when he comes to Iraq. And we too must change a bit, to understand him, because we can't have life without a common language between us. You must pay, and I must pay also." The professor smiled and stood up to leave. "And believe me, Iraqis are all good and nice and simple."

There was no flowering in Baghdad. It was too soon, and things were too unsettled. And perhaps Iraqis themselves weren't prepared or even capable yet. One day, as I was driving down Saadoon Street in the city center, I noticed a theater called the Nasir. Inside, the director, whose name was Abdulillah Kamal, sat smoking with a group of actors in the front office. Kamal was white haired and pink skinned, heavyset in sweatpants, with a shaggy mustache and reading glasses dangling around his neck. He was about to resume performances of the hit play that had been showing until April 9. "A nuclear fantasy," he called it, with the title *I Saw by My Eyes, Nobody Told Me*. It had filled all two thousand seats. I asked why he didn't stage something that he couldn't do under Saddam, something new—for example, a satire of the occupation. He brushed the notion aside. "We can't find a sadder story than the street to put on as a play," he said. "The play is out on the street. All Baghdad is a theater. We are the audience. We don't need to do a play."

But it would pack the house, I said, and it would give Iraqis something they needed—the chance to see their common experience through the bonding medium of art.

"Can I talk about Bremer and Bush?" the director demanded. "Can you give me guarantees?" He mentioned a newspaper that had been closed for inciting Iraqis to kill Americans. I tried to explain that this was different. In the end I was unable to persuade Kamal that he wouldn't be shut down—but I also sensed that my idea made him uneasy for deeper reasons. It would demand an act of imaginative courage that was beyond his power. Finally, Kamal confided that he had already written his next play. It was called *Masonica*, which crossed "America" with "Masonry" (a word one often heard in Iraq, having some obscure relation with Zionism). The play would reveal, he said, "the hidden thing that happened in America on September 11."

When Saddam ruled Iraq, the Baath Party's intelligence offices kept track of the rumors that were making their way through the streets. The documents were compiled annually in forty thick volumes that convey all the obsessive fascination of a police state. "Very confidential—to the President through the Office of the Secretary of the Security Council. The subject is Rumors," began one report written a few weeks after Saddam emptied Iraq's prisons in October 2002. "The political prisoners weren't set free, and they were executed by the Iraqi government." A second document declared: "It's about a fight between the two sons of the President, God praise him. It's about receiving power. Qusay Saddam Hussein was hurt. This rumor was discussed at Baghdad University in the College of Business Administration. October 6, 2002." The informer who was the source of the report was then named. Another rumor, originating in Hilla, said that Ariel Sharon was going to destroy Palestinian homes in Jenin to weaken the Iraqi economy, and that Saddam would give gifts of cars to foreign Arabs who had been living in Iraq since before the 1991 intifada, known as "the Page of Treachery and Treason." The king of Jordan would allow the Iraqi opposition to enter from his country and give them his support. The American invasion would come on the day of Saddam's reelection, to end the celebrations. The invasion would come on September 11, 2002, one year after the attacks in America. The United States would attack all the mosques in Iraq, with the excuse that the Iraqi government was hiding its WMD there in order not to attract attention. The aggressors would attack Iraq with a new weapon, a gas which, inhaled, would put Iraqis into a coma lasting more than eight hours. The invasion would be completely different from other military operations, and it would come in two stages, one secret and one public. The invasion would come in three places, each with a code name: in the north, "The Rabbit's Jump"; in the south, "The Movement of the Tortoise"; and in Baghdad, a special operation, "Pulling the Molars."

Most of the rumors originated in poor neighborhoods. In a sense, they were a normal expression of the experience of people undergoing the extreme stress of awaiting war and fearing their rulers—of coping with powerlessness amid constant violence. Many of the rumors were actually planted by the Baath Party, so that Saddam, having turned Iraq into a nation of spies, was tracking the progress of germs he himself had introduced into the body politic. He and his countrymen were joined in a closed system, a circle of paranoia. Survival depended on believing that anything was possible—the more unlikely, the more likely. To try to live outside the circle was a risky, even fatal, effort, and only the extraordinary were able. "Every Iraqi is a Baathist," Saddam liked to say, and even after he was gone from the scene, many of them acknowledged that he continued to inhabit their souls. The Iraqi who showed me the rumors, a sophisticated, artistic-minded woman whose whole family had gone into exile while she stayed behind with her husband and children, kept muttering oaths and trying to pull the volumes away. "I'm sorry, George, I hate government documents," she said. "Imagine living like this for thirty years. Surviving."

I had been in Iraq less than two weeks when Saddam's sons, Uday and Qusay, were killed in a safehouse in Mosul after an extended firefight with American soldiers. Uday in particular had been possessed of a psychotically cruel temperament. One of his former bodyguards, a bluff, good-natured man named Emad Hamadi, told me a story to illustrate what it was like working for him. Uday was frolicking in a swimming pool one day with a group of young women. He summoned Emad, who was wading nearby in his swimsuit, to bring him a whiskey. As soon as Emad handed over the glass, Uday forced his head under

water and pinned it between his knees. Emad knew that if he struggled at all it would be the end of his life, but the game went on and
on, for half a minute, a minute, until he felt he was about to die anyway. Emad resigned himself to his fate, but as he started to lose consciousness his arm instinctively moved from side to side to indicate
that he couldn't endure any more. He felt himself released, and when
he came to the surface, Uday was laughing along with his consorts.
"You're a good man," said the heir apparent, and he insisted that Emad
have a whiskey as well. Uday was probably the most despised man in
Iraq—even more than his father, who at least had climbed on his
own to the pinnacle of power and kept himself there with impressive
mastery.

The night of the firefight in Mosul, there was so much celebratory
gunfire in Baghdad that an American foot patrol I was accompanying
near the river had to call off the mission and return to base—the
rounds were falling dangerously close. But in the days that followed,
Iraqis began to wonder if Uday and Qusay were really dead. The
corpses presented to the media had been cosmetically repaired in
a way that looked waxen and unreal. I heard various theories from a
range of Iraqis. A woman who held a high position in the America-Iraq
Friendship Federation told me that she didn't believe it. "People haven't
seen any evidence that they are they," she said. "DNA, dental—can
these really identify them? Pictures can be manipulated. I heard a
story that the house where the sons were killed belonged to an anti-
Saddam sheikh. Why would he receive them?" And then there was the
father's mysterious silence. "If someone killed your two sons—I'm
sorry, would you sit back and say 'Okay, no problem'? So why hasn't
Saddam Hussein done something?" Her colleague suggested that
Bush was trying to secure his reelection. My driver had heard that
Uday escaped to Spain after the fall of Baghdad. Uday's jeweler, whom
I met at a party a couple of nights later, didn't believe it, either. He had
set hundreds of thousands of dollars worth of diamonds in rings, and
if he'd been short .000001 carat in his work he would have been killed.
He accepted the fact of all of Saddam's and Uday's crimes. Still, if
Uday now came to him for help, the jeweler said that he wouldn't turn

him away. Uday had his positive qualities: He was straightforward—if he didn't like you he killed you, if he liked you he treated you well. Uday had never personally wronged the jeweler, and it was a code of honor not to turn him in. His refusal to believe the news seemed like the expression of a wish: It would be humiliating if the Americans killed Uday and Qusay that way. In others it reflected fear: The young monsters were bound to return and inflict more pain. And in everyone it was the natural skepticism of people who had known only an official culture of lies. One old man, having seen Tony Blair discuss the event on television, became convinced that it was true, for Blair was smiling in a way that couldn't be faked; the old man had learned to read the truth from facial expressions after spending the years of the Iran-Iraq War watching Saddam on TV.

Over time, when Uday and Qusay did not reappear, and their deaths became accepted facts, the disbelievers turned into believers, without ever pausing to recalibrate their sense of their own ability to judge.

"THEY LACK THE POWER to experience freedom": The phrase, from Dr. Butti's proposal for the Gilgamesh Center for Creative Thinking, captured a truth about Iraqis in the months following April 9. It helped to explain one of the great mysteries after the fall of the statue: why the moment of good feeling was so short. The thousands of foreign soldiers, officials, contractors, and humanitarians who had poured into Iraq to rebuild the country found themselves in the position of the American sea captain in Melville's "Benito Cereno," who exclaims to the Spaniard he's rescued from a slave mutiny, "You are saved, you are saved: what has cast such a shadow upon you?" Iraqis were told they were free, they expected to be free, they had been waiting for years to be free—but they still didn't feel free. And so a reaction set in almost at once. Aqila al-Hashemi, a former diplomat who in July became one of three women appointed to the interim Governing Council, told me, "We are still under the shock, we are still afraid. We are still living the same—I was fifteen in '68, now I'm fifty. You see? You can imagine—can I change in two days, in two months, in two years? We need to be re-educated, rehabilitated." Iraqis who longed for freedom, she said, "were happy after the fall of the regime. But then there was an act of sabotage against this joy, against this happiness. It's not accomplished, you see. This feeling you have—ah, yes!—but then it's not accomplished. This is frustrating."

The "act of sabotage" was many acts: the outbreak of chaos, the return of Baathist violence, the reality of occupation—but also the ingrained sense of powerlessness. With it came an outsized expectation of what the superpower could achieve, and the disturbance in Iraqis' minds was only heightened by the performance of the Americans. If Saddam could restore the country's utilities within a couple of months of the end of the Gulf War, with all the destruction done by allied bombing, why was the power grid still deteriorating after four months, when they had left the infrastructure intact this time? One month before the war, President Bush had declared in a visionary speech at the American Enterprise Institute that Iraq would become a democratic model for the Middle East. Iraqis heard him, and as an unemployed electrician named Tariq Talib told me, "We expected the Americans would make the country an example, a second Europe. That's why we didn't fight back. And we are shocked, as if we've gone back a hundred years."

Rumors spread that the American forces were cutting electrical lines to punish Iraqis for staging attacks, and that they had brought Kuwaitis up with the invasion force to instigate the looting in revenge for the Iraqi occupation in 1990. "Our people don't understand what's going on, so they think the Americans are deliberately creating this chaos," Dr. Butti told me. The conspiracy theories were an attempt to make sense of the absurd. He himself didn't know what to think. "We don't want to believe it's not intentional—the greatest power on earth can start a nuclear war." The notion that bad planning, halfhearted commitment, ignorance, and incompetence accounted for the anarchy simply wasn't believable. How were Iraqis to grasp that the same Washington think tank where Bush offered Iraq as a model for the region had contributed to the postwar collapse by shooting down any talk of nation building? Deliberate sabotage made more sense.

Dr. Butti introduced me to several of his old classmates from the Jesuit-run Baghdad College. They were trying to set up an organization with a vague idea of improving social knowledge in Iraq by making contact with counterparts in America. We sat in a sweltering living room in Karada, the middle-class and commercial district on the eastern bank of the Tigris: There was a urologist named Nimat Kamal, who looked like Ed Asner when he scowled, and a fire safety engineer with a softer manner named Mohamed Abbas. Dr. Kamal was livid at his treatment by Americans. There were three tanks positioned outside his hospital, and every day soldiers searched him and his car—every day, even though they knew him. "They don't distinguish between a doctor and a terrorist." One of his distant relatives and his neighbor's twelve-year-old boy had been shot to pieces recently when they inadvertently drove into a street that soldiers had cordoned off. At the same time, the urologist wanted more security from the Americans.

Abbas, the engineer, compared their situation to that of the Palestinians. "Same soldiers, same Apaches, same way of apprehending people. Iraqis are becoming more aggressive, because they make the connection."

"It needs time for things to be settled, we know that," Dr. Kamal said. "We are unlucky to be living in this boiling period. But people like us are in a layer of society that is very conservative. We have an unconscious fear of politics—we don't like to get involved. The Americans won't protect us." Educated, professional Iraqis were lying low while others—the poor, the religious, the armed—took to the streets.

"I had conflicting feelings during the war," Abbas said. "I wanted both sides to lose. I don't like American occupation, and I don't like to live under Saddam's rule."

I asked whether they would share information about insurgent activity with the American military if they had it. None of them would, and not only for fear of reprisal.

"It is also my conflict over the American presence," Abbas admitted. "To be very objective."

Dr. Butti, who had brought us together, suddenly looked at me with concern and apologized. He hoped that I wouldn't take it personally. I pointed out that all of them were still trying to make connections with Americans.

"There's no love that doesn't come after a quarrel," Dr. Kamal said, finally smiling. "Maybe we will learn to love each other."

"THE HUMAN COMMITTEE FOR PRISONNERS AND LOSS-NERS INTERNATIONAL" said the sign on a side street, not far from the bombed-out headquarters of military intelligence in Kadhimiya, an old neighborhood in the city's north with a famous market of gold-smith shops and one of the holiest shrines in Shiite Islam. The sign indicated a two-story building that was office and home to Sheikh Emad al-Din al-Awadi.

The chaos following liberation that had upended so many lives also created opportunities. There was, in fact, a kind of revolutionary situation in Iraq. Those who reacted first and fastest were the country's long-oppressed Shiite clerics: They filled the vacuum with energy and organization, taking over hospitals and schools, providing social services to the poor, and imposing their Islamic code on daily life, while more secular Iraqis, doctors and engineers and artists, moved about in a daze. The sheikh had spent almost ten years in Saddam's prisons, where he formed a clandestine prisoners' group. Now that Saddam was gone, he was becoming an important man.

On April 12, word reached the sheikh that the central market building in the expensive Mansour district was on fire. Before the war, the security police had stowed millions of prisoner files in the building's base-ment for safekeeping. Now the Baathists were trying to destroy them, and the sheikh and a handful of associates, armed with knives and stakes, raced across town to salvage the evidence of Saddam's largely success-ful attempt to turn all of Iraq into a prison. Other groups were already on the scene, fighting for possession of the records, including members of Ahmad Chalabi's militia. The INC seized millions of documents around Baghdad, but the sheikh's group managed to carry away carloads of files and microfilm to Kadhimiya, along with a partially melted Canon mi-crofilm reader. The sheikh understood that these documents in soft pink and green folders represented not just the past but also the future.

They now filled old metal filing drawers stacked to the high ceiling of his office, they sat in nylon grain sacks under the banana tree in his yard, they baked on his rooftop under the sun. More were arriving from various locations every week. And they were a tiny fraction of the full record of imprisonment and execution left behind by the old regime. American soldiers hauled off nineteen truckloads for central storage. In the offices of a rival prisoners' association set up by former members of Hezbollah (the two groups traded accusations of file theft), I stood in a large room heaped waist-deep with loose documents and felt sick at the sheer anonymous quantity of it. Other regimes have created instruments of internal control as elaborate and meticulously documented, but even the files of the East German Stasi don't tell such unhappy tales as Iraq's Mukhabarat.

File: Saleh Issa Ali
Sentenced to Death
Serial #580392669
Republic of Iraq, Ministry of Justice, Prosecution
Department: Secret Pen
Date: 16-1-90

It is sent to the Ministry of Labor and Social Affairs. Its theme is execution.
Following the telegraph sent by the Presidential Board #368 on 8-1-90, we send you the order of execution of the following convicted persons:

1. **Karim Issa Ali**
2. **Saleh Issa Ali**
3. **Khaled Abdul-Rahman Ismail**

They should be hanged until death.
With best regards,
Minister of Justice Akram Abdul-Khader Ali

The exterior walls of the sheikh's building were papered with photocopies of old black-and-white snapshots of young men, most of them wearing the hairstyles of the 1970s and '80s. Men and women came from all over the country to the office and combed through the files that the sheikh's followers had alphabetized, hoping to discover the fate of a lost son or a cousin who disappeared two decades ago. One afternoon, a doctor arrived from Baquba, a town about an hour northeast of Baghdad. His name was Yousef Ibrahim and he was an otorhinolaryngologist—an ear, nose, and throat specialist—with the highest postgraduate degree in his field. One night in 1995, local Baath Party officials came to his house with orders for the doctor to go to the hospital and perform an emergency operation. Dr. Ibrahim was to cut off the ear of a young army deserter. "I told them it is not probable to do this at night, and I am not ready for this psychologically. They told me, 'You must cut it even if you are cutting it with your teeth—or we will cut your ear.'" The idea was Uday's, and in the months during which it was implemented, before Uday turned to other ideas, the doctor severed forty-seven ears. "I felt a feeling of nonexistence, a feeling of guilt," Dr. Ibrahim explained, "but I am trying to satisfy myself that I had no choice." He had come to the sheikh's office looking for information about his brother, an emotionally disturbed man who was arrested in 1992 for cursing Saddam. "I think he was still alive until last year." The doctor left without finding his brother's file.

On the same day, one of the sheikh's best friends from prison had come for a visit. He was also a doctor, with hooded eyes and a calm, weary manner, named Saad Baghdadi, and when I told him about the ear doctor, he said, "If for me, I will not do it. What if he ordered you to kill these forty-seven? Will you do it?" Saddam had not been so savagely brutal from the beginning, Dr. Baghdadi said. "But when he found they obeyed him, Saddam increased his cruelty gradually. I'm very sorry, but if from the beginning no one obeyed him . . . in jail I and others disobeyed him in many things."

The sheikh said, "I used to read seventeen hours a day—do you know what it means to read seventeen hours a day?—and I couldn't find anyone, a king or a sultan, who hurt people like Saddam."

The sheikh was in his forties, short, round bellied, dark complexioned. He always wore a black cloak, white vest and pantaloons, pointed slippers, and the white turban that signifies a Shiite not descended directly from Mohamed. Though he kept his wife strictly hidden away and his forehead bore the dark bruise of fervent prayer, and in his inner office there was a portrait of Ayatollah Khomeini, the sheikh was a worldly man, a bit of a sensualist, a lover of impish jokes. The bushy beard, the full lips, the bug eyes behind thick black-rimmed glasses, and the sonorous voice put me in mind of Ayatollah Allen Ginsberg. He often dropped hints that he wasn't a rigid interpreter of his faith. Once, when we were talking about dogs, he said that under Islam two kinds of dogs were sanctioned: guard dogs and hunting dogs. I said that my dog was a pug with no skills whatsoever other than companionship. Was this *halal* (lawful) or *haram* (sinful)? He thought for a moment. "It is neither *halal* nor *haram*," he said. "It is allowed."

The sheikh received me on several occasions in his pale-green sitting room, where we were served vast lunches and tea lasting hours. "I am one of the regime's victims," he would begin—whereupon the power failed, his fan died, and the sheikh continued, "and one of the facts of the new regime is that the electricity has gone off." He sat with his legs drawn up in a vinyl swivel chair, sweat now pouring from under his turban, and I felt compelled to apologize on behalf of the Americans for the terrible state of Iraq's utilities.

The sheikh was born near the south-central town of Hilla into a family of tribal chiefs, and he grew up studying religion with the Hawza, the Shiite school of theology in Najaf. His intellectual pursuits were broad—Catholic doctrine, the writings of Nostradamus, Arabic poetry, Greek philosophy (he taught Plato and Aristotle to his religion students every morning)—and there was a streak of mysticism in his brand of Islamic thought. But in Najaf he also met and admired Khomeini during the ayatollah's exile in the 1970s. It was the beginning of widespread Shiite political activism in Iraq, much of it inspired by Ayatollah Mohamed Baqr al-Sadr, and in 1977 the sheikh was arrested at a demonstration in the holy city of Karbala. After a year he escaped prison and fled to Kuwait, then to the Shiite-dominated part of Saudi Arabia, where he had friends and supporters. But the Saudi government betrayed him to Iraqi intelligence. He was drugged and sent back in a box to Baghdad, where he endured a year of interrogation at General Security Headquarters before trial. His own court-appointed lawyer recommended the death penalty, but the sheikh was sentenced to life. Before being sent to Abu Ghraib prison, he was beaten with cables for three days. "They wanted to make me taste torture, to give me an idea about torture, so that I would know this is a terrorist jail."

The sheikh spent seven and a half years in a special internal ward, sharing a cell the size of his sitting room with fifty other men. It was so crowded that they took shifts lying down, sitting, and standing; those lying down had to sleep on their sides. There were no visitors. "For seven and a half years I didn't see anyone. We didn't see the sun. We didn't see the moon." The guards themselves were punished if they failed to show sufficient cruelty. Pen, paper, books were all forbidden.

"Why do you forbid these?" Dr. Baghdadi, the sheikh's cellmate, once asked a prison guard.

"We want you to go outside after years here," the guard replied, "and you'll forget not only your sciences, but even your own name."

"But we have many prisoners here who are depressed. This would help."

"We want them to be depressed. This is our purpose."

Yet the sheikh described his prison years with an unmistakable nostalgia, and listening to his tales I began to understand why the religious Shia were the first Iraqis to seize the new opportunity with purposefulness. In prison the sheikh became a leader. He settled differences that arose over food, sleeping space, and the inevitability that a sleeping prisoner would embrace the man beside him, believing him to be his wife. When the guards distributed oranges on Baath Party holidays, the sheikh saved the rinds to treat his own and others' stomach troubles, and distributed the seeds as a psychological panacea for insomnia. He composed a book of theology on nylon sacks using the broken edges of tubes of distilled water. And when the known Baathist spies were asleep, he preached to his clandestine group. By chance, I met a man named Abdul-Jabbar Doweich, who had shared the sheikh's cell through the 1980s. At forty-one, Doweich was a rare Iraqi with almost no gray hair. "In prison I was happy," he explained, "because I lived under Islam." It was the sheikh who taught him and the other prisoners about *wilayat al-faqih*, the rule of the jurisprudent under Islamic law.

International pressure after the first Gulf War forced Saddam to release thousands of political prisoners, among them the sheikh. He spent the next decade under house arrest, with another year in prison for refusing an offer of money in exchange for supporting the regime. Just days before the most recent war, some of his followers from prison warned him that the government had plans to kill him. He took refuge in his sister's house until the fall of Baghdad.

The sheikh was utterly realistic about the Americans. He regarded them as neither liberators nor occupiers, but as a fact of life that could be turned to good or ill. He wanted them to leave fairly soon: "There's a saying that when you visit somebody once a month you'll be as lovely as the moon." Meanwhile, he had established good relations with the Army captain responsible for security in his area and gotten what he could out of him—a faulty generator.

The sheikh had an agenda: He wanted me to introduce him to important Americans. At our first meeting, he asked, "Did they come here to pay a visit, or did they come to put their hands on the country?" My answer didn't satisfy him. "You're running away from the question." Later, when he described a pornographic videotape of a Sudanese diplomat lured into a love nest by a Baathist agent, I asked how he'd gotten a copy of it. "We have our ways." I pointed out that he was now the one running away from the question. The sheikh smiled through a cloud of cigarette smoke. "You taught me how."

At our second meeting, he welcomed me with a kiss on both cheeks and said, "I like you. I feel that I've known you for years." At our third, during a relative's funeral under a tent in a Shiite slum, he gave me a silver ring with a black stone inscribed with a verse from the Qur'an. "There are hidden bodies swimming in the sky," the sheikh said. "Maybe our hidden bodies met in the sky before we met each other, and that's why we get along so well."

I had an agenda, too. The sheikh's work illuminated the shadow of the past that lay so heavily on Iraqis. But it also made him a man to whom they brought their problems and requests. Though he denied having any political ambitions, I wanted to know what he wanted, what idea he had for Iraq's future. The sheikh was careful not to let me know. His way of sizing me up with a sidelong look, eyebrows arched, amusement playing on his mouth, suggested from the start that our relationship would be marked by seduction and manipulation.

IN THE LATE AFTERNOONS, I often stopped by a hotel called the Hamra in southern Baghdad. Like other hotels, it was staffed by the same habitually surly Mukhabarat employees who had kept an eye on clients before the war and who were now trying to adjust and function as normal waiters and desk clerks. The Hamra was a hangout for Western journalists, Iraqi businessmen, and off-duty Australian soldiers from the embassy next door. For me, the whole point of the Hamra was its swimming pool. The sensation of plunging headfirst from the heat and noise of the city into the silence of that chlorinated submarine world was the closest I came in Iraq to ecstasy.

One afternoon, I saw a familiar balding head moving behind the deck chairs on the far side of the pool. It was Kanan Makiya.

He had driven up from Kuwait in April. He was staying at the hotel while waiting for a civil affairs battalion to vacate the modernist house that his father had built on the Tigris, in what was now the Green Zone, and that had been seized by the regime in 1972. Makiya and I made plans to get together. It was strange to see him again and be reminded of our lofty conversations in Cambridge and London—years ago, it seemed.

He had thrown himself headlong into a new project. It was called the Memory Foundation, and it was to be a kind of Yad Vashem, a Holocaust memorial, as well as a museum and archive of the thirty-five years of Baath Party rule. With the help of a civil affairs captain, Makiya had uncovered enormous troves of party files, along with the private library of the party's founder, Michel Aflaq, beneath his tomb, which had been slated for demolition. As enterprising as the sheikh, but with different ideas, Makiya ultimately carted seven million pieces of paper over to his father's house, including the binders of rumors, meticulous records of the political orientation of every high school student in Iraq, and a top-secret archive labeled "Jews." He was desperately trying to keep the occupation authority from tearing down and destroying the thousands of grandiose tributes to Saddam and the Baath all over Baghdad and Iraq. His own grand ambition—he was busy negotiating with the occupation authority—was for his museum to be housed at the Victory Monument itself, the crossed swords of the parade ground, about which he had written an entire book more than a decade before.

On an infernally hot day, Makiya took me on a tour of the monument along with Mustafa al-Kadhimi, his friend from London, and two other returned exiles involved in the memory project. The parade ground itself was a road about a quarter mile long, and at the midpoint, from the reviewing stand, the pair of saber-wielding arms rising out of the pavement in the distance at either end simply looked like arches. Up close, the forearms cast from models of Saddam's own on a scale of forty-to-one were so massive that every vein and hair follicle was visible. Nets made of steel cables hung from the hilts of the swords, which had been forged from melted-down weapons and crossed at a point a hundred feet overhead against the staring sun. From the nets down below poured dozens of helmets of dead Iranian soldiers, all welded together like a cluster of grapes. The helmets had been carefully selected, many of them perforated with bullet holes. At the base of the monument, this text, from Saddam's speech announcing the project in 1985: "One of the worst things that can happen to anyone is to pass under a sword that is not his, and to be in a situation beyond his control. Using their swords, the Iraqis have written in history a record of heroism defending their land. I have slain the invaders and severed their heads, and I made out of their severed heads an arc of triumph, and here we are passing under the eye of God, who will protect the Iraqis from harm and who will not show any mercy to the evil ones." American soldiers had scrawled graffiti across some of the Iranian helmets embedded in the ground: "PV2 Evans KIA 25 May 03 We will rember 977 MP Co."

"I had seen pictures, I knew it was obscene," Makiya said, "but frankly I didn't know how obscene it is. The worst thing is the helmets of the dead that you step on. That is taking obscenity to new heights, if you would allow the contradiction."

"Saddam is claiming divine status," Hassan Mneimneh, a Lebanese friend of Makiya's from Cambridge, said. "The hand on the sword, it's a masturbation image." The rigid symmetry of the monument oppressed Mneimneh; the form was fascist, he said, and he hoped that one of the swords could be taken down or replaced with something else to destroy the majestic effect.

"It's the perfect place to remember the misery, in the same place where he felt his greatest power," said Ammar al-Shahbander, a young exile I'd met in London along with Mustafa. "To make one of the most sacred and prohibited places in Baghdad a public museum. You can't imagine how good it feels to stand on the same place he used to sit and watch the troops."

Makiya wanted to leave the monument as it was. In a white short-sleeve shirt and dark trousers, he was walking and talking at an excitable clip in the heat as the rest of us trailed behind. There could be a park for children here, a restaurant, school field trips. Turning the vast marbled rooms of the palace behind the viewing grandstand into a museum and library would cost thirty to fifty million dollars. One room could have Baath-era paintings and statuary, another the regime's instruments of torture. "They've got the mincing machine," he said. "Bremer told me. It's not an urban myth."

The project would create a different vision of Iraqi history: not a tribute to the great achievements of the Babylonian, Arab, and Islamic past, but a humbler reckoning with the recent decades in which Iraqis had done such terrible things to one another. "Ultimately and in the very long run," he said, "it's about reshaping Iraqis' perceptions of themselves in such a way as to create the basis for a tolerant civil society that is capable of adjusting to liberal democratic culture. The premise is that forgetting the past, or trying to sort of work with half-cobbled versions of the past, is actually only likely in the long run to engender variations of a repeat of it. We need to deal with it, face up to it frankly, so future generations can in a sense exorcise it from their system."

In addition to his memory project and his plans to take over the family house in the Green Zone, Makiya was hoping to receive a position on the preparatory committee for the new constitution. His return to Baghdad after thirty-five years had put him in the grip of new ideas, and he was literally breathless with nervous energy. An odd condition had set in somewhere inside his chest, a chronic spasm that forced hiccups upward in the middle of a sentence. I wondered if the tic might be part of a struggle, an unconscious one, to fend off a realization that he didn't want to confront. Makiya was consumed with thoughts about the past and the future; I wanted him to acknowledge that the present was a disaster. Phrases like "tolerant civil society" and "liberal democratic culture" did not inspire me in Baghdad in the summer of 2003. They sounded abstract and glib amid the daily grinding chaos of the city, and they made me angry at him and myself—for I had had my own illusions.

Makiya was clinging to the idea that if only the Americans had brought a few thousand armed Iraqi exiles in with them, as he, Chalabi, and others had advised, everything would have gone all right. Given how bitterly most Iraqi "internals," as they were called, spoke about the exiles who had ridden in on the back of American tanks and appropriated properties and jockeyed for political power, I found the argument unconvincing. It sounded like an excuse for all that he'd gotten wrong. Iraqis, it turned out, were not who he had thought they were. They were not Kanan Makiya.

The returned exiles in Baghdad lived in a world apart. They went to one another's dinner parties, they traveled easily in and out of the Green Zone, they had contacts in the occupation authority, they hatched political plans and business schemes and visionary ideas for transforming Iraqi society. The event that had crashed like a bomb in the lives of other Iraqis, shattering the state and leaving them stunned in the smoke and debris, was to the exiles the opportunity of a lifetime and the fulfillment of a dream.

A few of them took in the reality of Baghdad. One evening, I had dinner at an outdoor restaurant near the river in southern Baghdad with Mustafa al-Kadhimi and Ammar al-Shahbander, the two exiles I'd met at the London opposition conference in December. Mustafa was working on the new television and radio network that the occupation authority had set up; Ammar, a young freelance journalist who had come down through northern Iraq with Kurdish *peshmerga* forces during the war, was running the Baghdad office of a foundation whose projects included the restoration of the southern marshes that had been drained by Saddam. Both of them were also helping Makiya with the Memory Foundation. They had left safety and comfort and their wives in London and come back to Iraq with high hopes. But as soon as we sat down and ordered *masghouf*—fish from the Tigris grilled on a spit—they began to tell me what was on their minds.

"We were living in a dream," Ammar said. "Our idea of Iraq was the opposite of reality. We always thought Iraqis lack knowledge but they have the will—so if we provide them with the knowledge and expertise, they will catch up basically, because they have the will. But what we discovered actually was the other way around. The Iraqis have the knowledge. They know what is right, they know what is wrong. But you know what? They don't care. They are too tired, they are too occupied with putting themselves together. They don't have the will to do what is right. They know that they should park the car this way"—in an orderly fashion when they lined up for gas—"but who cares? They don't have a good enough reason to try."

Mustafa described the murders going on every night that no one talked about, most of them revenge killings of Baathists. He knew a popular Shiite cleric who was approached every day with requests for religious sanction to kill. Criminal gangs had begun to kidnap professional or wealthy Iraqis and hold them for ransom. "The thinking of the people really surprised me," Mustafa said. "I know it's bad, but I never never never thought it was this bad."

Ammar said, "They are so normalized to the Baath and the fear and the death and the terror that they can't see the advantages now. When you tell them they have such a great opportunity to express their opinion, they don't give a damn. It means nothing to them, they don't have anything to express, they have no opinion." A slightly malicious smile appeared on his face. "Have you seen *The Truman Show*? The Iraqis believe they are this guy and everything around them is a conspiracy. The only difference is they think they have discovered the conspiracy."

The fish was served, but I was the only one who began to eat.

The problem wasn't only the Iraqis here, Mustafa said—far from it. "When Bremer arrived," he said, "the electricity was eighteen hours a day. Then it started going down." The American contractors working on the media network were grossly overpaid and incompetent. The programming was a disaster and no one watched it; al-Jazeera and the Iranian antenna network al-Alam had already won the war of the airwaves. The Americans were afraid of failure, and as a result they had failed to achieve anything; many potential supporters had already turned against them. And then there was the behavior of the returning exiles. Mustafa once saw a man he'd known in London kicking a low-ranking official of the former regime. A woman friend of Mustafa's remarked, "I've now seen Uday again, this time in a democracy project." As for Chalabi, whom they both considered the likeliest man to lead Iraq in a democratic direction, Ammar said, "Back in London he thought because the Pentagon supported him he'd be brought in and put in power. We told him over and over, 'Don't count on it.' But he did. And this is the second mistake: He is surrounded either by idiots or by opportunists."

The conversation came around to Makiya. I mentioned that he had told me 95 percent of Iraqis were glad to have the Americans here.

"Kanan is living on another planet," Ammar said. "He doesn't have a clue. He drives to the Green Zone and back to the hotel." Ammar had tried to open Makiya's eyes by telling him that Baghdad's garbage collectors sang songs while riding *inside* the back of the garbage trucks. They loved garbage. Makiya didn't believe him.

We got in Mustafa's four-wheel drive and sped through the streets toward my hotel. There was a ten o'clock curfew and we didn't have much time; Mustafa was staying at his sister's house in a dangerous pro-Saddam neighborhood all the way out in western Baghdad. The streets were dark and nearly empty, with no police anywhere. Cars approached at top speed, as suspicious of us as we were of them. Mustafa's brother's BMW had been shot up a few nights before—targeted, he believed. "George, did you know Fedayeen Saddam yesterday said they would kill people who work with Americans?" Mustafa said. These were the paramilitary terrorists trained under the old regime. "I think about death every day."

The floodlit facade of my hotel came into view. I felt myself relax.

"I'm saying a sentence over and over to my wife," Ammar murmured in the backseat. "'Never afraid of Saddam—beaten by the mentality of the Iraqi people.'"

6

THE PALACE

THE COALITION PROVISIONAL AUTHORITY was headquartered about a mile beyond the Assassins' Gate, down a road of eucalyptus trees and bombed state buildings and concrete barriers. The Republican Palace, protected by a high iron gate and sandbagged machine-gun positions, was a sprawling two-story office building done in the Babylonian-fascist style favored by Saddam, with Art Deco eagles spanning the doorways. Evenly spaced along the top of the facade were four identical twenty-foot gray busts of Saddam himself, staring straight ahead, his eyes framed by an imperial helmet. Beneath these Ozymandian tributes to the deposed leader, twelve hundred officials of the CPA went about the business of running the country.

Getting in to see one of them, a senior adviser to Bremer acknowledged, was "like a jailbreak in reverse." That was in the first months of the occupation, when it was still possible for my driver to clear security at the Assassins' Gate after searches of the two of us and the car, navigate the barriers on the road down to the palace, obey the signs warning him not to drive too fast or too slow or under any circumstances to stop, then park in the big dirt lot full of gleaming white SUVs that bore no relation to the vehicular character of Baghdad. I crossed the road and presented myself for another search and ID check to the soldiers under the massive hedge that grew beside the iron gate. But I wasn't in yet: I still had to locate my contact in the palace. My satellite phone could be relied on to work pretty well outdoors, but the cellular network that MCI had set up for the occupation in Baghdad was spotty, and I usually got a recorded voice telling me that the number was not in service at this time. Because appointments were so hard to make and hard to get, I dialed the number over and over; in the end, more often than not, I got through. After ten or fifteen minutes—which I spent watching dozens of people with more privileged status walk or drive into the palace complex with just the flash of an ID—my escort emerged from one of the doorways under the Art Deco eagle and walked past the desiccated fountain and the garden of eucalyptus and date palms to greet me and usher me into the mysteries of the occupation.

This was the drill at the beginning; it now seems shockingly porous. Over the next year the rules kept tightening, until I couldn't get within a mile of the palace without an escort who had the highest security clearance.

The jailbreak analogy worked both ways: For officials to leave the Green Zone required a two-vehicle military escort, which had to be arranged forty-eight hours in advance, assuming the soldiers and Humvees were available. In order to get their jobs done, some officials broke the rules and went in ordinary cars with no security out into the "Red Zone," that is to say, Iraq. Others—and over time their numbers increased—hardly ever ventured out. I met a British coalition official working on human rights who had left the Green Zone three times in five weeks. Though it was in the geographical heart of Baghdad, the CPA sat in deep isolation.

Hume Horan, an Arabist and retired ambassador whom Bremer had brought back into service "to be my pet bedouin" at the CPA, described what it was like to leave the Green Zone after long confinement. "It's an epistemological problem: What's going on out there?" he said. "You sniff, and then once you're out you overanalyze everything. It's like being in one of those sensory deprivation suits, one of those black suits, and then you're dropped in the water to see what you can feel."

Horan and I were sitting, literally, in a hall of mirrors, on gilt-trimmed green sofas, in a marbled alcove off the main rotunda of the palace. (A brigade commander once told me that one of the worst things about the Baathists was their taste in interior decorating. The Republican Palace, one of the dozens of presidential palaces that Saddam seldom used, was furnished like the others in the incredibly vulgar manner of an ersatz Versailles.) While Horan and I spoke, the little MCI cell phone on the sofa beside him kept ringing. On the other end was an Iraqi who had an appointment with Horan and was having trouble finding his way into the palace. In a series of increasingly agitated calls, Horan tried to determine the man's location and direct him to the main gate. Finally, Horan's secretary came over to report that the man's current position was next to a high black wall somewhere with no soldiers around. "I think he should stand down for today," Horan told his secretary. I had gotten in, but this resident of Baghdad and citizen of Iraq, who had probably gone to great lengths to secure the appointment, lacked the wherewithal—the language skills, or the confidence to approach heavily armed Americans for directions. Perhaps he returned another day and succeeded, or perhaps this became one of those failed connections in the early days of the occupation, when many Iraqis were still trying to meet the foreigners who were now governing their country, for which there would not be a second chance. I watched Horan's face—he was an elderly blue-eyed man with liver spots and a shock of gray hair, wearing sandals and short blue socks that revealed a pale stripe of ankle below his slightly tattered khaki cuffs—when he declared that the visitor should go home. His expression closed up with a sort of grim disappointment. I remember thinking that it seemed a bad omen.

The size of the rooms matched the palace's original purpose of leader worship rather than serious administration. Off the rotunda there was a room with a soaring octagonal dome depicting horses rising upward into a trompe l'oeil sky, and on opposite walls murals in the shape of altarpieces, one showing Scud missiles taking off into the sky, the other the al-Aqsa mosque in a Jerusalem without Jews; the room had been turned into a chapel. Around the corner there was an even vaster hall, on the proportions of a basketball arena, where the coalition's hundreds of officials took their meals cafeteria-style, with replicas of the Ashurbanipal friezes over the dining tables. The offices of Governance and Strategic Communications, or Stratcomm, were located in grand high-ceilinged meeting rooms, with officials seated at desks half hidden by partitions spread out across an immense floor space. As the CPA grew, the palace's broad hallways were divided by makeshift walls to create more offices.

There were a number of British officials in the palace, a few from other countries in the coalition, the Iraqi-Americans organized by the Pentagon just before the war, a security detail of Nepalese Gurkhas, and for a while a unit of Italian carabinieri around the main gate, looking far more chic than their counterparts from other countries in tight black T-shirts, sunglasses, and leather gloves. But no visitor to the palace could have any doubt about which country was in charge of Iraq. The composition was overwhelmingly American: half civilian, half military, with men and women from the Departments of State, Treasury, Defense, and other agencies, wearing casual office clothes—khaki pants and blue shirts, it always seemed—mixed with young soldiers in desert camouflage, emptied M-16s slung over their shoulders. There were bomb shelters hard by workout rooms. The intimate mingling of bureaucracy and war made for a strange sight. One CPA official described the palace as being full of "people who were typical pasty-faced bureaucrats, overweight middle-aged people, midlevel paper pushers, but all wearing body armor, helmets. It's like a play: There's this weird alter-world that you're in, where if they go out on a routine visit they've got to don body armor and face the prospect of being wiped off the face of the earth."

Amid the grotesque faux-baroque furnishings, the palace was a hive of purposeful activity. The scale of the place so dwarfed its human inhabitants that it was impossible not to think in insect metaphors. The atmosphere, in Horan's words, was "very heavily operational." Americans were constantly typing away at computers or hurrying to and fro across marble floors or taking quick breaks under the great granite columns, working late into the night seven days a week with a kind of fresh optimistic energy that could not have been in sharper contrast to the exhausted country outside the security perimeter into which they'd been air-dropped. Most of them seemed to be Republicans, and more than a few were party loyalists who had come to Iraq as political appointees on ninety-day tours. They were astonishingly young. Many had never worked abroad, few knew anything about the Middle East, and that first summer only three or four of the Americans spoke Arabic. Some were simply unqualified for their responsibilities. A twenty-five-year-old oversaw the creation of the Baghdad stock market, and another twenty-five-year-old, from the Office of Special Plans, helped write the interim constitution while filling out his law school application.

But they believed in what they were trying to do, which was rebuild Iraq as a democracy. They were trying to do it under fire, in a badly fractured country, with a governing authority that more and more Iraqis saw as illegitimate. A senior administration official said, "We sent an inexperienced, youthful, full-of-zest, full-of-courage team to do what seasoned professionals would have found extremely challenging, if not impossible. Instead we sent a third team, or a fourth team, or a fifth team." One of the few "seasoned professionals" in the CPA admitted, "None of us knew what we were doing at some level. We didn't have good enough information." Most of them didn't even know what they didn't know. They were always stretched thin, and there were never enough of them, nor enough vehicles and phones and bodyguards and money and time. Trips out of the Green Zone were constantly canceled for lack of escorts. In the summer of 2003 the CPA was less than 50 percent staffed, and it never rose above 70 percent; turnover was extremely fast, and hard-won knowledge was short-lived.

In late July, I met Meghan O'Sullivan at the palace. She had survived an unhappy experience under Jay Garner and become one of Paul Bremer's key advisers on political matters. She was wearing jeans and a lime-green top under a long-sleeve shirt; her pale, thin face was lightly made up, her auburn hair pulled back, her toenails painted. I had the sense that keeping up appearances was part of maintaining morale. She was working eighteen hours a day, with no days off; she usually got to bed around one a.m., and the phone started ringing at six. "There is very little to do for pleasure here," she said. Some of her colleagues who had come in with Garner were already gone and others were finishing up their tours, but O'Sullivan had signed on for the duration, though it meant turning down a position at the NSC. She wanted the whole picture, she said, and she could make a greater difference in Baghdad than in Washington.

We sat in the echoing emptiness of the chapel, and with a faintly amused smile she told me about her dreams. In one, the palace was filling up with smoke, there was shooting, she couldn't find the way out, and she calmly told herself: All right, this *is* dangerous, I *could* get killed. In another, a Black Hawk helicopter dropped her in the middle of the desert and took off, leaving her alone. She woke up from that dream yelling. "Then I tried to remember where I was," she said. "I was in the middle of the desert—alone." She was living on an upper floor of the Rashid Hotel, at the edge of the Green Zone. Although the room was more comfortable than a trailer, she was uneasy staying there: The CPA had intelligence that the Rashid was a security risk. Early one morning a few months later, in October, while Paul Wolfowitz was staying at the Rashid, the hotel was hit by half a dozen rockets. O'Sullivan's door was sealed shut by the force and heat of the blast, and the room began to fill with smoke as in her dream; when the noises of flight and rescue out in the hall died down and no one came to save her, she climbed out of her window ten floors up onto a narrow concrete overhang, inched her way across to the next window, which happened to be open, and saved herself. By 8:30 in the morning she was at her desk, working on requests from Bremer in Washington.

O'Sullivan was completely absorbed in the CPA's high-level policy work, and yet a part of her mind remained open to the skepticism that would press on any thoughtful person. At the outset, Iraqis had approached her in the street to thank her for their liberation. She found—it was hard to acknowledge—that they wanted to be given instructions, and Garner's team had made the enormous mistake of trying not to act like rulers. The looting and power vacuum of the early days continued to undermine the work of the occupation, from the smallest logistical detail to the great question of whether Iraqis would support the American project. Was America capable of nation building on this scale? Or should the Iraqis be the ones in charge? Yet the embryonic Iraqi institutions that the CPA was trying to set up were always on the verge of collapse.

ON THE DAY THAT SAIGON FELL to North Vietnamese troops in 1975, the British writer James Fenton found a framed quotation on a wall of the abandoned and looted American embassy: "Better to let them do it imperfectly than to do it perfectly yourself, for it is their country, their way, and your time is short." The words were from T. E. Lawrence.

The failure of the first weeks, and the replacement of Garner with Bremer, produced a new vision of the American role in Iraq. The Pentagon had prevented a serious strategic plan from ever being written. Now, the CPA under Bremer began to plan in earnest, essentially forcing the White House and Pentagon to go along with initiatives taken in Baghdad. The CPA was going to fill in all the blanks left empty back in Washington by the war's visionaries who had imagined that freedom and democracy would appear spontaneously in Iraq. The new plans included goals and timetables for the training of Iraqi security forces, the writing of a constitution, the creation of new government structures, economic reform, legal reform, education reform: nothing short of an overhaul of Iraqi society from top to bottom, culminating in the return of sovereignty at an indeterminate date.

Brad Swanson, an investment banker who arrived in Baghdad some months later to work in the CPA on economic development, described the reversal this way: "First there was the arrogance phase, and then there was the hubris phase. The arrogance phase was going in undermanned, underplanned, underresourced, skim off the top layer of leadership, take control of a functioning state, and be out by six weeks and get the oil funds to pay for it. We all know for a variety of reasons that didn't work. So then you switch over to the hubris phase: We've been slapped in the face, this is really much more serious than we thought, much more long-term, much more dangerous, much more costly. Therefore we'll attack it with everything we have, we'll throw the many billion dollars at it, and to make Iraq safe for the future we have to do a root-and-branch transformation of the country in our own image." The two approaches seemed like opposite extremes, Swanson added, but they had this in common: "They're very conceptual, ideological. They're not pragmatic responses to a detailed understanding of facts on the ground."

With such an ambitious undertaking, the CPA faced, and in some ways didn't face, a paradox that was unavoidable. The Americans were trying to rebuild Iraq in a way that allowed Iraqis, for the first time in their history, to take control of their own destiny. But if the power, the money, the guns, and the ideas remained with the Americans, how would all the plans ever lead to Iraqi control?

On the second floor of the palace, where the senior advisers to the ministries had their offices, Drew Erdmann was trying to negotiate the paradox every day, and the effort was wearing him down. People he hardly knew were telling him, "You look beat." His temper was worse than it had ever been in his life.

"The thing that I am constantly struggling against," he said, "and this is the American part of you, whether it's a national attribute I don't know—you just want to get things done. But of course you can't just keep doing that, you can't just keep doing it for these people. And you've got to let them fail sometimes. And you know it's going to happen." He gave me an example: At a recent meeting on budgets, one university president had requested a doubling of his faculty over the next six months. "In a situation where the country just went through this. What do you think? I mean, why even . . . you know, come on. It defies . . . what planet are these people on? It reaches the level of literally defying common sense. It doesn't pass anyone's laugh test anywhere in the world. But then you have to work through it." With so many highly educated and technically skilled people in Iraq, Erdmann had concluded that the administrative incompetence must be a product of "the absolutely pernicious effects of living in this police state that has beaten people down so much."

Erdmann decided from the start to put as much authority as possible in Iraqi hands. In May, after he convinced all the university presidents appointed under Saddam to resign, Erdmann announced that their replacements would be chosen in open elections by the faculties. He came to this decision only after intense debate within the CPA, his team of mostly Iraqis, and himself. These would be among the very first votes in Iraq, and some in Washington and Baghdad feared that Baathists or religious extremists might be able to hijack any elections. But Erdmann concluded that entrusting the Iraqi faculties themselves, though not without risk, was the best option available. With communications nearly impossible in large parts of the country, the CPA had little idea who the best candidates might be. That was the practical reason. The principled reason was to get Iraqis involved quickly, to give them the feeling that a new era had indeed begun. If the newly arrived administrator vetoed the idea, Erdmann had made up his mind that he would have to resign, since his credibility with the Iraqi educators would be gone at the start. But with Bremer's backing, the votes went forward in mid-May.

On May 17, seven hundred faculty members packed the sweltering theater of Baghdad University, along with al-Jazeera, CNN, and other media. Sweating in his poplin suit, Erdmann stood up to make a few opening remarks. "It's time to mark a fundamental change and a liberation of the academic establishment from the old order," he said. "And part of that is new leadership. There was a regime change, and this is a tremendous opportunity to bring in a new era." Then he stepped aside, to let the Iraqis run the process of nominating, voting, and counting ballots. The winner was a biochemist, Dr. Sami Mudhafar, respected for his integrity under Saddam.

At the College of Dentistry, students insisted on attending the vote. Erdmann resisted—all sorts of groups wanted to pack the halls and influence the outcome—and then agreed to bring one student in as his guest. The election was by secret ballot, and as the votes for the two front-running candidates were tallied on the blackboard of the stuffy lecture room, the student at Erdmann's side began to cry. He had never seen anything like it. "This is an answer to my prayers," he said. "We prayed for this, to see this."

Erdmann had gambled, and the gamble paid off. There was a safety net—if a college made a selection the CPA deeply disapproved, the nominee would have been struck down—but allowing a free choice and then interfering might well have been worse than never going down the road at all (this happened early in the occupation, when Marine commanders in Najaf organized an election for provincial government, only to have the CPA in Baghdad call it off at the last minute, prompting the outraged people of Najaf to question the Americans' true commitment to democracy). The trade-off between control and legitimacy was the recurring dilemma of every CPA decision, and there were dozens made every day by fallible human beings, and each one was going to push the project in one direction or another. Iraq was still fluid, Erdmann said, still plastic and malleable, but it would harden soon. The psychological demands of the occupation were daunting. "It comes down to judgment," he said. "Some people can navigate it, some people can't. Some people can make a mistake and recalibrate, others can't. On both sides. So much of this is up to the wisdom of people, their prudence, their judgment."

THE LEISURE READING of Americans in Iraq tended toward unhappy analogies—guerrilla wars and botched peaces. Colonel William Grimsley, an infantry brigade commander, was reading *A Savage War of Peace*, Alistair Horne's study of the French-Algerian conflict: "Lots of similarities to this place." In the tent of Jordan Becker, a twenty-four-year-old lieutenant up in Kirkuk, there was a shelf with several books on Kurdish and Iraqi history, a book about Algeria's recent civil war, and *Four Hours in My Lai*. Drew Erdmann was bogged down in David Fromkin's *A Peace to End All Peace: The Fall of the Ottoman Empire and the Creation of the Modern Middle East*, as well as John Maynard Keynes's account of the 1919 Paris peace conference. No one at the CPA had much time to read, though, or to think.

On the first floor of the palace, off the rotunda, past the metal detector and the bodyguards, Paul Bremer's long, high-ceilinged office was lined with bookshelves that were nearly bare when I visited. Rudolph Giuliani's *Leadership* stood on one shelf, and a book about the management of financial crises on another, near a box of raisin bran. On Bremer's desk, next to a wood carving that read "Success Has a Thousand Fathers," were several marked-up reports about postwar

Iraq, and on the coffee table lay a pile of maps: Iraq's power grid, administrative districts, railroad lines. At sixty-one, Bremer had the thick hair, boyish eyes, and willful jaw of a Kennedy. Like his reading, he came across as operational, a disciplined man with an even temperature.

He had served as a State Department counterterrorism official and ambassador to Holland, then became the managing director of Henry Kissinger's consulting firm. He was also "a bedrock Republican," Bremer told me, with strongly conservative values. This background made for an interesting mix that eluded the simple Washington categories of neoconservatives and realists, Defense and State. He was acceptable to both departments, but he would report to the secretary of defense, and at the start he would carry out policies that had originated in the Pentagon. Bremer was driven and hard charging, with no shortage of self-confidence. Though he admitted privately before leaving for Baghdad that he had questions about the wisdom of the war, he would approach the running of Iraq like a demanding corporate executive, insisting on fast and quantifiable results from his staff, hating surprises and setbacks, imagining that he could prevail over adversity on the strength of his character. Those who worked for him described Bremer as a ferocious boss—one of them spoke of being "Bremerized" in meetings—and they tried hard to make him happy even when the facts didn't warrant it.

He arrived on May 12 knowing almost nothing about Iraq, and before he had been in Baghdad four days Bremer made three momentous decisions: He dissolved the Iraqi army, he fired high-ranking Baathists from the civil service, and he stopped the formation of an interim government. A more cautious viceroy would have gauged the lay of the land and spoken with a range of Iraqis before taking such far-reaching steps. Bremer arrived amid general collapse, and his first moves left no doubt that he was now in charge. But his decisions changed or reversed the hastily drawn policies approved by the president a week before the war, as well as the ones that Jay Garner had been improvising on the ground. When Garner objected to the depth of debaathification, Bremer refused to amend the policy. "Look, I have my instructions," he said. The decisions on the Baath Party and the army reflected views held by the administration's neoconservatives (as well as Chalabi), while the indefinite postponement of an interim government was anathema to them. So the CPA was launched with a hodgepodge of improvised moves that reflected no one agency's strategy, no considered strategy at all other than a belated assertion of American control. People who knew him said that Bremer would never have accepted this nearly impossible job if he hadn't secured wide latitude to carry it out as he saw fit. In this, as in everything else, he was the opposite of his predecessor.

Jay Garner, who had surrendered the reins to Bremer, later told me that he woke up on the morning of Saturday, May 17, to find "three or four hundred thousand enemies and no Iraqi face on the government."

Garner's approach had been to slice off as little of the old regime as possible, removing a handful of senior Baathists at the top and trying to work with the rest. The idea, Barbara Bodine said, was to accept anyone who was competent and not tainted by crime or corruption. This had led to some embarrassments, as when a Baathist chosen to run the Ministry of Health had to be removed when doctors staged protests and the minister refused to renounce the party. But the Americans were treading with care, until Bremer's Debaathification Order on May 16 barred from government service the entire top four layers of the party, down to *firqa* or divisional level, meaning those in charge of up to fifty lower-ranking members—regardless of whether they were implicated in actual crimes. At least thirty-five thousand mostly Sunni employees of the bureaucracy, including thousands of schoolteachers and midlevel functionaries, lost their jobs overnight. And American officials who had begun establishing relations with Iraqis in the ministries and other offices were suddenly partnerless. The order allowed Iraqis to appeal and, in principle, regain their jobs, but the CPA was unequipped to hear the cases fast enough to prevent thousands of people from hanging in limbo with no position or pay.

"Bremer likes to say, and I think he's right, that it was the most popular decision he ever made," one of Bremer's top advisers told me. "But the people it was popular with were already on our side. I think that base was pretty solid. If you want to come in and restore things, you want to come in with malice toward none and charity toward all—you want to take a Lincolnian approach. You don't want to take a carpetbagger approach. People in Falluja told me, 'We were happy when you threw out Saddam. It's what you did after you threw out Saddam that's pissed us off.' Our whole approach was wrong."

The alternative would have been to try those Baathists accused of crimes, vet out the corrupt and incompetent on a case-by-case basis, retain the rest, and organize a nationwide truth-and-reconciliation commission along the lines of the South African experience. But debaathification had been a consistent theme of the Iraqi exile groups and their allies in the Pentagon. The obvious precedent was denazification in Germany. Yet not even the Report on the Transition to Democracy in Iraq suggested anything as deep as Bremer's order; Kanan Makiya had primarily focused on the need to cleanse Iraqi society of Baathist ideology, which would be a project of many years. Douglas Feith told me that the policy of cutting down four levels in the party hierarchy originated in the Pentagon. Some observers also saw the hand of Ahmad Chalabi, who soon gained control of the Debaathification Commission and used it to squeeze his political enemies.

In Kirkuk, in northern Iraq, I met a leather-faced father of nine with Coke-bottle glasses named Othman Ali Sadiq. He had worked as a technical supervisor for fire and safety at the oil company, until Bremer's order left him unemployed. Sadiq's twenty-eight years at the company were four fewer than his service to the Baath Party, in which he rose to a level that made him responsible for keeping tabs on two hundred families. "Every country has its system," he said. "In Iraq it was the Baath Party." He described his party job as a kind of civic duty, like serving on the board of aldermen. He got nothing for his pains except fired, he said. He never wrote a bad report on anyone; he never saw evidence of Baathist crimes. "What I heard is these mass graves are thousands of years old." His only way to feed his family now was to drive a taxi. If he were younger, he implied, he would pick up a gun and fight the occupation. No one at his level of the party had clean hands; morally, the Debaathification Order seemed unassailable. Such things were clearer before the insurgency ignited and Bremer's critics began to point to the May 16 order as an aggravating factor. It was the policy of an occupier that didn't think it needed to worry about making enemies. Drew Erdmann liked to say that American foreign policy at its best went by the dictum that what is right is also what is wise. In occupied Iraq, this became harder and harder to do.

For Erdmann, who had to fire seventeen hundred Baathist university professors and staff, the German analogy was apt. He bristled at any notion that academic freedom might be at issue. "In June 1945 you're not going to have a discussion about the legitimacy of the Nazi ideology and the legitimacy of the Nazi Party and you're sitting in Germany," he said. "It's not academic! Hello? It's only a few months ago, the people are still living next door, they're still working next door, they're still on campus, they're still around, they're still threatening."

Erdmann explained his support for debaathification by telling me about the Saddam bonus. On the scale of the dictator's crimes, the Saddam bonus was a minor atrocity. Under Iraq's college admissions system, students were ranked by test scores, and with thousands applying for a limited number of openings, a few points made a great difference. The Saddam bonus awarded five extra points to high school boys who married widows of the Iran-Iraq War, women often twice their age. "This is just the beginning of this fucked-up example," Erdmann said. The last Baathist minister of higher education under Saddam had withdrawn the points of certain applicants after determining that the marriages were fraudulent. "These guys came to me so they could get back their bonus points," Erdmann marveled. "Me, the American coalition guy! They think I'm going to give them the fricking Saddam bonus points for a fake marriage? To war widows? This is my example of how it penetrated in such a twisted way, and you multiply this by how many times to understand how deep this goes and how dark and twisted it is."

The dissolution of the army was harder to justify even at the time, and it came to be seen as one of the disasters of the war. With a stroke of the pen, Bremer put several hundred thousand armed Iraqis on the street with no job and no salary. It could have occurred only to an occupying power that was sure its enemy was beaten. The order was immediately unpopular with officers of the American military, who had no trouble grasping the likely strategic consequences in a country where unemployment was somewhere over 50 percent.

Douglas Feith and others would later say that the Iraqi army had already demobilized itself with the arrival of the invasion forces, when soldiers went home rather than putting up a fight. The dissolution order simply made it official. Walter Slocombe, a rare senior Democrat in the CPA, who had been Clinton's Feith and whom Feith asked to rebuild the Iraqi military after the war, told me, "There wasn't any army left. The assumption we had, which was that we were going to have substantial intact units, was wrong. What are we going to do? There was nothing to decide." It would have been impossible as well as stupid to summon the units back to duty, Slocombe said. The mostly Shiite conscripts were happy to be home and couldn't have been called back for love or money; and an Iraqi army composed of the remnant of a mostly Sunni officer corps would have driven the majority of Iraqis into opposition.

In the first two weeks of May, Colonel Paul Hughes, Garner's planning chief, was meeting with a group of eight Iraqi generals and colonels to organize the distribution to ordinary soldiers of twenty-dollar salary payments. Hughes and the Iraqi officers met at the Republican Guard officers club, an elegant plate-glass structure that had been partially looted. The Iraqis, remnants of a defeated army, wore coats and ties and looked anxious. "They knew I had them by the balls," Hughes said. "I told them that the future of Iraq belonged to their children. It was evident to me they as officers had no loyalty to Saddam Hussein, otherwise they wouldn't be talking to me. I said, 'You guys had best not be Baathists, because if you guys are Baathists I'm gonna come get you.'" The Iraqis wanted to cooperate, and after four meetings they had collected the names of one hundred thousand soldiers. Hughes felt a level of trust in American goodwill. He began the process of securing the money at the CPA. No one in Washington seemed to care one way or the other.

"Anyone who's done postconflict work says do not get rid of the military," Hughes told me. "You've got to control them—if you don't control them, you don't know what they're going to do. As long as we paid them twenty dollars, they were going to dance a jig for us."

In mid-May, Hughes went home on a brief leave for his daughter's college graduation. The day before returning to Iraq, he turned on the TV and heard the news that the Iraqi army had been abolished, with no provision for soldiers to be paid. Back at the Republican Palace, three officers from the group that he'd been meeting with at the officers club came to see him. Hughes went down to meet them in the rotunda. "I couldn't look them in the face. I was completely discredited in their eyes." Hughes assured them that he would somehow find a way to cover the salaries. The Iraqis thanked him. "They were complete gentlemen. That was the thing that just broke my heart, that I had built trust with these guys and people had taken steps to break it."

To Hughes, the dissolution of the Iraqi army was a decisive turn in the American presence in Iraq. "From the Iraqi viewpoint, that simple action took away the one symbol of sovereignty the Iraqi people still had," he said. "That's when we crossed the line. We stopped being liberators and became occupiers." A fatal riot of cashiered soldiers at the Assassins' Gate forced the CPA to begin paying off the men it had just fired.

The two orders had their origins in the Pentagon, and, probably, the vice president's office. Bremer's decision to break up the Iraqi leadership group that Garner had been organizing and to amass much more authority under himself and the CPA was his own initiative. After the occupation went bad, neoconservatives in and out of the administration would accuse Bremer of being responsible. If their idea of installing the exiles under Chalabi in power early on had been followed, they argued, America would not have become an unwanted occupier. The most basic of this argument's many flaws is that everything Bremer did was approved by Rumsfeld, who had laid claim to the postwar in Iraq. A senior official involved in Iraq policy said, "It is absolutely ludicrous for someone in Rumsfeld's office to say, 'Oh, well, gee, if only we'd been in charge.' They were in charge. That's the other side of the coin. Bremer increasingly turned himself into a viceroy answerable only to God, and the control freak let him get away with it. It's stunning."

By midsummer, some of Bremer's aides were privately acknowledging that the early orders had been ill considered. "He was a very dynamic person, very capable guy, very sincere," a top adviser said. "But he's a man in a hurry, and he made decisions quickly." The adviser saw in some of those decisions the origins of the insurgency: "Over time I think we all came to believe that we were creating enemies in Iraq. My personal belief is that the insurrection in Iraq is a result of those initial policy mistakes—failure to stop the looting, failure to establish firm control right away, and the initial decisions which were made when Bremer came in that pissed off Iraqis." Bremer himself never admitted any such thing. He struck visitors from Washington that first summer as absolutely sure of himself, too sure—depending largely on speculation because he didn't know the country, surrounded by aides no better informed than he, imagining Iraq as postwar Germany or postcommunist Europe, charging ahead with plans to apply economic shock therapy and privatize state industries despite the soaring unemployment, carrying out the ideological vision as if only will and determination were what mattered. By the end of the CPA's tenure, an Iraqi politician who knew Bremer said that he had begun to understand his early mistakes. Over time, his decisions became less ideological, more practically attuned to the reality in which he found himself. He put aside the privatization plans, he partly reversed debaathification. If he had waited a few months, Bremer might not have made the fateful choices of his first days in Baghdad.

IRAQ WAS A NONSTOP CRISIS, and the CPA existed in a temporal as well as spatial bubble; any attention to a past or future beyond thirty days was a luxury. When I went to see him in mid-August 2003, Bremer was completely immersed in the details of running the country. A question I asked about the historical precedents for his position led him almost directly to the urgent need for a 20-kilowatt generator at the oil refinery in Basra. That week riots had broken out in Basra over long fuel lines directly related to the electricity shortage, which was reaching a critical state. Bremer, wearing a white shirt with rolled-up sleeves, khakis, and combat boots, leaned over the coffee table where we sat and spread out his map of the electrical grid to show me why the existing system was in such disrepair and demand still exceeded supply. The CPA now had a plan for increasing megawattage, he said; unfortunately, it would cost billions of dollars. Meanwhile, Iraqis were growing unhappier and blaming it on the Americans.

Bremer spoke directly to Iraqis every week in television and radio addresses, as well as in meetings with dignitaries around the country. He was personally popular, especially with women, and he enjoyed the approval of twice as many Baghdadis as disapproved, according to a Gallup poll (higher than the CPA's ratings, and far beyond those of President Bush, who was not regarded favorably in the capital). His approach to the awesome task of leading a foreign country, in which Americans were still at war, through a political, social, and economic revolution was largely technical. Under pressure or criticism, he resorted to figures. Through the harsh summer, Bremer explained over and over that the power outages came from a lack of capacity in the system, aggravated by looting, sabotage, and the collapse of civil administration. Somehow, the message never got through. He reminded Iraqis just as often that they now had their freedom. This, too, sometimes failed to sink in.

"You have to understand the psychological situation that Iraqis are in," he said when I asked why they appeared to appreciate so little of what the CPA claimed to have achieved in its first months. "They went from this very dark room to the bright light in three weeks. It's like somebody just threw a switch. And so this is pretty jarring psychologically anyway. And your mentality, if you're an Iraqi, still is: It's the government that fixes things. And here comes a government that can throw out our much-vaunted army in three weeks, so why can't they fix the electricity in three weeks?" The failure to communicate, Bremer pointed out, "isn't a technical problem of tuning a television to get the right channel. It's psychological and intellectual."

He stood up, went over to his desk, and brought back some of the studies of postwar reconstruction that he was reading when he had time. "What I tried to do was study the relevant sort of reconstruction examples, of which there are four or five. There's Japan and Germany after the war. There's Bosnia, Kosovo. To some extent Afghanistan. And of those, the ones that are probably most relevant are Germany and Japan because they involved a war followed by a physical military occupation of those countries."

He opened a heavily underlined pamphlet written by a group of British experts and began to read aloud. "'In the immediate postwar period, security and the rule of law are essential.' Okay, well, that's true." Bremer had no interest in looking back at the looting and the failures of postwar planning. "I frankly don't have time to go back and reread what we knew and didn't know," he said. "I've got to worry about tomorrow. There'll be some great PhD theses that can be written on the subject." He read aloud again: "'Security means civilian policing, ability to arrest, detain, and try offenders. Minimize arrogance.'" He laughed. "Here's vetting—decontamination and debaathification. 'One of the lessons from particularly Germany was, typically, a deep process of vetting out occurs first and is best performed with speed.' Which is exactly what we did. We took it down and then we can build it back up, and of course we're turning it over to the Iraqis."

Bremer tossed the pamphlet on the coffee table. He was growing restless; he had things to do. I thanked him and said goodbye. There had been no small talk whatsoever, no curiosity about my own observations, and (this was quite striking in Iraq) no tea or other refreshment brought in. He made no effort to charm, and there was little evidence of wit. Bremer was already back at his desk by the time I was escorted out of the office.

THE PROBLEMS OF PSYCHOLOGY and intellect cut both ways. Almost all of Bremer's confidants were Americans. The Arabic-speaking ambassadors with years of experience in the Middle East had less access to the administrator and less work to do than his small coterie of trusted aides from Washington. An Iraqi who was close to the CPA told me that, in general, the less one knew about Iraq, the more influence one had.

When Bremer left the palace, it was necessarily under heavy security. One searing day, I joined his press pool and followed the administrator by Chinook helicopter as he hopscotched across the scorched southern desert. The first stop was a maternity hospital in the town of Diwaniya. Bremer, who forced himself to endure a suit and tie at all public appearances throughout the summer months, was received by local dignitaries in kaffiyehs and mustaches. He told them, "We of the coalition are glad that we were able to provide you with your freedom from the dictatorship of Saddam Hussein. You now have that freedom and you now have a better hope for the future." He went on, "All of Iraq's two hundred and forty hospitals are now operating. Ninety percent of the health clinics in the country are now working. The budget for the second half of this year is an increase of three thousand percent in health-care spending in Iraq. In May, five hundred tons of drugs were shipped in. Last month we shipped thirty-five hundred tons—a seven hundred percent increase in shipments in three months."

The dignitaries listened and applauded. In turn, they presented Bremer with lengthy supplications. Then he paid a visit to the wards upstairs.

Bremer traveled with a sizable contingent of aides and civilian bodyguards with MP-5 automatic weapons and wraparound sunglasses; along with the journalists in tow, this phalanx swept down the second-floor hallway past startled doctors and into rooms where even more startled mothers and infants lay in beds. His aides gave him stuffed animals to present to the patients. In one room, a withered and skeletal premature baby lay in its mother's arms. On a nearby bed, a child of about three had its head lolling back against its mother's body, mouth open. This was sickness, maybe even the approach of death, not childbirth. The smile died on Bremer's face as he realized where he was. "I don't like seeing this at all," he said, and asked the photographer to stop taking pictures.

Disturbed, I broke away from the group and went back downstairs. I fell into conversation with a couple of young doctors. They said that the electricity was on only because we were here—it had been off all week. The interruptions to power had doubled infant mortality here: Without proper incubation, the rate was now seven to ten deaths per day. The hospital had several broken generators. A Marine reservist had told me that with twenty thousand dollars in repairs the generators could provide the hospital all the power it needed for twenty-four-hour service. The doctors said that the generators could cut the infant mortality rate at least in half.

One of Bremer's press aides, Chris Harvin, gravitated toward us. "Are you happy with Saddam gone?" he asked the young doctors, pushing the conversation back on message. "Things are better now?"

"Yes," Dr. Kassim al-Janaby said, mustering a smile. "Yes."

"What's the best thing about Saddam being gone?"

"I can't understand your question," said Dr. Mohamed Jasim. Harvin had to repeat it three times. "Only one, I think only one," Dr. Jasim said. "Only the free talking. Only only only. But no doing. No doing."

"Do you think over time it gets much better?"

"Yes, we are thinking the next time it gets better."

"Patience? Yeah?"

"We need continuous electricity," Dr. Janaby said flatly. "Security in our city also is not until now. That's it. Also the salary."

Harvin, a veteran of the Bush 2000 primary campaign in South Carolina, which had sought to make hash of the reputation of John McCain, was undeterred by the young doctors in Diwaniya. "But don't you think with time it will get better? What do you think? What can we do?"

"Security," one of them said.

"Americans? Iraqis? Both working together?"

"Yes."

"So . . . the economy will stabilize the looting?"

THE CPA'S GOOD NEWS didn't always bear scrutiny. Again and again, Iraqis were told that the electricity output would soon be increased. But it didn't reach even prewar levels until a year after the Americans arrived, and meanwhile the hardships intensified. Naturally, this inclined the Iraqis to greater skepticism about their occupiers. The health figures that Bremer cited at the hospital in Diwaniya were somewhat undercut by a chance conversation I had the next day with Dr. Jean-Bernard Bouvier of the British medical charity Merlin. The Ministry of Health had become a hollow shell, without any central control, Bouvier told me. Nobody had any information about inventory at the warehouses of the Central Pharmacy. "They said they've put out six hundred tons—of what? If it's twelve trucks of IV fluid, I don't give a damn. Where? For what?" Sixteen tons of drugs were dumped on a single clinic, and the stacks of boxes left no room for patients. Bouvier had drawn up an "Emergency National Distribution Plan for Drugs"; after two months there was still no response from the coalition. A veteran of many disasters, he found that the expertise of NGOs like his kept falling into a void at the CPA. "This is missing in their experience. They don't see the fragility of the system. And they don't see the emergency of the situation. It's not that children are starving yet, but it's a structure that is slowly crumbling. It's just falling apart, without the impact showing up yet." He added, "You can degrade a society slowly bit by bit, but then you reach a point where you just crash."

The CPA's isolation behind security perimeters and the difficulty of communications made it a fairly opaque institution, to Iraqis and journalists alike. The inaccessibility was also partly deliberate. "I've just reorganized the strategic communications center here," Bremer told me a day after ordering Meghan O'Sullivan not to speak with me about anything (as a result of our conversations, she fell temporarily out of his favor). Stratcomm functioned as an offshore extension of the White House press office, relentlessly on-message. Its chief concern was to control the perceptions of the American audience in the twenty-four-hour news cycle, not to develop a source of information that could compete over the long haul in the reality of Iraq. I once received four separate CPA press releases announcing "Ruptured Baghdad Water Main to Be Quickly Restored"; when it was not restored as quickly as promised, Iraqi discontent inevitably rose, while Americans back home were none the wiser.

The CPA's own news outlet for Iraq became an unmitigated fiasco. The $82 million contract for the Iraq Media Network had been awarded to a San Diego company, Science Applications International Corporation, with no relevant experience in media but with relevant ties to the office of the secretary of defense. SAIC paid its American "media advisors" more than two hundred thousand dollars a year while nickel-and-diming the network, which produced a mix of official CPA announcements and Arabic singing. This reminded Iraqis sufficiently of TV under the old regime that most of them turned instead for their information to the inflammatory broadcasts of al-Jazeera and the Iranian antenna station. The CPA squandered the early opportunity, which would not come again, to begin the civic education that would be vital for Iraq's transition to democracy. Everyone in Baghdad knew that the media project was a disaster; in London, Tony Blair knew, and he was tearing his hair out trying to get it fixed. But as with so many other aspects of the occupation, the origins of the problem lay in Washington: The insipid programming reflected the Pentagon's desire to proclaim freedom in Iraq without doing the harder, riskier work of helping Iraqis create the necessary institutions, which would have meant giving up a measure of control. Even as Bremer and the CPA began to resurrect Iraq physically from its long decay and sudden collapse, the intellectual failures of the planning continued to haunt the occupation.

The manager of the media network traveled to Washington and warned Paul Wolfowitz about this unilateral disarmament in the battle for hearts and minds. Wolfowitz, the architect of the administration's democratic strategy for Iraq and the Middle East, replied that the Pentagon had full confidence in its contractor and brought the matter to a close. The manager was replaced and didn't return to Baghdad. These were the priorities chosen, the chances missed, the decisions made and not made, largely out of public view, in the occupation's early months when everything was still up in the air, as Drew Erdmann said, still fluid, before it all began to harden.

I WENT BACK AND FORTH between the Green and Red zones, between the CPA and Iraq, feeling almost dizzy at the transition, two separate realities existing on opposite sides of concrete and wire. The CPA insisted that progress was being made; the Iraqis didn't see it. An Iraqi on Erdmann's staff told him, "Look, if I didn't work with you I wouldn't want you Americans here. I see what you guys do, but the rest of society doesn't. What they know is there isn't electricity. And you're not convincing. You're not making the case. They don't feel there's a plan."

The furious activity of the Americans in the heat of Baghdad put me in mind of someone trying to dig his way out of a hole as the earth kept collapsing under his feet, or spinning his wheels in sand and sinking deeper. And yet in those first months I saw no alternative to the CPA. It was better than the power vacuum of April and May, and it was better than any Iraqi entity I could think of. The exile politicians were manifestly unpopular, perhaps even less popular than the Americans. The "internals," as they were called, had no viable organizations, and the shoots of local government that I was watching grow around the city were barely alive. I was slow to grasp the possibility that a weak, feuding, and corrupt Iraqi government might be better than an isolated, illegitimate American one.

One evening I had drinks at a hotel with a young official of the United Nations team in Baghdad. He described the complaints that the UN was hearing from Iraqis: the detainees whose families could get no word of them, the ostracism of Iraqis associated with the old regime, the heavy-handed manner of American soldiers, the bad Arabic spoken on the CPA's TV network. I listened with growing impatience. Were these really the most important things going on in postwar Iraq? Was I supposed to feel sorry for a Baathist who had done God knows what while he was in power and had now lost his job? What about the enormous crimes of the Baath Party and the chance Iraqis now had to move past them?

"They're under occupation," the UN official said. "They're not happy about it."

On one of my visits to the office of Sheikh Emad al-Din al-Awadi, a fellow ex-prisoner named Abdul-Zahra Abid, a stout middle-aged man with thick glasses and a broad Olmec nose, took me aside and told me about the case of his nephew, a banana importer. The nephew had been arrested by American soldiers at his office, along with nineteen other men, even the tea server. The soldiers also took twelve thousand dollars in Iraqi dinars and the company's BMW. Now the relatives of the nephew couldn't find out anything about his fate. They went first to the Assassins' Gate, hoping to get into the Republican Palace, but they were stopped by soldiers who said that they had no information. The soldiers suggested that the relatives try the airport, where high-value detainees were being held at the vast American base. At the airport the relatives were turned away as well. They went to a central police station where they had heard there were lists of names, but the nephew's name wasn't on them. The next day they drove past a sentry into the American base near the Olympic Stadium. A soldier pointed a gun and ordered them to leave, and they thanked the soldiers, got back in the car, and left. They tried the airport again, without luck. Under the old regime they would have known whom to bribe for information, but after four days of searching all over Baghdad, the family didn't know where to turn.

Abdul-Zahra Abid, who had spent a year and a half in prison for cursing Saddam's regime, told me this story as we stood in the anteroom to the sheikh's office, sandwiched between floor-to-ceiling metal shelves that were crammed with the pink and green folders of former prisoner files. "I'm not defending him. But even if he was involved in something, from a humanitarian point of view they should inform the families," Abid said. "They arrest people, they don't give information to families—like the Baath. The past and the present—there's no difference. There should be a difference."

Then Abid softened. He wanted to thank both George Bushes: the father for exerting the pressure that had led to his release from prison, the son for getting rid of Saddam. "Americans are humans like us. We're no better or worse. They make mistakes."

A couple of days later I was allowed to sit in on a commanders' meeting at the headquarters of the First Armored Division's Second Brigade. The intelligence officer in charge of the PowerPoint display showed satellite photographs of a banana importer's office that had been raided; the targets were financing insurgent activity, he said. The officers around the table joked about the insurgency's reliance on bananas. The case came up again the next day at the convention center, which was the one place where Iraqis who made it past the triple layers of searches and ID checks on the way in could present a problem directly to the occupation authority. At the Iraq Assistance Center I ran into a man named Raad Shaker Abid. He was the brother of the banana importer, and his odyssey had taken him here after the International Committee of the Red Cross told him that it could do nothing until the Americans allowed the ICRC itself to see detainees. From there he had gone to an ex-prisoners' association that was a rival of the sheikh's, and one of their members had brought him here.

It was chance that I kept crossing paths with the case of the banana importer, and it was chance that a CPA official named Dave Hodgkinson was at the convention center at the same moment that I met the detainee's brother. Hodgkinson told the brother to go see the colonel at the civil-military affairs headquarters near the Republican Palace. So the search for the detained man finally led his relatives back to where they had started, the Assassins' Gate. As Hodgkinson and the brother spoke, I noticed a sign on an easel propped up near the information desk: "CMOCS, HACCS, CIMICS, CMACS, ALL YOU EVER WANTED TO KNOW." "It was only by an improbable accident or extraordinary perseverance that an Iraqi could negotiate the forest of American military acronyms and armed gatekeepers to find the piece of information he needed, such as the whereabouts of a relative; most of them gave up long before. I never learned the banana importer's fate.

Hodgkinson was the CPA's adviser on "transitional justice." This meant that he, like the occupation authority in general, was more concerned with the past crimes of the Baath Party than the present predicament of Iraqi detainees. He was a young ex-Army JAG with the blond good looks and breezy manner of a fraternity president. I told him about the sheikh's group, and he expressed interest. The sheikh was one of the Iraqis who had quickly sized up the American occupiers for his own interest, and he'd been urging me to set up a meeting with someone from the CPA who funded groups like his, pumping me for advice on how to handle it. "Forget your American citizenship for thirty minutes and take my side with them," the sheikh pleaded.

On the drive from the Green Zone to Kadhimiya (CPA officials still made such trips without security in the early months), Hodgkinson said that "the word on the street" had the sheikh aligned with extremist Shiite tendencies, perhaps with the radical young cleric Moqtada al-Sadr, the son of a martyred ayatollah, and his Iranian backers. I asked if that would keep the CPA from funding him. "Only if the money would go for bazookas," Hodgkinson said. "If he's just anticoalition, if he wants us out, all the better."

The sheikh was waiting for us on his swivel chair in the sitting room. He greeted me effusively. "George must have some Arab blood!" The arrival of these important people from the CPA, with tens of thousands of dollars to distribute, made the sheikh nervous. "George speaks well of you, Mr. David. Did you pay him?" He showed us the ring he'd put on for the meeting. "I wear this ring for courage—like when I have to talk to my wife." As he had done with me the first time, he reeled in his new visitors with the story of his years in prison: the terrible overcrowding, the physical and psychological tortures, the man who sliced up his own shoe and ate it in a sandwich. At one point he was so overcome that he had to excuse himself. When he opened the door to his inner office, I noticed that the Khomeini portrait had disappeared.

Five minutes later he came back. "I'm sorry to bother you with this conversation."

"It's very important for us to hear," Hodgkinson said.

"Let's talk about the prisoners' association."

"Perfect."

"Do you want me to continue the story," the sheikh asked, "or talk about the association?" And there was another half hour of personal history.

The subject of the files created some awkwardness. Hodgkinson wanted the sheikh to acknowledge that they belonged to the Iraqi people.

"We ask humanity to work together to keep these documents," the sheikh said. "They don't belong to any one person, or even to the Iraqis, but to all humanity. Maybe Bush is a second Saddam, and maybe he's better."

"The Iraqi governing body, with the coalition's assistance, will use the documents to prosecute crimes or tell the story for the whole world to know," Hodgkinson said. "There are currently projects in place to centralize evidence."

"But this will take many years, many files will be burned, and many heads will be cut off. So I want to build a storehouse to keep them in—it will be safer because it will be under the care of my tribe." There was also a lack of office equipment, he added.

The meeting ended with no specific promise of money but a sense of mutual goodwill. Hodgkinson said, "I'm glad to get out of the CPA."

"It's a big jail," the sheikh said.

"You were in prison and now you're free. We've left our prison to come share your freedom."

Among the foreigners in Baghdad whom the sheikh was trying to cultivate was a UN human rights officer named Elahe Sharifpour-Hicks. The sheikh had given her a wish list without a budget: It included eight computers, four vehicles, a guard, a generator, an air conditioner, and a new building. Sharifpour-Hicks found the sheikh charming and dangerous. She had grown up in Iran as a member of the revolutionary generation; she had taken part in the overthrow of the shah and then seen the mullahs break all their promises to bring freedom and democracy. She was certain that the same thing was happening in Iraq.

"This ayatollah is hooking the international community by using prisoners," she said. "No one should underestimate these ayatollahs, and I'm afraid the Americans are doing this." As we spoke over lunch at the UN cafeteria, she became upset. "There are many like him. The dream, the model, the idea is to come to power the same way as in Iran. I can see with my eyes the same things as in the revolution." She found the Americans' reluctance to interfere maddening; the religious factions were growing stronger, while secular groups were too frightened to make noise. "The Americans are very shy and timid to look like occupiers. They say, 'Oh, we want the Iraqis to lead.' But what kind of Iraqi should lead? It is so painful, at the end of the day I am in tears."

The last time I went to see the sheikh that summer, I asked him what kind of government he wanted for Iraq. He ignored the question; there were three CPA cell phone applications he wanted me to fill out, for himself, his wife, and his six-year-old son. For the first time in my presence, he unwrapped his turban—and suddenly he was a balding, sweaty, pushy man. Our mutual enchantment was coming to an end.

I finished the applications. "Dave Hodgkinson heard you might be a follower of Moqtada al-Sadr," I said.

"Moqtada al-Sadr! He's a small man. He doesn't have a fraction of the level of my religion." The sheikh was convincingly outraged. "Those who said it to Mr. David are my enemy."

I said that Hodgkinson and the CPA didn't seem to care about his politics.

"That's good. But we must fix this idea about me." I knew that he was worried about his funding. "If it's proved I follow some line or am a member of any political party, I will stop working and sit at home."

I asked what he thought of Iran's system.

"Are you working for an intelligence agency?" the sheikh demanded, staring at me with no hint of the charmer's smile. "I have a mind and a heart. My heart is calm with you. My mind tells my heart to be careful."

What was the proper role of Islam in a democracy?

"After I answer this question, will you free me for God?" It was the hour of prayer. The sheikh took me rather roughly by the chin. "I'll make you calm by this answer, I'll cool your heart. Trust me, and I'll tell you honestly: I believe in Socrates and his circle. There's a line in the middle." He drew an imaginary line across a wooden coaster that was on his desk. "One side is hot, the other cold. This is the middle. As the philosopher believed, the best is the middle. Is that enough for you, or do you have other questions?"

A few days later, I received an e-mail from Elahe Sharifpour-Hicks. She had gone to see the sheikh that day: The CPA had given him forty-three thousand dollars. "He is in good shape," she reported. "He has now at least two computers and a generator."

DREW ERDMANN left Baghdad in late July, for meetings in Washington and to see his wife in St. Louis. They spent a beautiful Saturday morning walking through the dazzling green of an organic market, but he felt remote, as if he were looking at the world through a thick pane of glass. He woke up every morning before dawn, just as he did in Baghdad, feeling the stress of what remained to be done. It was nearly impossible to tell his wife what he'd been doing. When they went out with friends, he couldn't sit still for the conversation. He felt physically dizzy, his hands shook with nervous energy, and he wanted to get back.

In Washington, Erdmann was offered a position at the National Security Council, as director for Iran and strategic planning. His conversation with Condoleezza Rice at the White House lasted only a few minutes. "They don't like us much, but they like the alternatives less," he told her. Rice looked surprised, but the conversation moved on. Back in Baghdad, he told me that he didn't want to leave Iraq, he had never experienced anything like this work, he liked operating with pressure and uncertainty, and higher education was one sector that was showing signs of success. But because it meant being closer to his wife, he would take the job in Washington.

On one of his last days with the CPA, I accompanied Erdmann to the campus of Baghdad University. Until that morning, I had never quite understood his constant tension, his irritability, his ferocity about remnants of the old regime, the sense he conveyed that this was still a kind of combat. His team traveled in two civilian cars, staying in radio contact; in the seat next to me, Erdmann shoved a clip into his 9-mm. Beretta. The campus was largely empty—in spite of war and looting, the universities had completed their academic year in July—but there was a group of about thirty men standing under a tree in the plaza near the parking lot. They were debaathified professors, and as Erdmann walked past, his pistol hidden under his shirt, three of them fell into step with him.

"Are you Dr. Andrew Erdmann?" one professor said. "We have some forms." The men looked middle-aged, neatly dressed, and downcast. They displayed copies of the Agreement to Disavow Party Membership, with their signatures.

"The only exceptions are granted by Ambassador Bremer," Erdmann told them.

"We need your help about the situation."

"I understand the disruption in your life. But I hope you understand the coalition's May 16 proclamation."

"But we've done absolutely nothing that—"

Erdmann said that he couldn't promise anything. "Some of your colleagues don't deserve exemption. Some should return and some should not."

"I realize that," the professor said. "But our income now is absolutely zero. In this time, in this age, we can do absolutely nothing. There is no job we can do."

The men under the tree were watching us. One of Erdmann's Iraqi colleagues from the CPA said, "Let's keep moving."

Another Iraqi was approaching. "Let's get out of here," Erdmann said. "I'm about to have a serious sense-of-humor failure." We walked away, toward a white pillar at the edge of the plaza. Behind it was the glassed-in cafeteria. An anti-Baathist poster was taped to a wall: "THERE IS NO ROOM HERE FOR THOSE WHOSE HANDS DRIP WITH THE BLOOD OF INNOCENTS."

"This is where it happened," Erdmann said. "This corner. The body was lying there. I pulled the car up here."

Around noon on July 6, while Erdmann was meeting with UNESCO representatives in the building across the plaza, one of his military escorts, Jeffrey Wershow, walked alone into the cafeteria with his helmet off and bought a ginger ale. Wershow was twenty-two, a specialist in the Florida National Guard, an only child, a lawyer's son with an interest in politics. The soldier was holding his ginger ale near the white pillar when a man approached and shot him once in the head at point-blank range. The shooter, who was thought to be a Yemeni engineering student, disappeared into the crowd of students. By the time Erdmann sprinted across the plaza, shouting, gun drawn, soldiers had cleared out the crowd and wrapped the soldier's head wound. They placed the body in the back of Erdmann's Chevy Suburban, and he drove out of the campus to an improvised landing zone. The wounded soldier was stable when the helicopter arrived, but he died before reaching a military hospital.

That evening, Erdmann tried to clean the bloodstains out of the car with detergent. He decided to go back to campus the next day. "I can't let the last image of us be tearing out of town, throwing someone in the back of my Suburban and driving away." He had to request an escort from soldiers in the dead man's unit. "I'm the civilian and one of them got killed because of me. That's the way I feel. I don't necessarily think that's the way they feel—I wouldn't put that on them—but that's what happened." Erdmann smiled in his mirthless way. "Guy got killed so I could go and talk to some people from UNESCO."

The main reason for visiting the campus on this morning in mid-August was to say goodbye to Dr. Sami Mudhafar, the biochemist who had been elected university president in May. Mudhafar, in his sixties, was wearing a navy blue suit and had the hair and thick glasses of Henry Kissinger. He and Erdmann, thirty years younger and wearing olive khakis and a blue polo shirt, sat down in the president's office and went over the week's business. Erdmann reported that the State Department was resuming Fulbright scholarships for Iraqis. Mudhafar complained that professors suspected of working in bioweapons were being arrested on campus. Erdmann promised to take an application for an air-conditioning system in the political science department to the CPA.

"I wanted to tell you that I'm going back to the U.S.," Erdmann said.

Mudhafar looked stunned. "For a visit?"

"Permanently." Erdmann said that he was leaving just when the hard work of rebuilding the universities was paying off, and the focus could now turn to curriculum reform, which was his real interest. "I don't want to leave."

"I'm sorry to hear this news," Mudhafar said. "We've gotten used to you. We will miss you, really, because you are a good man and I wish you a good future. You have done the best you could. We have come through very serious days, and really very dangerous. We have argued, we have eaten together—and that's life."

Each of them had separately criticized the other to me. Erdmann complained that Mudhafar demanded independence from the CPA but lacked the nerve to fire bad administrators on his own. And Mudhafar once said that Erdmann had not always known how to deal with Iraqis, recalling that during the May 17 vote, when the noise got out of hand, the young American had screamed at the theater full of Iraqi faculty members, "*Shut up!*"

On this day, they seemed affectionate and nostalgic, bound together by shared experience. Mudhafar reminded Erdmann of the ordeal of simply finishing the academic year on time. "Many people were hoping we would not succeed. Especially those people from the past regime, and also some countries around Iraq. They were hoping it would not be completed."

Erdmann said, "I hope we'll both be able to look back in a few years and say we did good work."

"Don't forget us there, at your new position."

I saw Erdmann again in September, back in Washington. He was wearing a blue business suit and a White House pass draped around his neck. Iraq was not his portfolio, but he was soon drawn back to working on it again almost full-time. Erdmann found that no one, in or out of government, really understood what it was like in Iraq. The gap between headquarters and the field was profound. "I sound like, 'It's Khe Sanh, damn it! Charlie's inside the wire!'" he said, laughing grimly and adopting a Dennis Hopper tremor. "*You don't understand, man!*" He said that he was still unable to think as a historian. He joked that he hoped never to write a book on Iraq called *Strange Defeat*. But it made no sense to claim any certainty about how Iraq would emerge from the ordeal. "I'm very cautious about dealing with anyone talking about Iraq who's absolutely sure one way or the other."

BY LATE AUGUST, Paul Bremer was ready to lay out an ambitious vision for the CPA in Iraq. It would require spending tens of billions of dollars, which the American public and Congress had no idea they would be asked to pay. And it would mean a seven-step political process—writing a constitution and organizing several stages of national elections, before turning sovereignty back to Iraqis—that might last another year or more. America finally had a plan for Iraq.

A new entity called the Governing Council had been established in July, composed of twenty-five Iraqis and dominated by former exiles, but its power was unclear, its visibility poor, and ordinary Iraqis felt little connection to it. To create the Governing Council, Bremer had relied on the help of the United Nations mission in Baghdad, led by the secretary general's special representative. Sergio Vieira de Mello, a career UN diplomat from Brazil, had reluctantly left his new job as high commissioner for human rights in Geneva to take a temporary post in Iraq whose authority and purpose were worryingly vague. The Bush administration decided soon after the fall of Baghdad that, whatever its rhetoric about a "vital" role for the UN, the country that had waged the war should control the postwar and enjoy its benefits. No incentives were offered to countries that had opposed the war to involve their own troops and money in the reconstruction. Bremer saw no reason for internationalizing Iraq as time went on, and whenever a colleague—usually British—brought up the UN at a meeting, Bremer would roll his eyes as if the subject were a waste of time. The occupation would remain an American affair, and its legitimacy would depend on America's legitimacy.

Sir Jeremy Greenstock, the British UN ambassador who came to Baghdad in September as Tony Blair's envoy, told me, "The UN wouldn't have begun to be capable of keeping the lid on this. A, they were unpopular before it began. B, they don't produce that kind of leadership. Third, you can't have this kind of exercise being run by committee like the Security Council. I've been on it for five years—I know where the capability of the UN runs out, and so does Kofi Annan. He's never looked to be in charge of this theater." Between UN control and American control, there was always a third option: the early formation of an interim Iraqi government, not by the Pentagon with its hand-picked favorites, but by a national conference under international su-pervision, with Iraq's many constituencies, including the Sunnis, represented. Bremer never seemed to consider it; he was moving ahead resolutely with his own plan.

But the small UN team in Baghdad brought certain virtues that the CPA lacked. One of them was experience in the nation-building ef-forts of the nineties that the Bush administration considered irrele-vant and worse than useless for Iraq. Another was a corps of Arab officials who knew the region's politics. The team also had an ability to reach out and listen to a broader array of Iraqis than the Americans seemed able to. UN officials traveled to the disaffected Sunni prov-inces, where violence against the occupation was beginning to grow serious, and heard the complaints of Sunni Arabs who felt marginal-ized by the dissolution of the army and debaathification. Vieira de Mello himself met personally in the holy city of Najaf with Grand Ayatollah Ali al-Sistani, Iraq's highest Shiite cleric, who commanded vast support among the country's religious majority. Sistani refused to receive CPA officials. He made it clear from the beginning that he wanted elections in Iraq as soon as possible, and he issued a fatwa in-sisting that the new constitution must be written by an elected, not an appointed, body. Banners repeating the words of his fatwa hung from walls throughout the Shiite districts of Baghdad. But when people who had audiences with Sistani at his rented house in an alleyway in Najaf tried to convey the importance of the fatwa to Bremer, the ad-ministrator brushed them off. "Sistani is saying different things in pri-vate," he assured a visiting delegation. One ayatollah wasn't going to tell the occupation authority how to run the country. With the forma-tion of the Governing Council, Bremer seemed to regard the UN's role as finished. By the time I met Vieira de Mello in August, he no longer knew exactly why he was still in Iraq. His mandate would expire soon, and he would return to Geneva.

Nobody searched me on my way into the Canal Hotel, the UN's three-story headquarters on a lonely stretch of highway east of downtown Baghdad: two guard booths, but no searches. Vieira de Mello's staff occupied a hall on the third floor, but before going to his corner suite I stopped to talk with his political adviser, a Lebanese professor and former culture minister named Ghassan Salamé. Vieira de Mello and Salamé had both been students in Paris during the events of May 1968, but they had met only a few months ago, when the career international civil servant from Brazil asked the political veteran from Beirut to help him in what seemed an impossible assignment. "He said he knew nothing of Iraq," Salamé said, "and less of me."

It was the last week of my first stay in Iraq, and a particularly bad one: continuing power failures, numerous ambushes, explosions at an oil pipeline in Kirkuk and a water main in Baghdad, fatal riots in Basra, a devastating car bomb at the Jordanian embassy. Though I didn't know it then, two days before my visit to the Canal Hotel, the UN had received intelligence reports of an imminent bomb attack.

In spite of all this, Salamé, who occupied the office of the former UN weapons inspector Hans Blix, was thinking historically. "My deep feeling is that the problem is not in Baghdad, but in Washington," he said. "Those who decided this war and did it and won it are not the type of Americans Arab countries have been used to in the past fifty years or so. This is not the Corps of Engineers, this is not the American pragmatist problem solver." Salamé, a brusque man with thick black eyebrows, was fiddling with a strand of gold worry beads. "They are new Americans, unknown Americans, Americans with an ideology, with a master plan, with friends here, not open to everybody, with interests—somehow missionaries."

I pointed out that these new Americans were not unlike some of the old Americans who had fought the ideological Cold War in Europe and Asia. Salamé seized on the comparison.

"When I listen to Mr. Wolfowitz, I feel that he mistakes Baghdad for Berlin in 1945. He doesn't know the place." Salamé went over the main decisions taken by the CPA, singling out the plans for economic reform and a new investment code. "This country does not need at all the kind of sweeping privatization that these guys back in Washington are looking for. Either it's ideological, or they have an interest—they want to sell away Iraqi properties before there is a legitimate Iraqi authority." Ideology, he said, accounted for debaathification and the dissolution of the army, which led to security problems and ongoing sabotage. If only the Americans in Baghdad could liberate themselves from "this ideological-industrial complex" in Washington, Salamé said, "they would be able to do a much better job."

The special representative's office was at the end of the hall, overlooking an access road and a new security wall of hollow concrete blocks built to within a yard of the Canal Hotel. The section of wall just below the office was still unfinished—it reached only seven feet of an intended thirteen. Vieira de Mello had his jacket off, but as he sat down across from his corner coffee table from me, the perfectly pressed suit pants and sky-blue shirt, the sleek gray hair, above all the emphatic film actor's voice, made him every bit the elegant diplomat of reputation. Vieira de Mello's UN career had taken him from Cambodia and Angola to overseeing the early reconstruction of Kosovo, and finally to playing the role of Paul Bremer in East Timor.

Upon arriving in early June, Vieira de Mello tried to help the Americans out of the trap in which they found themselves and to help the Iraqis at the same time. Bremer, having taken charge of a project in jeopardy, seemed unwilling to loosen his grip. An advisory council of Iraqis with no substantive powers was the only proposal on the table other than complete American control.

"My message from day one, to them and to Jerry in particular, was this won't fly. It didn't fly in my experiments elsewhere, and I'm sure it won't fly here in the circumstances." Vieira de Mello told Bremer that the council needed to have executive powers. "You've got to give them responsibilities, even though you might be ultimately challenged. Iraqis are traumatized, Iraqis feel humiliated, rightly so. Iraqis feel, you know, orphaned—there is a huge power vacuum there. They might be happy that Saddam is gone forever, thank God, but they're not happy with this kind of situation."

Vieira de Mello, Salamé, and others began to hold a series of conversations around the country with leading Iraqis. Gradually, the ranks of the original group of exiles and Kurds were expanded with Iraqis who had lived under Saddam. The negotiations with the CPA became more informal and took on their own momentum, as Iraqis began to influence the selection of names. Vieira de Mello spent hours persuading a representative from the main Shiite party that joining the council would not be political suicide. When Bremer objected to the appointment of a communist, Vieira de Mello argued that secular Iraqis who didn't speak for sectarian groups would be vital. Ghassan Salamé came up with the Arabic term *majlis al-hokum* in place of the CPA's toothless "advisory council," and in early July the Governing Council became the first indigenous authority in Iraq since the fall of Saddam. "Over half would not have been there if Jerry could have had it his own way in the first half of June," Vieira de Mello said. The council functioned, he admitted, "in a kind of cocoon." Still, he thought that it would ultimately succeed. "I wouldn't be touring countries in the region trying to sell the Governing Council if I didn't believe what I'm saying, because the last thing I need and the organization needs is to be marketing the interests of the United States." He hoped for a fast political timetable, with a constitutional referendum, national elections, and a return of sovereignty by early spring. Occupation would soon become untenable.

As the secretary general's representative in Iraq, Vieira de Mello had every reason to snipe at the Bush administration, which had spent much of the past year ridiculing, bullying, and snubbing the UN. In Iraq its profile was so low that Vieira de Mello admitted feeling irritated and embarrassed by "the total lack of authority." But because he was pragmatic, and because he had once been in a role like Bremer's elsewhere, he refused to be churlish. "I don't want to be unfair to people who are up against an almost impossible task, having myself done similar things," he said. "Criticism can be made in a constructive way, but simply to criticize without telling people how to do it better is pretty irresponsible, because you're sitting on the fence and nothing is easier than to criticize those who actually are confronted with the challenge."

Bremer, Vieira de Mello suggested, had two sides: a more internationalist face, which perhaps came from his years in the diplomatic corps, and a more hard-line face that reflected the administration in Washington. Their relationship had recently been getting rockier, as what he called "the more neocon side of Jerry's personality" started emerging. But even when I threw what I thought was my fattest pitch and asked whether greater UN involvement early on might have prevented some of the CPA's mistakes, Vieira de Mello was modest.

"Yes, we could have helped, and we would have been only too happy to do so, also pointing to our own mistakes—because unless you admit why things went wrong and why it is you are now offering a lesson, you won't be heard. You see? And we could probably have done that. We still can. There's still time."

He looked at his watch: In a few minutes he had a press conference downstairs.

Six days later, at four-thirty on the afternoon of August 19, the day I left Iraq, an orange flatbed truck moving at high speed down the access road pulled up along the new security wall under Vieira de Mello's corner office. American forces had blocked off the road with a five-ton truck, but because it was uncomfortable with a heavy military presence, the UN had asked that the obstacle be removed, along with an observation post on the roof and armored vehicles in front of the compound.

Sergio Vieira de Mello was sitting at the coffee table with several staff members and visitors when the one-ton bomb exploded. Ghassan Salamé, with glass in his hair, ran down the hall and found that Vieira de Mello's office had collapsed two floors to the ground. "Sergio, *courage*," he called down, in the French they used because of the shared experience of May 1968. "We're coming to help you."

A shaft of light shone down through the destroyed outer wall, and though Vieira de Mello didn't answer, Salamé saw him wave his right hand.

"Sergio, answer me, are you alive?"

"*Oui*, Ghassan."

Two floors had fallen on his legs. Soon American soldiers arrived and hustled Salamé out of the precarious building. From outside, he helped in the effort to remove debris. He kept talking so that the wounded man wouldn't lose consciousness, but after a while the voice stopped answering. At eight-fifteen that evening, soldiers finally succeeded in clearing away the rubble, and Salamé identified the body of his friend.

Twenty-one others died with Vieira de Mello, including close aides, foreign humanitarian workers, and Iraqi employees of the UN. Elahe Sharifpour-Hicks, the Iranian-born human rights official, had left her office directly below Vieira de Mello's a few minutes before the blast to get coffee, and so she survived. Al-Qaeda claimed responsibility, but there was also suspicion that some of the building's guards, holdovers from the former regime, might have been involved. Ten days later, at the end of Friday prayers, an even more powerful car bomb killed Mohamed Baqr al-Hakim, spiritual leader of the largest Shiite party, and almost a hundred others outside the holiest mosque of Shiite Islam, in Najaf. And on September 20, Aqila al-Hashemi was shot in the stomach as she left her house to drive to a meeting of the Governing Council; she died five days later. Within two months, the number of foreign UN personnel in Iraq would dwindle from 650 to about forty, with none in Baghdad.

Paul Bremer was among those at the airport who said farewell to Sergio Vieira de Mello's coffin as it was loaded onto a plane for Brazil. Then he returned to the Republican Palace and the job of governing Iraq alone.

7

THE CAPTAIN

SHORTLY AFTER THE FALL OF BAGHDAD, CNN aired footage of a Marine, confronted with a crowd of angry Iraqis, who shouts at them, "We're here for your fucking freedom! Now *back up!*"

When the war of liberation turned into an occupation, tens of thousands of soldiers who thought they would be home by June saw their rotations out postponed, and then again, and again. They soon became the occupation's most visible face. Combat engineers trained to blow up minefields sat through meetings of the Baghdad water department; airborne troops used to jumping in and out of missions in a matter of days spent months setting up the Kirkuk police department; soldiers of the Third Infantry Division who spearheaded the invasion passed out textbooks in a Baghdad girls' school. The peacekeeping missions in the Balkans had given some of them a certain amount of preparation, but there was never any training for the massive project that fell on the shoulders of soldiers in Iraq. The CPA was months away from setting up provincial offices. Ray Salvatore Jennings, a consultant to USAID, who wrote one of the forecasts on postconflict Iraq that ended up on Bremer's desk, kept coming across young officers trying to establish government in midsized cities who told him, "I'm doing the best I can but I don't know how to do this, I don't have a manual. You got a manual? Anything you can offer me I'd be profoundly grateful for." A civil affairs captain asked Jennings's colleague Albert Cevallos for training in Robert's Rules of Order 101. Donald Rumsfeld's nightmare of an army of nation builders came to pass all over Iraq.

A rifle company commander named Captain John Prior showed me his war log for the spring of 2003. After Charlie Company of the Second Battalion, Sixth Infantry Regiment, First Armored Division had fought its way up from Kuwait to the Baghdad airport, Captain Prior's unit began an odyssey around central Iraq that lasted the better part of three months, before finally arriving at its permanent location in south Baghdad. Prior's war log tells one story of soldiers coming to realize that what President Bush, on May 1, called the end of "major combat operations" was only the beginning.

Prior was a twenty-nine-year-old from Indiana, six feet tall and stringy (he lost twenty-five pounds in his first five months in Iraq). He had joined the Reserve Officers' Training Corps at a small engineering college in Indiana, then decided to make the military his career. His undergraduate's face, deadpan sarcasm, and bouncy slew-footed stride did not prepare you for his toughness. "Some people are just born to do something," Prior said. By his own account, he loved Army life, the taking and giving of orders. "The sappy reasons people say they're in the military, and people say, 'Nah, they can't be'—those are the reasons I'm in the military. When Peace Corps can't quite get it done and diplomacy fails and McDonald's can't build enough franchises to win Baghdad over, that's when the military comes in."

Charlie Company's first mission after the fall of Baghdad sent Prior west to the city of Ramadi, to evacuate the body of an Argentinian journalist named Veronica Cabrera who had been killed in a highway accident. Prior and his soldiers were the first conventional forces to enter Ramadi, which was already—in late April—becoming a center of Baathist resistance. They were asked by Special Forces and the CIA to stay on for a few days and help patrol the town. As Prior's convoy of Bradleys, Humvees, and armored personnel carriers drove down the main east-west road, a mosque began blaring anti-American rhetoric, and soon a crowd of three or four hundred Iraqis gathered. Prior and his soldiers found themselves in the middle of a riot, with insults, fruit, shoes, two-by-fours, rocks, and finally chunks of concrete flying at them and their vehicles. The Americans didn't shoot and no one was seriously injured; in his log Prior commends his soldiers for their restraint. That night, Prior sent out another patrol along the same route, "to show the population of Ramadi that we are tougher and more resilient than they are and that we are here to stay." This patrol came under small-arms fire from dark alleyways, but the shooters melted away before the Americans could find them.

In the following days in Ramadi, and then in nearby Falluja, Prior records a series of raids on houses and weapons markets. "Our soldiers are becoming experienced enough to know the difference between being nice and cordial to people and when it is time to not be nice and throw people to the ground." Charlie Company is making the difficult transition from combat to stability operations—from Phase III to Phase IV—and Prior is pleased with his soldiers' resourcefulness. Then something new and strange enters the margins of his account: Iraqis.

In Ramadi, a man who speaks broken English among other Iraqis suddenly pulls Prior to the side, cups his hands around the captain's ear, and whispers in flawless English, "I am an American, take me with you." When Prior tries to learn more, the man slips back into broken English and then clams up. On another day, another man, accompanied by his wife and small child, approaches a soldier at the gate of the university. Speaking perfect English with a British accent, he tells the soldier his story: He went to school in England, returned to Iraq in 1987, and has been unable to get out ever since. The man warns the soldier not to trust Iraqis, that things are not what they seem. Suddenly, a white truck pulls up and seven well-dressed men get out. The man at the gate quickly disappears with his wife and child before the Iraqis can speak to him. Prior and his first sergeant, Mark Lahan, track him down at home to find out whether he and his family are in danger. Now using broken English, the man tells them that everything is fine.

In another mysterious incident, an Iraqi approaches Lahan on a night patrol and bluntly asks, "How are things in Baghdad? Have there been any suicide bombings? Have any Americans been killed?" When Lahan replies that nothing of the sort has happened, the man looks surprised. Prior notes in his log, "It is interesting to see that here, after the bulk of the fighting is done in this country, the disinformation campaign by Iraqi hard-liners is still in effect, it will be a long time coming to get these people to be able to trust [one] another again and to understand how a government and law and order is supposed to work." In fact, it isn't disinformation from regime diehards. The guerrilla war is about to begin.

"The entire situation seemed very weird," Prior writes on April 26, after five days in Ramadi. "It is clear now that they are not as happy as they say that we are here. For the first time in awhile, I felt extremely nervous being in such close proximity to Iraqi nationals. I do not trust them." In another entry, from Falluja, he writes: "The Iraqis are an interesting people. None of them have weapons, none of them know where weapons are, all the bad people have left Falluja, and they only want life to be normal again. Unfortunately, our compound was hit by RPG fire today so I am not inclined to believe them."

Ramadi and Falluja are the major cities of Anbar province, a vast western desert region of conservative Sunni Arabs, home to large numbers of Iraqi military and intelligence officers. Anbar was the last province to fall to coalition forces, and it did so without a shot being fired. By the time American soldiers arrived, local leaders had taken control of the towns and prevented looting. Anbar is where the insurgency began, and tribal sheikhs later told me that it had all been unnecessary. The province was ready to cooperate with the coalition. If only the Americans had remained outside the cities, then crowds wouldn't have gathered to protest, and soldiers wouldn't have fired on the crowds, as they did in Falluja on April 28 and 30, killing eighteen civilians, and Iraqis wouldn't have retaliated with grenades and automatic weapons, and the second war wouldn't have begun.

There is a bit of truth to this account. The American units that took control of Ramadi and Falluja—the Third Armored Cavalry Regiment and the Eighty-second Airborne Division, respectively—were ill suited to urban operations, didn't want to be there, and overreacted when they were provoked. "I was not impressed with the 3rd ACR's operations in Ramadi," Prior wrote, "they did not seem to have any idea what was going on, there was no sense of urgency, no one knew what the situation was anywhere in sector, none of the senior leadership could provide any guidance or answers." Having arrived in Iraq too late for the war, amid sand and heat and unfriendly locals, the regiment seemed unable or unwilling to adjust to Phase IV: "They did not appear to be ready for nor understand the urban/peace operations mission they had been assigned. Their attitude in terms of Rules of Engagement suggested to me that they had not made the change from combat operations to stability operations." Nor did it help that the house of a tribal leader in Ramadi, who had been cooperating with the CIA for years, was hit by an American air strike that killed him and seventeen members of his family. The Eighty-second in Falluja, clueless about Arab culture and lacking any civilian expertise (the CPA didn't come to Anbar until August), refused to compensate the families of the dead from the late April killings. By the time the Marines took control of Falluja in early 2004 and belatedly offered blood money, half the families refused it.

But Prior's log also shows that Anbar was set up for American failure. The CIA agents and Special Forces that first entered Falluja found no one to work with. "The local clerics, sheikhs, and government leaders have been complaining for some time that they need help to clear out the bad elements of their city," Prior wrote, "this has been their major reason for not providing more assistance or why they have been dragging their feet on getting anything done." But when the American agents summoned a small infantry unit for support, it was met with a riot, and the Eighty-second Airborne had to be called in to take control. Some American military analysts would later say that the problem in Anbar wasn't too much force but too little, and too late. The calibrations had to be finer than even the best-prepared units could make, and then each mistake played its part in deepening the ill will and hastening the insurgency.

Prior's soldiers drove a vehicle through a gate and smashed down a garden wall on their way to raiding the wrong house; when they hit the right house, which was next door, they picked up only two of the five brothers they were looking for. Prior recorded the raid as a success. But a few days earlier, he noted that professors at the bleak, sand-blown university in Ramadi, who had protected the property themselves with their own weapons, blamed the Americans for breaching the perimeter wire and inadvertently allowing looters in. No one was using the phrase "hearts and minds" yet, but Prior, unlike some of his superiors in Qatar and Washington, knew that it was a missed chance: "The university people seem neutral to the American cause and appear to be the typical university types, liberal, not appreciative of the military and looking to play both sides of the equation. The impression I got was that they did not care if Americans were there or if Fedayeen were there, they just do not want the university looted any more. Their loyalties appear to be able to be purchased for the protection of their university."

Prior was among the first soldiers to encounter the hidden nature of things in an Iraq that was neither at war nor at peace. Nothing was as it seemed. Firepower and good intentions would be less important than learning to read the signs. Prior saw himself as a liberator, but there were people out there whose support remained to be won or lost, and nothing would come easily, and every judgment he made would have its small effect on the outcome. Iraqis, no longer the cheering crowds that had greeted the company on its way up to Baghdad, were now going to play an intimate role in Prior's life.

The raids in Ramadi and Falluja lasted almost a month; then Charlie Company was recalled to Baghdad. There Captain Prior's log ends. "We put trouble down, we left," he told me later, "trouble came again."

CHARLIE COMPANY spent its first month back in Baghdad billeted at the zoo (the soldiers had already been there once in mid-April, on a mission to escort a truckload of frozen meat marked "A gift from the Kuwaiti people to the Iraqi people"). The unit spent a month pulling security in the area and setting up a neighborhood council. Then, in late June, the company was moved again, to a military academy in south Baghdad (the barracks were festooned with crepe-paper decorations from the last Ramadan), next to the bombed ruins of a vast military camp and airfield that had become home to five thousand displaced persons, looters, and criminals. The brigade's original lines hadn't been drawn to coincide with Baghdad's administrative districts, and Prior's unit lost crucial momentum. "We've been planning this war since freaking 12 September and it might have helped if someone had drawn a map before the war and figured out where everyone went," he said. "All that stuff you did—you gotta move. So at the time it was not that cool. We'd made friends there."

According to the brigade's original calendar, Baghdad's infrastructure would be rebuilt in August, elections would take place in early September, and the soldiers would leave the city in October. This brisk forecast was soon abandoned, of course. Prior and his soldiers weren't able to start serious work in their permanent location until early July. Because of the confused planning, it wasn't until August— four months after the Americans arrived in Baghdad—that Charlie Company's activities began to yield tangible benefits for Iraqis. And there was no time to lose. Throughout the summer, electric power operated sporadically, violence of all kinds kept rising, and Iraqis who could have been won over to the American side were steadily lost.

One morning in early August, I sat in the base-camp canteen with Prior, First Sergeant Lahan, and their translator, Numan al-Nima, a gray-haired former engineer with Iraqi Airways. Prior opened a coalition map of Baghdad's security zones and showed me the piece of the city he "owned"—a rectangle of Zafaraniya, a largely Shiite slum in south Baghdad. Roughly 250,000 people lived in the area. In addition to being charged with security, Prior chaired the neighborhood council and oversaw small reconstruction projects such as renovating schools. He was also responsible for sewage and trash in his battalion's entire zone, which contained half a million people.

"Infrastructure is the key now," Prior said more than once. "If these people have electricity, water, food, the basics of life, they're less likely to attack." Sewage, he realized, was the front line of nation building. When I met him, he was trying to get two hundred thousand dollars into the hands of Iraqi contractors as fast as he could.

"This is the answer," the translator urged Prior. "Show us something. People are hungry, starving. They don't believe they got rid of Saddam. If they got rid of Saddam, give me something to eat. That's why people hate Americans. We don't hate them because they are Americans. It is because they are the superpower, but where is the superpower? Show it to us."

I looked at Prior. "So it's all on you."

He said, "We've known that the whole time."

We went out into the streets of Zafaraniya in the usual two-Humvee convoy, complete with gunners manning the heavy .50-caliber machine guns. When Prior's jug-handle ears and boyish haircut disappeared under a U.S. Army helmet, his face underwent an instant transformation into a seasoned soldier's. His mission this morning was to visit nine pumping stations, which directed the district's untreated sewage into the Tigris and the Diala rivers. Iraqi poverty, in such sharp contrast to the grandiosity of Saddam's palaces and monuments, made a deep impression on soldiers from small towns in Indiana and Oklahoma, and for many of them the desire to help was the only impulse that argued in favor of their prolonged deployments. To tour a Shiite slum through its sewage was to understand that Saddam reduced those parts of Iraq he didn't favor to the level of Kinshasa or Manila. Green ponds of raw waste, eighteen inches deep, blocked the roads between apartment houses where children played. The open ditches that were the area's drainage system were overflowing.

"How foolish of me not to realize that the open sludge flowing past the children is the way the system is supposed to work," Prior remarked. A complete overhaul of the system was not his immediate priority. "I'm going to support their open-sewage sludge line and get it flowing." The heat rose, the streets stank, and Prior moved in battle gear at such a businesslike pace that two engineers from another battalion struggled to keep up. Each of the pumping stations, in various states of disrepair, was maintained and guarded by an Iraqi family that lived in a hovel on the premises, tended a lush vegetable garden, and kept an AK-47. Prior had never studied civil engineering—and he reminded me that his unit contained no former city planners—but he already seemed to have mastered the workings of the Zafaraniya sewer system. Lahan, a veteran of the Gulf War, told me, "People have said the Army's done this before, in '45 with Japan and Germany. Unfortunately, none of those people are in the Army anymore, so we have to figure it out ourselves."

With Prior there were no earnest attempts to win hearts and minds over multiple cups of tea. He was all brisk practicality, and the

Iraqis he worked with, who always had more to say than Prior gave them time for, seemed to respect him. "I will get you the money," he told a grizzled old man who was explaining at length that his pump was broken. "Six thousand U.S.? Yeah, yeah, great. Get started, get started."

Later, we visited Zafaraniya's gas station, another of Prior's responsibilities. Initially, he had devoted his energy to getting customers to wait in orderly lines. "In a lot of ways, you're trying to teach them a new way of doing things," he said. "'Teach' might be the wrong word—they're capable, competent, intelligent people. We're just giving them a different way to solve certain problems."

Prior's mission was to settle a price dispute between the gas station managers and the community, represented by several neighborhood council members. A meeting took place in the managers' cramped back office, equipped with an underperforming air conditioner. The council members wanted three hundred liters of diesel set aside every week for neighborhood generators. The managers wanted written permission from the Ministry of Oil. The council members pulled out authorizations signed by various American officers. Prior tried to move the discussion along, but the Iraqis kept arguing, until it became clear that the problem went beyond a dispute over diesel. One of the most hierarchical, top-down state systems on earth had been wiped out almost overnight, and no new system had yet taken its place. The neighborhood councils were imperfect embryos of local government. Confused, frustrated Iraqis, who had never before been allowed to take any initiative, turned to the Americans, who seemed to have all the power and money; the Americans, who didn't see themselves as occupiers, tried to force the Iraqis to work within their own institutions, but the institutions had been largely dismantled.

Flies were landing on Prior's brush cut. "Guys, we've been talking about this for twenty minutes," he said to the council members. "Do what I say. Go to the Oil Ministry. Just do it—just be done with it. Then you won't have to have slips of paper and we won't have to have this conversation."

Everyone was getting irritated. One of the neighborhood council members told Prior that other Iraqis suspected them of making millions of dinars off public service. They were considered collaborators; their lives had been threatened.

Prior changed his tone and lowered the pressure. "I would tell all of you candidly that you have a very tough job," he said. "We are not paying you, your people are angry and frustrated, and I know they take out their anger on you, and I really thank you for what you're doing. They may not understand or appreciate it now, but I'm telling you, your efforts, they're what are going to transform this country."

There was a commotion outside the office—loud, accusatory voices. Prior put on his helmet and flak vest, grabbed his rifle, and went out to the pumps. Customers waiting in the long line had left their vehicles, a crowd had formed, and it was getting ugly enough that the soldiers who had been standing by the Humvees were trying to intervene. Amid the shouting, Prior established that an employee of the Oil Ministry had come to collect diesel samples from each of the pumps for routine testing. One of the council members was accusing him of stealing benzene.

"No accusations," Prior declared. "Let's go see."

The crowd followed him under the blinding sun to the ministry employee's truck. Five metal jerricans stood in back. Prior opened the first can with the air of making a point and sniffed: "Diesel." He opened the second: "Diesel." As he unscrewed the cap on the third jerrican and bent over to smell it, hot diesel fuel sprayed in his face.

Everyone fell silent. Prior stood motionless with the effort to control himself. He squeezed his eyes shut and pressed them with his fingers. The fuel was on his helmet, his flak vest. A sergeant rushed over with bottled water. Then the chorus of shouts rose again.

"Everybody shut up!" Prior yelled. "I'm going to solve this. What is the problem? No accusations." His face wet, he began to interrogate the accusing council member, who now looked sheepish. "Go get the pump operator who sold him the benzene."

"I could only catch the guy who gave him the diesel."

"So how do you know someone gave him benzene? This is a great object lesson, everybody!" Prior was speaking to the crowd now, as his translator frantically rendered the lesson in Arabic. "You came out here and said this guy's a thief, and everybody's angry and he's going to get fired—and now you're backing down."

"It wasn't just an accusation," the council member said. "The guy drove up on the wrong side—"

"But what proof do you have that he did it? Wait! Hold on! I'm try-ing to make a point here. How would you like it if my soldiers broke into your house because your neighbors said you have RPGs, and I didn't see them but I broke into your house—how would you feel? Stop accusing people, for the love of God!"

"I caught him red-handed," the council member insisted.

"No, you didn't."

"Okay, no problem."

Prior wasn't letting it go. "There *is* a problem. The problem is that you people accuse each other without proof. *That's* the problem."

Prior's treatise on evidence gathering and due process ended. The crowd dispersed, and the meeting resumed inside. Prior tried to laugh off the incident and spare the accuser a complete loss of face. "Who doesn't like diesel in their eyes? I mean, everybody does." Later, he told me, "I wish I hadn't lost my temper. It wasn't the diesel—it was the way they kept bickering."

That afternoon, two of the council members, Ahmad Ogali and Abdul-Jabbar Doweich, invited me for lunch. Both men were poor, and neither had a house he wanted to bring me back to, so we ate in the living room of Ogali's brother-in-law, sitting on cushions. Before it became too risky for both them and me, I was invited to take meals in the homes of a number of Iraqis, and the famous hospitality of the Arabs always meant that we would sit for several hours sweating our way through multiple courses of hummus and flat bread, cold appetiz-ers, bean soup, chicken and rice, sweets, tea, and Pepsis (these last had been unavailable under Saddam and were points of domestic pride). Far more was prepared by the invisible women of the house than anyone could eat, and huge quantities of food were thrown out.

Toward the end of the meal, Ogali, a thirty-three-year-old gym teacher who was the council chairman, said, "It's a good thing John Prior lost his temper. Today was a small problem. If I told you about our problems, you wouldn't believe it. They exhaust us." The council members were working without pay—they couldn't even get cell phones or travel money from the CPA. The house of another member had been half destroyed (and six of his neighbors killed) by an errant missile that American soldiers, disposing of unexploded Iraqi ordnance, had set off by mistake; his efforts to get compensation had been checked at every turn. "Prior is doing more than his best," Ogali said. "But he's also controlled by his leaders."

Doweich, an unemployed father of four, had spent eight years in prison under Saddam for belonging to an Islamist political party (where he had met Sheikh Emad al-Din al-Awadi and heard him preach the system of rule by the clerics). Though it wasn't possible yet, he still hoped for an Islamic state in the future—as did 80 percent of Iraqis, he added.

"That's his personal opinion," Ogali said. "It's not eighty percent."

For now, Doweich saw working with Captain Prior on the neighborhood council as the best way to serve his country. The expectations of Iraqis were falling on the council members' heads, and Doweich believed that at levels well above Prior, American officials had no interest in solving problems.

"The people are watching," Ogali said. "When I come back at night, they're waiting. They want to know what we're doing. Last week, I told them about the schools, the sewer projects. They were happy—but these are very old projects, they were promised for a long time."

Doweich suggested that the Americans give a hundred dollars to every Iraqi family. That would take the edge off people's frustration. "I can't say why the Americans don't do these things," he said. "Iraqis have trouble understanding Americans."

Nor, said Ogali, did Americans understand Iraqis very well. "The Americans didn't come here to understand the people. They came here to do a job, and that's what they'll do. Iraqis work closely with them, but they don't try to understand us." As a result, Ogali said, the Americans' accomplishments in Iraq would be limited.

AMERICAN SOLDIERS had a phrase for the Iraqis' habit of turning one another in. Prior once used it: "These people dime each other out like there's no tomorrow." With these betrayals, Iraqis played on soldiers' fears and ignorance, pulling them into private feuds that the Americans had no way of navigating.

The night after the meeting at the gas station, Prior and a couple dozen soldiers from Charlie Company went out in two Humvees (lacking armor and even, in one case, doors) and two Bradleys to look for a suspected Fedayeen militiaman. For such missions, Prior used a different translator: Instead of the fatherly Iraqi Airways engineer, whose cultural insights were invaluable during daytime meetings, the nighttime translator was a strapping young guy with an aggressive manner. I expected to see the rougher side of Prior and Charlie Company that night—these were soldiers, after all, not civil engineers.

The suspect happened to be named Saddam Hussein, and he was High Value Target No. 497. It would be the Americans' second visit to his house. The tip had come from an informant Prior called Operative Chunky Love, whose picture showed a plump young man posing in a tuxedo against a studio backdrop of pink hearts. Chunky Love's intelligence had already rolled up three men in the neighborhood, including his brother-in-law. Tonight, Chunky Love was supposed to show up at his sister's house, near Saddam Hussein's, in an orange garbage truck loaded with weapons—a sting operation. Lahan warned me, "Out of a hundred tips we've gotten from Iraqi intelligence, one has worked out."

Recently, Prior had experienced what he called an epiphany. He and his soldiers were searching a man's house on what turned out to be a false accusation. "And I just realized: We're on top," he said. "Rome fell, and Greece fell, and I thought: I like being an American. I like being on top, and you don't stay on top unless there's people willing to defend it." It was a feeling not of triumph but of clarity, and a limited kind of empathy. "I thought: What if someone did this to my family? I'd be pissed. And what if I couldn't do anything about it? And I thought: I don't want this to happen to me or my family, and we need to maintain superiority as the number one superpower."

Tonight's target was a village along a dirt road, on a peninsula where the Diala River doubled back on itself. At sunset, Prior pulled up before a yard where a cow was grazing. A middle-aged woman came to the gate. She was the sister of Saddam Hussein and the wife of one of the men picked up on Prior's last visit.

"Saddam Hussein?" she said. "The president? He's not here." She laughed nervously. Prior did not; his dry humor was not in evidence tonight. "Saddam Hussein moved out with his wife and children," she said. "I don't know where they went."

"She's lying," the translator told Prior in a thuggish tone. Prior told the woman that he wanted to search the house. A younger woman who looked ill was trying to calm a crying baby.

The search of the bedroom turned up nothing: pictures of a young man with his girlfriend, love notes, Arab girlie photos. "Ah, that's nice," Prior said. "It's a freaking bra wrapped in plastic."

I went back into the living room, which was nearly bare except for a television. An old Egyptian movie was on, without sound. The woman with the baby was retching in the doorway. Speaking Arabic, the middle-aged woman said, "We were happy when you Americans came to get rid of the dictator, and now here you are searching our house. It's surprising." Her two sons, about six and ten, were standing against a wall and staring at the soldiers. They would never forget this, I thought—big strangers in uniforms, with guns, who had already come once and taken away their father, speaking a strange language, walking through their house, removing things from closets.

The bedroom that Prior had searched turned out to be the wrong one. Saddam Hussein's bedroom was locked, and the woman couldn't produce a key. A soldier arrived with an axe; three blows with the blunt end broke open the door. The younger woman's retching grew louder. This search, too, was fruitless. Saddam Hussein was long gone.

Night had fallen while we were inside. As we left, the translator taunted the woman: He said her brother was wanted because his name was Saddam Hussein. When Prior heard this, he snapped, "Tell her the truth—he's wanted for being Fedayeen." By morning, I was sure, the translator's remark would have made its way around the neighborhood as an example of American justice—baseless arrest, accusation without proof.

"Why did you take my husband?" the woman demanded of Prior.

"Because he's Fedayeen. He's Baath Party."

"No! No! No!"

"Tell her he's in detention," Prior instructed the translator. "If he's guilty, he'll be kept there. If he's not, he'll be processed and released." (A few days later the husband was let go.)

Out on the road, Prior shone his flashlight on an old man sitting on the ground. "Why did you lie to me last time we were here and say he was just gone for the day? Tell Saddam Hussein that he's a fugitive from coalition justice, and when he returns he should turn himself in to coalition forces immediately. Let's go, we're out of here."

We drove farther down the road and parked in front of a tall hedge. The house behind the hedge was owned by Chunky Love's sister. Prior and another soldier moved along the hedge under the palm trees and a full moon. A breeze was blowing off the river. Prior called out into the silence, "*Salaam alaikum*"—Peace be with you.

The translator turned to me. "Like Vietnam."

I was having the same thought. I knew that it was a limited analogy, more useful for polemic than insight, but at the moment Iraq *did* feel like Vietnam. The Americans were moving half blind in an alien landscape, missing their quarry and leaving behind frightened women and boys with memories.

There was no sign of Chunky Love or his orange garbage truck full of weapons. His sister hadn't seen him in a month; when she did, she told the translator, she would kill him for turning in her husband.

Prior realized that he'd been pulled into a family feud. The sister was told that her husband would be released. Prior called this the "hearts-and-minds moment," but the sister did not look grateful.

"What do you think, First Sergeant?" Prior asked Lahan on the way back to the base.

"I think we should disassociate ourselves from any information from Chunky Love," Lahan said. Operative Chunky Love had gone from informant to fugitive.

Prior marveled over how many flatly contradictory stories he had heard from the same people during his two visits to the neighborhood. He admitted that he would never get to the bottom of it. "I'm not freaking Sherlock Holmes," he said. Then he deadpanned, "I'm just an average guy, trying to get by."

THE WORLD OF THE SOLDIERS was unfamiliar to me. It was a world unto itself, with its own strange language and gear and endless rules and codes. I was frequently "sirred" and almost always made to feel welcome in their insular ranks. They enjoyed talking about what they were doing, which made them rather similar to the Iraqis and which more than anything else explained why I kept returning. They *were* average guys, and yet whenever one of them spoke about his other life back home—his favorite pizza, his degree in history—I experienced a slight jolt at recalling that these men and (a few) women, who enjoyed almost no personal freedom and privacy, who were generally more conscientious than anyone their age I'd ever met in America, who seemed to face the daily prospect of danger and death with businesslike aplomb, came from my own self-seeking culture. Prior's salary as a captain in charge of 150 men was $53,100. He and Lahan once told me that they never worried about dying, *ever*. This was their job, what they were trained to do, and they couldn't do it if they allowed normal thoughts to arise. They were molded to live for the unit and the mission, the greater good. Military life made them peculiarly un-American.

I can count my unpleasant experiences with soldiers on one hand, and they were essentially the same. One day, my driver and I got lost amid the ruins of the vast Rashid air base in south Baghdad, with its thousands of squatters picking through bombed-out military buildings. We were trying to find the entrance to Prior's camp, and we could locate only an opening in a chain-link fence along a berm where military traffic was entering and exiting. As we approached, two soldiers appeared on the berm. I got out of the car (an old, typically Iraqi Chevy Caprice that was useful for keeping a low profile) and waved, shouting to them that I was an American. One of them raised his M-16 and drew a careful bead on me, while the other instructed me to come forward with my arms raised. It was unnerving to be in the sight of that weapon while walking the fifty yards toward their position and trying to keep a friendly American smile on my face. Once the misunderstanding was cleared up, they pointed out the main entrance gate a half mile up the road. On another occasion, we were waiting to meet someone at the checkpoint next to the 14th of July Bridge into the Green Zone, which would become the scene of several suicide bombings. I noticed the red-lettered sign in English and Arabic promising deadly force against anyone who stopped exactly where our car was idling only when a soldier stalked up to my window and started screaming that he had been about to shoot. On the highway down from Kirkuk to Baghdad, a different driver and I ran into a huge backup at an American checkpoint. The driver decided to cut the line, and as he was speeding along the dirt shoulder a soldier stepped out and aimed his rifle at us. We stopped and I got out with my press card, but the sight of it only enraged him more. "You're going to get me killed!" he shouted. "They see me letting an American go through and they want to shoot me. Don't do that again! No, don't try to shake my hand, they'll see you. Just get back in the car and get in line." He was new in the country and rattled: To him Iraqis were already a threatening "they." The closest call came when I was driving toward Baghdad on the desert highway from Jordan and traffic came to a near standstill behind an American convoy. Against the instructions of everyone in his Suburban, my driver, a Jordanian in a hurry, kept approaching the rear vehicle, whose gunner, a visibly frightened teenager, kept waving us back. Suddenly there was gunfire—the warning shots hit the asphalt in front of us. Before long we pulled over with a flat tire halfway between Ramadi and Falluja. While the driver was changing the tire, a black BMW, with four men inside staring hard at us, appeared on a dirt road parallel to the highway. For ten minutes, the car cased us, passing in one direction, then another. We waited inside the Suburban, helpless. Finally the car seemed about to draw alongside us when our driver's cousin pulled up, and the BMW moved on like a thwarted shark swimming away from prey.

Each of these encounters resulted from the absurd proximity of heavily armed soldiers and free-floating journalists in what was still, after all, a war zone, where no one really understood the rules. If I had been Iraqi, or if any of the incidents had happened a few months later, the outcome would have been worse.

The behavior of American soldiers toward Iraqis was usually less restrained. As time went on and suicide bombings increased, checkpoints became the scenes of great danger. Far too many Iraqis, sometimes families with children, went down in a hail of gunfire when they failed to understand the bewildering array of signs and hand signals and orders shouted in English. No one knows how many Iraqis have died in such situations, because the American military makes a point of not keeping track of civilian deaths and conducting investigations only under extraordinary pressure. But leaving aside these tragedies, even the daily screaming of obscenities and the spectacle of men thrown to the ground and zip-cuffed played a crucial part in fixing Iraqis' early impression of the occupation. It was often their first direct encounter with any of the thousands of Americans in their country.

The American presence in Iraq must be one of the most isolated occupations in history. There was no real way for soldiers and Iraqis to mix outside the context of their jobs. Baghdad was a long way from Saigon; there were no bars where soldiers could unwind and get into trouble. Relationships with Iraqi women were prohibited by the military and nearly impossible anyway, given the social restrictions. Everyone knew that intimacy was dangerous, and it somehow wasn't surprising when an Iraqi woman who was working at an American base went into the barracks of a soldier with whom she was presumably having an affair and ended up dead from a gunshot to her head. Prior, who worked as closely with Iraqis as any soldier in the country, entered someone's home as a guest on only one occasion during his fifteen months in Iraq, when he dropped by the house of his translator and close friend Numan al-Nima. The sight of two military vehicles parked outside and surrounded by half a dozen soldiers drew the attention of the translator's neighbors. He asked Prior not to repeat the visit.

The stress of doing regular patrols, raids, and checkpoint duty, while coming under increasingly frequent attack from Iraqis who didn't wear uniforms and drove unmarked cars, brought out a degree of brutality that was probably inevitable. But some of it was avoidable and had more to do with individual pathology and poor leadership than the nature of occupation and guerrilla war.

One night, when I was in the northern city of Kirkuk, I went out on patrol with soldiers from the 173rd Airborne Brigade, which controlled the city. At one police station, the local cops had arrested a pair of Iraqi men in their late twenties, who had been blindfolded with strips of cloth, their white shirts torn and bloody, their backs scraped and bruised. The cops said that the two men had tried to run their checkpoint and crashed the car. A search had turned up a pair of ancient-looking fragmentation grenades. One of the men, a taxi driver, insisted that the grenades were for fishing; the other said he had been a passenger in the car and knew nothing about the grenades. They were now suspected insurgents, and the Americans took them to the airfield, where there was a temporary prison with about a hundred inmates.

The airfield was crisscrossed with wire and floodlit. Across a dirt field from the boxlike detention cells there was an outdoor holding pen made of metal bars and concertina wire. The suspects, hands zip-cuffed behind their backs, were put in the pen. It was after eleven, and the soldiers on guard duty weren't happy to see more work arrive. One young soldier in a green T-shirt, with dark brows and delicate pretty-boy features, directed a stream of abuse at the holding pen.

"I will fucking kick your ass," he snarled. "I will cut you up." One of the prisoners, the passenger, looked confused and a little scared. He indicated that he needed to urinate. "What's the matter, can't hold it? You a fucking pussy? You a cooze? Man, you are a dumb motherfucker. I could be in bed by now, dumb piece of shit."

The leader of the patrol, a young sergeant named John Adams, called for the driver to be brought over for processing.

"Hey, retard, get up here," the pretty boy yelled. "No, the next person—yeah, you, you fucking retard. Stand up, stand up." The driver was brought out of the pen and his cuffs removed. He didn't look at all frightened—there was a trace of cockiness on his face—which only enraged the pretty boy. "I'm gonna break your freaking head."

Sitting at a picnic table, Adams began to question the driver and fill out paperwork. Where did he get the grenades?

"That one is mine. That one was put in my car by the police," the driver said, and he reached to point at the grenades on the picnic table.

The pretty boy grabbed his arm and yanked him away. "Next time he touches that grenade I'm going to break his fucking hand." A white thread was stuck in the driver's hair, and the soldier who was tagging him with his prisoner number pulled it out. "That's sweet," the pretty boy sneered.

"Did you serve in the army?" Adams asked the driver. He had served less than a year before deserting. "Baath Party?" The driver made a quick, firm gesture of wiping his hands clean of the Baath Party, followed by a short monologue.

Before the translator could render it in English, the pretty boy broke in. "He's saying all that shit just to say no? I can't speak Arabic except to tell him to shut the fuck up."

"This one is very thirsty," the translator said, indicating the passenger. "He needs water."

"He'll get it when he kneels down. Tell him this is not no 7-Eleven. This is prison—we're not here for your fucking convenience."

It wasn't Abu Ghraib, just the ugliness of a bored and probably sadistic young man in a position of temporary power. But I left the airfield that night with an uneasy feeling. I'd had a glimpse under the rock of the occupation; there was bound to be much more there.

IRAQIS LIKED TO COMPLAIN that the Americans didn't know how to be occupiers. The British troops in the south, many of them veterans of Northern Ireland, seemed far more comfortable with the inherent ambiguities of police work and civil affairs. Americans were both too soft and too hard. Niceness and nastiness seemed to be two conjoined sides of their personality: Love me or I'll kill you. They had allowed the looting, Iraqis said, and they were allowing criminals and extremists to have the run of the country. At the same time, they turned friends into enemies with impulsive, violent reactions. *The New York Times* told the story of a fifty-one-year-old merchant with heart trouble who was kicked, beaten, and urinated on by the soldiers arresting him; then he was sent to a military hospital, where he was treated just as well as the wounded American in the next bed. He told the nurse, "I'm really confused. At the base, they beat me and tortured me. Here they treat me like a human being."

I once sat in on a meeting between three American junior officers in Kadhimiya and two Sunni tribal elders from Adhamiya, the district just across the river. Rockets were being fired from their neighborhood over the Tigris into the Americans' base, and the officers wanted the elders' help in stopping it.

One of the elders, wearing a gold-bordered brown robe and a kaffiyeh, lit a cigar and urged the Americans to emulate the British down in Basra. "I don't mean to hurt your feelings, but you don't have any experience here," he said. "You have to study the psychological way, study the community and the faith. That's why they have no problems."

"The reason is they have a long history of colonialism," the American captain said. "We have no interest in this. We don't want to stay here and run Iraq."

The elder puffed on his cigar and smiled. "The Americans need a lesson from the British."

The elders launched into a familiar litany of complaints: the power outages, the security situation, the checkpoints, the abuse of women during raids, the Americans' aggressiveness, the Americans' passivity. The soldiers sweated heavily in their flak vests, with helmets and M-16s at their sides. Every now and then one of them tried to mount a defense.

"There are explosives on the highways," an elder said.

"We can't watch every inch of road," the major replied. "This is where we need help we're not getting."

The elder ignored him. "And four a.m. is too early for the curfew to end."

Finally, one of the elders seemed to take pity on the American officers, who were so much less skilled at this old game of negotiation that was apparently a specialty of tribal sheikhs and British colonial officials. He put an end to the criticism with the faintest possible praise: "If we have to choose between the former regime and this one, we choose this one."

"But it's not a regime," the captain said, rousing himself. "We're here helping. That's important to understand. We are not here to impose a regime. I'd love for my job to be taken by someone from Kadhimiya and go home."

The elder recited an enigmatic aphorism. "If you're piloting a boat, why burn it?"

The meeting ended in the handshakes, the hands on hearts, the elaborate displays of cultural sensitivity and mutual respect with which such encounters always began and ended. I imagined the officers going back to their base in a rage. The whole point of the meeting—the rocket attacks—had barely been mentioned.

THE SOLDIERS were out on the streets, and so they began to grasp the difficulty of the occupation much earlier than the CPA in the palace. They were on the front line of complaints: It was the lieutenant on foot patrol, not the senior adviser to the Ministry of Electricity, who was asked by the woman standing outside her house why the electricity kept going off and who had to explain that he couldn't do anything about it. The soldiers were also less invested in their ideological preconceptions, and though they were often woefully ignorant of the country and the region, the nature of their work forced them to be pragmatists. Debaathification and the dissolution of the Iraqi army were generally unpopular with the American military; soldiers sometimes lost their hardest-working counterparts just as they were beginning to form a relationship, and soon found that the same Iraqis or ones like them were now shooting at them. In the absence of guidance from the center, commanders in the provinces, such as the 101st Airborne's Major General David Petraeus in Mosul, moved ahead with forming councils, finding business partners for reconstruction, training security forces, even setting local economic and border policy. They were in a hurry, and they often didn't bother to coordinate their work with the various international organizations and occupation officials who were working on the same problems. Meanwhile, the CPA was still drafting its blueprint for the future of Iraq. A lieutenant colonel in Kirkuk showed me a chart of projects—police stations, fire stations, schools, parks—that his brigade was ready to start. I asked how much money had been allocated by Baghdad, and he held his thumb and finger up in a zero. "I could do so much in this town with a frigging bag of money!" He was afraid that the new Kirkuk police force, which the battalion he commanded had already set up, would have to be scrapped when Bernard Kerik—the colorful former New York police chief, whom President Bush sent to Iraq to rebuild security forces—finally got around to announcing his national plan. Instead, Kerik spent his time in Baghdad going on raids with South

African mercenaries while his house in New Jersey underwent renovation. He went home after just three months, leaving almost nothing behind, while the lieutenant colonel spent almost a year in Kirkuk. Among some soldiers, the occupation authority's initials stood for Can't Provide Anything.

The civilians in the palace saw it differently. At the end of his day-long tour of southern Iraq, Paul Bremer urged me to look into just the kind of reconstruction projects that I had already seen consuming John Prior's energy. "That money that we're putting out through the brigades and the divisions is the fastest-spent dispersing money I have," Bremer said. The CPA handed out money from seized assets of the old regime in lump sums of half a million dollars at division level and two hundred thousand at brigade. When the unspent amount approached zero, the sum was audited and replenished. The Commanders Fund had gone through twenty-three million dollars by mid-August, in more than two thousand reconstruction projects. "We can't even keep track of how many," Bremer said. "It's small things—sewers, opening amusement parks, fixing schools, clearing out drains." These were the most visible achievements of the early months, and at times it seemed that the CPA could point to nothing else when Iraqis wanted to know what the occupation was bringing them.

But twenty-three million dollars in four months was a very small amount of money—less than a dollar for each Iraqi. It stood no chance against the gathering sandstorm of expectation. Officers in Iraq and officials in Washington, including Wolfowitz and Rice, accused Bremer of being far too slow to release control of the money in the Commanders Fund. Iraq's infrastructure had been deteriorating for years—an American development expert once told me that, if Iraq were a used car, Saddam got rid of it at just the right time—and with the collapse of the regime, along with the departure of its top managers, the jury-rigged machinery seemed to give out. By the end of the summer, Bremer understood both the extent of the problem and its political urgency. He went to Washington and let the White House know that Iraq was going to cost America tens of billions of dollars. Iraqi oil money and seized assets wouldn't come close to covering it. The reassuring forecasts of Cheney, Rumsfeld, and Wolfowitz went into the dustbin of history.

President Bush broke the news to the country on September 7, 2003, and Congress quickly passed an $87 billion appropriation bill that included $18.4 billion for Iraq's reconstruction. Much of the money was earmarked for the huge infrastructure projects—power plants, water and sewage treatment, telecommunications—that only large multinationals could carry out. There was much criticism of the restricted- or no-bid contracts that went to American companies with Republican Party ties, but the problem wasn't so much the coziness of Bechtel and Halliburton with the Bush administration as the kind of projects they contracted to undertake and their execution in Washington and Baghdad. The projects were so big, and the official American procurement regulations so cumbersome, that the money made its way into Iraqi society at the pace of tar poured on a cold day. By August 2004, ten months after the appropriation, only $400 million of the $18.4 billion—barely two percent—had been spent. By the time Iraqi subcontractors saw any of the money, all but a small fraction had been lopped off in overhead, security (as much as 40 percent of any contract), corruption, and profits. The CPA kept promising Iraqis that the spigot was about to be turned on and the country was going to be flooded with lifesaving cash that would put tens of thousands of people to work. It never happened.

Part of the problem lay in the business-as-usual attitude back in Washington. Rumsfeld, still technically in charge of the postwar, set the tone: In mid-September, just a few days after Bush's televised speech, the defense secretary said, "I don't believe it's our job to reconstruct the country. The Iraqi people will have to reconstruct that country over a period of time." He even offered the Iraqi people a reconstruction plan of sorts: "Tourism is going to be something important in that country as soon as the security situation is resolved, and I think that will be resolved as the Iraqis take over more and more responsibility for their own government." Key officials who might have been able to negotiate the byzantine guidelines for congressional expenditures never went to Baghdad. On one of his trips to Washington, Bremer approached the acting secretary of the Army, Les Brownlee, and confessed, "I have no contracting expertise over here at all. I am going to be in deep trouble. Can you help me?" With the approval of Wolfowitz, the Army dispatched forty contracting officers from the Corps of Engineers to Baghdad. Halfway through the life of the CPA, it was the beginning of the Project Management Office. "It didn't work very well," a senior administration official told me. "They were too scared. They were scared to death to let that money go out because they already saw what was happening with some of the Iraqi money"—accusations of waste and corruption were beginning to plague the CPA—"and they were already being visited by congressional delegations." The failure to spend Iraq reconstruction money wisely, or quickly, or at all, became one of the less publicized but more significant scandals of the occupation. In the end, the CPA inspector general's report found that nine billion dollars in Iraqi funds had gone missing on Bremer's watch, and this was only a preliminary figure. "Someday, somebody is going to sit down and figure out how much damn money was wasted," the senior official said. "You can sit there and say, 'Kofi, you really didn't waste a whole lot, considering the normal corruption and profligacy and stupidity of international programs.' I believe in Iraq we wasted more than Kofi did." He added, "If you're past the political and security breaking point, all the contracts in the world won't help you."

Jerry Silverman, a former official of the U.S. Agency for International Development who worked in Vietnam for four years, found himself, two decades later, in Iraq. The assumption behind the development efforts in both wars, he said, was that "if you do good things for people, it will result in political support. There's no evidence for that. The Viet Cong sent their kids to the schools we built, and they shot us during the day anyway." But in Iraq, unlike in Vietnam, the political war was still to be won or lost at the outset. If the Americans had established security early on, Silverman said, "It's possible—not inevitable, but possible—that reconstruction could have taken hold. It's been impossible since then." Compared to the American soldiers and civilians in Vietnam, he went on, the ones in Iraq were not prepared to take the kind of casualties necessary to secure the cities and the highways so that reconstruction stood a chance of succeeding. "Our troops are in force-protection mode. They don't protect anyone else. They're another private militia." Vietnam and Iraq, he said, were cases of "different mistakes, same hubris."

FROM THE FIRST DAYS of the invasion all the way through the occupation, a controversy persisted in Washington about whether there were enough troops in Iraq. Beginning in May 2003, Powell told Bush several times that there were not, and each time the president heard him out and then followed the advice of his secretary of defense instead. Whenever the question was put to Rumsfeld, he simply repeated his generals' assurances that no additional American divisions were needed. General John Abizaid, Franks's successor at Centcom, and Lieutenant General Ricardo Sanchez, McKiernan's successor as commander of ground forces in Iraq, said again and again that they had enough troops to do all the missions they had been assigned. This had the sound of a reply with a catch—for what were the missions? The debate in Washington was fixed, the answer predetermined by the phrasing of the question. One of Paul Bremer's aides said that the administrator never looked worse than the day he was told by Rumsfeld in a video teleconference that he couldn't have any more troops. After leaving Iraq, Bremer criticized the troop levels, but while he was in Baghdad he never publicly broke with the administration's united front that preserved the fiction. Some champions of the war, such as Senator John McCain, Robert Kagan, and William Kristol, began to get nervous as summer turned to fall and the forces that the administration assumed would be provided by foreign countries never materialized. Other neoconservatives remained sanguine. Danielle Pletka of the American Enterprise Institute spent a few days in Iraq in September and published an op-ed in *The New York Times* expressing her satisfaction with troop levels. Richard Perle asked me rhetorically, "What would be accomplished by having patrols up and down the highway? The point of our presence there, it seems to me, is not to make sure that all the highways are open all the time. That isn't how this is going to be won, in my view. This is going to be won when we have a flow of intelligence that identifies the guys we're fighting."

Unless you had an ideological stake in it, this controversy didn't survive your first contact with Iraqi reality. There weren't enough troops to patrol the road between Baghdad International Airport and the city center so that visitors didn't have to take their life into their hands upon arrival. There weren't enough troops in the city streets to act even as a deterrent to someone who wanted to steal a car or shoot up a convoy or assassinate an official. There weren't enough troops to guard a fraction of the million tons of munitions left lying around in dumps all over Iraq that were being steadily looted by insurgents. There weren't enough troops to provide a token presence along Iraq's borders with Syria, Jordan, Saudi Arabia, and Iran, which might dissuade some jihadis and intelligence agents from infiltrating across. There weren't enough troops to prevent militias from gaining control of entire provinces. There weren't enough troops on the major highways to keep bandits and insurgents from terrorizing the truckers carrying essential goods, such as reconstruction materials or even food for the Green Zone. There weren't enough troops to allow CPA officials to do their jobs.

Perhaps the connection between patrolling highways and winning the war was too abstract for those supporters of administration policy who never went to Iraq, and for a few who did. It shouldn't have been that hard. Why would Iraqis join the American effort when their personal safety, or even a minimum of public order in their country, couldn't possibly be upheld by the occupying forces?

The number of American soldiers in Iraq, which hovered around 135,000, sometimes spiking or dropping by ten or twenty thousand in response to events, reflected nothing other than Rumsfeld's fixed idea of military transformation. If more troops had to be found and sent, the direction in which he wanted to take the twenty-first-century military would be called into serious question. It's hard to imagine that Rumsfeld suffered even private doubts about this: He had a vision, and the messy aftermath of the Iraq War wasn't going to turn him aside. General Richard Myers, chairman of the Joint Chiefs of Staff, had the legal authority under the Goldwater-Nichols Act to ask for a meeting with the president in case the secretary of defense rejected his advice. "Myers knows—he's got to know by now," a senior official said. "He's got a goddamn Marine as his vice chairman. They should have gone over and said, 'Mr. President, we don't have enough troops,' and suffered the consequences. The consequences, in my view, would have been the president and the vice president siding with the secretary of defense and the chairman leaving. But at least he would leave with the idea that 'I've exercised my right under Goldwater-Nichols and I feel better.'" Instead, Myers kept his counsel and his job. There was always the example of General Shinseki to dissuade him and other senior officers from excessive candor. A few of them found ways to get the point across privately. Officers in Iraq talked off the record about the need for two more divisions. As Senator Joe Biden was boarding a helicopter at the end of one of his visits, a Marine general rushed up and said, "Senator, if anybody tells you we have enough troops over there when you get back, tell them to go to goddamn hell."

The top civilians in the administration, and the top brass at the Pentagon, and the top officials in Iraq all held on to their positions and failed the men and women they had sent to carry out their policy. They failed in the most basic obligation to give those men and women what they needed. The slow, mismanaged arrival of armored vehicles and bulletproof plates for flak vests was only the most conspicuous demonstration of how the Iraq War, like every war—just or unjust, won or lost—became a conspiracy of the old and powerful against the young and dutiful.

As the war went on, I noted how often Paul Wolfowitz traveled to Iraq. Sometimes he was accompanied on these three- or four-day excursions by a coterie of sympathetic journalists who then filed stories about how well it was all going. But it was impossible not to see that Wolfowitz himself was deeply moved by the commitment of soldiers in mess halls and combat hospitals, how (he said) they buoyed his morale rather than the other way around, how well he listened to them (the battalion commander I met in Kirkuk was disarmed by the deputy secretary's attentiveness when they had a few minutes together), how poignantly he spoke, ashen faced, after the rocket attack on the Rashid Hotel that killed an Army lieutenant colonel on the floor just below his. Then Wolfowitz's visit would end, and he would return to Washington, where he was never able or willing to do the most important thing he could for the soldiers, which was to give them what they needed. Over time, it became hard to think of the dedication of soldiers like John Prior, the resourcefulness and good faith with which they undertook their task, and not feel a particular bitterness.

IN THE SUMMER OF 2003, morale in Prior's battalion was under serious strain. In their first six months in theater, some soldiers had a total of three days off. Others were stretched so thin that they had begun to report "ghost patrols" back to headquarters—logging in scheduled patrols that didn't actually take place. Few junior officers in the battalion planned on staying in the Army after their current tour. Alcohol use, which was illegal for soldiers stationed in Iraq, had become widespread, and there had been three suicides in other battalions at the base. Relations between young Americans at the end of a four-day patrol rotation and the host country nationals tended to deteriorate, according to one officer, into "guys kicking dogs, yelling at grown men twenty years older than they are, and pushing kids into parked cars to keep them from following and bothering them." In September, soldiers in a platoon from Charlie Company beat up a group of Iraqis they'd caught moving around the perimeter of their outpost in Zafaraniya; the soldiers were disciplined with loss of rank and, in one case, confinement. Everyone suffered from the stress of heat, long days, lack of sleep, homesickness, the constant threat of attack (about which they were fundamentally fatalistic), and the simple fact that there were nowhere near enough of them to do all the tasks they'd been given.

A soldier in Prior's battalion wrote me a lengthy account of the problems:

> The reason why morale sucks is because of the senior leadership, and
> by this I don't necessarily mean the battalion commander or company
> commanders, but the brigade and division commanders, and probably
> the generals at the Pentagon and Central Command too, all of whom
> seem to be insulated from what is going on at the ground level. Either
> that or they are unwilling to hear the truth of things, or (and this is the
> most likely), they do know what is going on, but they want to get

promoted so badly that they're willing to screw over soldiers by being unwilling to face the problem of morale, so they continue pushing the soldiers to do more with less because Rummy wants them to do more with less and get us out of here quickly. These people are like serious alcoholics unwilling to admit there even is a problem.

The soldier wasn't a defeatist. He was simply describing what anyone who spent time with American troops in Iraq knew. His letter concluded:

I'm not pessimistic about the country of Iraq because things are getting better and will continue to do so, albeit slowly. There are great things we're doing here, much has already been done, yet much more remains to be accomplished, and what we need now is the money, people, and most importantly, time to do it. We'll win, that's for sure, and this won't be another Vietnam; I truly believe that.

John Prior was also a believer. The Army was going to be his career, and in Iraq, which he called his first "real-world deployment," he was gaining invaluable experience doing things that were not taught in basic training but that would be increasingly central to the missions of the American military and its next generation of leadership.

I once asked Prior whether his night work, the raids and arrests, threatened to undo the good accomplished by his day work—if, essentially, the mission was impossible. He didn't think so: As the sewage started to flow and the schools got fixed up, Iraqis would view Americans the way the Americans saw themselves, as people trying to help. But Prior was no soft-shelled humanitarian. He called himself a foreign-policy realist. Fixing the sewer system in Zafaraniya, he believed, was an essential part of the war on terror. Terrorists depended on millions of sympathizers who believed that America was evil and Americans only wanted Middle Eastern oil. "But we come here and we show that we're honest, trustworthy, we're caring, we're compassionate," Prior said. "We're interested in them. We're interested in fixing their lives. Not because we have to, but because we can, because we can be benevolent, because we *are* benevolent. Then you start denying them refuge." Once, while monitoring one of the local mosques during Friday prayers, Prior heard the imam say that some Americans who weren't Muslims followed the tenets of Islam better than some actual Muslims in the Arab world. The Zafaraniya sewer system was worth dying for, Prior believed, because fixing it reduced the chances of terrorists striking Boston, where his fiancée lived.

I never think about John Prior without remembering one particular incident. On the canvas of the war and occupation it was a tiny speck, but it stayed with me as other, more significant events have not. I was riding in Prior's Humvee when we got stuck in a mass of cars at an exit off a Baghdad highway. In the usual chaos of the roads, drivers were swinging over from the far lanes to jump the exit line, which was backing up traffic well down the highway. After a few minutes, Prior got out of the front passenger seat and, walking briskly among the stalled cars, positioned himself at the head of the off-ramp, where the cheaters were trying to slip into line. He held up his hand and directed them to continue along the highway. Reluctantly, one after another, they began pulling out of the line, and the backup eased. But one man kept inching ahead toward Prior, who finally slammed his hand on the hood of the car, glared at the man through the windshield, and swung his arm around to point down the highway. "Come on, guy, what're you doing?" Prior muttered. The man stared back in fury, and I thought he might keep moving forward until he ran Prior over. Instead, he braked, hung his head, and left the line. It was an amazing display of nerve—Prior was completely exposed, with none of his men beside him, a foreign soldier taking it upon himself to impose order. The drivers he prevented from exiting no doubt resented it, but other drivers waved thanks. I wondered how many soldiers would have done the same thing. Most American convoys hurtled through Baghdad, chewing up asphalt and curbs, with little concern for the rules of the road or Iraqi drivers. At that moment I felt the whole American project in Iraq depended on such actions and reactions, all of them idiosyncratic, unpredictable, hair-trigger.

In late October 2003, I spoke with Prior on the phone from Baghdad. The sewage ponds had been cleaned up, and security in his sector had improved with better intelligence. The council members were being paid sixty dollars a month and ran their own meetings. Abdul-Jabbar Doweich had a job as a security guard. But, for various reasons, the money in the Commanders Fund for reconstruction had been shut off—something to do with a lawsuit by disabled Gulf War veterans, or recalcitrant new cabinet ministers. Current projects were quickly running out of money; some of Charlie Company's contractors were being threatened by loan sharks, and much of the work was coming to a halt. Hearing this, I remembered something Prior had said as we were driving into Saddam Hussein's village. "The most frustrating thing is we can't do more for them. My hands are tied, everybody's are." And he added, "It's hard to know at what level the hand tying starts."

8

OCCUPIED IRAQIS

"WE MUST GO OUT OF IRAQ! We must travel! We must see America! Can you give us hope?"

A young woman named Aseel and one of her coworkers planted themselves in my path one day in a hallway on the campus of Baghdad University. Aseel was a pale, pretty twenty-eight-year-old computer programmer. Her cream-colored veil seemed incongruous with her vitality, and in fact it was just a prop: She wore it to keep from being killed by fundamentalists. "They speak in name of God," she said. "Before, they spoke in name of Saddam." There were many fears in Aseel's life. She was afraid of kidnappers: A group of them had snatched her friend as she got off the bus; Aseel had barely managed to run away. She was afraid of her neighbors, who threatened her with harm if she ever took another picture of American soldiers. She was afraid of the woman who ran her office, a former Baathist who used to wear a uniform and sidearm to work, and whose three framed photographs of Saddam were still propped up on the floor, facing the wall. Aseel complained that Dr. Sami Mudhafar, the new university president, was too weak to get rid of the Baathists. They still had the run of the place.

"Do you feel danger here? I feel danger," Aseel said as we spoke in her office. "I feel a life in prison—after liberation! I want to see the world, I want to learn more, I want to feel I'm getting something important for my life. When you visit countries, that's a simple thing of having freedom. That's the thing I lost for my life. The danger is still in the streets. In this room. Especially in this room."

The Baathist office manager walked in and glared. She told Aseel that I would have to leave.

"We are in prison here," Aseel whispered. "I have no freedom."

I offered to drive her home. She lived with her parents, her brother, and a maternal uncle who had gone mad after imprisonment and torture. Their modest house, on an empty street in an underbuilt new neighborhood of eastern Baghdad, stood baking in the relentless yellow light of midday. The power was out, and because the phone didn't work, Aseel had been unable to warn her mother, so the family served me a simple dish of rice and beans in the darkened room. On one wall Aseel's mother had written a Qur'anic verse in chalk during the war, a prayer for safety that the family recited together. On another wall hung a photograph of her mother's parents, from 1948—a man with a small mustache, a woman with bright lipstick.

"During royal times, the people were more modern than now," Aseel's father said. He was an architect in the Ministry of Information, nearing retirement. In 1965, he had studied in Manchester, England, but the family now belonged to Iraq's beaten-down middle class, crushed by two decades of wars and sanctions. At one particularly desperate moment in 1993, her mother had sold most of her gold at a low price. Before the most recent war, Aseel's pay had been six dollars a month; it wasn't enough money to buy a shirt. The family had lived with her father's relatives in Adhamiya, the middle-class district on the Tigris that was Iraq's historic center of Arab nationalists, dating back to the officer class in the last days of the Ottoman Empire. A few months before the arrival of the Americans, her father's Baathist brother, knowing that Aseel's family didn't support the Saddam regime, threw them out of the house in Adhamiya. In their new home, Aseel wept watching the war on TV, urging the Third Infantry Division on to Baghdad; the bombs exploding outside gave her heart. Aseel said, "We thought everybody would be happy. But it was not like that."

Aseel's family passionately supported the Americans. If this was colonialism, she was ready to be colonized. Every Saturday, the family sat down together and listened to Bremer's weekly address. "I feel him very close," Aseel said. "Even his way, I like it—he's a simple man." Her salary had been increased to one hundred twenty dollars a month, and her brother had just been hired as a translator, but the reason for Aseel's sympathies went much deeper. She showed me a copy of the letter that she had sent to President Bush by way of a surprised American soldier: "Mr. President you were honest with us and you did every thing you said. We are a nation suffered so much from bluffing, your policy we are seeing our country's future and it will be prosper," she wrote. "I hope that things will be back to normal soon and you may visit Iraq with a great welcome party."

"The Americans should change the region," Aseel's father said. "Not by war, but by Iraq. Iranian people, if they saw what happened in Iraq, and we progress by liberation and wealthy life, they do the same."

Her veil off, Aseel wore her hennaed hair in a long braid. She brought out her large collection of American movies—she had learned English from watching Nicole Kidman in *Moulin Rouge* and Sharon Stone in *The Quick and the Dead*. She said, "It needs time, I think, a very long time, to make connection between the two civilizations. To make us civilized, I mean."

Aseel sat on the couch between her sad-faced parents and talked excitedly about her future. "I'm always saying to my mother, 'I lost my life.' And she says, 'No, you're young, there's still time.' And I say, 'Maybe.' Maybe now I'll catch the rest of my life to see the world." She went on, "I want to leave Baghdad, I want to be free to do what I want. Just improving myself—my mind, my way of life. I'd like to meet people from different countries, know how they live, what they do, what they believe."

Her mother was on the verge of tears; her parents were afraid for her to leave Iraq. Aseel put her arm around her mother and touched her father's hand. "He believes in me," she said.

They were Shiite Muslims, but on the drive from the university Aseel had hinted about a secret in their background. After lunch, when she went into the narrow kitchen to make tea, I followed her and started to broach the topic. Aseel's eyes shifted away: Her father was standing in the doorway, watching us closely. "I can't talk of it," she said. "My father says it's long ago, let it go. We've lived like this for so long."

At the end of the afternoon, when I rose to leave, the family offered me their silver heirlooms. I declined by saying that the gifts would be confiscated at the Jordanian border. Outside, the mad uncle was pacing with a glass in his hand. I was thinking how isolated the family seemed. They had no political party or religious militia, no ayatollah or tribal sheikh; they had only the Americans, who didn't know of their existence. Aseel had never spoken to a foreigner before the morning we met. She wanted to travel, but she was too frightened to go into town and set up an e-mail account at an Internet café. The pressure of her yearning filled the small room.

At the door, Aseel smiled. "Do you think my dreams will come true?"

I RETURNED TO IRAQ several times during the year of the occupation, and I always made a point of seeing Aseel. The status of her dreams became one index for me of the status of America's vision for Iraq. Aseel was one of its most ardent supporters, and she never lost her faith. Over time, the family's fortunes improved, and they began to reverse twenty years of decline and climb back up toward middle-class comfort. The brother's salary from a large contractor allowed them to begin building a new two-story house in the narrow space between their old one and the garden wall. The ceilings were high, the floors tiled, and Aseel chose the color green for her new bedroom. She threw away her *hijab* when she started to see more and more young women going unveiled on the street, and she wore trousers outside the house. The family acquired a satellite dish; although electricity was still four hours on and then four off, the home telephone was working again after being out of service for months due to war damage and looting; and once there was sporadic cellular coverage around Baghdad and a few other cities, Aseel carried a mobile phone. She opened an e-mail account and enjoyed going to the Internet café and logging on to chat rooms, where she would madden young men from across the Arab world whose chief purpose was to meet girls online and who instead got an earful of political taunts from this fiercely opinionated Iraqi. She once commented that Americans and Israelis seemed to care about Iraqis more than other Arabs did.

An Egyptian wrote back: "Aseel, the Arabs are like brothers with one blood like a wall of stone. No Arabs want to kill Muslims. The Arabs refuse what is happening in Iraq because we are brothers."

"You are bad people," she replied.

"Wait, Aseel. Iraqis are the best people."

"You're a liar."

"But you Iraqis are with America and Israel."

"I'm proud of that. But Hosni is in Israel. Goodbye."

"No, no, wait."

But Aseel's life wasn't changing fast enough to suit her. It remained impossible to get a passport because there was no such office yet, and a scholarship for study abroad was just as out of reach. Iraq seemed as isolated as ever. The academic exchanges, the shipments of books, the visiting lecturers that Baghdad University had hoped for in the first months of the occupation never materialized; instead, the university campuses had been taken over by religious groups, with their ubiquitous banners and portraits of martyrs. The explosion at the UN, and then the steady rise in terror bombings and insurgent violence through the fall and winter, drove all but the bravest international organizations out of Iraq. On the morning of January 18, 2004, Aseel's brother was in a line of cars outside the Assassins' Gate, waiting to get into the Green Zone, when six cars ahead of him a thousand-pound bomb exploded with massive force, killing two Americans and twenty-three Iraqis who worked for the occupation authority. A minibus full of young women directly in front of Aseel's brother took the force of the blast, and he was able to drive home with cuts in his face from shattered glass. Six weeks later, on Ashura, the holiest day of the Shiite calendar, Aseel and her mother were standing in a throng of worshippers outside the shrine of Kadhimiya, Baghdad's old Shiite district. The sun beat down, Aseel felt hot, and they moved a hundred yards away into shade. Fifteen minutes later, a man detonated himself in exactly the spot they had left; several more explosions followed almost instantly as the panicked crowd began to stampede. The same thing was happening around the same time at the holy shrines of Karbala, south of Baghdad. At least 180 pilgrims died in the Ashura bombings.

Aseel's attitude toward these near-death calamities was the same as that of other Iraqis: When it's your hour, there's nothing you can do. Meanwhile, she chafed at the constraints on her life.

"If the Americans want to do us a favor," she said, "they can make us free to leave Iraq. The minds are locked here. It will take about twenty years, I think. And I don't want to lose my life here."

Her mother suggested that I take her to New York and put her under glass for public display: "An Iraqi girl!"

Being an Iraqi girl was itself a kind of confinement. Aseel and I couldn't go alone to a restaurant, couldn't talk alone in her house, couldn't exchange the kisses on both cheeks that every other member of her family gave me. For all of her insistence on free thinking, free dressing, free reading, and free moving (she longed to ride a bicycle around the city, something no woman could do without drawing unwanted attention or worse), I had the sense that Aseel accepted these taboos as the way she had to live. When she was sixteen, an older cousin had danced with her at a wedding, and the touch of his hand on her back was like nothing she'd ever felt. Then he went away to school, and soon he was married, and that was the end of the first and last love affair of her life. She prayed infrequently, she went to the mosque only on special occasions like Ashura, and her attitude toward religion was more mystical than doctrinal. But she still wanted to be a good Iraqi girl.

IN THE WEST, Iraq had a reputation for being the most secular country in the region; its people were thought to be educated, cosmopolitan, modern. The reputation turned out to be decades out of date. After the oil-rich, freewheeling 1970s, when women wore miniskirts and alcohol flowed liberally, the effect of endless war, steady immiseration, and the Islamic revolution next door in Iran made Iraq far more conservative than most people on the outside, including Iraqi exiles, realized. Especially among the poor Shia, women disappeared under the *hijab*, or veil, and the *abaya*, the full-length black robe. The Shiite clergy became Saddam's most serious internal opposition. To shore up his power with his own Sunni base after the disaster of the Gulf War, the newly pious dictator launched a campaign of Islamization: The words *"Allahu akbar"* were added to the Iraqi flag in Saddam's own script, a copy of the Qur'an was written in his own blood, and gigantic Sunni mosques began to go up around Baghdad, beginning with the Mother of All Battles mosque. Many of them remained unfinished when the Americans arrived, and across the city's horizon you could see the hulking shells of half-built domes encased in scaffolding, like the monuments of a warlike civilization that ended with some sudden catastrophe. In the ruins down below, the Shiite masses were coming out to claim the streets.

March 2004 roughly coincided with the first lunar month of the Muslim calendar, Muharram. For the Shia, it was a tragic month, an unlucky month, Sheikh Emad al-Din al-Awadi told me, when no religious Muslim would get married or make an important decision. The tenth day of Muharram was Ashura, the anniversary of the death in A.D. 680 of Imam Hussein, grandson of the Prophet, and the massacre of his followers at Karbala, where Hussein had come to stake his claim as leader of the faithful. Those who killed them immediately repented. They became the Shia, or "partisans" of Hussein's father, Ali, who believed that the caliphate passed down through his descendants, as opposed to the Sunnis, whose caliphs were chosen from within the circle of religious authority and who located the Abassid caliphate in Baghdad, where it remained until the city was sacked by Mongol invaders in 1256. Beginning with the death of Hussein and continuing down through the history of the Arab Muslim world, the Shia were the great losers of this schism, enduring under the religious yoke of the Sunni caliphate, until it was abolished by Atatürk in 1920, and then under the temporal power of Sunni kings and dictators in the new Arab nation-states. In the light of this history, the most significant result of the American invasion of Iraq, and the larger American project of bringing majority rule there, was that, for the first time in their history, the Shia were going to take power in an Arab country.

And now, 1,324 years after Karbala, Baghdad was festooned with the symbols of Shiite piety and penitence—the red flags of Hussein's blood, the green flags of Islam, the black flags of grief bearing messages such as "Hussein Taught Us to Become Victims in Order to Gain Victory." The chants, the parades, the beating of chests, the flaying of scalps and backs in ceremonies of atonement, also became displays of collective power. For the first time in more than two decades, the Shia were free to celebrate Ashura in Iraq. So the holy shrines of Baghdad and Karbala were unusually crowded with black-clad Shiite pilgrims from around the country, Iran, and the far-flung corners of the world, and, anonymous among them, a few Sunni jihadis wrapped in explosives.

The Baghdad morgue became a charnel house filled with bodies, heads, limbs, and buckets of flesh. Outside the squat yellow two-story building, in a decaying neighborhood near the Tigris called Medical City, a man waited to enter and look for an eleven-year-old boy, a neighbor, whose father lay wounded in the hospital. Others were leaving with rags pressed to their faces. The authorities were rushing to complete the process of identification. There would be no forensic autopsies of the victims, I was told by Dr. Bashir Shaker, the young forensic-medicine specialist on duty. These followers of Hussein were the newest Shiite martyrs, and Islam forbade the violation of their bodies.

On the day of my visit to the morgue, another death had come under Shaker's review. "An interesting case," he told me, more so than the terrible carnage of the Ashura bombings. The body of a woman, forty-one years old and never married, had been discovered with six gunshot wounds in the chest. Shaker's initial examination found that she appeared not to be a virgin. This was what made the case interesting.

Before the American invasion, the doctor said, one violent death a month arrived on the tables of the city morgue. This number revealed two conditions of Iraqi life under Saddam: The state owned a near monopoly on violence and most of its victims disappeared without a trace in unmarked mass graves. One effect of Iraq's liberation from Baathist tyranny was the widespread dispersal of violence, and its utter unpredictability. In occupied Iraq, between fifteen and twenty-five murder victims arrived at the morgue every night, most of them with gunshot wounds. Every two weeks, the unclaimed bodies were released to the authorities for obscure burial. Shaker estimated that five cases a week involved Baathists executed in reprisal killings; their families typically retrieved the bodies without informing the police. With barely functioning courts, a weak, ill-trained, and often corrupt new police force, a foreign occupier that was failing to provide security, and a general atmosphere of lawlessness—kidnappings, carjackings, highway banditry, shootings by jumpy American soldiers at checkpoints, suicide bombings, urban firefights, murder for revenge, for money, for every reason or no reason—Iraqis didn't expect to start receiving the justice that was denied them throughout the Saddam years anytime soon.

The details of Dr. Shaker's "interesting case" cast suspicion on the dead woman's family. The number of gunshots suggested something other than the new gang style of killing. The doctor called such a crime "washing the shame." Honor killing was an old tradition in Iraq, he said, though in this case with a new element: Before the war, the family would have burned or drowned the woman to disguise the murder. "Now you can kill and go," Shaker said. "No need to cover the crime." The standard prison sentence for "washing the shame" was six months.

The woman's case was referred to a committee of five doctors, including Iraq's leading hymen expert, who had done his advanced research and taken his board degree in the subject. The committee found that the woman's hymen was extremely thin but intact. Case closed. The family would not be investigated, and, without the means to find other leads, the police would seal the woman's file.

Down the hall from the morgue, housed within the same Medico-Legal Institute where Shaker was on staff, was another examination room, with a reclining chair and stirrups. This was where virginity exams on living subjects took place. Before the war, when there was rule of law of a sort, Shaker performed five or six a day—most of them on suspected prostitutes, but also on runaways, kidnap victims, and girls who had suffered some accident and whose parents, for the sake of marriageability, wanted a medical certificate establishing their chastity. These exams could have explosive consequences, and their results had to be carefully guarded. Women were shot dead by relatives on their way out the institute's front door; in cases when a husband killed his bride on their wedding night and the exam showed that she was one of the 40 percent of Iraqi women with a condition known as "elastic hymen"—that is, she was still a virgin—the danger of reprisal came from her family. An entire subspecialty of forensic medicine in Iraq dealt with virginity. In any criminal case involving a woman, it was the most important piece of information. "It rules our life," Shaker said. The most surprising thing about these details of his profession was their ordinariness.

In March 2003, a week before the start of the war, a sixteen-year-old girl whom the former regime's police had found wandering disoriented through the streets was brought to the Medico-Legal Institute. Upon examining her, Shaker found that her virginity had been recently and violently taken. The girl, named Raghda, was beautiful, with pale skin and large, dark eyes, and she was so miserable she could hardly speak. Raghda seemed nothing like the teenage prostitutes Shaker examined, and he gently persuaded her to tell him what had happened.

Raghda had gone to audition as a television introducer at the studio owned by Saddam's psychopathic older son Uday. Along with the six other finalists, she was taken to a room where Uday—crippled from a 1996 assassination attempt—was seated in a chair, holding a pistol in his lap. He ordered the girls to undress and walk in a circle around his chair. When one girl begged to be excused, Uday raised the pistol and shot her dead. After that, the other girls, including Raghda, did as they were told. In the following days, Uday (who was committing some of his last crimes in power, while an invasion force gathered along Iraq's southern border) raped the girls one after another, then threw them out on the street, drugged, with a wad of cash, which was how Raghda was found by the police. When she told them her story, they gave her a beating and then brought her to the Medico-Legal Institute.

"If you want to help me," Raghda told the doctor, "go tell my parents their daughter was found dead."

On March 18, the day before the war started, Shaker completed Raghda's paperwork. "Notice that there is the appearance of complete hymen rupture from the top to the base. This is the result of an erect penis or a tool of the same quality. It occurred not long ago—about two weeks or more, and cannot say exactly when. In conclusion, the hymen membrane was ruptured longer ago than two weeks and cannot say how long. End of report." Raghda was returned to the police. Shaker never learned her fate.

Over the course of his career, Shaker served in the Iraqi army and took part in the occupation of Kuwait, a period he would only describe as an existence utterly separate from the rest of his life. His testimony in trials sent homosexuals to execution. At the morgue he handled the nightly traffic of violent death. A bloody Friday that March of 2004 brought thirty-two bodies, including two German and Dutch water engineers gunned down by insurgents on a road south of Baghdad, and two Iraqi journalists shot to death by American soldiers as they drove away from a checkpoint. For Shaker, such cases were purely intellectual matters. The effect of this dispassion showed in the cold, handsome gaze of his blue eyes, in his blunt uninflected manner of speaking, in the way his smile turned almost automatically into a sneer. But he never got over Raghda.

WHEN I MET HIM, Dr. Shaker was looking for a change in his life. "Any change," he said, "better or worse." He had a restless mind and hated boredom, and since the Americans represented something new, he welcomed spending time with me and became my guide to Baghdad's morbid underside. I assumed that this forward-thinking man of science, with a flat-top haircut and a clean-shaven jaw, wanted a relatively secular, liberal Iraq. I kept waiting for him to catch my eye in the middle of one of his clinical descriptions and shake his head over the backwardness of a society obsessed with virginity and prostitution. It never happened.

Shaker was born in 1968, the year the Baath Party came to power. "For thirty-five years, I feel I was dead," he said. "Only these last weeks I'm beginning to live." The fall of Saddam and the arrival of foreign occupiers—who happened to be the makers of his favorite old movies—had, at last, brought the chance for a new life. Eager to obtain travel documents and venture outside Iraq, he sold his private dermatology practice and a piece of land he'd received as a soldier. His first foreign trip was to Amman, Jordan, where he had arranged to meet an Iraqi girl who was living in exile in Amsterdam. They married after two days. "Like a movie," he said. Without consummating the marriage, because it had not been an Islamic service, they went back to their respective cities and waited for the situation in Iraq to become more stable.

But these same foreign occupiers now presided over the chaos that created the brisk business Shaker saw every night at the Baghdad morgue. On a morning when I was allowed inside, the wet blood on the floor and on the empty stretchers was drawing flies. The stench of death was real enough that I had to breathe through a bandanna. The morgue had the filthy, improvised atmosphere of a front-line hospital, and nothing was less ceremonious than the dead themselves. In the hall, bodies lay uncovered on tables. A man with a broad mustache, his throat slashed so deeply that he had almost been decapitated, found naked under a pile of garbage in a middle-class district. A man with a gunshot wound in his head, his blue eyes open and filmy, the orange plastic tip of a breathing tube stuck in his mouth like a whistle. The small, blackened corpse of a woman burned over most of her body. In the gloomy chill of the refrigerated room, six naked bodies lay sprawled on the floor, two women and four men. One of the women, believed to be a prostitute, had been shot through the nipple—by a relative, Shaker assumed. Some of these corpses, he said, would never be claimed; there would be no washing of bodies, no Muslim burial rites, only disposal.

On the way out, I passed a well-dressed man who was staring down at the waxen face above the slashed throat. He was the dead man's cousin; he had searched all the hospitals before ending up at the morgue. When he looked up, our eyes briefly met. He seemed at a loss, as if he were seeking an explanation. He shook his head once and turned to leave, talking frantically to himself.

While the morgue overflowed, the examination room down the hall, with its reclining couch and stirrups, was usually empty. Before the war it had been the other way around. These two sections of the Medico-Legal Institute didn't just occupy the same floor; they existed in a kind of fragile moral relation, as if the social control of virginity offered the last defense against the anarchy that led to murder. Shaker, a religious Shiite, wondered if the Iranian method of public whippings might be the answer to Baghdad's prostitution epidemic which, he said, was flourishing in the lawlessness of the occupation. "It's strict, it's horrible, but it has good results," he said. "Prostitution now is normal." He blamed the Americans, and especially Bremer, who had threatened in February to veto any interim constitution that declared Islam to be the principal basis of law. Personal freedom, Aseel's most ardent desire, was a moral disaster to Bashir Shaker. "When they give everybody their rights, it's causing bad things in society, it's corrupting us," he said. "If Islam is the main source of law, none of these things would happen."

It was one measure of America's inability to achieve its goals in Iraq that a man like Bashir Shaker, who had everything to gain from the overthrow of Saddam and the opportunities it opened up, now felt himself pulled toward a harsher brand of Islam in reaction to the pervasive insecurity of the occupation. The doctor said that he belonged to "the middle level of mind" in Iraqi society, between the strictly religious masses below him and the secular elite above. "There are many Iraqis like me," he said. In Iraq, there was nothing unusual about a doctor who loved Marilyn Monroe and Cary Grant, advocated the public whipping of prostitutes, and believed that executed homosexuals got what they deserved. But the middle level of mind meant inner conflict. Shaker feared the effects of living outside Iraq, and of the images transmitted into his house by the satellite dish that he installed on the roof when it was still illegal and highly dangerous under Saddam. He had fallen in love with an independent-minded Iraqi who grew up in Holland and wore low-cut shirts; if she came to Baghdad, he wanted her to start covering her hair and acting like a more traditional Muslim woman. His work fascinated him, but he worried that his daily immersion in death would coarsen his soul. "The doctor of forensic medicine deals only with bodies," he said. "So maybe in the end I will become like you—an existentialist."

Shaker lived with his mother, brothers, and sisters on a tidy side street in the vast, impoverished, overwhelmingly Shiite district of two million people in northeastern Baghdad that some Baghdadis still called by its original name, al-Thawra, which means Revolution. Saddam, who was as hated there as anywhere in Iraq, inflicted his own name on the place; immediately after his fall, residents proclaimed that Saddam City was now Sadr City, after Grand Ayatollah Mohamed Sadiq al-Sadr, a leading Shiite cleric who was assassinated in 1999, almost certainly on Saddam's orders. Sadr's uncle, Ayatollah Mohamed

Baqr al-Sadr, the greatest Shiite scholar of the previous generation, had been tortured and killed along with his sister in 1980. Saddam's brutal suppression of the uprising that followed the Gulf War in 1991 shattered the established Shiite clergy in the holy city of Najaf, a center of the rebellion: Grand Ayatollah Sayyid Abu al-Qasim al-Khoei died soon afterward, and Ayatollah Ali al-Sistani was placed under house arrest. Saddam picked Mohamed Sadiq al-Sadr, imprisoned at the time, to take over the leadership of Iraq's Shiite community. So Sadr was elevated with Saddam's blessing and Baathist money, and through the 1990s he built up a network of thousands of followers whom he recruited among young, poor, and uneducated Shia in the countryside, gave six-week religious instruction in Najaf, and then dispersed throughout the largely Shiite cities of the south, as well as Baghdad's al-Thawra. Sadr's message was a Shiite blend of nationalism and populism: He spoke for the dispossessed and blamed the troubles of Iraq's Shia on the fact that so many of their religious leaders, such as Khoei and Sistani, originally came from Iran. Sadr's followers attributed superhuman powers to him. One of Shaker's younger brothers told me that, on Judgment Day, God will see everyone as he truly is: A liar will appear to God as a dog, an arrogant man as a tiny insect, a drinker as a pig. But Ayatollah Sadr saw human beings this way while he was still alive.

By the end of the '90s, Sadr began to challenge the regime that had made him a leader. He disparaged Sistani and the politically quietist, "silent" Hawza (the school of Shiite theology) in Najaf, and identified himself with the "speaking" Hawza, who believed, with Iran's Khomeini, in the clergy's central role in politics. In a series of Friday sermons at the shrine in Kufa, a few miles outside Najaf, Sadr used metaphors and double meanings to deliver attacks on the Baathist tyranny. These speeches, which were secretly recorded and distributed, greatly enhanced his reputation, and they also led to his martyrdom, which in many ways must have been the desired end, as it had been for so many figures in Shiite history. Sadr and two of his sons were ambushed and shot on the road between Najaf and Karbala. His youngest son, Moqtada, a seminary student, remained alive to claim his father's mantle and his following.

A round sticker affixed to the wooden front door of the Shaker house bore an image of the white-bearded Sadr, along with a quotation from one of his sermons, insisting that women be veiled. The living room was decorated with pictures of Sadr, Moqtada, and Imam Hussein crossing a river on horseback by moonlight, like one of the Christian saints. Compact discs containing forty-five sermons by Ayatollah Sadr were stacked inside the family's TV cabinet, alongside a pile of back issues of *al-Hawza*, the fiercely anti-American newspaper published by Moqtada al-Sadr's movement. Shaker told me that he got his television news from al-Jazeera and Iranian broadcasts—he never watched Iraq's American-run state network. His main source of information from the non-Islamic world, I realized, was old Hollywood movies. That wouldn't offer him much help in parsing the truth of a story I noticed in *al-Hawza*. The newspaper had reprinted side-by-side photographs of President Bush and President Clinton holding up their index and pinkie fingers; the accompanying article offered the images as evidence of a Zionist-Masonic conspiracy.

Shaker's younger brothers, Ali and Samir, joined us in the living room. Ali was a secondary school math teacher; Samir, an unemployed telecom repairman. Unlike their dirty-blond, fair-skinned older brother, they were dark and bearded—respectful, serious, slightly wary.

"Samir is closer to God than me," Shaker said. "Ali is like me—flexible." Ali and Samir were devoted followers of Moqtada; they shared his hostility toward the occupation. From time to time, someone knocked on the inner door, and one of the brothers would get up to receive a tray of Pepsis from the hands of an unseen woman.

Ali brought up the Ashura bombings. "Ninety-five percent of Iraqis knew the main purpose of this was to start a religious war between Shia and Sunnis," he said. He was skeptical of the Americans' assertion that Abu Musab al-Zarqawi, the Jordanian terrorist with ties to al-Qaeda, who had recently written a long letter to Osama bin Laden advocating a strategy of fomenting civil war in Iraq, was responsible for the attacks. "This Zarqawi—it's only a game that the Americans use," Ali declared. "Before the election of Bush, they'll show Zarqawi on TV. Just like Saddam—they captured him months before they showed him."

The brothers told me a joke about the occupation. An American soldier is about to kill a Shiite, who cries, "Please, no, in the name of Imam Hussein!" The American asks who Imam Hussein was and then decides to spare the man's life. A few weeks later, this same soldier is sent to Falluja, where he's cornered by a Sunni insurgent. The soldier thinks fast and cries, "Please, no, in the name of Imam Hussein!" The insurgent says, "What? You're an American *and* a Shiite?" and blows him away.

There was a moment of laughter in the living room.

I had been collecting Iraqi jokes, and I weighed telling the Shaker brothers one. There was the joke about the newlyweds in Falluja (Falluja jokes abounded in Iraq). The man asks his new bride to suck his dick. "No, no," she says, "it's *haram*." "We're married now," he says, "please, please do it." "I can't, it's *haram*." "*Please*." "Okay, if you cover it in honey, I'll do it." "Are you kidding? If I cover it in honey, *I'm* sucking it." A glance at the faces of somber Ali and devout Samir made me file the Falluja joke away. Then there was the joke I'd recently heard, from an Iraqi Shiite, about Ayatollah Mohamed Baqr al-Hakim, the spiritual leader of the Tehran-based Shiite political party, who had been killed by a car bomb in Najaf in August 2003. In the joke, he is blown into so many pieces that his body can't be identified. Finally investigators bring a severed penis to his widow and apologetically ask her whether she can make a positive identification. The widow glances at the object and says, "That's not my husband. That's his driver." This joke was so *haram* that I felt a quiver of fear just thinking about it. Finally I remembered a repeatable joke. Ten Kurds locked up in a mental hospital spend six months fighting one another to look through the tiny hole in the wall of their cell. A doctor, curious, enters the cell and asks to have a look. He puts his eye to the hole for ten minutes: nothing. "There's nothing there," he says. One of the patients answers, "We haven't seen anything in six months—you expect to see something in ten minutes?" But by the time I remembered the Kurdish joke, the moment had passed.

Ali, sitting cross-legged on a rug against the wall, looked directly at me. "Before this war, I was waiting for the Americans to come, and now I feel sort of cheated. All this talk about rebuilding Iraq, and all we see is a couple of light coats of paint. And they say they renovated Iraq."

Samir spoke in darker tones, with a faint smile. He had never had any illusions. "No enemy loves his enemy. We know very well that the Americans don't intend us any good."

I pointed out that the Americans had at least gotten rid of Saddam.

"That's not enough," Ali said. "Now things are worse. We can't go outside at four in the morning, as before."

If within a year there were free elections in Iraq, I asked, would they be satisfied?

"Yes," Samir said.

Ali disagreed. "I don't think the people will be satisfied. What if we have a president? The mobile phones we have here don't work. Why can't it be like the Gulf countries? Maybe in generations after generations. But we won't be here then. It pisses me off."

Shaker asked to borrow my satellite phone and disappeared up on the roof, to call his new wife in Amsterdam.

ON THE FRIDAY following the Ashura bombings, I went with Shaker to hear prayers in Kadhimiya. Along a broad pedestrian market street that ended in the square in front of the sixteenth-century mosque, cordons of grim-looking young men in black, carrying Kalashnikovs, searched the throngs of pilgrims for weapons. These were the local security force of the Mahdi Army, the armed followers of Moqtada al-Sadr, named for the twelfth Shiite imam, the hidden imam, who is expected to return as the messiah and usher in the Apocalypse. There were no Iraqi policemen or American soldiers on the streets. One militiaman, who was eighteen years old, told me that the Americans had prevented the Mahdi Army from carrying their weapons on Ashura. This was a foolish decision, he said: If the militia had been armed, it would have been able to hold back the surges of worshippers that day and catch the suicide bombers mingling in the crowd. After the explosions, Iraqis had greeted the soldiers who rushed in to evacuate the wounded with a storm of rocks and shoes.

While Shaker went into a shop to wash himself before prayers, a local cleric named Sheikh Mohamed Kinani told me that the bombers were Wahhabi members of al-Qaeda, working in concert with an

American soldier employed by the John Kerry campaign. "I believe John Kerry is behind this so Bush will lose his presidency and look bad in front of the world," he said. "But it's the Iraqis who pay for it." The traffic in conspiracy theories had grown so heavy that an American intelligence unit began putting out *The Baghdad Mosquito*, a daily compendium of rumors currently in circulation, not unlike the records kept by the Baath Party. According to men I spoke with in Kadhimiya, Wahhabi had light-colored beards and were the enemies of true Muslims. A merchant on the pedestrian market street said, "We caught a Wahhabi from Ramadi an hour ago." The captive was wearing a short dishdasha, in the Wahhabi style, and while his feet were dirty, his body was suspiciously clean. A search of the Wahhabi man turned up blank paper and a map. Local people took him to the police station, where he would be tortured until he confessed.

Prayers began beneath a hot noon sun. The shrine itself, with its splendid golden dome and minarets, its tiled arches soaring over the wooden front doors, was closed because of bomb damage. Men filled the square; holding black signs and pictures of Shiite martyrs, they shook their fists and chanted, "Pray to Mohamed and the followers of Mohamed and hurry the damning of our enemies. Give victory to Moqtada! We follow *Moq-ta-da!*"

The doctor knelt in the front row and prayed. He seemed alone in the crowd, the only worshipper who wasn't chanting.

One of Moqtada's aides, Hazem al-Araji, delivered the sermon. He was a thirty-five-year-old sayyid, or descendant of the Prophet, with a salt-and-pepper beard, who had spent two years in exile in Vancouver before the war. Later, in conversation at his office, he proved to be a smooth, smiling politician who Googled himself several times a day to keep up with his press and who made a theocratic Islamic state sound not very different from a parliamentary democracy. But in front of the crowd of worshippers outside the shrine, Araji let loose an incendiary and conspiratorial analysis of the violence in Iraq. The attacks came from four sources, he declared, none of them Iraqi or Muslim: It was the Jews, the Americans, the British, and the Wahhabi. The Jews—who had been warned to stay away from the World Trade Center on September 11, so that not one Jew died—"want Iraqis to die." America, the devil, allowed the violence in order to have an excuse to continue occupying Iraq. The British, America's partners, were more directly responsible, since they invented Wahhabism and, therefore, al-Qaeda, which have "nothing to do with Islam."

Shaker knelt, slump shouldered, and gazed down at his clasped hands, muttering prayers. He looked puzzled, as if he were trying to figure something out. I wondered if the cleric's ranting embarrassed him.

"If you read the modern books of history," Araji proclaimed, "Wahhabism started in 1870 by the good graces of the British government in order to go against Islam, to make Islam look bad, to make Muslims fight each other. Those who know—good. Those who don't—know now."

Araji was referring to *Confessions of a British Spy*, an apocryphal memoir attributed to a British colonial officer of the early eighteenth century named Hempher (Araji was off by 150 years). Going undercover, Hempher befriends a gullible, hotheaded Iraqi in Basra named Mohamed ibn Abd al-Wahhab and tempts him into founding a heretical sect of Islam that will bring disrepute to other Muslims and turn them against one another: "We, the English people, have to make mischief and arouse schism in all our colonies in order that we may live in welfare and luxury." But Hempher cannot conceal his admiration for the spiritual grandeur of Islam, which more than once nearly causes him to abandon his mission. *Confessions of a British Spy* reads like an Anglophobic variation on *Protocols of the Elders of Zion*, the labor of a Sunni Muslim author (probably Turkish) whose intent is to present Muslims as both too holy and too weak to organize anything as destructive as Wahhabism on their own (or, Araji's listeners could deduce, to pull off a crime as appalling as the Ashura bombings, which took place two centuries after Wahhabis, on the same holiday, had sacked the Shiite shrine at Karbala, slaughtering two thousand citizens). With its subtext of powerlessness, the "memoir" is a confession of Muslim humiliation, a text that was bound to find an audience in occupied Iraq, where, in spite of a pronounced streak of anti-Shiism throughout the book, the name Hempher was beginning to circulate among militant Shia.

"America, England, Israel, do whatever you have to do, build more missiles, more explosives, more terrorism all over the world," Araji said. "But it's not going to stop us."

The crowd chanted: "Yes, yes to Islam!"

"Just a speech," Shaker scoffed as we drove out of Kadhimiya. "If I knew this man is going to deliver the Friday prayers, I would not go." He would have preferred to hear Moqtada himself. If Moqtada had come, he said, there would have been less talk and more action.

ON THE NIGHTS around Ashura, the Shia prepare large quantities of food, visit friends and neighbors, and stay up together until dawn watching for the spirit of Imam Hussein to pass by. I was invited to spend one night at the house of a theology student named Ali Talib. He lived just off a highway in eastern Baghdad, on a narrow street amid a warren of houses, all of them flying tattered little black, red, and green flags above their rooftops. Ali was outside when I arrived, stirring a cauldron of steaming porridge with a wooden paddle twice the length of a baseball bat. All along the street, his neighbors were doing the same. It was already late evening—the curfew would soon make it impossible for me to leave until early morning. I had never spent the night in an Iraqi home before, and Ali made a point of putting me at ease from the start by handing me the paddle and insisting that I stir. I was to help feed the passing spirit of Imam Hussein.

Ali was in his early thirties, a fleshy man with a severe limp, nearly bald, a light growth of stubble on his cheeks—doctrinally correct, he insisted, since what mattered was having enough facial hair to be unmistakable for a woman, not having a full beard. Ali was warm, ebullient, constantly touching my shoulder for emphasis or laughing with startled delight at something I said. "I wish one day would be forty-eight hours instead of twenty-four!" he cried. "I can't sleep quietly— this week I slept eight hours, because of the Internet." The dial-up connection, a present from his family, allowed him to study night and day in the absence of expensive books. "I'd love to be in NASA and see this world from the sky," he said apropos of nothing. "I want to live it second by second."

Ali's family tried to make his life as easy and fulfilling as possible, because it wasn't clear how long he would live. Since childhood he had suffered from a disease of the left leg. He lifted his dishdasha to show me: The leg was horribly swollen and discolored, with knots of bulges up and down the thigh and calf. An operation had been unsuccessful; the doctor had told him that unless he went abroad for treatment, the disease would eventually kill him.

"The reason I'm patient is that I know Imam Hussein suffered much worse things," he said. "The killing of Hussein led to a revolution. But this revolution was not one of blood—it was of the spirit."

The two-story house was built around a small inner court that was open to the night sky. A bird fluttered in a cage, a boom box played rhythmic chants of self-flagellation, and Ali, his uncle, and I sat talking in the court while neighbors came and went. Ali was an ardent student of Islamic philosophy. For years under Saddam, he had gone down to Najaf, not telling his parents, and pursued a course of study with the leading Shiite clerics of the Hawza. The government monitored the students, and two of Ali's teachers were eventually executed, but he had always been plagued with hopelessness, and what he was learning in Najaf made life not just bearable but ecstatic. "The whole world is built on the love of God," he said. "Not just human beings— everything you see in life, every living organism." He became a follower of the seventeenth-century Persian mystic Mullah Sadra, an idealist philosopher in the spirit of Neoplatonism, who taught the unity of all existence. "He built this road, Mullah Sadra, and all the scholars after him built the same road, and I wanted to follow him, but Saddam and my uncle wouldn't let me take that road."

Ali's uncle, an old communist who was not particularly religious, said, "We didn't want him to follow it, because at that time just listening to this music would have killed him, and the punishment would have been for the whole family."

Eventually, Ali's health and the dangers forced him to stop attending classes in Najaf. He kept studying with a secret group of friends in Baghdad. The hardest part was finding and buying books. In his bedroom upstairs Ali had Machiavelli's *The Prince*, a brand-new copy of Mullah Sadra's *Philosophy of the Principles and What Is Promised*, and other texts, but it was never enough. The Internet had become his obsession—it was, he said, Bremer's greatest gift to Iraqis. On his desk there was a picture of Grand Ayatollah Sistani.

We talked on into the night: about Mill's idea of liberty, Islam and democracy, the role of women in religion and tradition, the leading Iraqi politicians, the place of the clerics in the future government. Ali's ideas were half formed; at times he came close to advocating Iranian-style *wilayat al-faqih*, at other times he wanted to keep religion and politics separate. He asked me a thousand questions. What did I think of *The Passion of the Christ*? Had I met anyone famous other than Bremer? How could I separate what was the government's business from what was Allah's? Would the Americans let Iraqis write their own constitution? It was a rare and bracing conversation, for Ali was open to every idea; nothing was out of bounds.

The Shiite surge during the days of Muharram in Iraq had all the heat and fervor of a long-suppressed desire, but it was not a tolerant month. Students were threatening academic deans for taking down their religious banners, and Moqtada's followers were conducting themselves more and more like a fascist militia. Mustafa al-Kadhimi, the exile I first met in London, who in his youth had been a member of the Islamist Dawa Party, once explained that this religious explosion was not just a reaction to the Baath Party's repression but a version of the same dictatorial mentality, for the generation of younger Shia had grown up knowing nothing else. It would take two or three years to spend itself, and in the meantime a lot of mischief would be done. As for Ali Talib, he didn't know exactly what he thought, but how he thought was self-critically, with a touch of metaphysical joy.

We even talked about sex. The mutual friend who introduced us had told me that for six months Ali had been carrying on a semisecret affair with a widow. The Shia sanctioned a practice known as *zawaj mutea*, or pleasure marriage. It was based on a verse from the Qur'an and had all the trappings of conventional Islamic marriage: There was a contract, payment up front, consent of both parties, approval of the woman's family, and clerical blessing (the woman couldn't be a prostitute). The difference was that *zawaj mutea* was temporary: It could last anywhere from one hour to twenty years, and it was indefinitely renewable. I had heard that there were rooms in Kadhimiya rented out for just this purpose, and imams with albums full of pictures of good

men and women for their flock to choose among. "But there's a sensitive point," Ali cautioned. If the woman was still a virgin, "You cannot
have sex with her—you can only touch and kiss." He explained, "It
would be a disaster for that virgin because her brother would kill her.
It isn't Islamists who would kill her—she would be killed by tradition."
(In the case of widows and divorcées the restriction was lifted.) But if
you clicked on www.sistani.org and looked up the grand ayatollah's
teachings on the subjects of oral and anal sex, you realized that thousands of young Shia were well advanced in the arts of love before they
ever married in the traditional manner. Ali described the practice as a
doctrinal act of kindness. "We Shia don't want to have forbidden sex,
so we have *zawaj mutea*. It's like having mercy, so that he or she
wouldn't suffer inside, to make it easier for them."

All the while we talked, the women of the household—Ali's mother,
sister, cousin, and neighbor—were cooking holiday dishes just a few
feet away in the kitchen. The younger women kept coming to the door,
dressed all in black for Muharram but unveiled and extremely curious,
and made eye contact with me before retreating to whisper among
themselves and giggle. I told them that they were making me feel like
an animal at the zoo. On any other occasion, Ali said, they would not
have shown me their faces at home, but this was a feast day and I was
an honored guest.

His sister Ibtisam, a volleyball instructor at a local college, finally
stood in the doorway, her face half hidden by the jamb, and engaged
me in something like a conversation. She asked why the American soldiers no longer smiled and waved as they used to after the liberation.
She wanted me to know that after a year they had seen nothing from
the occupation. And women, she said, wanted their rights. "We want
to take part in the elections."

"Nobody said you can't vote," Ali told her.

"We want higher education," she said. "We want better jobs. And
respect in society." With that, Ibtisam retreated to the safety of the
boiling pots.

Around three in the morning, I followed Ali up the exterior stair-
case that ran from the court to the second-story roof. A cool breeze was

blowing. Down below, the penitents on the boom box were still chanting and beating themselves. Under the stars and a half-moon, palm trees and lights stretched out across the city. All of Baghdad seemed to be awake, waiting for Imam Hussein, and at this distance, on this night, it was a magical place. Ali and I said goodbye just before dawn.

AS THE MONTH WORE ON, Iraq became noticeably more dangerous for someone like me. On March 9, a young CPA official who had been working with women's groups, a colleague of hers, and an Iraqi translator were chased down and shot to death on the road between Karbala and Hilla by five men wearing Iraqi police uniforms. An hour earlier, I had been driving back to Baghdad on another road a few miles away. On March 15, four Baptist missionaries were killed by automatic weapons fire in Mosul. The next day, two foreign water engineers were gunned down in a roadside shooting near Hilla. Their corpses became part of the nightly work at Dr. Shaker's morgue. Perhaps as a warning, he gave me the clinical details of the Dutchman's case: A Kalashnikov bullet fired at a distance greater than six feet shattered the right ankle; a second entered the back of the right thigh, tore off the scrotum, and exited through the left thigh; a third penetrated the right kidney with shrapnel; a fourth entered the left side of the neck and exited with part of the lower jaw, causing death.

I was staying at a small family-owned hotel on a side street in the commercial district of Karada. Its clients were mostly Turkish, Arab, and Iranian businessmen. The low visibility of the place seemed safer as well as more congenial than the big downtown hotels surrounded by blast walls, which were widely known to house Western journalists and contractors. My room was off the street, and I had scoped out an emergency exit through the bathroom window. Nonetheless, the explosions that went off two or three times a night were making it harder to sleep. One night in the middle of the month, around midnight, a bomb somewhere in the city rattled the windows and walls of my room just after I'd slipped into unconsciousness. You could never tell where it came from or how far away—the blasts always sounded much closer than they were. I tried to fall asleep again, but it was no use. I pulled on my clothes and went out to the street.

The security guard, Saad, who had one AK-47, was standing outside his booth with the night manager, Dafir. Dafir reassured me that the explosion had come from the direction of Liberation Square, a mile or so north. Both men were in their forties but looked the usual decade older, underpaid and underdressed on a chilly night. They invited me to join them. I knew that I wasn't going back to sleep, so I stood with Saad and Dafir while a movie about the martyrdom of Imam Hussein played on the DVD. They began to reminisce about their experiences in the eight-year war with Iran.

"Saddam destroyed me." Saad lifted his shirt to reveal a nasty eight-inch vertical scar on the right side of his stomach. He had been wounded in the battle of Majnoon. The Iraqi soldiers used to find the hands of the dead Iranians still clutching keys, to get into paradise. Dafir had also seen action in Majnoon, as well as other battlefields along the border. His job had been to test the air for safety after the chemical weapons attacks by the Iraqi army that turned the tide of the war.

I asked Dafir what they had been fighting for. "No, the government just told us to fight." He quoted the words of a Moor who had led the conquest of Spain in the eighth century: "The enemy is in front of you, the sea is behind you. Nothing to do—you must fight." He added, "We fought against Iran and now here we are, making fifty dollars a month." They laughed heartily. Dafir, a man of painstaking dignity, wrote out daily news summaries of Iraq's calamities for me in his self-taught English. Tonight he was wearing a sheepskin coat given to him by a Kuwaiti guest; Saad had no coat.

The movie about Imam Hussein ended in martyrdom and lamentation. Saad took it out and replaced it with vintage Iraqi porn. A man was undressing a woman in a seedy-looking bedroom. The production values were quite low, but Saad was more attentive now than he had been during the Karbala movie. I ribbed him that Moqtada al-Sadr would have him punished. He waved off Moqtada and pointed upward. "Allah," he said. It was between him and his God.

After an hour with Saad and Dafir I felt much better.

A few nights later, a huge car bomb destroyed a hotel a dozen blocks away. The Mt. Lebanon matched the profile of mine perfectly. Iraqis speculated that the bomb had detonated prematurely, that the intended target had been one of the Western hotels. Nonetheless, I didn't think it was wise for me to stay at a hotel whose only protection was Saad and his AK. The next morning, Dafir asked for no explanation as he wrote up my bill, but it was hard to look him in the eye. I had the feeling that I was abandoning them.

Foreign journalists were beginning to realize that they might be specifically targeted as Westerners, which elevated the risk far above the bad luck of being blown to pieces by a stray mortar round that happened to land next to you. And since journalists spent a good deal more time wandering around Iraq's streets and highways looking for Iraqis to talk to than either CPA officials or private contractors, many decided that they needed more protection than simply keeping a low profile afforded. Those with bureaus in Baghdad had the means to hire security consultants and buy armored cars and even build blast walls and watchtowers around private compounds. I had no bureau, no staff—whenever I went to Iraq I had to cobble together a team of driver and translator almost from scratch.

I decided to hire a bodyguard. The man I found for the job had relevant work experience and was currently underemployed, having formerly served as one of Saddam's, and later Uday's, bodyguards. Emad Hamadi was a short, broad-chested thirty-four-year-old with a Fuller brush mustache and mirthful eyes. He was spending his days sitting at home in Qadisiya, one of the newer Baathist neighborhoods on the western side of the river (Saddam liked to bestow them with Arab nationalist names: Qadisiya for the seventh-century Arab victory over the Persians, reprised for the Iran-Iraq War; Andalus for the Arab conquest of Spain; Jihad for jihad). One or two days a week, Emad ran intergovernmental mail from the Ministry of Foreign Affairs, where, owing to family connections, he had worked before the fall of the regime. For this sinecure he was still earning a hundred dollars a month, as much payoff as salary. As far as I knew—and I had only his and a few other people's word for it—Emad was staying out of the insurgency.

His family was Sunni Arab, from Falluja and the small towns of Anbar province. All his relatives had battened off the old regime. A brother had worked in the now-defunct Ministry of Military Production and also owned a trading company that had once done brisk business through government cronies, but with no contracts coming from the CPA, he had closed his shop in Mansour. A cousin had been a decorator of the hideous guest rooms in one of Saddam's palaces, now accommodating American soldiers; another had been laid off by the Ministry of Health. Emad's nephew, the son of a diplomat at the Iraq UN mission in New York, had been working at a Brooklyn deli when federal agents arrested him, just after the invasion, on a visa violation in a sweep of suspect Iraqis, jailed him for four months, and then deported him to Iraq. Emad's family was just one small block of Saddam's vast edifice of patronage and control that the war had sent crashing to earth.

In the past few months, half a dozen of Emad's friends from the old regime had been bumped off in mysterious circumstances. One of them, a notorious womanizer from Tikrit, had said to Emad shortly before being killed, "What's happening? The world has turned upside down." But Emad was too good-natured to express any bitterness. When American soldiers came through his neighborhood searching houses, he burned his snapshots taken with Uday, Qusay, Arafat, and Qaddafi; they were of strictly sentimental value. Emad was one of the thousands of younger Iraqis who came after Saddam's generation and who had no ideological attachments, simply using a regime that had turned into a criminal operation for personal gain and pleasure. Emad was about the same age as Ali Talib and Bashir Shaker and his brothers: Though they had lived on different sides of its fault line, they all knew nothing but the rule of Saddam. Now Saddam was in American custody, having been caught in a hole in the ground looking like a homeless man.

Since the present had grown so bleak, Emad lived happily in the past, the good old days when he could fuck a woman behind a tree in Zawra Park, get into a fight with a group of men who tried to take their turn with her, shoot one of them in the leg, and then be sprung from jail by Uday himself. Women and booze were easy to find, the problems they led to could be solved by pulling the right strings, and justice was done within the extended family. After deserting from military college during the war with Iran—he couldn't take the drills, and he wasn't used to washing his own clothes—a chance family connection to Saddam's private secretary landed Emad a place as one of the thousands of men on the president's personal security detail. The first line of guards consisted entirely of Saddam's cousins, favored with a piece of land and a yearly car, empowered to remove even a minister; the second line was distant relatives, who could place a phone call and move an entire division. There were five lines in all, and Emad was in the third.

Saddam loomed over Emad's life as an awesome but just god. "From what I saw and heard, Saddam was a man of mercy," Emad told me. "He didn't punish—he forgave, he gave gifts. Let me tell you this as an example. One of the guards at the gate, who controlled the spikes in the road—he saw Saddam coming out of the palace, and when he saluted he stepped on one of the spikes. Saddam stopped and asked him, 'Why did you do this?' 'I don't know,' the guard said. 'It's the first time I saw you.' He was crying the whole time." Saddam ordered medical treatment and gave the injured man money and a Toyota Corolla. Emad's direct encounters with Saddam were few but memorable. There was the slow Friday afternoon when he and his mates were lounging around outside the palace in their underwear, when two cars pulled up. Saddam was in the backseat of one. "We didn't expect him, we didn't know what to do. We stood and saluted." Saddam's much-feared first secretary promised the guards extreme punishment. But Saddam let them off. "It's Friday," he said. "They didn't know." Most unforgettably, during the American bombing of Baghdad in 1991, Emad and a few other guards stayed in the presidential palace while others fled the explosions. Saddam handed out gold watches and Browning revolvers to the loyalists. Emad was trembling in fear—less of the bombing than of the president. Saddam laid his hand on Emad's head. "His presence was something abnormal," Emad remembered, "like a magician's."

Emad was well aware that the regime he served massacred thousands. He once spat out the worst epithet imaginable in Iraq for the whole Baathist elite: "They were criminals, sons of dogs." But it was the life he knew, and leaving aside the occasional whipping or incarceration for one infraction or another, he had done well by it. Emad made a point of insisting that he had never committed murder. He swore up and down that, during the intifada that followed the Gulf War, he had refused an order to shoot a rocket-propelled grenade into a house in Karbala with women and children inside, for which he was flayed with a cable and hose. I had no way of judging the truth of this. In my dozens of conversations with servants of the old regime in Iraq, none of them ever admitted to having harmed a soul.

The rough experience in Karbala led Emad to request a transfer, and he ended up on Uday's detail. Uday was a source of constant, dangerous fun. Emad freely acknowledged that he was insane, his mood swinging wildly from hour to hour, especially when he drank. His generosity was as overwhelming as his cruelty. When things turned dark inside the head of the first son, Uday would pull out his pistol and no one knew whether he was going to shoot out a ceiling light or the brains of someone who had displeased him. Emad spent two years in Uday's pleasure palaces and nightclubs. It was the swimming pool incident that prompted him to try to leave the service. This was nearly impossible to do, but after several attempts and interventions by high-placed connections, Emad was allowed to retire on his memories.

By the time he entered my employ, Emad was past his prime. With a 9-mm. pistol tucked under his Hawaiian shirt, he needed constant reminding to walk behind me and to keep an eye on more than just girls. Still, I enjoyed his company. Amid the humorless righteousness of Muharram, it was a relief to travel around with a steady source of jokes. Emad felt a fond nostalgia toward Baathist corruption and decay, and he looked with disapproval on a city—his city—so thoroughly transformed, its walls draped in black banners of Shiite faith, its streets taken over by youth militias in green headbands, the familiar names of its bridges and neighborhoods changed to religious ones. Emad was outraged that a friend of his had been stopped on his way to Basra at a Shiite checkpoint outside Najaf and, when militiamen found a case of whiskey in his trunk, had been beaten forty times with a length of rubber hose. *Zawaj mutea*, Shiite pleasure marriage, was a source of particular amusement to Emad. "Ask a Shiite if you can have his sister for a month," he said. "He'll go crazy." It was better to be a bad Muslim and admit it than to pretend to be good. "All Iraqis are going to hell," Emad told me on our last day together. "I know I am. So why not sin?"

THE MORE DANGEROUS Iraq became, the more I depended on the Iraqis I worked with: to overhear hostile comments in a restaurant and decide that it was time to pay the bill and leave, to talk us past police checkpoints and divine the real from the fake, to scope out the mood of a crowd before bringing me onto the scene, to lend me a jacket that allowed me to blend in. Eventually, I couldn't cross the street by myself.

I hired several different translators. Because each visit seldom lasted more than a month, after my departure they always got snatched up by other journalists with permanent bureaus in Baghdad, and on the next visit I had to find someone new. The skills required for the position went far beyond fluency in English and Arabic. The wave of kidnappings placed a high price on every Westerner's head, and simply working for a foreign journalist endangered an Iraqi (many local employees of Western news organizations were threatened, and a few killed). So the relationship between journalist and translator was forced onto ground where mutual trust became essential, and the balance of power equaled out. I was the boss and paid the salary, but it was his country, his language, and my scalp was more valuable than his. There was a running joke between me and my driver, Qais, who worked with me on each trip and displayed fanatical loyalty: If I didn't come to his house and have dinner with his family, he'd turn me over to the jihadis.

I was well aware that by employing these young men I was forcing them to choose every single day whether or not to say a few words to a cousin who had a friend who had a friend in a criminal gang and, just like that, collect ten or fifteen thousand dollars. One translator who worked for me seemed a little unstable. He sometimes swore to himself when there was nothing obviously wrong, and he had a tic of snapping his head back on his neck with a groan as if he were in mental pain. He also lied to me about work more than once (I would never have known if Qais hadn't told me—such was the state of ignorance in which we

Westerners spent most of our time in Iraq). One day I suddenly stopped trusting him, and from that moment until my departure I was aware of every chance the guy had to turn me over—all he really had to do was speak English in public in a loud voice. Fortunately, I left a few days later and never saw him again. But some of the news bureaus were virtually hostage to gangs of drivers and security guards, most of them blood relatives, who couldn't be fired because the risks were too great.

When one party to a relationship has the power of death over the other and, at great financial sacrifice, steadily chooses not to exercise it while at the same time risking his own neck just by the fact of working together, the personal bond grows strong. I never left Iraq without feeling a little emotional about the young men who had kept me safe.

The best translators in Baghdad weren't professionals (these were mostly the corrupt middle-aged minders from the previous regime) or graduates of the College of Arts with textbook English. The best had been doing some other kind of work and fell into the job by accident after the arrival of the Americans, sometimes by a chance conversation with a journalist on the street. They were quick-witted, resourceful, more than a little brave, and had to thrive on the pressure of moving between our world and their own. They harbored a sort of double consciousness, interpreting Iraq for us while belonging to it, accepting that nothing in their country of holies was going to be sacred, sharing our nonstop patter of profanity and sex talk, our mockery of sheikhs and imams and *zawaj mutea*, then going home to shrouded mothers who hardly ever left the house. The translators were ambitious, they knew that the opportunity wouldn't last forever, and the best learned fast enough to grow restless in the job, perhaps even a little resentful that we needed them so much and that they got so little glory. As the insurgency became more brutal, news organizations began to rely on local staff to go out and do the reporting for them, first in no-go cities like Falluja, and then, once the kidnappings started, almost everywhere. After a few cases that amounted to literary theft in the pages of America's leading dailies, followed by bitter complaints, the Iraqis began to receive professional credit. What they lacked in training they more than made up in street knowledge and willingness to risk their lives.

One of my best translators was a young doctor named Ali. He was half Sunni, half Shiite (he called himself a Sushi), and a year before the war he had fled to Yemen when the security police got wind of the fact that he was running a side business making copies with a banned color printer (Saddam had declared Hewlett-Packard office equipment to be "Jewish"). Ali came back after the invasion, dug up the printer where he had buried it in his yard in a watertight wooden box, and soon abandoned medicine, which bored him, for a desultory career working with and then abruptly leaving some of the best journalists in Baghdad. He was that rare thing in Iraq, a free spirit as well as a daredevil, willing to smuggle Westerners into Falluja at the height of the fighting there. He had good contacts among the insurgents and sympathized with their resentment of the occupation, as well as with the civilians suffering in the war zones. We once stayed up half the night arguing whether the young judge in the case against Saddam should be considered a national hero. I thought so—he represented the new value of law against the old object of power worship. For Ali it was too soon. Such a man was too close to being a collaborator, the sting of humiliation was still more compelling than the principle of democracy. But Ali's own life had opened up under the Americans. He liked the soldiers individually, and he was restless enough to apply for one of the newly available Fulbright scholarships so he could study journalism in the United States.

Ali bought a suit and wore it to the Green Zone for the finalists' interview with State Department officials. Afterward, he called me in New York on his cell phone from the checkpoint outside the convention center. He was in despair. One of the questions had been, "Do you consider America to be a liberator or an occupier here?" Every other young Iraqi candidate had answered the former, but when it was Ali's turn he had said "occupier" and felt a chill come over the interview. He was sure that his honesty had cost him the scholarship. Ali was impressed when the U.S. government gave him a Fulbright anyway. He arrived in Philadelphia determined to learn how Americans managed to do what Iraqis were increasingly incapable of doing: to break down their group identities, to become individuals, to live together. Ali had become a harsh critic of the Sunni insurgents, the Shiite militias, and their uses of Islam.

My first translator in Iraq, and the one I got to know the best, was a Kurd whom I will call Serwan. He was thirty-three years old when I met him that first summer, with a skinny, angular frame, a right shoulder that had an agonizing habit of dislocating (it happened one day when Serwan, Qais, and I were swimming in a lake above Suleimaniya), and a scar on his forehead just above one of his black brooding eyes. He liked to drink beer, and he liked the feel of his 9-mm. pistol in his hand and the businesslike metallic sound when he shoved in the clip (I wouldn't let him carry his gun on the job). He had the coiled, intense air of a former intelligence officer, which he was, and which women found attractive. He felt that he had been born in the wrong country, that his hard life as an Iraqi had been a mistake.

Serwan was the older son of a powerful tribal leader in Suleimaniya, in the foothills of northeastern Iraq. He was adored by his mother and bullied by his father, who considered pleasures like bicycles and musical instruments unworthy of a boy of Serwan's station. He grew up with a sense of grievance, and when he was eighteen it found a focus larger than his father. A friend recruited Serwan into a small underground political party. "What do they want?" Serwan asked. Kurdish independence, the friend said. Suleimaniya was a Kurdish town under the control of Arab Baathist security police who had a license to arrest, torture, kidnap, rape. Throughout the eighties, with the intensification of the guerrilla war in the mountains and the Baathist campaign of destroying villages, the repression in Suleimaniya grew worse. Serwan joined the party, and at secret meetings its politics quickly got into his blood. "I was crazy," he said. He began to carry around a concealed bomb, keeping others in his room. "I was ready to do anything. I was ready to kill. It was very easy for me to do it if they asked me, but they didn't."

One day in 1989, when Serwan was nineteen, security officials dressed in policemen's uniforms approached him on the street. They were very nice, very polite; no need to call his family, they only wanted to talk to him for ten minutes; would he come with them? They brought Serwan to the security headquarters, an ugly concrete structure the color of dried blood, called the Red Building. Everyone in Suleimaniya knew it—the name alone terrified people. Kurds disappeared inside the Red Building for weeks, and if they came out, they came out destroyed. The security officials told Serwan, "We have a report you were in an organization against the government. Maybe they fooled you, you're a good guy, we know for sure you're an honest Iraqi person. But the truth is you're helping some guys against Iraq."

"I don't know what you're talking about," Serwan said.

"Yes, you do. Here's paper, pen—if you need tea or cigarettes just tell us. Write down who you know."

"I don't have anything to write."

"Take your time."

Serwan had been told by his friends that to make any confession would mean the end for him, and so he didn't. What happened next I didn't learn until I had known him for a year; Serwan had told me his life story during one long night that first summer without mentioning it. The normal experience of Kurdish youth was to join nationalist politics, to be arrested, to face torture, and someone like Serwan had had occasion to ask himself how he would hold up under it. He knew that no one could stand the pain for very long, but an older friend had told him to make sure he was always hungry in prison so that he would faint soon after it began.

The Red Building, which the Kurdish government has turned into a museum, was a warren of dim interrogation rooms and narrow cells, the walls chalked with despairing graffiti, extending too far back from the street for passersby to hear what was happening inside. The interrogation rooms were bare except for a metal desk in the corner and a chair. An exposed cast-iron pipe ran beneath the ceiling, with a piece of steel rebar welded around it in the shape of a hook. Serwan was taken into one of these rooms. He was made to stand on the chair with his arms tied behind his back, suspended over his head from the hook. An interrogator kicked the chair away, then grabbed him by the waist and pulled him down hard, and the violence of the jolt jerked his right arm out of the socket, and he fainted.

The torture continued for seven days. The torturers were professionals: After each dislocation, as Serwan lay unconscious on the floor, one of them would shove his arm back into place. "All their life this is their job, this is what they know." Serwan tried to get through it, telling himself: It's temporary, you will get hurt, they will make you scared, just try to handle it, be brave, handle the pain, it's temporary, everything will be okay, after that you will forget. What also helped the pain, he found, was the thought that these men were foreigners, occupiers, in his home, taking Kurdish land, killing Kurdish villagers. "You know, I just—I was hating them. Till now I am hating them. I hate them. Sometimes when you are in front of your enemy, you decide not to be weak."

After two weeks, Serwan was released. The security officials told him, "Okay, you're a good guy. We're sorry, we didn't know, there's a confusion with another name."

In 1991, at the end of the Gulf War, when the Kurds and Shia rose up against the regime, Serwan was among the fighters who stormed the Red Building and killed dozens of Baathists inside. It was the happiest day of his life. But he was not cut out for lasting happiness, even during the years that followed, when Suleimaniya flourished under the protection of the no-fly zone into a prosperous, modern-looking town. First, he married the wrong person—a very nice, high-strung girl, the daughter of a politically powerful family. Serwan was still involved with his small party, doing intelligence work, and when his in-laws offered him jobs and foreign visas if he joined the ruling elite, he refused. Kurdish security officials tortured him once, too: A blow just above his eyebrow popped one of his eyes out of the socket, dangling from a nerve. Tensions increased with his wife, and after eight months they agreed to divorce.

Then there was his father. After the divorce their quarrels grew worse, and life at home became intolerable when his mother, whom he loved more than anyone, died of cancer in 1997. One night, Serwan left his father's house with the equivalent of four dollars in his pocket. "If you go out of this house, you will die of hunger," his father said. "You are not used to a hard life."

"We will see."

Serwan went to Erbil, the capital of the other Kurdish region, under a different party's control. He was completely alone now, determined to defy his father's prediction, to make his own way, a strange thing for a man of his lineage and a very difficult thing in a country like

Iraq where everyone relied on family and tribe and connections. There were days and nights of hunger, when he lived on three daily pieces of bread and jam. He smoked by his watch, one cheap cigarette every two hours. "I was not ready to lose. And I didn't lose, but I paid so much, I killed all the nice things in myself. No girls, no love, no music, no picnics. No happiness. Every moment in my life was challenge."

After two months he found a job in an Internet center, and he was still working there in the winter of 2003 when foreign journalists began arriving in Kurdistan in advance of the American invasion. Two Australians hired Serwan as a translator in spite of his rough English, sensing that he was trustworthy and tough, the kind of man you would want by your side during a war.

Serwan went on to Baghdad to pursue this new work. But liberated Iraq was still Iraq, a closed, narrow place, afflicted—as he saw it—with political Islam, with corrupt mullahs and parties, with constricted relations between men and women. Iraq had a hundred free political parties, but the problem was inside people's heads. You could change teachers in a classroom, but if the students were crazy they still wouldn't learn anything. So it would be for another fifty years, and he didn't want to lose another half a life. What he wanted was to fall in love, but he made another mistake: He fell for an American correspondent, who soon left him and Iraq. Aseel, whom Serwan met through me, seemed like a kindred spirit, another oddball with a strong will, but to Serwan she was an Iraqi woman living with her parents, which meant that true understanding, true freedom, would be impossible together.

Serwan had a dangerous secret: Jewish ancestry. It was on his mother's side, generations ago. His mother had mentioned it when he was young and the subject interested him intensely. As a Kurd in the Arab world, he identified with Jews and admired Israel, which had supported the Kurdish cause; he wanted to live there, to marry an Israeli and raise Jewish children. Nothing could have set him more apart from other Iraqis. Once, in Suleimaniya, we visited his mother's brother to find out whether there were any records. The uncle, a writer who had come within a few days of being executed when the 1991 uprising saved him, was a depressed man in pajamas, and he had bad news: The regime had burned all the relevant documents after 1948, when Jews left Iraq en masse. Most of the uncle's childhood friends were in Israel now. The Suleimaniya synagogue was turned into a mosque.

I introduced Serwan to some American neoconservatives in Baghdad, knowing that this Jewish Kurd who wanted to go to Israel would be of interest to them. But the story was always the same: Without documentary proof, it would be difficult, if not impossible. So Serwan continued to live as a foreigner in Baghdad. He still had no contact with his father. He channeled his anger into his work, going into the most dangerous cities, driving the tense roads at night. He would calmly translate while an Arab claimed that no chemical weapons had ever been used on Kurds, and on our way out he would turn to me, his black eyes like glowing coals: "Did you hear that son of a bitch?" We attended a funeral once with Sheikh Emad al-Din al-Awadi, where Serwan and I shook the hands of dozens of men with different varieties of facial hair. At one point Serwan smiled mischievously and whispered, "These guys don't think we're real men because we don't have mustaches. [pause] And they can only have sex once a month. [pause] And what would they do with me if they knew I was a Kurdish Jew?" I once asked him if oral sex was *haram* in Iraq. He replied, "Everything nice is *haram*." At times he seemed to be at war with the whole world and only I was on his side. He openly wished that an insurgent would take a shot at him so that he could have an excuse to carry on his own private struggle. When I suggested that some of the insurgents might see the Americans the way he had seen the Arabs in Suleimaniya—as foreigners occupying their homes—he wouldn't hear of it. "Always they saw their self powerful. They lost it. What do those guys have to believe in to fight for? Saddam? Baathists? Islam? Why they didn't fight for Islam during Saddam?"

In a sense Serwan was yet another child of Saddam, on yet another side of the fault line. The regime was gone, and with the Americans his life had undergone great change. But the essentials were still the same. "Suleimaniya was a jail for me," Serwan said. "Now it's all of Iraq. I can move around, and it's a big jail."

BAGHDAD WAS HAUNTED by its Jews. According to some accounts, until the pogroms of the 1940s and the exodus that followed the creation of Israel, Iraq's capital was one-third Jewish. By the end of Baathist rule, the Jewish population of Iraq, the oldest continuous settlement in the world, had dwindled to about two dozen. In all the major cities, the former Jewish districts were the old neighborhoods, with their narrow streets, tradesmen's shops, and Ottoman balconies of wooden latticework. You could still find abandoned synagogues, and the mayor of a small town south of Hilla was keeping watch over the twenty-five-hundred-year-old shrine of Ezekiel until the Jews returned. There was a sharp generational divide between those Iraqis who had breathed in the air and light of pre-Baathist Iraq and those, like Emad, Bashir and his brothers, and Ali Talib, who had not. Older Iraqis were likelier to speak English, to have traveled, to be secular. And nothing dramatized this divide more than the attitude toward Jews. With a few exceptions, younger Iraqis, raised on virulent propaganda in a country that had no more Jews, talked about them as if they were devils incarnate. The insurgents called American soldiers, civilian contractors, and eventually just about anyone working with the occupation "Jews." Once, when a Sunni tribal sheikh was demonstrating his open-mindedness by telling me that he didn't care if the next Iraqi president was Kurdish or even Christian, I asked provocatively, "What about Jewish?" A man in the gathering exclaimed, *"Gawad!"*—You *pimp*! Even as gentle and questioning a soul as Ali Talib believed that the Jews sought world domination. But urban Iraqis who were roughly fifty or older had memories of Jewish friends and neighbors, and those memories were bathed in affection. The Jews seemed to represent the time when Iraq was cosmopolitan and no one cared who was Muslim or Christian or Jew, let alone Sunni or Shiite. One night, when my driver's family threw me a birthday party, his father, a retired artillery colonel, sat in the living room with his fist against his forehead in deep thought. Suddenly he looked up: "Doris Day—Jewish?" Disappointed, he went back to thinking. Then: "Gene Kelly—Jewish?" Finally I confirmed that Danny Kaye had indeed been Jewish, and the colonel was satisfied.

Thousands of Iraqis had Jewish ancestors, but if they knew it they kept it a closely guarded secret. The whole subject of the population that had mysteriously disappeared from Iraq was hidden in mystery and fear. Among the millions of documents that Kanan Makiya had obtained, the most sensitive were the Mukhabarat's files on Jews. When I visited his father's house on the Tigris, Makiya took me on a tour of the archive. Baath Party binders filled shelves as dense as the stacks of a research library. While we were walking through the basement, my cell phone rang: it was Aseel. As soon as I hung up, Makiya said, "Who was that?" He wanted to meet her: He needed to hire more staff for the vast work of scanning the documents.

A few days later, I brought Aseel to the Green Zone. She had never been inside its fortified perimeter, and as we walked toward Makiya's house down quiet tree-lined streets, past crew-cut soldiers jogging in their regulation shorts, past the trickling fountains of villas occupied by American NGOs, Aseel was amazed. "It's a whole new city," she said. "It's a different country."

The interview took place in Makiya's conference room, with his books stacked on the table. He told her about his Memory Foundation, questioned her about her office skills (Aseel's knowledge of software reflected the fact that Iraq was at least a decade behind the West), and finally he said, "If you work here you will hear things about me. For example, you will hear that I've been to Israel."

Aseel looked him in the eye. This wasn't customary for Iraqi women, least of all in conversation with someone important. But she wasn't easily cowed, and she had something to say. "I want to have a stamp in my passport saying I've been to Israel, just to show it's allowed." Then she recounted her family's story. When she was five, her father's mother told her that in the 1920s the family had been attacked because they were Jews. They were hidden in the house of a Muslim family, and they decided that it was safer to become Muslims themselves than to risk more attacks. "When I asked my father about it, he said not to repeat it to anyone," Aseel recalled. "He said, 'The old ones would hate you, and the new ones would hate you.'" Her father meant Jews and Muslims alike. This was the secret that Aseel had hinted at on the day I met her. Speaking of it had become the ultimate test of whether she could be free.

There was another woman in the room during Aseel's interview. Wallada al-Sarraf was in her early fifties, a small, attractive, blunt woman with dyed hair who smoked and wore jeans and a suede jacket. There was a melancholy defiance about Wallada. She came from a family of wealthy Shiite bankers in Najaf, and as a teenager in Baghdad she collected Beatles and Stones records and traveled in the same circle of Jesuit high school friends as Makiya—the vivacious rich girl and the bookish boy from humbler stock. His architect father designed the Sarraf house. Makiya left Iraq for good in 1968, the year that he turned nineteen and she seventeen and the Baath Party took power. Then, one by one, her entire family, twelve brothers and sisters, went into exile. Wallada married a businessman and stayed behind. She had three sons, and she survived the growing repression, the wars, the decade of sanctions that destroyed the family fortune. She created her own protected world, an internal exile of poker games and art salons where friends trusted one another enough to say what they thought. She drove her boys to swimming lessons and squash games in the heat of summer so that they would expend their energy and be too tired at night to think—too tired to hate the regime, or be seduced by it, or turn to religious fanaticism like so many other Shia their age. Wallada once said to me, "Imagine living in a country where no one is allowed to discuss God or sex." She lived there her whole life, doing all she could to preserve the atmosphere of her own youth while Iraq went backward. Then came the Americans and Kanan Makiya. Now she was working with him at the Iraq Memory Foundation.

Toward the end of March, I took a trip with Makiya and Wallada to Kurdistan. He wanted to look at a piece of land his father owned in the mountains near Dohuk and talk to Kurdish human-rights officials about documents from the Anfal, before continuing north to give a speech in Ankara. I wanted to get out of Baghdad, which was becoming more tense by the day.

We traveled with an old Kurdish friend of Makiya's named Shirku

Abid and his *peshmerga* bodyguard. Shirku, whose name means "mountain lion," was an imposing man, with brush-cut white hair and a powerful nose under thick black eyebrows; he was a veteran of the Kurdish struggle who had lived in England for years and was now running an Internet company in Baghdad. As soon as we crossed the green line into the hills above Kirkuk, we all began to relax and chatter in loud voices. I could almost feel the pressure leaving my lungs. The hills were covered with spring wildflowers, and there were wedding parties in the fields, the Kurdish women dancing in bright red and green robes with their hair uncovered, and families were picnicking in celebration of Now Ruz, the Zoroastrian new year.

"We were Zoroastrians before we were Muslims," Shirku said. "And it's a pity we didn't stay with this civilized religion. Instead we went with this backwardness."

"I feel safe here," Makiya said.

Shirku said, "We waited so long for this great day. I'm only sorry for the comrades who didn't live to see it. The achievement is magnificent— the end of backwardness. Not only Saddam, but backwardness. And we mustn't stop, we must keep on struggling against the backwardness, in the mosques, everywhere. We must begin Iraq's true liberal party."

The next morning we woke up at a hotel in Dohuk and did something that was impossible down south: We took a long walk. The mountain air was fresh, the lake was brilliant blue, and in the distance to the north was the snow-capped ridge that marked the border with Turkey. It was hard to believe that forty miles away, in Mosul, a war was going on. As long as we stayed on the trail to avoid old land mines there was absolutely nothing to fear. Shirku and Wallada walked ahead, and as Makiya and I followed, he told me what had happened in his life since his return to Iraq.

When they were teenagers, he and Wallada had loved each other. But he was too shy to speak up, and some perverse instinct had compelled her to flirt with another boy on the last occasion they were together. Makiya made up his mind to forget her, and he left Iraq for college in America. When Wallada's sister visited him in Cambridge a couple of years later, she found Makiya with an Iranian woman and wrote to Wallada that he had gotten married. It wasn't true, but now it was Wallada's turn to plunge into despair and try to forget. So she accepted a marriage proposal. Her husband-to-be asked, "Is there anyone else?" Wallada replied that she loved Makiya but he was now beyond her reach. She thought that she would learn to love her husband, but it never happened, and she never got over Makiya. Two and a half decades passed, in which they saw each other twice briefly outside Iraq. When Makiya returned to Baghdad in April 2003 after thirty-five years away, they met at a dinner party and realized that nothing had changed. He was in the process of getting a divorce from his second wife, but Wallada was still unhappily married. They were working together now, traveling together, and enmeshed in a secret relationship that satisfied neither of them. As we caught up with Wallada and Shirku, Makiya said that he had seen the same thing happen in places like Lebanon: During historic upheavals, people's personal lives underwent their own revolutions.

We drove farther north, to Amadiya, a walled Ottoman city on a hilltop at the foot of the steep mountain range along the border. We sat at an outdoor restaurant with a view across a plunging ravine of Amadiya and the spectacular white peaks beyond it. There were Arab families here on vacation from the south; I'd heard that doctors and other professionals from Baghdad were taking cuts in salary and status to come work in the safety of Kurdistan. As we ate, I watched Makiya and Wallada, realizing now that her wry deflating tone, her refusal to grant him his lofty thoughts—"Kanan doesn't know this country, he thinks they want what he wants"—expressed the opposite of contempt. She wanted him, not Iraq; but she had them together, and it was terrible.

Shirku took in the sublime landscape with a sweep of his hand and cursed. "Bloody British! Couldn't they see this isn't Iraq?"

Our destination was the old border town of Zakhu, where Makiya and Wallada would spend the night before crossing into Turkey. As we finished the last part of the drive in darkness, Shirku told us the story of his student years in Baghdad, when he was both a communist and a Kurdish nationalist. It was 1963, and the Baath Party, having taken power for the first time in a coup, was trying to wipe out its enemies. Shirku was arrested and thrown in jail. The Baathists had many enemies, and they kept the Nasserists in one cell, the communists and

Kurds across the corridor in another. Shirku endured several days of beatings, of being hung in the air from his wrists with his arms behind his back. He had expected to be arrested and tortured ever since he was recruited into the Kurdish movement by an older man named Mohamed Sadiq, and he found that he was able to endure it. Sadiq himself had disappeared. One day, jailers threw a body into the cell—barely a skeleton, skin on bone, with blood all over the face and the eyes gouged out. "I was afraid to look," Shirku said. The small shape of the head was familiar. "I had a feeling it might be him." Shirku approached the body and whispered in the ear, "Mr. Sadiq, this is you and this is me. I'm Shirku here."

Shirku gave him water. Sadiq could hardly speak, but in a croaking voice he said, "I'm going to die. And I tell you, I didn't confess, I didn't say anything about you or your other comrades. But that means that your life belongs to me. My life is in your hand now. You have to work all your life for the thing I died for."

Sadiq made Shirku repeat an oath, which Shirku repeated to us thirty-one years later in the car: "I swear on my honor and the honor of Kurdistan and my people that I will always be frank and truthful with what I think, what I do, to keep distance from whatever makes me weak, to strive to succeed with my struggle, and not to separate my life and my fate from the poor people of this earth. I will not be afraid of anyone on this earth, and I will not bow my head to anyone on this earth. I will dedicate my life and my fate for the unification and liberation of Kurdistan."

Sadiq was taken away the next morning to die. Shirku was eventually released, but he left jail with an insatiable desire for revenge. It wouldn't leave him alone; he couldn't live with it. After the Baathists were thrown out of power toward the end of 1963, he heard that one of his torturers had been arrested. Shirku lied his way into the prison and found the man in his cell. He kicked him hard in the stomach until the jailers intervened. It didn't satisfy Shirku completely, but he found that he could live again.

Makiya, who had been listening carefully, said, "It's interesting, Shirku. You don't like weakness in other people, do you? But we're weak, we human beings."

"That's true," Shirku said. "I don't like it."

I asked Makiya what kind of oath he would take if his life were on the line.

"Mine would be as close as possible to an idea," he said. "It would be a liberal idea, it would be an idea that started in Iraq but extended to the rest of the Arab-Muslim world." He had advocated this idea in all of his books, he said, but now he was tired of simply writing: He wanted to live it, here in Iraq. "Now here's a problem I have, you see. I, unlike Shirku, have grown deeply aware of my own weaknesses and my own frailties. It's difficult in conditions like that, when your idea rests on a notion of our frailty as a species, to swear allegiance to an ideal. Because the premise is our weakness, our inability to hold up to impossible ideals."

Makiya's answer didn't completely satisfy Shirku. "George, for forty years I wanted to take over the machine that tortured me and reverse-engineer it, crush it, and then make it work for me."

I asked him what he meant.

"You have to protect the liberal values with that ruthlessness," Shirku said, and in the darkness of the car I could almost feel his fist clenching. "We are talking about defending a future of generations, and that cannot be done just by some slogans. You've got to protect it. You cannot escape from that, especially in a society like Iraq. It's impossible to escape. It means you are not serious about your liberal ideas if you don't protect it." This ruthlessness involved forcefully pushing liberal ideas, but it also meant, as he put it, stopping certain people from breathing—thugs such as Moqtada al-Sadr. "Then you will attract a lot of militias, people in parties, intellectuals, attract them into this momentum and then give them direction. If they know the direction has also strength behind it, force behind it, there's hope of reverse-engineering this process of madness, backwardness— getting out of this backwardness. There's not any other way you can do it. But now, in the absence of that, this backwardness is flourishing here, and it's truly a disappointment to thousands, tens of thousands, hundreds of thousands of liberal and forward-thinking people in Iraq."

A week later, I was back in Baghdad. On the day before my departure from Iraq, the CPA closed down Moqtada al-Sadr's newspaper *al-*

Hawza for sixty days for inciting attacks against coalition forces. But as a show of strength it only revealed weakness, for the Americans hadn't prepared for what followed. That night, thousands of Moqtada's militiamen took to the streets. Their chants could be heard all over the city. Wallada, who had also returned to Baghdad, was driving home when she ran into a mob of young men in black brandishing Kalashnikovs. American soldiers were trying to block the militiamen, and they looked as scared as she felt. Wallada quickly threw a scarf over her hair and somehow managed to reach the house, where she was trapped. It was the first night of an insurrection that would last the better part of two months. By the end, much of what the occupation had been trying to achieve in Iraq lay in ruins.

9

INSURGENCIES

CAPTAIN JOHN PRIOR'S TOUR in Iraq was scheduled to end in the middle of March, almost exactly a year after he entered the country with the invasion force. Prior made the final rounds of the humble offices where he'd put in so much time: the gas station, the propane station, the sewer department. His Iraqi counterparts didn't disguise their feelings: They were dismayed to see him leave. "We were like wounded people thrown in the road, and no one would stop," the director general of the district sewer department told Prior, "and you came along and picked us up and saved us. This is how we look at it. Religion, nationality—none of this matters."

I accompanied Prior to his last meeting with the Zafaraniya Neighborhood Advisory Council that he had helped coax into existence. The NAC (Prior was now pronouncing it with a soft *c* after learning that "nack" was Iraqi slang for "fuck") met at the unlovely concrete housing project for employees of the Atomic Energy Commission. The sewage swamps of the previous August were gone. Prior sat down in a cramped office with nine or ten council members. They were unhappy to be losing him, but the council members spent their last two hours with Prior complaining bitterly. "Our authority as the NAC is still shaky," Ahmad Ogali, the chairman who had invited me to lunch in August, said. "I don't want compliments and nice phrases. People don't trust us. They come up to us and ask for something, and we can't do anything for them. It makes us look bad."

In fact, because of a dispute with the Governing Council, Paul Bremer had let months go by without signing the legal order drafted by the CPA in late 2003 that would spell out the authority of the local councils. This delay, along with the two-and-a-half-month stoppage of the military's emergency funds, left the councils and the soldiers working with them in limbo, bringing reconstruction to a near stand-still, and preventing local government from developing into a power center that could compete with the militias and the insurgents for popular support. All of this was far above Prior's level, but as the American in the room he was the one to hear about it.

When the meeting ended, Prior stood and said with a touch of ceremony, "I leave here knowing that the job is not finished. There will always be a hole in my heart because I couldn't see it through to the end. But I leave knowing that Baghdad and Zafaraniya are in good hands, because they're in yours." He presented the council members a certificate of appreciation. "I hope to come back someday with my family to see my friends here," he said, "and I promise not to wear tan or green."

A councilman said, "We give you thanks, and apologies for any mistakes we might have made."

"No apologies necessary. If anything, we are guests in your nation and we should be apologizing for our flaws."

Prior left Iraq for Germany, then went home on leave to see his fiancée. In early April, violence exploded all across Iraq. The two precipitating events behind the uprisings had come in the last days of March: the closing of *al-Hawza* by the CPA on March 28, and the killing of four American private security contractors by insurgents in Falluja on March 31, their bodies subsequently charred, hacked to pieces, and strung up from a bridge over the Euphrates by a delirious mob. The Falluja incident was a gruesome but predictable ratcheting up of the war in the west. The newspaper shutdown was a self-inflicted American wound. But the origins of the crisis that followed lay further back and deeper down than the two events at the end of March. The decisions surrounding both of them showed how precarious American control in Iraq had grown during the year of the occupation, how badly all the gears were meshing—between Americans and Iraqis, between military and civilian, between Baghdad and Washington.

THE GUERRILLA WAR that followed the invasion of Iraq caught the U.S. military by surprise. It shouldn't have. The CIA issued several secret prewar intelligence reports warning of the possibility of an insurgency. During the sprint from Kuwait to Baghdad, the Fedayeen Saddam, the paramilitary forces led by Saddam's younger son Qusay, harassed the invaders' supply lines with hit-and-run attacks and intimidated Iraqi civilians by publicly and brutally murdering those who welcomed the Americans. Lieutenant General William Wallace, the commander of V Corps, observed, "The enemy we're fighting is a bit different from the one we war-gamed against." The first suicide bombings hit American checkpoints around the time Baghdad fell; a few weeks after that, what the military called improvised explosive devices, or IEDs, began blowing up convoys in the capital. General Franks's achievement of toppling the regime in just three weeks, hailed at the time as a brilliant new form of warfare, allowed thousands of Iraqis to melt away into the population or go into hiding and fight another day. Franks and the administration's civilian leaders would later describe the chaos and insurgency that followed the fall of the regime as the inadvertent consequences of their war plan's "catastrophic success." As it turned out, there was nothing inadvertent about it.

When the chief weapons inspector, Charles Duelfer, released the final report of the Iraq Survey Group in late 2004, there were no weapons of mass destruction to be described. Saddam had never rebuilt his programs after they were destroyed by inspections, sanctions, and bombings in the 1990s; in the madhouse logic of his late rule, he had pretended to possess the weapons in order to deter an Iranian attack, in some cases fooling his top officers, in other cases being fooled by his top scientists. The American military's greatest concern in Iraq had been a phantom. But the report also found that guerrilla war had been the enemy's plan all along. "Saddam believed that the Iraqi people would not stand to be occupied or conquered by the United States and would resist—leading to an insurgency," Duelfer wrote, basing his conclusions on CIA interrogations of the top members of the regime, including the number one himself. "Saddam said he expected the war to evolve from traditional warfare to insurgency."

Before the war, Iraqi intelligence had trained foreign fighters in explosives and marksmanship at a camp southeast of Baghdad, in Salman Pak. (Douglas Feith's off-the-books intelligence shop and its friends in the Iraqi National Congress had described this operation as a terrorist training center, proof of the link between Saddam and al-Qaeda; instead, it was a training camp for the guerrilla war that the Pentagon had been unable to imagine.) Between August 2002 and January 2003, Iraqi commanders had removed weapons and equipment from bases and hidden them in farms and houses all over the countryside. On the eve of the invasion, Saddam had told his top ministers and commanders to hold out for eight days—"and after that I will take over." American intelligence officials later came to believe that Saddam and his top generals were studying Vietnamese manuals on guerrilla tactics. Knowing that he had no unconventional weapons, the Iraqi dictator was getting ready for a different kind of war, one at least as old as the Romans. The American war planners assumed that they would encounter the kind of resistance they could most easily defeat. They didn't want to fight a guerrilla war—after Vietnam it had ceased to be an option. In planning for the wrong adversary, they failed to follow the ancient military dictum to "know your enemy." It was another failure of imagination.

The Iraqi insurgents thus had time to prepare, they had the advantage of surprise, and they adapted quickly as the battlefield changed. In the early weeks of the insurgency, attacks against coalition forces tended to be straight-on assaults with small-arms fire and rocket-propelled grenades. These tactics got a lot of insurgents killed at the outset. In the Darwinian nature of such wars, the smarter fighters survived and made adjustments. The most lethal of these was the IED, a home-made bomb composed of an artillery shell or other military munitions (available at unguarded factories and ammo dumps throughout the country), buried in a hole on the roadside or hidden in trash, rubble, or roadkill, and detonated either by wire or remotely with a device such as a garage-door opener or mobile phone. By midsummer, IEDs and other forms of ambush were killing several soldiers a week, mainly in what had come to be known as the Sunni Triangle, the area of Iraq's center, west, and north between Baghdad, Ramadi, and Mosul.

In Washington, Donald Rumsfeld called these attacks the work of a few "dead-enders." The phrase suggested a handful of potbellied Baathists with dyed mustaches waging a pathetic last stand on behalf of some half-remembered notion of Arab socialist glory. Later, they became FRLs (former regime loyalists), then FREs (former regime elements), and finally AIFs (anti-Iraqi forces). "Now they're just POIs—pissed-off Iraqis," a senior CPA official said. "But there was always this desire to say that they were people that were bad guys, either diehard Saddamists or foreigners, not that they could just be regular Iraqis. It's not our fault they hate us—they're going to hate us whatever we do. There wasn't a recognition that our own tactics may be fueling the opposition."

Facing the American role in the growth of the insurgency beyond the initial core group first required facing the insurgency itself. But in Washington there had been no plan for a guerrilla war; a guerrilla war would change all the calculations about the military presence in Iraq; and so there was no guerrilla war. On the ground in Iraq, the consequences of this willful blindness were as real and dire as the months or even years of delay in supplies of armored vehicles and body armor reaching American forces whose "operations tempo" was increasing every week. After the Army ordered more bulletproof vests, it took almost half a year for the first shipment to reach Iraq. By December 2003, Lieutenant General Ricardo Sanchez, the top U.S. commander in Iraq, was writing to the Pentagon that the shortage of spare parts and other equipment was so severe that "I cannot continue to support sustained combat operations with rates this low."

T. X. Hammes, a Marine colonel who devoted his career to studying guerrilla war, told me, "I am willing to bet the captain you were with understood he was in an insurgency very early. Our leadership was absolutely unable to make that leap. Bad news was very, very slow to filter up." When President Bush stood on the deck of the carrier *Abraham Lincoln* on May 1 in front of an enormous banner proclaiming "MISSION ACCOMPLISHED" and declared the end of major combat in Iraq, Hammes said to himself, "'Oh, shit.' It struck me that, my God, we don't have any understanding at all of how bad this can be."

Hammes, a stocky, square-headed, blunt-spoken man, entered the Marine Corps a month after the fall of Saigon, and he spent the next three decades trying to figure out how an agricultural society of twenty million people had defeated the United States. It was not a question senior military leadership cared to explore. After Vietnam, "There was a pretty visceral reaction that we would not do this again. We stopped thinking about insurgency years ago. So even when we figured out Iraq was an insurgency, we didn't know what to do about it." Though the Marine Corps, as Hammes reminded me, had always been a "small-wars outfit" with a tradition of intellectual independence, he spent his career as something of an outlier. During a fellowship year, he studied the classic texts and cases of insurgency over the objections of his instructors, who told him, "You're crazy, we don't do insurgency," and urged him to study something relevant, like conventional war in Europe. Then he pursued practical knowledge in the dirty little conflicts of the late Cold War—Honduras, Angola, Somalia, Afghanistan. He picked the brains of U.S.-backed guerrilla fighters, assuming that sooner or later people like them would become America's main enemies. "I was sitting there thinking: If I'm a bad guy and I've got to fight the United States, that whole conventional thing doesn't look that good. If you want to study your profession, go to the other guy's side and look back." After Hammes set down his years of thinking about insurgency in a book, publishers told his agent, "Interesting book, well-written, but a subject nobody's interested in because it's not going to happen." *The Sling and the Stone* was finally accepted for publication in the spring of 2003, just as "it" started to happen.

The Iraqi insurgency soon took on the characteristics that Hammes had written about. It was a fragmented network, which made it inefficient in some ways but also difficult to defeat because there was no central node of command; it could survive great damage. Its members learned by experience, watching their own coverage on al-Jazeera; they also coordinated their efforts through the media. They used the population, mainly by intimidation, but also by luring the Americans into violent overreactions that swung support their way. They chose soft targets. They lacked a unifying ideology—Hammes identified at least five groups in Iraq with different goals—and yet the solution to this kind of war must be political. Iraqi institutions of governance and security would have to become capable of winning the population's allegiance. Meanwhile, the United States would have to make a long-term commitment to what was bound to be a protracted struggle. The ultimate arbiter would be the Iraqi and American publics.

None of this was good news at the technology-minded Pentagon. Franks's successor as chief of Central Command, General John Abizaid, an Arab American with a better grasp of the strategic dangers in Iraq than his predecessor, acknowledged on July 16, 2003, that American forces were faced with "a classical guerrilla-type campaign." He was directly contradicting his boss Donald Rumsfeld, who had said a couple of weeks earlier, "I guess the reason I don't use the phrase 'guerrilla war' is because there isn't one." The soldiers on the ground in Iraq were far ahead of the senior leadership in Washington in recognizing the seriousness of the enemy they now faced. But even the sharpest of them had no ready-made model for understanding the Iraqi insurgency. The battalion commander I met in Kirkuk, Lieutenant Colonel Dom Caraccilo, said that the American role as liberators, occupiers, and counterinsurgents in Iraq had no parallel in our military history. "It's hard to make a relevant comparison to anywhere. It's very unique." Postwar Germany and Japan, Vietnam, French Algeria—none was an exact template. "What we're seeing here is a different face. This isn't guerrilla warfare, it's not some Maoist thing. I personally don't think there's an organizational structure like the Algerian FLN. It's a hodge-podge. They didn't have a plan—there's no plan right now."

The Iraqi insurgency had no Mao, no Ho, no clear and popular political agenda. The killing of Uday and Qusay and the capture of Saddam had no strategic effect on it. There was little attempt to court the press (few Western journalists got anywhere close to the insurgents except by unpleasant accident or kidnapping, and even with arranged contacts they were sometimes lucky to return to their laptops). In Hammes's experience of the small wars of the eighties and nineties, modern insurgencies were likely to be composed of dispersed cells, criminal gangs, ethnic militias, and regional warlords, sometimes cooperating, sometimes not, all festering in a weak state with corrupt local officials. The absence of a manifesto and a charismatic leader didn't make them any less durable. What the Iraqi insurgency lacked in coherence it made up for in weapons, cash, and trained personnel.

The key military tool in counterinsurgency is intelligence. Because of the planning failures and the slow recovery, this was exactly what the United States lacked in Iraq. There were nowhere near enough Arabic interpreters for each battalion—the Pentagon contractor hired to provide them, Titan Corporation, was reviled all over Iraq for its sluggishness—and soldiers often went out on patrol with no way of knowing what was being said to them, let alone what was not being said. In September 2003, a staff officer in a battalion in Baghdad wrote me:

> Security is not really something you can do anything about unless you have an intelligence network set up, or some sort of security force is at the right place at the right time to catch the right criminal or terrorist . . . There aren't enough security forces, whether coalition or native, to do the job now. As it stands, a native-intelligence apparatus is non-existent. Our information comes from open-source intelligence, which means people walking up to the front gate and saying they have information and our intelligence officer debriefing him, or Iraqis who we deal with through the NACs offering up some information, which isn't always useful. Also, sometimes the locals use us to carry out grudges against their neighbors. One translator who worked for us got our guys to raid a house he said had RPGs and contained individuals carrying out attacks on coalition forces. Nothing was in the house and the guy sleeping with his family inside told us immediately who it was that had sent us; he owed the translator money and the translator said he would sic the Americans on him. Turns out he was telling the truth. We fired and arrested our translator instead.

The military kept claiming that its intelligence was getting better, tips were pouring in faster than intelligence officers could handle them. And yet the number of daily attacks kept rising and growing more sophisticated. In November, the bloodiest month since the invasion, the Pentagon estimated that the insurgency included five thousand fighters. This struck most people who had spent time in Iraq as improbably low. The United States still seemed reluctant to give this new, hidden enemy its due, as if, Hammes said, "This insurgency thing is an aberration, so we can get on with" the high-tech revolution in military affairs. He added, "There seemed to be kind of a feeling of 'So what if it's a guerrilla war?' It really shocks people when you say that superpowers are zero and five against insurgents."

Arguably, the only modern success has been the British victory over communist guerrillas in Malaya in the 1950s, which took ten years. More than a year into the Iraq War, Hammes wrote an op-ed for *The New York Times* about Sir Harold Briggs, the retired British general who devised the political-military plan that led to the defeat of the communists in Malaya. After it appeared, Hammes got a call from Douglas Feith's office: Would he write it up as a memo to the undersecretary by the following Monday? "Seems they'd never heard of Briggs," Hammes said. He duly wrote the memo and sent it to the Pentagon. By then Feith was traveling; time went by, and Hammes never heard back. "Maybe it was the ten-year number that soured them," he said. "But if they haven't heard of Briggs, we're in trouble."

Kalev Sepp, a retired Army lieutenant colonel who taught at the Navy's Center on Terrorism and Irregular Warfare, went to Iraq twice in 2004. In the late eighties, as a Special Forces major, he had served as an adviser to a Salvadoran army brigade in what was a qualified, if brutal, success in counterinsurgency, and then he analyzed the Central American wars in his dissertation at Harvard, where he met Drew Erdmann. Sepp, like Hammes, was one of the independent thinkers on the margins of the military who had watched senior leadership fail to understand America's strategic situation in the wars that followed September 11. (In Iraq, as in Vietnam, one continually found more insight among midlevel civilians and military than at the top—because the political pressure at that altitude was low enough for clear thinking to take place, and because their intellectual candor made professional advancement less likely.) Sepp was first recruited to study military intelligence in Iraq by General Abizaid, and he arrived at the palace in Baghdad in January 2004. He soon discovered that the officers working in the CPA felt a barely concealed or nakedly obscene contempt for most of their younger, inexperienced civilian counter-parts rotating in and out on ninety-day tours. He also found that Lieu-tenant General Sanchez, the ground commander in Iraq, and his staff had grown defensive to the point of paranoia toward anyone coming from outside. By then, things were going badly enough that any offer of help was seen as an attempt to place blame. There was plenty to go around—almost everyone realized that Sanchez was in way over his head—but relief of command at such a high level would have been an admission of failure, so Sanchez's job was secure (he would only be punished after Iraq, when he failed to get his fourth star).

At the palace, Sepp met an Army Special Forces colonel who sat two desks away from the door to Bremer's inner office. Sepp engaged the colonel in conversation, trying to get a sense of the CPA's strategic thinking, and at one point he used the word "insurgency." The colonel held up his hand. "There is no insurgency here," he said. "There's a high level of domestic violence." At V Corps headquarters out in Saddam's old lakeside hunting lodge by the airport, Sepp found an atmosphere that suggested the routine business of staff work back in Heidelberg rather than any reckoning with a worsening war. The party line in Baghdad reflected the unimaginative approach that Sepp had seen coming from the Rumsfeld Pentagon. It was "kill-capture": Success was measured in the number of insurgents and of top-level Baathists from the deck of playing cards who were eliminated. No one seemed able to explain why, with all the dead or detained, the number of in-surgents kept increasing. The strategy was all wrong, Sepp realized. Instead of an emphasis on threats, it should have been on effects, the desired end-state, which would have put the center of action in the lives of Iraqis. "The most important thing is security—the security of the people," Sepp said. "The problem was, we seized on the idea that *our* security was the most important thing. This is where there's some sacrifice involved. The people have to be secured first."

This was the meaning of hearts and minds (a phrase, Sepp re-minded me, first used by John Adams about the American Revolu-tion): the establishment of a government to which Iraqis would be willing to risk giving their allegiance. The insurgents understood bet-ter than the Americans that the battle was for the loyalty of the population. They began slaughtering police recruits in part to show Iraqis that the new institutions couldn't protect them. But the Americans, having dissolved the old Iraqi security forces, didn't adapt quickly, didn't seriously train and equip the new police, didn't ensure the safety of Iraqis who came forward with intelligence. The early training efforts were focused on the formation of a conventional Iraqi army— the lowest priority, with a hundred and sixty thousand foreign troops already in Iraq. The trainers weren't the experts from Special Forces, who were originally created to train foreign armies, but who were being used in Iraq to kick down doors. The Pentagon didn't want the job of training Iraqi soldiers, and instead it was done by the CPA using a private contractor. Walter Slocombe, Bremer's adviser on security, told me, "If we had been able to say at the beginning that training up the Iraqi army is a military mission, that would probably have been a good thing. The military didn't want to do it." A private corporation called Vinnell, a subsidiary of Northrop Grumman, was hired on a $48 million contract. "They were supposed to train twenty-two battalions," Sepp said. "They trained six—half of the soldiers deserted, and the remainder were judged untrained." An officer on Abizaid's staff came to inspect Vinnell's work. "He was furious, he was *furious*, at how bad the training was and how bad the equipment was that Vinnell was giving the Iraqi soldiers." The military took over the job from its inept contractor, but precious time had been lost, and with it the confidence of the Iraqi public.

The Bush administration, seeing an exit strategy, wanted to claim high numbers of trained forces in a hurry and went for bargain-basement soldiers and police. Sepp said, "It was a failure of military leadership to look at political leadership and say, 'I appreciate that there's a presidential election coming up, but this is how it has to be done.'" The Pentagon and the occupation authority kept issuing utterly misleading figures on manpower and training. Even in 2003, Rumsfeld and Bremer threw around numbers in the range of 150,000, but in June 2004, the small print of a CPA report on the new police force revealed that fewer than six thousand out of almost ninety thousand had received serious academy training lasting more than two or three weeks. As a result, during the April uprising the undermanned, under-equipped police abandoned their stations all over the south, and the new soldiers trained by battalions like Prior's collapsed; national guardsmen refused to board helicopters that would ferry them to join the fight with Americans against fellow Iraqis.

T. X. Hammes volunteered to go to Baghdad in January 2004 to work on training and found that the American operation was staffed at less than 50 percent. There was no system for printing out Iraqi ID cards in Arabic or getting cash salaries to soldiers in an efficient way. By September, when recently promoted Lieutenant General David Petraeus was trying to make up for all the lost time, the level of staffing was still only 60 percent. It was the same problem of bureaucratic inertia in Washington that was bedeviling the reconstruction. "It is clear that the only way you get out of Iraq is to train Iraqi security forces," Hammes said. "This administration absolutely failed to do that." Because of manpower regulations, Hammes was recalled to Washington after two months even though he'd volunteered for a year, knowing as well as anyone the importance of the training to counterinsurgency in Iraq.

"The U.S. failed to treat the Iraqis as partners in the counterinsurgency effort for nearly a year, and did not attempt to seriously train and equip Iraqi forces for proactive security and counterinsurgency mission until April 2004," Anthony Cordesman of the Center for Strategic and International Studies, who followed the training closely, wrote in July 2004. This failure followed directly from the Pentagon's original sin of willful blindness in the face of the insurgency. "The U.S. wasted precious time waiting for its own forces to defeat a threat it treated as the product of a small number of former regime loyalists (FRLs) and foreign volunteers, and felt it could solve without creating effective Iraqi forces." The new Iraqi security forces, resenting their low pay and inferior equipment, seemed to feel that they were being asked to fight for the United States, not Iraq. Without the brutal discipline of Saddam's army, most of them were incapable of becoming cohesive fighting forces and quickly fell apart under fire. A CPA official once said to me that a lot of the bravest, most dedicated, most idealistic Iraqis seemed to be fighting on the other side.

THE SUNNI INSURGENCY fed on the unhappiness of a minority group that had essentially run Iraq since its creation and foresaw a diminished role in the new order, especially after the abolition of the army and debaathification made the point clearer than it needed to be. The insurgency's backbone—its organizers, financiers, suppliers—were officials of the Baath Party and the regime's many intelligence and security services. Shadowy messages began to appear bearing the name "Party of the Return." But from early on, the character of the insurgency was more complicated than the rearguard action of a ruling party whose moment in history had passed. What could be called Sunni nationalism took root in some Iraqis who had never greatly benefited from the Baath Party. Their motives were various and overlapping: patriotism, religion, personal resentment over some injury done by American soldiers. The insurgency remains poorly understood in part because it defies easy categorization.

I met a tribal sheikh from Ramadi named Zaydan Halef al-Awad, who had fled the American military to Amman, Jordan. A traditional man, he had seen the Americans as partners who could benefit his tribe, and he said that he had joined the insurgency only when their behavior made it impossible to cooperate. "We Iraqis have a nature, which is revenge. If my cousin kills my brother, I have to kill him. If the Americans come from thousands of miles away and dishonor our women and hurt our children, how can I spare them?"

He had almost nothing in common with the young Iraqi a reporter for the London weekly *Observer* met in Baghdad. He had been a fan of Bon Jovi and American movies before the war and had welcomed the invasion, imagining a new life of freedom, travel, and consumer goods, until the spectacle of civilian deaths and looting turned him into a full-fledged insurgent in an independent seven-man cell (while he continued to hold down his day job in a government ministry). This fighter's grievances were a mix of economic hardship and national pride that amounted to no clear political agenda. He found the foreign jihadis in Iraq too bloody and irrational to work with.

Iraq's Sunnis were the country's modernizers, and in the cities they tended to be more secular than the Shia. But Islamist ideology, which had taken hold in other Arab countries with repressive and corrupt secular regimes, quickly spread through occupied Iraq in a particularly virulent form, the default worldview of a suddenly dispossessed group. A friend of one of my translators, who had been a partying and carefree student before the invasion, fled to Yemen, grew his beard, and became a collector of beheading videos. Sometimes the transformation happened in less than half an hour. *The Washington Post* reported the story of an overweight and unemployed thirty-two-year-old college graduate who spoke some English and lived with his mother in Adhamiya. Until the night American soldiers raided the house, he had accepted their presence in Iraq. But that night they humiliated him by mockingly spreading his secret girlie magazines across his bed next to his Qur'an. Twenty minutes later the soldiers were gone, and the young man began to slap his mother, screaming that Americans were devils. He spent the night in the mosque, and when he came home the next day he threw out all the foreign-made cheese in the refrigerator, burned all the Western images in the house, and forbade his mother to watch Western news or movies. When she brought home antianxiety medication for her troubled son, he refused the pills: The yellow ones were from Jews and the red ones from evil foreigners. As the world would discover with the Abu Ghraib prison scandal, military occupation and sexual shame are a combustible mix. In the eyes of Iraqi men, the trespasses of the soldiers frequently crossed a line into the most sensitive realm. Raids sometimes caught the women of the household in their nightgowns, and there was a persistent rumor that night-vision goggles had see-through capabilities. The young man in Adhamiya probably suffered the same psychological troubles as his overweight, unemployed, living-with-mother counterpart in America. But in Iraq there was a violent ideology ready to answer his moment of crisis.

The Iraq War proved some of the Bush administration's assertions false, and it made others self-fulfilling. One of these was the insistence on an operational link between Iraq and al-Qaeda. In fact, Saddam had always kept a wary distance from Islamist terrorist groups; he co-opted conservative Sunni imams in Iraq only to use them as window dressing. But after the fall of the regime, the most potent ideological force behind the insurgency was Islam and its hostility to non-Islamic intruders. Some former Baathist officials even stopped drinking and took to prayer. The insurgency was called *mukawama*, or resistance, with overtones of religious legitimacy; its fighters became mujahideen, holy warriors; they proclaimed their mission to be jihad.

The first terror bombing hit the Jordanian embassy in Baghdad on August 7, 2003, and was soon followed by the devastation of the UN mission. In October, as violence surged across Iraq with the start of the Ramadan Offensive, the Red Cross and several police stations in Baghdad were blown up on a single bloody morning. In November, a suicide bomber drove his car into the Italian base at Nasiriya and killed nineteen Italians. In January, more than two dozen people were blown to pieces while waiting to enter the Assassins' Gate. These bombings were widely believed to be the work of foreign fighters affiliated with al-Qaeda and led by the Jordanian terrorist Abu Musab al-Zarqawi, who had migrated to Iraq after al-Qaeda was routed in Afghanistan. The strategy was clear and largely successful: Isolate the American occupiers in Iraq by driving other foreigners out of the country and intimidating any Iraqis who cooperated with them. No one knew how many jihadis were slipping across Iraq's unguarded borders; the American military put the number in the hundreds. They introduced forms of violence that the Baathist and Sunni nationalist insurgencies, as brutal as they were, stopped short of, but their tactics advanced goals that were shared by the local fighters. Eventually, the jihadis began targeting Iraqi civilians with massive explosions simply for being Shia or Kurds, as in the Ashura bombings. The Shia were considered non-Muslims by Sunni extremists and were feared by larger numbers of Sunnis as Iraq's democratic majority; the Kurds were regarded as agents of the Americans and the Jews. Zarqawi appealed for the blessing and help of Osama bin Laden in a letter that was intercepted and made public by the U.S. military. It revealed a strategy of fomenting ethnic civil war in order to prevent the emergence of a democratic government. The foreign jihadis came to be intensely hated in Iraq—even in Falluja, where they assumed more and more control leading up to the April violence—but they also served a useful purpose, for both Iraqis and Americans. If it was Sudanese, Algerians, Egyptians, Syrians, Saudis, and other Arabs who were turning thousands of Iraqis into scattered bits of flesh, then the country was enduring international terrorism, not the civil war that everyone dreaded. Even after some terrorists were positively identified as Iraqis, local people continued to insist that no Iraqi would do such things. The terrorists had to be foreigners—either Arab jihadis or American agents seeking to perpetuate the occupation.

Among young Iraqis who now had access to new media, a morbid interest arose in DVDs and Web sites that featured footage of attacks on American soldiers, beheadings, outtakes from Baath-era crimes, and other grotesque entertainments, in what was becoming a subculture of death. The atmosphere was so brutal that the news of mass murders became numbingly routine. Personal anecdotes that came my way somehow hit harder. They suggested an epidemic of violence that was going largely unreported. My driver's sister, a gerontologist at a public clinic, told me that a woman had come in the day before with severe shock: Her husband, a translator at an American base, had been shot dead before her eyes. One of my translators, also a doctor, had a friend from medical school, a Shiite, who had gone to work at a clinic near Ramadi in order to be with his fiancée. Local people immediately suspected him of being a spy—why else would a Shiite want to work in a wild place like Anbar province?—and the doctor and his fiancée were beheaded. A factory owner in Mosul appeared in a documentary film saying that the fall of the regime had improved his business. The film was shown several times on Arab satellite TV, and soon afterward the factory owner's uncle was kidnapped; when the family ransomed his release, he was returned without eyes or hands. And there was this leaflet that an Iraqi-American woman working with the CPA picked up in Kadhimiya and showed me:

IN THE NAME OF GOD THE MERCIFUL. THIS IS A FINAL WARNING.

To the spies at the local council, to all the translators and coordinators who work with the occupation forces: we are warning you that you should go back to your God and to the people. Otherwise your fate is known ahead of time and your punishment will be just, because you are informing on our sons and our brothers and they are being arrested now, and if they are exposed to any danger we will take justice into our own hands in order to defend our people who reject the traitor even more than the occupier. If you don't stop after this warning we will tell your families that you are spies and your families should disown you because you are traitors and have sold out our land and our honor. We will tell your families to kick you out of your homes publicly, otherwise they will be like you and they will also be responsible.

GOD IS GREAT. MAY BELOVED IRAQ LIVE LONG WITH HONOR AND DIGNITY. MAY THE CURSE OF GOD BE ON ALL WHO EXTEND A HELPING HAND TO THE AGGRESSORS.

The Sunni insurgency never articulated a political vision that could win over Iraqis in large numbers. Its rhetoric was nationalist and Islamist; its strategy was increasingly sectarian. But what it really excelled at was fear.

THE SHIITE INSURGENCY was fundamentally different. It began on April 10, 2003, in Shiism's holiest shrine, the tomb of Imam Ali in Najaf. Ayatollah Abdul-Majid al-Khoei, the son of a grand ayatollah who had been Sistani's predecessor as Iraq's leading Shiite cleric until his death in 1992, returned to Iraq from exile with American support in early April and entered his hometown of Najaf. Khoei had run a human-rights foundation in London, and he wanted to guide Iraq's Shiite majority in a democratic direction. His appearance in the holy city was taken as a direct challenge by Moqtada al-Sadr, himself the son of a late and revered ayatollah, but far more radical than Khoei in the theocratic mold, with Iranian backing. On the morning of April 10, Khoei went to the shrine to make a conciliatory gesture toward its Baathist *kilidar*, or keeper. A mob of Sadr followers gathered outside and besieged the mosque office. The keeper was murdered on the spot; Khoei, who fired a gun in self-defense, was bound, beaten, and dragged by the mob to the door of Sadr's headquarters. I spoke with the young judge, Raed Juhi, who investigated the case (he would later read charges to Saddam Hussein at his first court appearance). Eyewitnesses told Judge

Juhi's investigation that when Sadr appeared at the door, he was asked by the mob what should be done with Khoei. The witnesses reported Sadr answering, "Take this person away from here and kill him."

The investigation was conducted two months after the murder, and in order for there to be an autopsy on Khoei, who was buried inside the gates of the shrine, the police, having secured the permission of the victim's family for this most un-Islamic deed, exhumed his body in the middle of the night. The severed finger, lacerations, stab wounds, and bone fractures confirmed the witnesses' testimony about the manner of Khoei's death (the corpse was returned for reinterment several nights later under cover of new burials). Juhi issued arrest warrants against Sadr and two dozen others. But rather than executing all of the warrants, the CPA placed Sadr's under seal.

The murder of Khoei was an ill omen of the political violence to come. In Kuwait, Jay Garner's inner circle received the news without concern. "Oh, it's just them killing each other," one of the retired generals said. But Sadr had struck an audacious early blow in what was essentially an internal Shiite power struggle, and the Americans' refusal to confront him only emboldened Sadr to push harder. Shortly after the murder of Khoei, his followers even surrounded the small rented house of Ayatollah Sistani in Najaf, but armed tribesmen from the region drove them away. Sadr's main rivals were the other leading clerical families—the Khoeis and the Hakims—who were vying for leadership and who were more willing to play by the CPA's rules. Sadr was around thirty (his exact age remained a mystery—some said he was still in his twenties), with a cleric's black turban and bushy black beard, but without the scholarly credentials; his slightly cross-eyed scowl and demagogic outbursts left most observers unimpressed. Some Iraqis thought Sadr mentally ill, and one called him a "Mongolian," by which he meant Mongoloid. But Sadr had two weapons that made it unwise to underestimate him: his father's mantle, and his father's following among young, poor, dispossessed Shiite men, the generation created by Saddam, whom Sadr's aides organized and armed as the Mahdi Army. They took over schools and hospitals, intimidated the staffs, assaulted unveiled women, set up kangaroo sharia courts that issued death sentences, repeatedly tried to seize control of the holy shrines, ran criminal gangs, firebombed liquor stores, and were often drunk themselves. They made themselves extremely unpopular among the middle classes of Najaf, Karbala, Basra, and Baghdad. Their tactics were those of fascist bullies; Sadr's father had at one time been Saddam's handpicked Shi- ite leader, and many of the men around the younger Sadr were former Baathists. In March 2004, they wiped a village of gypsies in southern Iraq off the map. But the fragile Iraqi police were unable or unwilling to constrain them (the Basra police chief and many of his officers were Sadrists themselves), and the occupation authority allowed Sadr's strength to grow unchecked while providing him with a rhetorical tar- get that was a far better recruiting tool than his attacks on other Shia. In October 2003, Sadr briefly declared himself the government of Iraq.

The CPA didn't know what to do with young Sadr. If he was arrested, there would be a backlash; if he was ignored, he would continue his campaign of intimidation. Sadr had been left off the Gov- erning Council, but now he was, in Lyndon Johnson's phrase, outside the tent pissing in, and the CPA had no channel to his movement, mak- ing or failing to make decisions, as so often, without enough informa- tion. Ambassador Hume Horan, Bremer's liaison to the Shia, said of Sadr, "His father would be so distressed if he'd seen his son. How can you do an Erik Erikson on Moqtada al-Sadr? Here's this unchurched son of one of the great churchmen who fills the role without any of the qualifications. What is he lashing out at? Is it his own sense of inade- quacy that is being projected out?" Horan, who committed suicide in 2004 while suffering from cancer, was an elder of the Presbyterian church and a bookishly eccentric retired diplomat who was reading a ten-volume French historical novel at the palace. His assignment in Iraq was to get to know the more moderate senior Shiite clergy—"these shaggy fellows," he called them. "I feel like a paleontologist. It's like a new frontier for an Arabist, to talk to Shia clergy. They've not been poi- soned by these anti-Semitic currents that have been washing around much of the Sunni world. I think their otherworldliness has given them some protection against the distemper. I wish them well. Innocence de- serves a break now and again." I asked Horan what the chances were of an Iranian-style theocracy being imposed by the Shiite majority on Iraq. "Absolutely zero," he said. "Not a chance in the world."

Paul Bremer finally decided to have Sadr arrested, and at least twice, Horan said, the CPA issued a general lockdown order to its personnel in advance of a move. "But the water receded without ever going over the sea wall." The brake was applied in Washington, several CPA advisers told me, where the fear of immediate violence overrode the long-term gain of enforcing the law and neutralizing a growing danger. It was just one of the many cases where domestic political calculations by the Bush administration undermined what its emissaries were trying to do in Iraq. Sir Jeremy Greenstock, Tony Blair's envoy in Baghdad from September 2003 to March 2004, told me that Bremer "was actually quite carefully constrained by an overambitious Washington from making his own decisions on the ground." But even as knowledgeable a diplomat as Greenstock had little sense of the extent of Sadr's following. "Tiny. And with no political impact," he told me in the last week of March, a few days before the April uprising.

So Sadr remained free, and the warrant stayed under seal. Cash poured in from Iranian backers, and his militia acquired heavy weapons. The Americans had turned over control of the south-central region to a multinational division under Polish command, but the mix of Poles, Spaniards, Salvadorans, Bulgarians, and Ukrainians was more useful as evidence of a coalition in Iraq than as a security force. A power vacuum emerged, and the Americans lacked the troops and the will to disarm the militias that were competing to fill it—not just Sadr's, but also those of his rivals in the more mainstream Shiite parties. The strategy was essentially to hope for the best.

On April 1, a CPA adviser on democracy, Larry Diamond of Stanford University, came back to the palace in Baghdad from a trip to Hilla, where he had learned that security across the Shiite center and south was deteriorating rapidly. He requested a private meeting with Bremer in his office. Diamond warned Bremer that the situation was dangerous, and he urged that five thousand Marines from the force that had just arrived in Anbar province be diverted to the south-central region immediately to do what the multinational division manifestly couldn't.

It was evening, and Bremer was eating a dinner that had gone cold on his tray. He had been in Iraq for almost eleven months, soldiering through crisis after crisis with unflappable determination, and he looked worn-out. When an aide once saw him remove his shirt to put on a bulletproof vest, Bremer's chest was skin and bones. "I don't know if you've noticed," he told Diamond testily, "but there is a war going on in the west." No Marines could be spared from Anbar. When Diamond pointed out what had always been obvious—that there weren't enough troops in Iraq, and everyone knew it—Bremer implied that it wasn't politically possible to get more. Diamond pressed again: At least send twenty Marines and two Humvees down south to protect CPA officials who had little in the way of security. "We don't *have* any more troops," Bremer shot back. If someone felt unsafe, he should go home. There was nothing more to be said.

FROM DECEMBER THROUGH MARCH—between the Ramadan Offensive and the nationwide uprisings—the CPA worked under the illusion that it was making real progress. Those were, relatively speaking, quiet months, when it was possible for officials in the palace to believe that the project of transforming Iraq was succeeding. In mid-November, Bremer, under pressure for different reasons from both the White House and Ayatollah Sistani, abandoned his seven-step plan for the restoration of Iraq's sovereignty. With Iraqi support for the occupation plummeting into the single digits in opinion polls, the transition had to be speeded up, and Sistani's basic demand that the constitution be written by an elected body, which Bremer had ignored for months, must be granted. The November 15 agreement, which the CPA wrote and then obliged the Governing Council to sign, speeded up the return of sovereignty to a fixed date, June 30, 2004. Both the CPA and the council, which most Iraqis correctly saw as unrepresentative and ineffective, would then dissolve. An interim assembly, chosen through a process of nationwide caucuses so complex that not even American officials could explain it, would govern Iraq until national elections in early 2005. The elected government would then write the new constitution.

Much of this plan eventually went the way of previous American blueprints, unable to survive prolonged contact with Iraqi reality. Sistani objected to the caucus system for the same reasons he had blocked Bremer's earlier plan—because it wasn't based on a democratic election. As before, Bremer and his aides in Governance clung to the scheme for months before finally giving up. Then the Bush administration, having spent more than a year pushing the UN aside, asked it to return to Iraq in the person of the Algerian diplomat Lakhdar Brahimi to oversee the transition. The United States simply lacked the legitimacy to manage the process itself. But one thing from the November 15 agreement remained sacred: the June 30 handover. Suddenly, the CPA had an expiration date.

The pace of hard work in the palace grew frantic. Meghan O'Sullivan and her colleagues invested weeks of time and enormous energy negotiating with the Governing Council an interim law by which Iraq would be ruled until the permanent constitution. Bremer issued a blizzard of legal orders covering everything from the registration of NGOs to the appointment of inspectors general in the ministries. The CPA opened training and resource centers around the country for businessmen, tribes, women's groups, political parties. Hundreds of "democracy dialogues" took place in dozens of cities and towns. Contracting officers poured into the Green Zone to hasten the spending of Congress's eighteen billion dollars. Ray Salvatore Jennings, who specialized in postwar reconstructions, described the CPA officials he knew as people underwater, sinking with the pressure, isolated, wearing down. "They talk to everyone else and each other by e-mail. And they worry that they're running out of time." Officials in Washington found that the CPA was becoming a kind of foreign government with power massed in one man's hands, unanswerable to the administration, ever more out of touch with Iraqis, and still insistent that it knew best. The two political decisions of the occupation that could be called successes—the November 15 agreement and the return of the UN to help with the transition—had to be forced on Bremer and the CPA by Robert Blackwill, a Kissinger protégé and former ambassador to India with a reputation for abusing underlings, who was appointed to serve under Rice at the NSC as a political czar on Iraq, in an effort to rein in the CPA. The flow of information from Baghdad to Washington was slow and sometimes misleading, and mutual antagonism filled the void. O'Sullivan, a rising young star under Richard Haass and then Bremer, was frequently criticized back in Washington for failing to see how little the Governing Council mattered to Iraqis—for not knowing how much she didn't know. During the long year at the palace, she and other talented officials seemed to become more and more enameled in the belief that they were succeeding, more and more impervious to dissenting views. Yet all the while, the country was slipping away.

In February, a fifty-year-old investment banker in Virginia named Brad Swanson got a call from his old friend Michael Fleischer, the brother of Ari Fleischer, Bush's bald and implacable former press secretary. Fleischer was working with the CPA on private-sector development—setting up a stock market, getting foreign investment, making loans to Iraqi businesses. But he was severely understaffed. Would Swanson come out to Baghdad and help? Swanson had been a foreign-service officer in Liberia in the early eighties, he had done investment deals in countries all over the world, but he had never worked anywhere like Iraq. He was a good-looking, thoughtful man who wore buttoned-down shirts, with a wife, three sons, two dogs, and a rambling old house in a horsey suburb outside Washington. He didn't need to jump-start his career, or earn a tax-free salary, or win his stripes with the Republican Party, or prove his courage. But the historic nature of what was happening in Iraq attracted him. Swanson's wife saw the excitement in his eyes and didn't try to talk him out of it, but his two younger sons, fourteen and eleven, were angry and frightened. Swanson told me, "If I'd been somebody who said, 'I am going to put the well-being or the composure of my family above everything else,' I wouldn't have gone."

Bureaucratic delays kept Swanson from reaching Baghdad until mid-March. He quickly fell into the intense rhythm of the palace, the mission culture, working absurd hours seven days a week, leaving the Green Zone in an unmarked pickup truck to meet Iraqi businessmen, at considerable risk to both parties, and negotiate loan agreements. There was still goodwill on both sides and a desperate need to get factories started up and Iraqis hired. But days went by, and then weeks, and nothing happened. The money from the eighteen billion, which included a portion for business loans, was bottled up by stateside procurement rules, with provisions for insurance and workman's compensation that made no sense in Iraq, and by turf battles between the various government agencies whose detailees staffed the CPA. Swanson didn't know whether the bureaucracy was simply incapable of working any faster, or the Bush administration didn't want to break so many rules as to create a sense of urgency that might raise public concern about how well Iraq was really going. But it wasn't until late October 2004, seven months after his arrival in Iraq and three months after his departure, that Swanson's first loan, to the owner of a factory that made plastic water bottles, finally came through.

Even in the heat of the effort, Swanson realized that the CPA was failing. He imagined Iraq as a patient lying on a table with his arteries open, and the Americans pumping in blood as fast as they could, and the blood pouring out as fast as it was pumped in. Late at night, out by the swimming pool behind the palace where officials could sit with a beer and relax, he would sometimes delicately broach the big questions—Was it really working? Did it all make sense?—but he seldom found takers and quickly backed off. "I think people either didn't want to admit it, or didn't want to talk about it, or couldn't concentrate on anything beyond their immediate environment." The determination to get the job done overrode everything else, and so no one asked whether the CPA had any business writing codes for Iraq that created a 15 percent flat tax, transparent accounting procedures, and new banking and commercial laws. "The quality of the fairyland that was created was very lovely. All these things were great laws, but they just had no application in the real world."

The word Swanson used to describe the mental atmosphere at the CPA was "groupthink": the uniform mind-set that takes hold of any hermetic, hierarchical institution with strong leaders and a sense of common mission, where bad news is unwelcome and no one wants to be the one to ask the truly unsettling questions. Swanson had seen groupthink once before, at the U.S. embassy in Liberia in the early eighties, where the American policy was to support a half-literate sergeant named Samuel Doe who had shot and disemboweled his way into power. As a political officer, Swanson sounded out a variety of Liberians about Doe, and they all said that if America continued to finance and arm him, Doe would bring the country to ruin. Swanson, the enthusiastic young diplomat in his first overseas post, argued that it couldn't be true, Doe was learning to be a good ruler, the IMF was coming in, things were getting better. But the Liberians were right: Within a few years, Liberia collapsed into a terrible civil war that destroyed the country and much of the region. "Something I'll live with the rest of my life," Swanson said.

In Iraq he was older, with more critical distance, and so he was able to recognize the telltale signs of groupthink, which had traveled the eight thousand miles from Washington and taken hold at the palace in Baghdad. Michael Fleischer, Swanson's friend and boss, was a true believer. The two men disagreed about the reasons for the ongoing war: In Swanson's view, part of the fault lay with the CPA, since the insurgency fed on the Americans' failure to spend money and even partially satisfy the expectations of Iraqis. To Fleischer, it was much simpler. "He believed that there were insurgents because in any population there was going to be a number of bloody-minded, psychopathic, terrible people." But the two remained good friends, and Swanson worked his heart out in spite of his misgivings. He didn't understand exactly *why* the CPA was a failure until he left Iraq at the end of July and rejoined his family on vacation in England, where he took long walks in the countryside and began to acknowledge the huge futility of what he'd been trying to do.

The problem lay in the hubris of the whole enterprise. "CPA was set up to do a root and branch transformation of the country, and that wasn't what was required," Swanson said. "What was required was to get two basic things right: security and economy. CPA was created to be a long-term institution, a MacArthur-type restructuring of the society. And then, when there was the abrupt decision in November to hand over in June, there wasn't the follow-through to pare down the CPA's activities and focus on one or two key things. Instead, this machine kept grinding on, creating structures as if it were going to be there for years to implement them. But then it just stopped, and the structures collapsed of their own weight with no enforcement, no real foundation."

Back in Virginia, Swanson set his thoughts down in an op-ed piece. When it was published, he sent a copy to Michael Fleischer. He heard nothing back, and several attempts to get in touch went unanswered. Finally, Swanson received a very brief e-mail from his old friend. "If we speak again," Fleischer wrote, "it will be sometime in the future."

IN THE GREEN ZONE, it was as if a construction crew was carefully applying the finishing touches to the interior of a new house without noticing the arsonists gathering outside. Politics was a game played out of public view. For example, the interim law signed by the twenty-five members of the Governing Council in early March was a real achievement, with a liberal bill of rights and hard-won compromises on the most intransigent issues, like the autonomy of Kurdistan and the role of Islam. The final negotiations lasted all night, with Bremer and other CPA officials sitting back from the table in silence while the Iraqis argued out their differences.

But the Governing Council was a creation of the CPA, and negotiating with it, one of Bremer's deputies said, was "like staring at your own navel. They had no relevance to the average Iraqi, and there was no way they were going to gain relevance, because they had no real authority." After the signing ceremony, the document was taken outside the Green Zone and presented as a fait accompli to the Iraqi people, who knew nothing about any of it. The CPA tried to mount a public relations campaign, but it was overwhelmed by the speed of the popular reaction, which was prompted in part by negative propaganda from the office of Ayatollah Sistani, who objected to the effective veto granted to minority groups over the permanent constitution. Not surprisingly, the sessions at which American and Iraqi officials tried to explain the law's contents and invited comment turned into angry denunciations. I sat in on the meeting of a district council in a palace that had belonged to one of Saddam's daughters. Two representatives from the Governing Council were shouted down by people in the room, who complained that Kurds received more rights than Arabs, Jews would use the law to return to Iraq and take over the economy, the law hadn't been explained in the media. Finally a man standing in the back of the room said, "Don't you think you should bring this to the Iraqis first, and then decide what you're going to do with the country?" The law hadn't come from them or anyone chosen by them—this was the real objection. The CPA sacrificed legitimacy for control, and it ended up with neither.

Moqtada al-Sadr quickly took advantage, organizing daily protests against the law in Firdos Square and claiming to be acting on behalf of Ayatollah Sistani, who in fact was his main rival for power among the Shia. Ethnic tension increased noticeably around the country. One day, when I went to see Bashir Shaker, the doctor from the morgue, at his house in Sadr City, his brothers had just come back from a demonstration where Kurds were denounced as infidels and traitors.

"The story will be like Lebanon," Dr. Shaker said. "A civil war."

Arab against Kurd?

"A strong possibility."

Shiite against Sunni?

"It's a possibility. The constitution will be the starting point, and then the event will be gradually increased."

Entire armies fighting each other?

"This is how I imagine it." The likeliest scenario of all, he said, was civil war among the Shia.

It was my last visit to the house. Later, neighbors belonging to Sadr's militia warned the doctor against having an American over.

THE DECISION on March 28 to suspend Sadr's newspaper for sixty days wasn't considered important enough to clear with Washington or even to involve Bremer. Bremer's top deputy, Ambassador Richard Jones, and his legal adviser, Scott Castle, were simply following a CPA policy against incitement. Other papers had been slapped for lesser deeds, and if *al-Hawza*, which printed lists of names of "collaborators," accused American soldiers of deliberately rocketing mosques, and charged Bremer himself with starving Iraqis, was allowed to go on publishing, the CPA would be playing favorites.

No one seemed to anticipate the consequences. When the Mahdi Army took to the streets, Bremer was still waiting for an operational plan from the military to neutralize Sadr and his followers. Sadr was unaccountably left free to direct the uprising, and four days later, at Friday prayers in his headquarters mosque in Kufa, just outside Najaf, he urged the faithful to rise up against the occupation and strike terror in its heart. The next day, April 3, Lieutenant General Sanchez informed Bremer at their morning meeting that his soldiers were going

to arrest Sadr's top lieutenant, Mustafa Yaqoubi, that same day in Najaf on an outstanding warrant in the murder of Khoei (Sadr's warrant
remained sealed, but the military had standing orders to enforce the
two dozen others). Fine, Bremer said. Some people at the meeting
thought Yaqoubi was an al-Qaeda operative.

The shutdown of the newspaper and the arrest of Yaqoubi were
never thought through and coordinated, within the CPA, between
Bremer and Sanchez, or between Baghdad and Washington. Yaqoubi's
arrest sparked a massive rebellion, which Sadr had obviously planned
in advance—a direct bid to seize power from the occupation forces.
Mahdi Army militiamen began pouring down from Sadr City to Shiite
towns across southern Iraq, and within a few days they had overrun
and trashed CPA offices in Kut and Nasiriya, where the Ukrainians
and Italians were unable to hold their ground. The Spanish in Najaf and
Bulgarians in Karbala would have been overwhelmed, too, if American
forces hadn't been rushed down to reinforce them. The whole multinational division proved to be a paper army that was no match for the
thousands of untrained, foolishly brave young Shiite militiamen who
fought out in the open with AK-47s and RPGs.

At that same moment, the chronic Sunni insurgency in Anbar
province suddenly exploded into full-scale combat. The mutilation of
the four Blackwater contractors on March 31 shocked the American
public. At the White House, President Bush declared, "I want heads
to roll." It was an impulsive reaction, based on the domestic impact of
the pictures from Falluja, as if Iraq were a shootout in which personal
honor was at stake (just as Bush's response to the initial stage of the insurgency had been to say, "Bring 'em on"). Officials in Baghdad called
this kind of long-range tinkering "the eight-thousand-mile screwdriver,"
and at the other end was a president who often said that the lesson of
Vietnam was that politicians shouldn't try to do the job of generals. The
order went down the chain of command for the new Marine division in
Anbar to surround Falluja, which had been left unpatrolled for weeks
by the Eighty-second Airborne, retake it, and hunt down the contractors' killers. The commander of the First Marine Expeditionary Force,
Lieutenant General James Conway, later said that he wasn't happy
about the order to attack a whole city in revenge for four deaths; the

Marines had come to Anbar with the idea of taming the rebellious province with a smoother, softer touch than the ham-fisted Eighty-second, and Conway wanted to handle the crisis with targeted operations. Bremer was also opposed, according to an official in Washington, but Rumsfeld overrode him, and Bremer's appeal to Bush was in vain.

Conway was unhappier still when, three days after the assault began, with the Marines approaching the city center in close fighting, the order came from the Pentagon to stop. Unconfirmed reports on Arab satellite TV of hundreds of civilian deaths in Falluja were inflaming opinion all over Iraq and the region; Lakhdar Brahimi, the UN special representative in Baghdad, said that his mission was about to collapse, and several members of the Governing Council threatened to quit. The fighting in Falluja, which spread to Ramadi, created for the first time an alliance of Sunni and Shia against the Americans: Shiite mosques organized blood drives and aid convoys for besieged Fallujans, and Sadr's picture appeared in Sunni mosques. There was even some tactical coordination between fighters. Most of the country now seemed to be in open rebellion against the occupation. The United States was fighting a two-front war without enough troops, and in the first two weeks of April, a year after the formal end of major combat operations, forty-eight soldiers were killed.

The Marines eventually withdrew from Falluja. The city was handed over to a contingent of former Iraqi soldiers called the Falluja Brigade, which soon lost control to the insurgency and in some cases went over to the other side. The Falluja Brigade was Lieutenant General Conway's idea; the CPA wasn't consulted. Falluja would become a Taliban-like fiefdom and base of operations for Iraq's most violent jihadis, foreign and local, until a new division of Marines would retake the city by frontal assault in November. Sadr's militia was soon repelled from Kut and other towns by American forces and armed tribes; under pressure from Shiite clerics and politicians, Sadr returned control of the holy cities to the Iraqi police. But the Mahdi Army was still armed and far from finished. It would take a second round of fighting in Najaf and Sadr City, Sistani's intervention, and then the beginning of serious negotiations and reconstruction projects, to persuade Sadr to end the Shiite insurgency and join Iraqi politics—a rare strategic success for America in Iraq.

"Six months of work is completely gone," said a CPA official who survived the April battles in the south. "There is nothing to show for it." By sheer fecklessness, confusion, and ignorance, the administration in Washington and the occupation authority in Baghdad had allowed Iraq to become explosive and had then triggered the detonator themselves.

During the violence of April and May, the credibility of the CPA collapsed. The civilian and military spokesmen, a Republican appointee named Dan Senor and a brigadier general named Mark Kimmitt, stood up at daily press conferences in the convention center and issued statements about the history of Sadr's arrest warrant and the coalition's intentions toward the rebels that were usually at odds with the facts, on occasion flatly untrue, and often in direct contradiction to statements made a day or a week earlier—all the while insisting that American policy remained firm and the violence was sporadic, minor, and under control. Senor and Kimmett were only repeating the blithe reassurance coming from the White House and Pentagon in the midst of a presidential campaign, but in Baghdad their words took on the tone of farce, and the audience that mattered most—the Iraqis—wasn't fooled.

The scandal of prisoner abuse, which had been going on for months but broke publicly in early May with the uprising still seething, became a microcosm of the larger failures. Bremer had known that the prison system was broken for some time, but an official who worked on the issue of detainees told me that Sanchez and the military steadily resisted the CPA's attempts to get information about the prisons or have certain prisoners released. The attitude was: This is our job, we know what we're doing, stay out. Bremer never publicly showed that the issue concerned him, and Iraqis, including those who could get no word about the fate of family members, believed that the entire occupation was to blame—which, in fact, it was. Bremer and Sanchez, the senior civilian and the senior soldier in Iraq, "literally hated each other," an official in Washington said. "Jerry thought Sanchez was an idiot, and Sanchez thought Jerry was a civilian micromanaging son of a bitch." So the CPA allowed the single worst stain on its reputation to spread indelibly.

"What's the moral difference between Saddam Hussein and us?" one soldier, who didn't find the abuse itself particularly terrible, wrote me in May. "Obviously a lot, I believe, but the problem is that those who don't know America aren't going to see it that way. It's set our work back a long, long ways, which is the greatest shame if you're like us and want to see Iraq succeed. That's the depressing part, its effect on everyone else, not what actually happened."

Over time, it became clear that the ultimate responsibility lay in Washington, at the Pentagon, the Justice Department, and finally the White House. The memos on torture and the Geneva Conventions written by the president's counsel Alberto Gonzales and others made abuses inevitable. One administration official who had served in Vietnam said, "There's no doubt in my mind as a soldier that part of the responsibility for Abu Ghraib and for Afghanistan belongs with the secretary of defense and the president of the United States. There's an old aphorism: Keep it simple, stupid. KISS is the acronym. You always have personalities in uniform—I had them in Vietnam—who will take advantage of any ambiguity, any lack of clarification in the rules of engagement,' and kill people, or whatever his particular psyche is liable to do. You don't have rules for your good people. You have rules for that five or six percent of your combat unit that are going to be weird. You need those people, because sometimes they're your best killers. But you need the rules. And when you make any kind of changes in them, any relaxation or even hint of it, you're opening Pandora's box. And I fault Gonzalez, the president, the vice president, the secretary of defense, the chain of command, Myers, Abizaid, Sanchez, the whole bunch of them."

All of these men kept their jobs. One was even promoted. The failure to hold anyone in authority responsible ensured that immoral and, from a practical point of view, worthless methods of interrogation would continue. Even after the world saw the pictures from Abu Ghraib, prisoners would go on being tortured in American custody.

The events of April and May 2004 showed that no one was making decisions based on a clear, realistic strategy. No one was really in charge of Iraq. Bremer acted without consulting Washington, Washington kept stepping in to overrule Bremer, the Pentagon was still battling State and NSC, the White House had its eye on the political calendar, Bremer and Sanchez were barely speaking, Sanchez left his division commanders to pursue wildly different tactics. When something went wrong, it was somebody else's fault—a psychopathic sergeant, or the press corps, or the Iraqis. And the Iraqis turned out to have their own ideas about their country's fate. Looking back, a senior CPA official said, "What they needed was somebody in charge in Washington and somebody in charge in Baghdad, and they needed to be twins, in the sense that they were really on the same wavelength. Rumsfeld was kind of washing his hands, it seemed. Jerry over time began dealing more and more with Rice and Powell. Unfortunately, by then you had a full-blown insurgency."

THE FIGHTING DELAYED THE REDEPLOYMENTS of twenty-five thousand soldiers for two or three months. The plan to reduce American troop levels to 115,000 was tossed out as the coalition once again had to improvise. Departing convoys of exhausted soldiers were turned around on the road to Baghdad International Airport. The First Armored Division was sent south from Baghdad to Najaf and other cities to take over from the overwhelmed multinational force. Within a few weeks of his departure, and hastily married, John Prior was back in Iraq.

Prior's battalion ended up at a base in a former chicken factory, twenty miles south of Baghdad outside a squalid town called Mahmudiya. Prior's war log for April 2003 recorded that thousands of jubilant Iraqis had thronged the main road in Mahmudiya as Charlie Company liberated the town on its way to Baghdad. The area was now called the Triangle of Death. The town was mixed Sunni and Shiite, but the outlying lands were largely Sunni, with a large number of former Republican Guard officers in houses built after 1991 by the old regime to create a line of defense between Baghdad and the Shiite south. Mahmudiya was dense with munitions factories, which had been looted after the invasion, and was now the scene of constant roadside explosions and even suicide car bombings. One car bomber drove into a checkpoint and blew up eight soldiers in an explosion so powerful that his steering wheel landed two hundred feet away and a thirty-ton Bradley was disabled. Insurgent attacks on Shiite policemen and pilgrims traveling to the holy cities were increasing, and Mahmudiya was also notorious for the shooting of journalists and other foreigners along the highway that passed through the middle of town. Mortar or rocket fire was directed at the chicken factory almost every night. Charlie Company was spending the last of its fifteen months in Iraq in a bleak, hostile place.

I went to see Prior there in the middle of June. Highway 8, the strip down from Baghdad, was closed to civilian traffic, and one section of the road, a bridge over a canal, had recently been blown up. The soldiers who escorted me down to the base made no secret of their feelings about the prolonged stay in Iraq. "I sympathized with the Iraqis when we first got here," said a young sergeant who had spent every day of the occupation in Iraq. "But now I'm cold, I feel no remorse. When you see some of your friends get killed, it changes you." I asked if he still distinguished between good and bad Iraqis. "How can you tell them apart? The same guy that waves at you can shoot you with an RPG."

At the base I heard the same thing from almost every soldier I talked to. The bitterness extended beyond Iraqis to their own chain of command. Rumsfeld, who had sent them out here without enough men and armor and then extended their deployment several times, came in for particular hatred, and even the president wasn't popular; a number of soldiers said that they intended to vote for John Kerry, who at least had served in Vietnam. Everyone was still doing his or her job, but the heart had gone out of it and a stale air of cynicism hung over the place as the soldiers waited for their orders to ship out. After the close relationships Prior and his lieutenants and NCOs had developed with their translators in Zafaraniya, it seemed an unfortunate development that the portable toilets at the base in Mahmudiya were segregated between American soldiers and Iraqi workers. The Americans complained that the Iraqis kept breaking the seats by standing on them. Thousands of years of civilization, the Americans said, and these people still didn't know how to use a sit-down toilet.

I spent several nights at the base. On the second evening, two mortar rounds flew overhead and exploded somewhere outside the perimeter, but otherwise my visit to Mahmudiya was quiet. One morning I went out on patrol in a convoy of two Bradleys and two armored Humvees (in Zafaraniya the thirty-ton Bradleys had stayed at the base, but here no one patrolled without them). The commander of the Humvee I rode in, Sergeant Scott McKissen, had seen his son a total of fourteen days in the boy's fourteen-month life. Another soldier had canceled his wedding three times. McKissen, a blond, good-natured thirty-one-year-old from a small town in Utah, was still doing his damnedest to complete the mission, waving at pedestrians on the main road who resolutely refused to wave back. Most Iraqis didn't look at the heavily armored vehicles lumbering through their town, but the few stares were hard; no one smiled, not even a child.

"The hardest thing is treating these people with dignity and respect," McKissen said, "because I haven't met one yet that I can trust. We know what they'd do if they got their hands on us. And the fatigue of being here so long and wanting to go home doesn't make you want to be friendly. I think the biggest battle here is just trying to be friendly with these people. You gotta try—it's the only way to fight the fight, trying to set them up with a democratic government. It's not going to work if you just shoot 'em. They've been living this way for centuries. Are we going to change that in a year? All you can do is try."

At the southern edge of town a tread fell off one of the Bradleys, and we stood out on the shoulder of the road in the summer heat, soldiers fanned out with guns at the ready position, while a mechanic lay in the dirt with a wrench. I started broken conversations with a couple of Iraqis walking by and took a perverse pleasure in the knowledge that I wouldn't have lasted here more than a few seconds on my own. Later, we heard over the radio that a car bomber was cruising the area. After an hour we moved on in what struck me as a pro forma patrol, speeding down the stretch of highway south of the city where IEDs were particularly bad. McKissen looked hard at every pile of garbage and dead dog on the roadside. The land was flat and dust blown, with lines of palm trees in the distance and fields of sunflowers wilting on their stalks.

We stopped by the railroad tracks, near a canal overgrown with papyrus rushes. A section of the line had been blown up near here two weeks ago. Eight lonely Iraqi national guardsmen were digging a trench in the dirt perpendicular to the tracks. The Americans stopped and got out to talk, but there was no translator with them. "Good idea, but it's facing the wrong way," a soldier tried to explain to the guardsmen. "You want to face toward the tracks."

It was a pathetic sight. A lot of sweating and digging had gone into the trench, but the sandbag and plywood reinforcements were next to worthless. The men themselves looked too skinny and too old for the work; a few had gray hair. They wore different pieces of uniform, some without regulation boots, none with flak vests. Their only protection was their AK-47s. The area was rife with insurgents, and within a couple of weeks these guardsmen or others like them would start to die five or ten at a time under daily attacks against which they would be practically defenseless.

McKissen was on the radio back to the base chuckling about the new fighting positions. An Iraqi explained with gestures that a nearby unit had been fired on a few minutes ago. "I'm not surprised," McKissen said matter-of-factly. "It happens often."

The Americans offered their counterparts a thumbs-up and headed back to the base. The Iraqis returned to digging.

That night, I shared a dinner of MREs around a table in Charlie Company's cramped tactical operations center, which doubled as Prior's sleeping quarters, with Prior, his lieutenants, and his new first sergeant. Mark Lahan had gone back to Germany, and his replacement, Karl Wetherington, a wiry thirty-nine-year-old, let me know what he thought about the people that the Americans had come here fifteen months ago to liberate. "An Iraqi came up to me and said it pisses them off to have to wait for military traffic. I told him, 'If you wouldn't blow us up with car bombs, we'd let you pass us.' Shitheads."

The men around the table, from small towns in Georgia, Minnesota, North Carolina, all had the same view: After working here for more than a year, they had concluded that Iraqi men were unreliable, didn't tell the truth, couldn't think rationally, never showed initiative. Prior had reluctantly come to believe that the religion, with its treatment of women and its pervasive fatalism, was a serious obstacle to democracy in Iraq—that it would take years and years. After relinquishing his company command he was going to study for a year on an Army fellowship at Harvard's Kennedy School of Government, and he imagined that the other students would think him a right-wing racist if he dared to utter these hard-learned home truths.

"During Vietnam, Americans were against the soldiers *and* the administration," Wetherington said. "Here at least the public supports the soldiers, even if they might not support the administration."

"Although that's changing with Abu Ghraib," Prior said. When he was in Boston in April, he had seen demonstrations and overheard bar talk that disheartened him.

"I'm sick of reading about what five people did to a bunch of shit-bag Iraqis," Wetherington said. One day, while he was driving in a convoy through Mahmudiya, children had lined the streets holding up newspapers with pictures from Abu Ghraib. "I mean, what they did was wrong. Just not representative."

Prior said that, compared with Abu Ghraib, the mutilations of the contractors in Falluja *was* representative. "It would be nice to let the American people know that the problems here aren't just because Americans have cultural flaws. It's because these people have cultural flaws, too." He added, "We can change a culture. We have to lean on it, and lean on it, and lean on it. And Americans want it to be done in three months. If people are getting killed, fuck it. And that's a cultural flaw."

Wetherington sat brooding. "I hate the motherfuckers. Muslims are worthless. I don't mind Iraqis—they're okay—just Muslims."

"What the sergeant means," Prior said in his deadpan way, "is that there are many challenges in understanding each other."

The soldiers of Charlie Company were still proud of what they had done. A sergeant named James Jett told me that, compared with other units that used rougher tactics, the restraint and respect shown by the company were the best way to win over Iraqis who were still sitting on the fence. That, even more than catching bad guys, was the thing that mattered most in winning the war—not turning friends or neutrals into enemies. Prior was pleased that during the year of the occupation only one of his soldiers had died and two had had to shoot Iraqis. Later, when we were alone, I reminded him of the speech on evidence and due process that I'd heard him give almost a year ago at the gas station in Zafaraniya. I suggested that he wouldn't give it now, at the end of his long tour.

Prior shook his head. "In my heart I believe everybody's American. George, I'm a complete idealist. All that stuff I told you in August—none of that has changed. My frustration with the Iraqi people, that has increased. But my attitude toward wanting to fix this place hasn't changed. I can't give up on them just because I'm frustrated. I would still give that speech today." What he wouldn't do, Prior said, was tell

Iraqis what he had told me tonight, because he didn't want to destroy their confidence. "Everything I told you in August was from my heart. Now I'm just more frustrated because they're not a Mom and apple pie people in my mind. But I still love my country, I still believe in public service, I still want to give back to my nation. And part of me giving back to my nation is me giving to other nations."

AT THE END OF JUNE I was back in Baghdad for the handover of sovereignty. To foil any attacks, it occurred unannounced two days ahead of schedule, on June 28, in a hasty private ceremony in the Green Zone, after which Paul Bremer and his top aides were spirited to the airport and flown out of Iraq. The sudden end of the CPA was in keeping with its short life.

The interim government of Prime Minister Iyad Allawi, which was to have been chosen by Lakhdar Brahimi's UN team, in fact was the result of a deal brokered between Washington and the Governing Council, with Ayatollah Sistani's blessing. The public seemed prepared to give it a chance. On a single Thursday a few days before the handover, at least a hundred people died across Iraq. Explosions and assassinations were now part of everyday life, and any change would be change for the better.

I visited several government offices and found Iraqis grimly determined to take on the new responsibility that most of them felt should have been theirs from the start. Every official, every secretary, every policeman, was risking his or her life just by leaving home in the morning. In his chambers at the Central Criminal Court, I asked Raed Juhi, the young judge who had issued the arrest warrant for Moqtada al-Sadr and was now leading the investigation of Saddam Hussein, what kept him coming to work every day. He had already survived three attempts on his life.

"If I stay at home, and you stay at home, and the other guy stays at home, who will build Iraq?" Juhi said, and he leaned forward and fixed me with a look. "This is a battle, mister. And we're all soldiers in this battle. So there are only two choices—either to win the battle or to die. There's no third choice."

10

CIVIL WAR?

IRAQ WAS CREATED by European diplomats in Paris after the First World War out of three Ottoman provinces: Mosul, Baghdad, and Basra. According to the secret Sykes-Picot Agreement of 1916 between Britain and France, Mosul, believed to have valuable oil fields, was to come under French control after the war, but Clemenceau graciously handed it over to Lloyd George. The first civil commissioner of the British Mandate, Sir Arnold Wilson (in a sense, Paul Bremer's predecessor in Baghdad), thought from the start that Iraq was too fractured to become a viable independent state. The Kurds in the northern mountains, part of the old province of Mosul, had expected to achieve an independent Kurdistan after the war; they suddenly found themselves ruled from Baghdad in the name of an overwhelmingly Arab entity. The Kurds "will never accept an Arab ruler," Wilson wrote to London. And there was another problem. The majority Shia would not accept Sunni rule, but at the same time, because the officer corps and the administrative class under the Ottoman Empire were Sunni, "no form of Government has yet been envisaged, which does not involve Sunni domination." Wilson's legendary assistant, Gertrude Bell, who had been traveling and writing in the region for years, was warned by an American missionary, "You are flying in the face of four millenniums of history if you try to draw a line around Iraq and call it a political entity! Assyria always looked to the west and east and north, and Babylonia to the south. They have never been an independent unity. You've got to take time to get them integrated, it must be done gradually. They have no conception of nationhood yet."

In Iraq, as elsewhere, the British brazened through the absurdities of their own making. They soon had their hands full with another, more immediate problem than the ultimate viability of Iraq, for one thing that seemed to unite Kurds, Shia, and Sunnis was their rebelliousness against British rule. In June 1920, a revolt began among the Shiite tribes near the holy cities and spread to the Sunnis of Falluja, while in the north the Kurds had been causing trouble for months. British troop levels were grossly insufficient to keep the vast territory under control, and in London there were serious misgivings about the wisdom of an occupation. A headline in *The Times* proclaimed, "Bad to Worse in Mesopotamia." It took additional troops from the Indian colonial army, British air bombardments, and the deaths of six thousand Iraqis and almost five hundred British soldiers to put down the revolt.

According to the historian David Fromkin's excellent account of the era, *A Peace to End All Peace*, Wilson found the uprising almost incomprehensible: "What we are up against is anarchy plus fanaticism. There is little or no Nationalism." The government in London saw the hand of various conspirators from outside Iraq: Turks, Pan-Islamists, Germans, oil companies, Bolsheviks, and Jews. But Gertrude Bell understood the force of Arab nationalism in Iraq, and she proposed to Winston Churchill, the colonial secretary, that Iraq be ruled not directly but as a protectorate, with the core of the old Ottoman Sunni elite built up into the administration of a modern state. In November 1920, she wrote to her father that the new Sunni-dominated council in Baghdad "has against it almost the whole body of Shiahs, first because it's looked upon as of British parentage, but also because it contains considerably less Shiahs than Sunnis. The Shiahs, as I've often observed, are one of the greatest problems." For their part, the Sunnis "are afraid of being swamped by the Shiahs," she wrote two months later. "The present government, which is predominantly Sunni, isn't doing anything to conciliate the Shiahs."

Bell died and was buried in Baghdad in 1926, probably a suicide, without resolving the problem that she had helped to create. The majority Shia and the Kurds fell under the rule of the minority Sunnis, first during the Mandate and then after independence in 1932. Shiite and a handful of Kurdish politicians served in the numerous Iraqi governments of the monarchy period, including several Shia as prime minister, and in republican Iraq after the 1958 coup that overthrew the king. Iraq's powerful Communist Party was largely Shiite, and in its early years the Baath Party had Shia in key positions. But during the decades of Baath Party rule, the Sunni came to dominate, and under Saddam the ruling class telescoped down to a clique of cousins and tribal relations from around Tikrit. When Islam became a political force among the Shia of Iraq in the late 1970s, Saddam repressed it brutally, and Shiite consciousness spread across the country's south. The Kurds had never completely stopped fighting since the creation of the state. So there was reason to worry that the American occupation would inherit three pieces that had never fit together and were bound to chafe until they combusted if they weren't separated.

The insurgency that followed the American invasion reminded some amateur historians of the 1920 revolt against the British. But there was this key difference: In 1920, it was Shiite tribal sheikhs who had first rebelled; after the invasion, very few Shia, other than the Sadr militia, took up arms against the Americans. The reason was obvious: This time, the heirs of Arnold Wilson and Gertrude Bell, the neoconservatives in Washington and the CPA officials in Baghdad, were determined to put power in Shiite hands. This had to do with more than simple majority rule; the Sunni Arabs of Iraq were regarded as one key source of the malaise of the Arab world, with its violent anti-Western ideologies. The main insurgency that began shortly after the fall of Baghdad and continues to this day was always Sunni in character.

During the first year of the war after the war, many Iraqis refused to speak in terms of Sunni, Shiite, and Kurd. People told me that the term "Sunni Triangle" was an insult—that the region was an American invention. As soon as I mentioned one of the unmentionable ethnic categories, I would be told (usually by a gray-haired gentleman in a suit jacket) that these were ideas imported by Westerners and Arab extremists, no one used to ask about Sunni, Shiite, or Kurd, all Iraqis suffered equally under Saddam, and the gentleman in the suit jacket himself had numerous cousins and neighbors in mixed marriages. There could never be a civil war in Iraq, because Iraqis didn't think that way. I always found myself thinking: If only it were true.

Iraq without the lid of totalitarianism clamped down became a place of roiling and contending ethnic claims. The surge of Shiite religiosity was also a political display, deeply disquieting even to Sunnis (as well as secular Shia) who had no desire to dominate. As Shiite officials, security forces, clerics, and pilgrims increasingly became the target of attacks, the sectarian character of the insurgency and of Iraqi politics in general overwhelmed the best intentions of those who insisted that they were all Iraqis. The CPA's failure to disarm the militias, as Bremer more than once vowed to do, left almost every city in Iraq under the real control of an ethnic group rather than the government. It sometimes felt as if a civil war had already started, which only the Sunnis were fighting. The great Shiite patience in not retaliating (apart from a campaign of assassination of former Baathists) had less to do with Iraqi nationalism than with the knowledge that majority power would soon be theirs. Communal violence and occasional terror bombings also erupted along the fault lines in the north where Arabs and Kurds came together. Kurdish separatism was such an obvious force that the only question seemed to be whether the Kurds would stay in the new Iraq or not.

Some American observers, such as Leslie Gelb, the former president of the Council on Foreign Relations, and Peter Galbraith, an ex-diplomat who was an adviser to the Kurds, looked at the mess and decided that only a separation of Iraq into three autonomous regions could prevent civil war. This was in direct opposition to the official American policy that Iraq's "territorial integrity" must be preserved. To Gelb, partition was the solution to America's problems in Iraq: Cut off the Sunni center, abandon it, concentrate troops in the south and north, and support democracies among the Shia and the Kurds. The

Sunnis, with no oil in their desert, could then decide whether they wanted to cooperate or fade away.

This scenario struck me as too remote from the texture of life in Iraq. The country was cobbled together almost a century ago; there are very few Iraqis alive who have any memory of the time before Iraq. The decades of living together wove innumerable personal ties and created a national consciousness that was badly damaged by Saddam, especially among the young, but was nonetheless real. There was nothing organically inevitable about Iraq's falling apart. If it fell apart, it would do so because of the folly of its leaders. Lakhdar Brahimi, the UN envoy in Iraq, who had seen terrible civil wars firsthand in Lebanon and his native Algeria, warned Iraqis, "Civil wars do not happen because a person makes a decision 'Today I'm going to start a civil war.' Civil wars happen because people are reckless, because people are selfish, because groups think more of themselves than they do of the benefit of their country."

As the violent year 2004 wore on, Iraqis talked more and more openly about the danger of civil war. Some people thought it was already happening; others said it could happen with a single spark. And almost everyone agreed that, if a civil war began, the place where it was most likely to begin was the ethnically mixed, oil-rich city of Kirkuk.

It was my favorite Iraqi city. Kirkuk was just as searing in summertime, as neglected and trash strewn and traffic choked, as any other place in Iraq. But from my first visit I found it charming, sometimes even magical, with the nostalgia of the past and the fearful complexity of the present layered like sediment in every narrow street; and at the heart of the city lay a mystery.

It was on my third and last trip to Kirkuk that I met Luna Dawood.

LUNA WAS TWENTY-FOUR YEARS OLD when Saddam Hussein paid a surprise visit to her house, but she reacted like a teenager. It was an October afternoon in 1983. Two presidential helicopters landed on an open field; tanks cordoned off the tidy middle-class streets of the Ar-rapha neighborhood, home to employees of the oil company; and the president, flanked by an enormous security entourage, showed up at the Dawoods' back kitchen door. The Baathists' long-standing war against Iraqi Kurds was intensifying, and it appeared that Saddam wanted to secure the loyalty of those who worked in Kirkuk's valuable oil industry. Two decades later, Luna still recalled Saddam's visit a bit giddily: He was handsome in his olive-drab military uniform, and he paused to admire the house and ask friendly questions. His cologne was so overpowering that, for days afterward, Luna couldn't wash the odor off the hand that had shaken the president's, and the living room sofa smelled so strongly that it had to be given away.

Saddam refused coffee and chocolates, but a painting of a woman drawing water from a tree-shaded river caught his eye—Luna's brother, who was serving on the front in the Iran-Iraq War, had painted it—and the president claimed it as a gift. The Dawoods were Assyrian Christians, not Arabs, and when Saddam addressed Luna's mother in Arabic she replied in the English that she'd learned from the British managers of the Iraqi Petroleum Company before it was nationalized by the Baathists, in 1972. "That time is gone," Saddam scolded her. "You must learn Arabic."

A presidential trailer was parked in the Dawoods' garden, and neighbors lined up to go inside for a private audience with the president. Those were flush days in Iraq, and Saddam's personal secretary, Barzan al-Tikriti, presented each petitioner with three thousand dinars from a bag full of money. To her everlasting regret, Luna was too timorous to enter Saddam's trailer. Her younger sister Fula did so, and she emerged with both the cash and a job at the oil company. One of Luna's cousins entreated Saddam to release his brother, who was doing five years in prison for comparing the face of a top Baathist official to that of a monkey. Saddam replied that he couldn't interfere with the judicial system. Then he came out of the trailer to tell the assembled residents that Iraq was at war with Iran to protect the purity of Iraqi women from Ayatollah Khomeini's rampaging troops. The helicopters took off, and everyone assumed that Saddam had left Kirkuk.

But the trailer remained in the Dawoods' garden; their phone was cut off, their kitchen full of security men. Without explanation, the family was told to spend the night on the second floor. At two in the morning, unable to sleep, Luna went to the window and looked down at the garden. As if in a dream, she saw Saddam step out of the trailer wearing a white dishdasha. The next day, he was gone.

The president visited Kirkuk again in 1990. This time, his helicopter landed in the square in front of the municipal building. By then, Luna was working there as an accountant in the finance department. Saddam announced a campaign to beautify Kirkuk: The walled citadel—the oldest part of the city, situated on a plateau across the dry Khasa River bed from the modern city—was going to be cleaned up, beginning with the removal of the eight or nine hundred mostly Kurdish and Turkoman families living in its ancient houses. The next day, fifty million dinars arrived at Luna's office from Baghdad. She had forty-five days to dig through title deeds, some dating back to 1820, and pay compensation to displaced homeowners.

The process of emptying out the Kirkuk citadel had nothing to do with urban renewal. It was the climax of a forty-year campaign known to Iraqis as Arabization. Beginning in 1963, and continuing up to the eve of the American invasion, the Baathist regime in Baghdad deported tens of thousands of Kurds—some Kurdish sources put the number at three hundred thousand—from the city and the surrounding province, forced other ethnic minorities from their houses, and imported similar numbers of Arabs to Kirkuk from the south. Luna's job required her to distribute lump sums of money to families forfeiting their homes, sift through crumbling property records, and handle the traffic of deportees at the municipal building. She was a bureaucratic expediter of ethnic cleansing.

A slim, energetic forty-five-year-old when I met her in the summer of 2004, Luna was unmarried, and, unlike most Iraqi women, she wore Western clothes and carried herself with self-confidence. She had wide, startled eyes and the kind of strong nose seen on statuary from Nineveh, and when she talked about Kirkuk's history under Saddam, her anxious smile flashed a row of crooked teeth. "It was a tragedy I don't want to remember," she told me when we met in her office. She then proceeded to remember everything. "They were poor people," she said. "Each one who came to take the money, in his eyes you saw the tractor coming to take his house." Crowds awaiting deportation filled the hallway outside her office; women fainted. Because Assyrian Christians comprised the smallest and therefore least threatening of Kirkuk's many ethnic groups, some of the deportees in Luna's office trusted her enough to curse Saddam. If the secret police instructed her to delay paying someone they intended to arrest, Luna would quietly urge the reluctant man to leave Kirkuk without his money.

At the end of one long day, an old Kurdish farmer approached Luna's desk. She presented him with a consent form that granted the government ownership of his family's land in exchange for several thousand dinars. The procedures were finished; all that remained was for him to sign.

"I would like some water first," the old man said. Luna gave him a glass. He drank the water, signed the form, and fell dead in her lap.

"The things I saw," Luna told me, "nobody saw."

A few weeks before the American invasion, the government in Baghdad sent a secret order to officials in Kirkuk: Immediately burn all paperwork related to the Central Housing Plan—the regime's euphemism for the ethnic-cleansing campaign. The Baathists were meticulous record keepers; outside the municipal building, officials torched three large garbage containers filled with papers, and the bonfire lasted almost twenty-four hours.

Luna decided to ignore the order. "I can't burn these things," she said. "How can we compensate these people if these documents are burned?" Her motives were not entirely altruistic. Luna was a Baathist (a requirement of the job), and she wanted to protect herself against any accusations of misappropriating funds. She was also an admitted busybody. "You know, I put my nose in everything," she said. "I want to know everything." So she lied to her boss, and instead of burning the files she secretly drove several carloads back to the house in Arrapha that she shared with Fula and another unmarried sister. When I met Luna, most of the documents were kept on the roof of city hall, in an airless slant-ceilinged storeroom to which only she had the key. A waist-high sea of paper and dust inside had yet to attract the interest of either Iraqi or American officials, although among the documents that Luna salvaged were secret letters that exposed the Baath Party's sustained effort to transform Kirkuk from Iraq's most diverse city into a place dominated by Arabs loyal to the regime.

Luna's files spoke about not just the past but the future. After the invasion, Kirkuk became the stage of an ethnic power struggle. Kirkuk was compared to New York and, more often, to Sarajevo. How the new Iraq corrected the historical injustices recorded in the files would reveal much about the kind of country Iraqis chose to live in—or if it would remain a country at all.

Inside the storeroom, Luna waded through the files and stooped to inspect them with a kind of wit's-end affection, like a mother with too many unruly children. "Look—look—how many people? This land—this land—how many people?" she cried. "How could I work this all? Do you know how much I have in my mind? All this! All this! I must get it out!"

KIRKUK SAT NEAR THE FOOTHILLS of the Zagros Mountains, not far from the southern border of Kurdistan, the autonomous region that broke free of Baathist control in 1991. During the decades of intermittent fighting between the Iraqi army and Kurdish *peshmerga* guerrillas, the regime regarded Kirkuk, with oil fields outside the city comprising almost 9 percent of Iraq's total reserves, as strategically vulnerable. In part, the Arabization program was aimed at securing Baghdad's authority over this valuable resource. But the essence of Arabization was ideological. The history and demography of Kirkuk were an affront to the fascist dreams of the Arab Baath Socialist Party. It was a dense, cosmopolitan city along a trade route between Constantinople and Persia, and its layers of successive civilizations had nothing to do with Arab glory. Around the city's markets and the citadel, residents still lived in close quarters, and a visitor found the variety of faces and dress, tolerant manners, public female presence, and polyglot street life of a mixed city. Kirkuk felt closer to Istanbul than to Baghdad.

One local historian, an elderly Arab named Yasin Ali al-Hussein, told me that Kirkuk was built by Jewish slaves of the Babylonian captivity. Although scholars doubt this version, until the creation of Israel in 1948 several thousand Jews lived behind low arched doorways in the city's twisted back streets, many of them near the old souk at the foot of the citadel. An Armenian church dated from the first millennium. (Christians made up roughly 5 percent of the population.) In the fourth century B.C., Xenophon noted the presence of an ethnic group that might have been Kurdish. Turkomans from central Asia, ethnically different from Turks, migrated to the region about a thousand years ago. During Ottoman rule, which was established at the citadel in the sixteenth century and lasted until the arrival of British troops during the First World War, many educated Turkomans became imperial officeholders, while Kurdish shepherds coming down from the mountains provided labor. More than a century ago, Arab immigrants began settling around Kirkuk, mostly in the farmland west and south of the city; these "original Arabs" were distinct in almost every way from those imported by the Baathist regime. E. B. Soane, a British intelligence officer who traveled through Mesopotamia disguised as a local in the years before the First World War, observed, "Kirkuk is thus a collection of all the races of eastern Turkey—Jew, Arab, Syrian, Armenian, Chaldean, Turk, Turkoman, and Kurd—and consequently enjoys considerable freedom from fanaticism."

Fanaticism became the legacy of the ethnic cleansing. After the fall of the regime, every aspect of Kirkuk's history was violently contested. Kurds, Arabs, and Turkomans all made claims of ethnic primacy in a city where there were only pluralities. (According to the 1957 census, conducted before Arabization began, the city was 40 percent Turkoman and 35 percent Kurdish.) The elderly Arab historian refused to answer whether the Turkomans had come to Kirkuk before or after the Ottomans—the question was too sensitive. Ali Bayatli, a Turkoman lawyer, insisted that his people were direct descendants of the Sumerians and therefore the first residents of Kirkuk, with unspecified rights. Kurdish politicians had two slogans designed to end any argument: "Kirkuk is the heart of Kurdistan" and "Kirkuk is the Jerusalem of the Kurds." Arabs, meanwhile, were angry about the sudden loss of power that followed the removal of Saddam. Luna Dawood's view of her city's future was grim. "It will be war till the end," she said. "Everyone says Kirkuk belongs to us: Arabs, Kurds, Turkomans. To whom will it belong? We want America to stay here and change minds, to teach what's freedom, what's human. That's what our people don't know. They are animals."

Fifteen miles outside the city, on a road heading northwest, I met

Mohamed Khader, a Kurdish farmer who was hoeing a vegetable garden next to a cluster of ruined-looking houses. Khader had recently returned to the area from Erbil, a city in Kurdistan, where he worked as a butcher. After the invasion, he and his two wives, their ten children, and twenty-five other families followed American and Kurdish soldiers south into Iraq, with the goal of reclaiming Amshaw, their ancestral village, from Arab settlers. Khader, who wore the traditional Kurdish pants that are drawn tight around the waist and ankles but hang loose around the legs, took me up into the surrounding hills. It was spring, and across the vivid green grass were patches of yellow wildflowers and bloodred roses, tragic emblems of Kurdish poetry.

"This was the village," Khader said, pointing at a pattern of grassy humps on the hillside. Shards of terra-cotta pottery lay in the dirt. "That was our house. Exactly here." Farther up the hill, a field of jagged headstones marked the village cemetery.

In 1961, the first phase of the long war between Iraq's central government and Kurdish *peshmerga* began. The rebel Kurds demanded linguistic and cultural rights, control over regional security and financial affairs, and authority over Kirkuk and its oil. In 1963, following the coup that first brought Baathists to power, Iraqi soldiers attacked Amshaw and other villages. Khader was three years old. "I remember it like a dream," he said, "a bad dream, with children crying and people fighting and dying." The villagers fled north and were forced to retreat all the way to Erbil. Amshaw was razed.

I asked Khader if his family was ever compensated for their loss.

"Are you making fun of me?" he said, staring in disbelief. "They took everything. You see how I am now? That's just how we left—no blankets, nothing."

For a decade, the central government and the Kurdish guerrillas alternated between fighting and negotiating. The issues remained the same, up until now, and the cycle of distrust and misjudgment and betrayal was never broken: Kurdish demands, Arab acquiescence out of military weakness, increased Kurdish demands, Arab betrayal from a position of strength. After the Baath Party returned to power in 1968, Saddam himself, in secret talks with the Kurdish leader Mustapha Barzani, committed the regime to nearly everything the Kurds were asking, in-

cluding a future vote on the status of Kirkuk after a census. The dwellings next to the vegetable garden where I met Mohamed Khader were
built during this rapprochement—ostensibly to house returning Kurds in
what was to be called New Amshaw. But the lands around Amshaw were
already being distributed to Arab tribes from the south. When negotiations collapsed and fighting broke out again, the houses in New
Amshaw were given to Arabs. In 1975, after the shah of Iran—prompted
by Henry Kissinger—signed an accord with Baghdad and withdrew Iranian support for the Kurds, resistance collapsed. Oil-rich and militarily un-
challenged, the regime began to Arabize Kirkuk in earnest.

SABIHA HAMOOD and her husband were Arabs who moved their family to Kirkuk from Baghdad in the late 1980s, lured by a free house and
ten thousand dinars. "Arabs like us are known as the benefiters," she
said. "We came here just to live in a house. My husband used to work
in the Ministry of Housing, but it wasn't enough money to buy a house."
Like Hamood, the overwhelming majority of the benefiters were Shia,
and many were employed in the military, the state security apparatus,
or the civil service. The house offered to Hamood's family was in a
middle-class neighborhood called Taseen, across the road from the
Kirkuk air base. It had been an almost entirely Turkoman neighborhood until, near the end of the Iran-Iraq War, the regime decided that
Turkomans posed a security risk to the base. There was no policy of
deporting Turkomans as there was of Kurds, so the five or six hundred
families bought out in Taseen were scattered around the city. Hamood
convinced herself that the former owner of her house had been hand-
somely compensated and bore no grudge.

Several doors down was the house that once belonged to the family of Fakheraldin Akbar, a Turkoman woman who worked with Luna
in the finance department. The house had been built by her father—
two stories, nine rooms. One day in 1988, the family received a government letter declaring that a railroad was going to be built through the
neighborhood. "They gave us three days," Akbar recalled. "On the second day, policemen were standing outside the door. We took our furniture and went to stay with an aunt on the road to Baghdad." The

family was awarded a sum that represented less than a quarter the value of the house. The railroad was never built. A few years ago, attending a funeral in her old neighborhood, Akbar decided to go and look at the house for the first time since the family's eviction. "I said to myself, 'Let me just walk past the door. I won't speak to them—why should I? I don't know them, they don't know me.'" The benefiters who were given the house had painted its beautiful wooden front door blue.

Ethnic cleansing in Kirkuk proceeded in piecemeal fashion, but the Baathists were following a master plan. The plan was to make Kirkuk a predominantly Arab city, with a security belt of Arab neighborhoods encircling it, especially along the vulnerable northern and eastern edges, which faced Kurdistan. Accordingly, Kurds were forbidden by law to build, buy, or improve houses in Kirkuk. Any Kurdish family that couldn't prove residence in Kirkuk from the 1957 census had no legal right to live there, which meant that thousands of Kurds were displaced to refugee camps in Kurdistan or else to inhospitable regions in the south. After 1980, the teaching of languages other than Arabic was forbidden in city schools. Kurds and other non-Arabs in Kirkuk were frozen out of government jobs; before the war, according to one Kurdish official, the oil company had eleven thousand employees, of whom eighteen were Kurds. The entire families of Kurdish *peshmerga*, of draft evaders, and of other security threats were deported. Kurdish neighborhoods were declared illegal and razed in order to widen a road, to build a munitions factory or a stadium, to expand a base—but always, to reduce the Kurdish population and replace it with Arabs.

Some Kurds were given a choice: Leave the city or else become an Arab. This was called "correcting" one's nationality, and thousands of Kurds and Turkomans agreed to undergo the humiliation in order to stay in Kirkuk or hold on to a job or obtain a business license. In Luna's office, I met a middle-aged Turkoman engineer named Abdulrahman Sadiq. "I'll tell you a nice story," he said. In 1980, Sadiq's family was displaced from a village called Bilawa, just outside the city limits near the air base, along with the other villagers, all Turkomans. His family, whose lands were given to an Arab, moved into the city. In 1999, Sadiq decided to buy a piece of land in Kirkuk. He was told that, in order to register the land in his own name, he needed to correct his nationality.

He swallowed his pride and became an Arab—only to be told that he still couldn't put the land in his name, because, although now an Arab, he was from Bilawa, not Kirkuk. So he had to register the property with his sister-in-law, who had also corrected her nationality but who was born in the city. The web of rules in which individual lives were caught, and the attendant indignities and absurdities, were an Iraqi version of apartheid.

In her downtown office, a Kurdish architect and lifelong resident of Kirkuk named Hawry Talabani unfurled a map of the Baathists' twenty-year urban master plan, drawn up in 1972 by a Greek company hired by the regime. The plan allowed for the city to be developed in one direction only—south, toward Baghdad. These became the Ara-bization neighborhoods, and they had a different feel from the old city—the lethargy of an overgrown village, with men wearing white dishdashas and women completely enshrouded in black *abayas*, the new buildings thrown up in graceless concrete along wide, empty streets. The few Kurdish and Turkoman neighborhoods in the center of town that survived demolition became strangled with traffic and were deprived of parks, sewers, and public transportation. The waters of the Khasa River were diverted west to irrigate Arab farmland, and the dried-up riverbed filled with garbage. While social engineering proceeded on a grand scale, the oil-rich city fell into ruin. "There was not a sincere thought of making Kirkuk a real city," Talabani said. "In-stead of development we are going back, every year."

A Kurdish journalist named Omar Abdelkhader took me around a very old neighborhood called Imam Qasim, along the riverbed just north of the citadel. He was born and grew up in Imam Qasim, the grandson of a mullah and the son of a teacher who led a clandestine Kurdish po-litical organization in Kirkuk. The father was arrested in 1986 and exe-cuted in 1987; in 1988, Abdelkhader and his mother and sisters were put in a government truck and dumped beyond the provincial border. Over the years, the cousins and neighbors he left behind were packed into smaller and smaller quarters; compounds built for two or three families had to contain ten or twelve. In the back streets of Imam Qasim, antique houses of stone and mud in the Turkish style, with painted spiral pillars on either side of the doorway and arches around an inner courtyard, were literally caving in from neglect. Even the hill-top Kurdish cemetery where Abdelkhader's father lay buried was as dense and confined as the city. "You can say Kurds were just surviving here. It wasn't a life," Abdelkhader said. "It's like plant or animal species under threat. What Kurds were doing here to survive—they were changing their nationality, they were hiding themselves, they were eating shit, they were doing the worst jobs. Anything just to survive."

The year Abdelkhader's family was expelled from Kirkuk, 1988, was the climax of the regime's persecution of Kurds. The destruction of Kurdish villages in the mountains—known as the Anfal, a separate effort from the ethnic cleansing in Kirkuk—reached genocidal proportions, with chemical weapons used against civilians in Halabja and elsewhere. Toward the end of that year, the governor of Kirkuk wrote a letter to the official responsible for Arabization, the general secretary of the Northern Committee, Taha Yassin Ramadan—who, in addition to being Saddam's close friend and cellmate from youth and, more recently, the ten of diamonds in the deck of most-wanted playing cards, was a Kurd. Iraqis knew him as "the Butcher." This letter, which was among the documents that Luna salvaged from city hall, offered a report on an intensive phase of the ethnic-cleansing campaign in Kirkuk, from June 1, 1985, to October 31, 1988.

"We would like to inform you that we have followed the strict orders and instructions that you made for our work, which pushed us to work harder to serve the citizens, the sons of the courageous leader of victory and peace, Mr. President the Patriot Saddam Hussein (may God save him)," the governor wrote. What followed was a detailed statistical account of three years of ethnic cleansing:

- 19,146 people removed from villages "forbidden for security reasons"
- registration documents of 96,533 people transferred from Kirkuk to Erbil province in preparation for removal
- 2405 families removed from villages lying near forbidden oil facilities

- 10,918 Arab families, including 53,834 people, transferred to Kirkuk from other provinces
- 8250 pieces of residential land and 1112 houses distributed to Arab families transferred from other provinces

The letter noted that these removals, transfers, and distributions created a net gain of 51,862 Arabs in the province and a net loss of 18,096 Kurds during this period, making Arabs the largest group in Kirkuk for the first time. In addition, seven measures were taken "to make the city more beautiful," including scattering all sellers of vegetables and fruits from the central city market to points around the city. "For any new building or service project that will be built," the governor wrote to Baghdad, "we will give the priority to the new neighborhoods." The letter concluded: "All this made it an easy matter to renew the surveillance process to prevent the leaking back in of families who have been included in the displacement, and also to prevent the leaking of saboteurs into the city . . . Now the displacement process from the city center is taking its course."

Two years later, just before the invasion of Kuwait, Saddam made his announcement outside Kirkuk's municipal building that all human life be removed from the citadel. According to Gha'ab Fadhel, the director of Kirkuk's archaeological museum, who oversaw the bulldozing of dwellings, the purpose of the citadel project was simply to excavate and restore ancient monuments. The 850 Ottoman-era houses on the site were ill kept, unhygienically crowded, and mostly occupied by poor renters. "Their removal had nothing to do with politics," he insisted. But the citadel was the heart of the city. On the Muslim holiday of Eid, Christians joined Muslims to celebrate at the Tomb of the Prophets, an ancient shrine where Daniel and Ezra were apocryphally said to be buried. On Christian holidays, the Muslims reciprocated.

At the souk below the citadel walls, the Turkoman owner of a women's dress shop recalled that, years ago, the citadel was the site of many feasts. In the quiet of summer evenings, he used to hear the sound of cooking oil, and the scent of grilled meat would drift down into the market. "From what I hear," he said, "Turkomans were living there."

"Why do you say that?" a Kurdish customer asked. "We were living there, too."

Across the alley from his shop, a Turkoman woman selling shoes and purses told me, "We were the last people to leave the citadel." Her father, a wealthy trader in seeds, had a large house by the western gate that overlooked the river. He built houses on the citadel for Jews whom he employed as scribes. "We had relations with so many people on the citadel," she said. "Like family, not neighbors." One day, Baathists knocked at the door: The family had a month to vacate their house. "The citadel was the most beautiful place," she said. "My childhood was there. I see it every day." She pointed to the remains of a stone wall, overgrown with yellow grass, just visible above the shops across the alley.

The Gulf War and sanctions delayed the final destruction of the houses until 1998. By then, the citadel had been empty for eight years, and no one was allowed up there except members of a Republican Guard unit, who were positioned on the citadel to suppress an uprising or attack. The attack came in April 2003, in a wave of Kurdish *pesh-merga* and American Special Forces soldiers sweeping down from the north, and the dream of Arab Kirkuk collapsed overnight.

A FEW WEEKS after the liberation of Kirkuk, a twenty-four-year-old lieutenant with the 173rd Airborne Brigade named Jordan Becker was told by his company commander to sort out a problem in Arrapha, the neighborhood where Luna Dawood lived. Among the thousands of Kurdish deportees who had come back to Kirkuk after the war to reclaim houses and land—in some cases chasing out Arab occupants, in others finding that the Arabs had fled—sixty-seven families were squatting in the fine houses abandoned by top oil company officials in Arrapha. The Kurds had been living for years in refugee camps in the hills around Suleimaniya. Becker, who had a shelf full of books on Kurdish language and Middle Eastern history in his tent at the American base, was given the mission to tell the Kurds that they had to vacate so that the oil officials could return and the industry could be revived. At the first house that he visited, the wife swore that if the Americans made her leave, she would light herself on fire.

The lieutenant returned to the base and conferred with his captain. They decided that he should go back and try again, but this time Becker, a blue-eyed southern Californian who was built like a cornerback, left his body armor behind. In this less threatening guise, he sat down with the family for two hours. "I knew their lives had been miserable," Becker said, "and I knew they were going to go on being miserable for a while. When you read about history and politics, you don't learn about the mentality of these people. And what I learned about these people is that they have a sense of history and historic patience. They have a sense of what's best for their community, and when you convinced them that they were going to drive a wedge between their community and the Arabs, and between their community and the Americans, they realized they didn't want to do that." Becker's argument to the Kurds was an abstract one: "If you have a house in a country that's unstable and violent, then all you have is a house. But if you have a house in a country that's stable and ruled by law, then you have a lot more than a house." Then he made his approach in more concrete terms. "I know you'll find a place to live, because you're Kurds, and you haven't had a place to live for twelve years, and you haven't had a country ever. But just because you won a war doesn't mean you'll get shit for free. But if you support law over victor's justice, you'll be investing in the future of Iraq." Becker smiled. "And they said, 'That's cool.' "

The Kurdish squatters left Arrapha. That was in the early weeks, when the Kurds regarded the Americans as saviors and were willing to postpone rectification a little longer. The paratroopers in Kirkuk were far out ahead of their counterparts in Baghdad that first summer. The companies lived in safe houses around the city rather than out at the isolated air base; Becker's battalion hired fifty translators locally because the American company with the contract was going too slowly; the soldiers moved around Kirkuk with ease, sometimes in SUVs; the battalion had already opened nine police stations with seventeen hundred cops chosen with a careful eye to ethnic balance and equipped with vehicles and weapons. The CPA was a distant nuisance that didn't approve plans or release money nearly fast enough to satisfy the 173rd Airborne Brigade. For the time being, Kirkuk felt like a city under control.

As paratroopers, they were used to three-week missions, and

Becker's battalion commander, Lieutenant Colonel Dom Caraccilo, a stocky, impatient, snuff-dipping forty-one-year-old from upstate New York, made no secret of his frustration at being stuck in Iraq for months on end. "If you're going in to kill something, you've got to set it up so when you leave you can achieve the goals and objectives you went in there with," Caraccilo said in his gravelly voice, as we sat in his quarters and he spat into a water bottle. "In the past we had this 'civil-affairs battalion will come in and take care of civil affairs.' That's bull-shit—it doesn't work. Why it doesn't work, I don't know." The soldiers who were trained to operate mortars and call in air strikes now had nothing to do, so they trained the police force. The signal operators worked with the fire department and emergency services. The support and transportation platoon resettled returning refugees. But the chief role that the Americans played in ethnically divided Kirkuk was, as one soldier put it, that of "a bouncer in the middle of a nasty bar fight."

When I went back to Kirkuk in the summer of 2004, a new unit had taken over, and the historic patience of the Kurds was running out. The rhetoric of the city's three major ethnic groups was growing extreme, and the prestige of the Americans had plummeted. Lieu-tenant Becker's speech to the family in Arrapha articulated better than any high officials the policy of the occupation authority: Old griev-ances must be settled according to law, not force. Until a legal mech-anism was in place, the status quo had to be maintained. Yet, more than a year after the removal of Saddam, the legal mechanism for re-solving individual property cases had barely begun to function. As for a larger political solution to the status of Kirkuk, the occupation authority avoided imposing one, and the interim constitution postponed it until an elected government could write a permanent constitution. Kirkuk remained dangerously stalled, while facts that could force the most extreme outcome steadily accumulated on the ground.

After the invasion, thousands of Arabs in the north were uprooted from their homes. A report by the refugee organization Global IDP put the total number at a hundred thousand, although the absence of in-ternational organizations in Iraq made it impossible to reach an accu-rate count. Northwest of Kirkuk, in the village of Amshaw, Mohamed Khader and the other Kurds expelled in 1963 had taken over the partly demolished houses of the Arabs who were brought to Amshaw in the 1970s. The houses were abandoned when the Kurds arrived, Khader said. I found those same Arabs squatting in the bombed barracks and helicopter hangars of an Iraqi air force base just west of the city, near the American base. Two old men who spoke for the fifty-two families there said that Kurdish fighters had chased them out of Amshaw at the end of the war.

"We have young men who believe Amshaw belongs to them," one of the Arab men, Ali Aday, said. "I tell them, 'My son, they say it belongs to the Kurds.' They say, 'How can it? We were born and raised in those houses.'" The old man pointed out that the number of Kurdish families who had taken over Amshaw was just half the number of Arabs who had fled—there were enough houses in Amshaw for twenty-five Arab families to return and live together with the Kurds. "We just want to know who will give us our rights," Ali Aday said. American soldiers in the area had given the refugees blankets and food and told them to stay put until the problem could be sorted out by law. "Where is the government that will give us our rights? Is it from America? From the Iraqi government? We don't know. It isn't possible to just leave us here without our rights."

A mile away, a forlorn camp of seventeen tents stood in a field next to a military pillbox. A ragged turquoise flag with a crescent moon and star—the symbol of the militant Iraqi Turkoman Front—hung limply in the heat. The camp was also symbolic—the tents were empty—but a handful of men were standing watch. They were Turkomans who had been expelled in 1980 from Bilawa, the village of the engineer who had corrected his nationality. They showed me copies of property deeds from 1938, black negative images of British documents; they also had Ottoman-era deeds, they said. Part of their land had been taken over by the air force base, and another part was occupied by a wealthy Arab supporter of the old regime, who refused to leave. The Turkomans also claimed the land where the Arab refugees were squatting in helicopter hangars. It was hard to imagine how all this could ever be worked out.

"The solution is for everyone to go back to where they're from," one

Turkoman said. "Before Saddam, where were these Arabs? This is the solution, exactly. We want it just like before Saddam."

On the other side of the city, hundreds of Kurdish families had taken up residence in the tunnels and under the grandstands of Kirkuk's soccer stadium, which was built in a razed Kurdish neighborhood. On a dusty plain beside the stadium, hundreds more families were living in tents. The director of a Kurdish refugee organization estimated that nine thousand families had returned to Kirkuk. Most of them were expelled more than a decade ago—taken by government truck beyond the provincial border and dumped in no-man's-land with the few belongings they had managed to salvage—and had lived in refugee camps ever since. More of them were pouring into Kirkuk every day—at the height of the return, as many as five hundred a day—even though living conditions were squalid and almost no help was offered by the Americans, international aid groups, or the city government. A Kurdish man named Farhad Mohamed echoed what the Arabs on the other side of the city told me. "I really don't know who will give us a house, because there are many many governments in Iraq," he said. "We hope the new government won't be like Saddam's."

The two chief Kurdish political parties, the Kurdish Democratic Party and the Patriotic Union of Kurdistan, began to accelerate the return of Kurds in advance of a census and elections. Government employees in Suleimaniya, northeast of Kirkuk, were told to return to Kirkuk and promised that their salaries would be sustained until they found new positions. In Erbil, forty Kurdish families originally from Kirkuk were ordered to vacate the government building in which they had lived for years as refugees and that a politically connected businessman planned to turn into a supermarket; they were given three thousand dollars apiece and sent back to their hometown. A month later, I found a number of them in Kirkuk, building simple houses illegally in the old Kurdish neighborhoods of Azadi and Rahimawa. Others without means were squatting in government buildings; others still, with political contacts or firepower, had chased Arabs out and taken back their old houses or simply laid claim to new ones. Some Arab leaders told me that Kurds, including ones who had never lived in Kirkuk, were moving to the city in order to tip the ethnic scale. One of them called the effort "Kurdification."

Meanwhile, Arab "benefiters" were leaving. Sabiha Hamood, the woman who moved with her family from Baghdad in the late 1980s into the old Turkoman neighborhood of Taseen, sold the house a few months after I met her, taking advantage of the inflated prices that Kurds were willing to pay. In Qadisiya, a neighborhood in the south of the city, I met a group of Arab men attending a funeral. They took me back to a dingy cinder-block house, into which three families who had been forced from their homes were squeezed. In the immediate neighborhood, they said, a hundred Arab families had sold their houses to Kurds and left the city. The men were Shia, former policemen and soldiers, now unemployed and filled with grievances. Riyadh Shayoob, who came to Kirkuk from Basra in 1986, when he was five, had been driven from his house in a Kurdish area and been refused employment by the new Iraqi police force. He was making a meager living selling trinkets in the souk, where he suffered contempt and threats from Kurds. Some of them, he said, mockingly sold CDs with images of Arab prisoners being tortured in Abu Ghraib. "They told me, 'Go back where you came from. Don't stay in Kirkuk,'" Shayoob said with a melancholy smile. "Before, I had Kurdish friends, but now they don't support me. They've turned against us."

Government jobs went to Kurds; the mayor and the police chief were Kurds; all the television networks were in Kurdish; the Arabs were being driven out of the city; the Arabs had no one powerful to back them: The list of Arab complaints was long, and it bore a striking resemblance to the predicament of the Kurds in Kirkuk under Saddam. To these men, the Kurds were now the benefiters. "There's more injustice now than under Saddam," a bearded, tough-looking man named Ethir Mohamed insisted. "Even if Saddam did these things, what's our guilt? We did nothing to them."

In Kirkuk, the Arab-Kurdish conflict was intensified by the insurgency. The Kurds were often considered collaborators of the Americans, while many of the imported Arabs sympathized with the Sunni or Shiite resistance forces. Moqtada al-Sadr often thundered that the Kurds were Muslim apostates and faced damnation; hundreds of

Kurds fled to Kirkuk from Samarra and other Arab cities after being denounced in Sunni mosques as traitors. The Arab men in the cinderblock house were followers of Sadr's representative in Kirkuk; their mosque had been raided by American soldiers who discovered a cache of weapons and arrested around thirty people. All of the men vowed to stay in the city. "Kirkuk has turned into a jungle," Ethir Mohamed said. "If someone comes to force me to leave, then either I'll kill him or he'll kill me. This is the law of the jungle."

Among imported Arabs, I heard that the chemical weapons dropped on Halabja were actually sacks of plaster dust. This theory was offered by a fireman employed by the oil company, whose house in Arrapha looked directly across a field at the former mansion of Ali Hassan al-Majid—known, ever since he directed the gassing of the Kurds, as Chemical Ali. An Arab woman who was a retired teacher from the southern city of Kut said, "Iraq is part of the Arab nation, not the Kurdish nation. The Kurds are guests in Iraq—and they want to kick the Arabs out?" What I seldom heard was any acknowledgment of the crimes committed against Kurds in Kirkuk, or any shame at having been the benefiters. This only deepened the sense among Kurds, especially among the deportees who were returning, that it would not be possible for them to live alongside imported Arabs in Kirkuk.

THE KURDISH PLAN for Kirkuk was absolutely clear. The imported Arabs had to leave, every one of them, even those born in the city. The government should compensate them, and perhaps find them land and jobs in their provinces of origin, but allowing them to stay in Kirkuk would be to endorse the injustice of Arabization. After Kurdish deportees had been resettled, and the earlier demographic balance had been restored, the province would hold a census. (The 1957 census showed that the provincial population was almost 50 percent Kurdish.) The outcome of this census was a foregone conclusion to the Kurds: They would be the majority group in the province. Equally predictable was the result of the referendum that would follow: The province would vote to join the autonomous region of Kurdistan, and the city of Kirkuk would go with it.

None of this was stated in Iraq's interim constitution. Article 58, which delineated "Steps to Remedy Injustice," was purposefully vague about the future of Kirkuk. It called for "the injustice caused by the previous regime's practices in altering the demographic character of certain regions, including Kirkuk" to be redressed. It stated that "individuals newly introduced to specific regions and territories . . . may be resettled, may receive compensation from the state, may receive new land from the state near their residence in the governorate from which they came, or may receive compensation for the cost of moving to such areas." (Not "must.") The status of contested cities like Kirkuk would be deferred until after the census and a permanent constitution, "consistent with the principle of justice, taking into account the will of the people of those territories." This bland language raised more questions than it answered. Did justice belong to individuals, or to groups? Did it require only the restoration of confiscated property, or did it also require the restoration of Kirkuk's demography to the period before Arabization? Wouldn't forcing Arabs to return to the towns "from which they came" create new injustices and perpetuate the cycle of revenge?

Although there had been nothing like the apocalyptic communal bloodshed that some predicted, Kirkuk suffered a steady rise in insurgent attacks and suicide bombings, and a campaign of assassination against the city's leaders. Most of the murdered officials were Kurds, though a few Arab politicians and a tribal sheikh who had occupied disputed lands around the village of Amshaw fell victim as well. Arrests were seldom made in these cases. Kurds in Kirkuk cast suspicion on Turkish intelligence agents and their allies in the hard-line Iraqi Turkoman Front. The Turkish government repeatedly asserted that a Kurdish power grab in Kirkuk would be regarded as a prelude to an independent state and therefore a threat to Turkey itself, with its own minority population of rebellious Kurds. The Turkish foreign minister, Abdullah Gul, compared Kirkuk to Bosnia and issued a veiled warning: "Everyone is aware that this is the issue that could end up being the greatest headache for Iraq."

Hasib Rozbayani was the Kurdish deputy governor for resettlement and compensation, the official responsible for the returning refugees.

Rozbayani was a leading spokesman for the emerging policy of reverse ethnic cleansing. He had spent years teaching social studies and statistics in exile in Sweden, and, with a head of unruly curly hair, spectacles, and a habit of mumbling questions to himself as he talked, he had a mild professorial air. When we spoke in his living room, he was barefoot in sweatpants and an untucked shirt, and he kept absently picking up the automatic pistol that lay on the sofa beside him, then startling himself and setting it down again. Propped against his stereo system was a Kalashnikov.

Rozbayani left no doubt about the future of the imported Arabs. Their departure from Kirkuk was necessary for a variety of reasons, he said, including psychosocial ones: The Arabs suffered from guilty consciences, since most of them were criminals and former Baathists, which would make them uneasy about staying; they knew they didn't belong in the city and had no friends among the other groups; their continued presence would be a provocation to Kurds, inciting social conflict. Moreover, unemployment was already too high in Kirkuk.

Those Arabs who hadn't left Kirkuk before the census and referendum would not be allowed to vote there, Rozbayani said. He did not expect many Arabs to be living in Kirkuk by then. "They have to leave," he said. Imported Arabs had to leave even if no one contested their house or land, because their fault was a collective one. After the census and the referendum on the status of Kirkuk, he told me, Arabs could return to the region—for a visit.

I told Rozbayani about a couple I'd met: The husband came from central Iraq in the 1960s; the wife was an "original Arab" whose family had lived in Kirkuk for generations. Their children grew up with playmates from a mixed Kurdish-Turkoman family next door. What should happen to this couple?

"They have to return," he said.

"The wife is a native of Kirkuk."

"She can follow him."

My questions struck Rozbayani as misplaced humanitarianism, and he threw them back at me. "Of course, I accept brotherhood and friendship," he assured me. "But we know openly that the Arabs have taken lands, occupied lands, they have gone to every house to investigate people, execute people, take their sons, their girls—and you will say, 'Welcome, Iraq is for all people'? It's funny, I say."

MUCH OF Rozbayani's and other Kurds' unhappiness was directed at the American-led coalition. They had expected something more than studied evenhandedness from the United States. A *peshmerga* living in an abandoned house in Amshaw asked me, "Why, when the Kurds are your friends, do you now treat us just the way you treat other Iraqis, including the Republican Guard?"

The first CPA representative in Kirkuk, and the most influential advocate for the city with Paul Bremer, was a slim, brown-eyed, thirty-six-year-old Englishwoman named Emma Sky. She spoke some Arabic and once worked with Palestinians in the West Bank; though she opposed the invasion of Iraq, Sky answered a request from the Foreign and Commonwealth Office for volunteers to join the occupation authority. Being English- and Arabic-speaking put her in the minority at the CPA, and she was also out of step with its ideological assumptions.

"Bringing democracy—to many Americans it's like the new religion," she told me in Baghdad. "People come here as missionaries. I've never had that as a mission. I don't have the sense of democracy as this good that we should be promoting around the world." Rather than ignoring or breaking down the undemocratic tribal structure of Iraqi society, she said, the occupiers should see it as a natural outgrowth of a harsh environment and find ways to allow more people to participate within it. She found American nationalism, with its sunny certainties and its zeal, a strange and troubling force. I reminded her that it was not entirely different from British nationalism, which had once conquered half the world (including Iraq) in the name of the white man's burden. "Maybe we had it in the UK forty or fifty years ago," Sky said. "Iraqis are always saying, 'Oh, the Brits, you know how to do this far better than the Americans,' as if it's something genetic that's been passed down to you. My generation have never grown up with ruling other countries." Yet she was well aware of following in the footsteps of her colonial forebears, and, as a result, of bringing a feel for Iraqis and their history that most Americans might not have. Perhaps because she knew the name of the British general who had "liberated" Baghdad from the Turks in 1917, Sky was better able to think skeptically about the current project than her American colleagues who did not. In Baghdad she visited Gertrude Bell's tomb; she was a little haunted by Bell and her suicide.

Upon arriving in Kirkuk, Sky saw that the most urgent task was to reassure alienated Arabs and Turkomans that the triumphalist attitude of their Kurdish neighbors did not mean there was no future for them here. As she traveled around the province, her prestige among Arabs soared. Ismail Hadidi, the deputy governor and an original Arab, gave Sky his highest praise: "We deal with her as if she's a man, not a woman." Sky believed passionately that Kirkuk could be a model for an ethnically diverse Iraq. "People have to move away from this zero-sum thinking," she said. "Kirkuk is where it all meets. It all comes together there. Yes, you can have a country of separate regions, where people don't have to deal with other groups. But can you have a country where people are happy with each other, where people are at ease with each other? I think Kirkuk is going to tell you what kind of country Iraq is going to be." She was instrumental in securing millions of dollars from Iraqi oil revenue to fund the new Kirkuk Foundation, which would give grants to local civic groups that were trying to avoid the logic of ethnic politics. Compared with the problems in Israel and Palestine, Sky said, Kirkuk's should be relatively easy to solve. "Kirkuk you can win. Kirkuk doesn't have irreconcilable differences—yet."

Over time, with no apparent solution to the legacy of ethnic cleansing, many Kurds began to regard Emma Sky and the CPA as biased toward Arabs. When she met the Kurdish leader Jalal Talabani in Suleimaniya, he snapped, "They call you Emma Bell." His gibe captured the full irony of Sky's situation. She was trying to bring Europe's postcolonial values—diversity, tolerance, a sense that people could solve their problems if they would sit down together and talk—to a place where zero-sum politics had been the rule ever since her ancestress Gertrude Bell had drawn the map and set up the modern state in such a way that Sunni Arabs became the holders of power and Kurds saw their dream of nationhood dissolved.

Nor did it help Sky's cause that the CPA's mechanism for untangling and redressing grievances in Kirkuk—the Iraq Property Claims Commission, which Sky helped set up—didn't begin to hear claims until April 2004 and still hadn't issued its first decision by early 2005. Azad Shekhany, a Kurd who once directed the commission, concluded that the whole thing was an elaborate stall to keep the peace, and he put the blame on the CPA. "I understand they don't want to send the Arabs back to their original places, but they don't want the Kurds to be unhappy as well," Shekhany said. "So they just delay everything by bureaucracy."

The commission was receiving far fewer claims than anticipated—exactly 1,658 as of the July morning in 2004 when I visited its well-equipped and nearly empty offices. Two Kurdish women in billowing black robes—Jamila Safar and her mother, Khadija Namikh—were seated at a desk making a claim. In March 1991, during the uprising in Kirkuk and the north that followed the Gulf War, Safar told me, her father died. On the day of his burial, March 13, she and her mother returned from the cemetery to find their house surrounded by soldiers, Baath Party members, and men with masked faces who worked for Chemical Ali. "Are you Kurds or Arabs?" the men demanded. Everyone in the neighborhood was out on the street—Kurds, Arabs, and Turkomans, grouped by ethnicity. Tanks blocked the streets and helicopters circled overhead as the Kurdish men, including Safar's older brother, were bound and taken away in buses. The women and children were loaded onto other buses and driven into the mountains, where they were dumped and told to walk north. As Safar and her mother walked, they were bombed by aircraft overhead, and several neighbors died in front of them. They stayed at the Iranian border for three months. When they ventured back to Kirkuk, their house—along with two thousand others in the neighborhood—had been destroyed.

"Thank God, all I found was dust," Safar said. "Thank God for our safety."

A staff lawyer was filling out a lengthy form for them. "Was the house brick or clay?"

"Brick," Safar's mother said. "Finish, please. I'm sick, I can't wait."

"Do you want to take the land or do you want compensation?" the lawyer asked.

"We want the land," Safar said.

The lawyer wrote that they wanted the land and money to build a new house. "Why didn't you go to the commission for people with damaged houses in 1991?"

"I did," the mother said. "I gave them an application, but they didn't give us anything."

An Arab man in his late thirties came over and said hello to the two women with a shy reserve. His name was Ayob Shaker and he had once been their neighbor. On the day of the deportation, he had helped other Kurds in the area load furniture on the buses. He was also a soldier in the Republican Guard, and when he came back to Kirkuk from Baghdad after the fall of the regime, he found a group of *peshmerga*, including another former neighbor, occupying his house. Though the property claims statute had been amended to allow Arabs displaced after the war to make claims as well, Shaker said that his children had been threatened by the *peshmerga*, and he was afraid to file for compensation.

"Believe me, nobody knows for sure, but mostly it's the Kurds who are running the city," he said. "For me as an Arab, if I want a job I have to get a paper from a Kurdish party saying I'm not a criminal." Chance had brought him to this office on the same day as the two women he used to greet every morning on his way to work. He felt that the very injustice he had once seen done to them was now befalling him. "The same thing," he said. "The government did it to them. The *peshmerga* did it to us."

The women agreed, and there was a moment of good feeling between the old neighbors.

"Only God and America can solve the problem," the Arab said.

What about the new Iraqi government? I asked.

"I don't know," the mother said. "Is there a government right now or not? I know nothing. I know there is day and there is night. I don't even remember my own name."

The staff lawyer finished filling out the form. The daughter smiled and said, "I think that's it—there will be justice and our case will be finished."

I asked the Arab if there will be justice in Kirkuk. He hesitated. "I don't think so. It's very difficult."

The daughter said, "Why are you making things hard?"

"Because those who are now in the city don't understand each other," he said. "I am a son of Kirkuk"—an original Arab—"and for thirty-five years nobody could hurt us. Now I'm feeling upset, because of my house."

I asked the women if Kurds would ever do to Arabs what Arabs had done to Kurds.

"No, they won't do that," the daughter said. "Believe me, I swear to God they won't do that."

"They've done *more* than the Arabs," Shaker said.

The daughter stiffened and coldly eyed her former neighbor. "Where is that?"

"I know one person who made half a tribe run away from their houses in the city."

The warm feeling was gone. The daughter pointed out that Shaker had already forgotten what happened to the Kurds in Kirkuk. Abruptly, she excused herself and helped her mother out of the Iraq Property Claims Commission.

BECAUSE KIRKUK wasn't yet the scene of large-scale combat, the city remained a hidden flaw in the broken Iraqi landscape. But what was a local dispute between neighbors would inevitably become one of the greatest obstacles to making Iraq democratic and keeping it whole. In the summer of 2003, I had a conversation with Barham Salih, who was then the prime minister of the regional government in Suleimaniya. A strong supporter of the American invasion and of Kurdish partic- ipation in a democratic and federal Iraq, he was also mindful of his con- stituents' ingrained suspicion of Baghdad and longing for independence. For twelve years, Suleimaniya was one of the two capitals of Iraqi Kurdis- tan, a de facto independent state under the protection of the allied no- fly zone. A generation of Kurds grew up speaking no Arabic and feeling no connection to Iraq, and the idea of rejoining a country that not long ago visited genocide and ethnic cleansing on Kurds was a hard sell.

"While I have accepted the fate history has landed my people with, I want to assure my kids and the new generations to come that the new Iraq will be fundamentally different," Salih said. "If the Arabs of Iraq do not have the courage to come to terms with the terrible past that we have had and make right those terrible injustices that befell my people, I would have extreme difficulty convincing the doubters in Suleimaniya's bazaar that Iraq is our future."

I went to see Salih again in June 2004, on his first day as deputy prime minister of the newly sovereign Iraqi interim government. After a year of occupation and insurgency, his mood was darker, and his interpretation of the interim constitution on Kirkuk was uncompromising. "The *indigenous* people of Kirkuk, the original communities of Kirkuk, should be the ones who decide the fate of Kirkuk—not those who were brought by Saddam or any outside power," he said. The imported Arabs were victims, too, "tools for a vile policy, for Saddam wanted to create the environment for a permanent civil war between Kurds and Arabs." But, Salih added, "Kirkuk is not Bosnia, and in fact the Kurdish leadership has demonstrated the utmost restraint in the way that it has handled Kirkuk. In Bosnia you'd have seen civil war."

I asked Rowsch Shaways, one of two vice presidents of the interim government, what would happen if the imported Arabs refused to leave Kirkuk. Would they be loaded into trucks and driven south to Basra and Kut?

"Well, there should be a continuous campaign to persuade them," he said.

Wouldn't the attempt to force Arabs out of Kirkuk lead to reprisals against Kurds in Arab regions of Iraq? "No, it's a different situation," he said. "Kurds who are living in the south, they were coming here very normally, not through a campaign of changing ethnicity." After the reversal of ethnic cleansing, Shaways said, "everybody can live where he wants. But before that you have to reverse the unjust policy which was done to strengthen the Baath Party and to change the composition of some regions." The Americans had waited too long to resolve the problem of Kirkuk, he said, adding, "This is my opinion: Kirkuk is a part of Kurdistan."

Of the top Kurdish officials, I imagined that the person who would find the question of Kirkuk most vexing was Bakhtiar Amin. He grew up in Imam Qasim, the old Kurdish neighborhood near the citadel. He and his family were expelled from Kirkuk during Arabization; his relatives were jailed and tortured. Amin, in his mid-forties, lived in exile for years, working as a human-rights activist in Europe and founding the International Alliance for Justice. He then became the first human-rights minister of a sovereign Iraqi government. But when we sat down in his spacious Baghdad office to talk about justice in Kirkuk, Amin made it clear that he was answering as a Kurd.

After recounting the history of Kurdish oppression in great detail, the minister warned me that the situation in Kirkuk was becoming explosive. The Americans, with their hands full in the rest of Iraq, "want to keep the calm there—the calm of a cemetery." Amin added, "It's important not to be naïve with your foes and Machiavellian with your friends. Patience has its limits for victims as well." The only solution, he insisted, was to return the demography of Kirkuk to what it was before Arabization, helping Arabs to resettle in the south.

I asked how he would answer an Arab youth who said, "Mr. Human Rights Minister, Kirkuk is my home. I don't have another. Why do I have to leave?" Amin replied that he would introduce the young Arab to a young Kurd who had lost his house and grown up in a tent, whose brother or sister had died of starvation or cold. He would tell the young Arab, "Your father, your mom, they are from a different area and they came here and they took these people's house, and this is what they did to those children. And I will help you to have a decent life where your parents came from."

KURDISH POLITICIANS and the constituents they represented wanted a guarantee that the future in Iraq would not repeat the past. After the fall of the regime, the Kurds negotiated hard with the Americans and their fellow Iraqis on two tracks: They sought as much power as possible in Baghdad and a strengthened autonomous region in the north. They understood that the interim and permanent constitutions would be the key to their desires, and they put their considerable skills to work on these documents, often outmatching the young, inexperienced Americans and divided Iraqis with whom they dealt. They were increasingly alienated from their American allies, who always seemed readier to soothe the recalcitrant Arabs than the dependable Kurds. Several Kurdish politicians told me that a repetition of 1975, when the United States withdrew its support and abandoned them to the Baathist regime, now seemed entirely possible. This kind of talk had the feel of an extreme reaction born of extreme experience, a kind of historical neurosis in which Iraq's Kurds and Arabs were both trapped.

Samir Shakir Sumaidaie, the interim Iraqi ambassador to the UN, said, "I cannot blame a Kurd for feeling anger. But I can plead with him to contain his anger, because angry people often do stupid things, and they end up hurting themselves. Arabs, on the other hand, must acknowledge the injustice that has been done to the Kurds. By acknowledging the injustice, you take the poison out of the system. I've told this to Arabs in Kirkuk: We must admit what was done in the name of Arab nationalism to the Kurds, and of which you were perhaps the unwitting instrument." Kurds' anger, he said, would cool only when they began to see justice done, "especially for the families that suffered most in Kirkuk." When Sumaidaie made these arguments to his fellow Iraqi Arabs, he told me, the response was grudging. Kurdish intransigence over Kirkuk, with occasional threats of war and separation, was having its answer among Arabs. "Nationalism ignites nationalism," Sumaidaie said. "I think we should get away from nationalism and move toward humanism."

A government official in Baghdad who was a self-described Iraqi liberal told me that more and more leaders were reacting to Kurdish threats with an attitude of "good riddance." The benefits in keeping the Kurds happy might not outweigh the costs. "The truth of the matter is, the Arabs of this country—eighty percent—are getting tired of these threats of secession," he said. "And one day their answer will be: 'Secede.'"

NEVERTHELESS, during three visits to Kirkuk, I kept meeting citizens of each ethnicity who still wanted to live together. In particular, Kirkukis who had spent their whole lives in the city seemed more willing to surrender part of their own historical claim to it in order to coexist peacefully with other groups. The idea of a multiethnic city, I realized, still existed in the minds of people in Kirkuk; it was not just a desperate piece of cheerful public relations from American and British officials.

An Arab in his twenties named Mohamed Abbas, whose family had come to Kirkuk when he was six for his father's military service, described to me the hurt of losing Kurdish friends after the war. "I don't want to leave because I've gotten used to this place, to the way of living here." He had recently been detained overnight by Kurdish police for having no ID card. "Maybe if this had happened during Saddam's time, I would have been locked up for days," he said. "And a Kurd might have been tortured." Abbas thought that Arabs and Kurds could live together in Kirkuk if the politicians allowed them to do so. "We're human beings and they're human beings," he said. "In my opinion, the city of Kirkuk, the Kurds have every right to it. They have more rights in Kirkuk and they deserve Kirkuk. But still, we can't just go anywhere and leave the house. Where would we live?"

On the other side of town, I met a young Kurdish engineer named Sardar Mohamed. He had somehow survived all the years of ethnic cleansing in the old Kurdish neighborhood of Imam Qasim, where he and his wife and children were squeezed into one house with his two brothers and their families. "If there had been no war, in fifteen years you would find no Kurds at all in Kirkuk," he said. When the American invasion seemed imminent, Mohamed went down into his basement and cut a square out of the plaster wall, behind which there was a concealed room. He planned to hide there if the Baathists started rounding up young Kurdish men, as they had done in 1991. Instead, the Baathists fled the city. After the fall of the regime, Mohamed's family experienced a rebirth of sorts. They built a new outhouse and extended the kitchen, and they filled it with new appliances. "It wasn't that I didn't have the money," Mohamed said. "But I wasn't sure I would keep this house. I didn't know if I'd need the money in the future for food." His wife had dropped out of school because there was no chance for a Kurdish woman who didn't correct her nationality to find a job. After the liberation, she reenrolled and obtained her degree. "Before, we didn't know when we'd be arrested or expelled," Mohamed said. "Now we have hopes for the future."

As for the Arabs who enjoyed all the rights and privileges that were denied his family, Mohamed was of two minds. It would be easier for everyone if they left. "But their kids, when they're born here, there's a kind of relationship to the land, and it's not those kids' fault that they're in love with the place where they were born," he said. "It's unfair for them to have to leave." The only reason for Kirkuk to join Kurdistan, he said, was that Arabs didn't treat Kurds fairly. The important thing was for Iraqis' minds to change. If the imported Arabs would just admit that they came to Kirkuk through Arabization and displaced the Kurds, "They can stay and even bring more Arabs," Mohamed said. If a government in Baghdad ensured that all Iraqi citizens would be treated equally, he would gladly live under its flag instead of in Kurdistan.

Kirkuk suffered inordinately from bad ideas, and the old ones had engendered some that were new: that the historical clock could be turned back forty years, or that Iraq could be carved among its Sunnis, Shia, and Kurds without enormous bloodshed and countless individual tragedies. The weakest idea in Iraq was the idea of Iraq itself. Barham Salih said, "There is no Iraqi identity that I can push my people to today. I want to have an Iraqi identity, but it does not exist." Samir Shakir Sumaidaie said, "To get away from what Saddam did, where ethnic identity is what mattered most, to a society where citizenship is what matters—that transition is not an easy transition. We have to make it, though."

The obsession with ethnic identity had become the ultimate legacy of Saddam's rule, his diabolical revenge on his countrymen. Nowhere could this be more strongly felt than in Kirkuk. "Saddam is gone, but we're not through with him," an Arab there said. "Even if he's not here, it's like he planted problems for the future."

ON MY LAST EVENING in Kirkuk I went to see the citadel with Luna Dawood. She wore high-heeled sandals; although her hair was uncovered, she had pinned it up as a gesture of respect. She had visited the citadel only once, in 1988; after the residents were removed and the houses destroyed, she developed an aversion to the place.

At sunset, we made our way through the souk, past little Kurdish shops that sold bread, yogurt, and ancient-looking tools, past a black-smith's forge, and then we followed an alley that led us to the top of the plateau. The citadel spread out before us, a vast and nearly empty field of dirt and dead grass and broken stones and scattered monu-ments. A pack of wild dogs roamed menacingly, and the sole human inhabitants were an old Turkoman and his family. They were squatting in the marble dwelling of a long-departed imam. The Turkoman told us that he had once lived in a house a few yards away. He brought his family back after the fall of the regime, and somehow he had been al-lowed to stay. "This is my original place," he said. "I'm a poor man, I have nowhere to go. Where should the poor man go?"

We crossed the field, toward an octagonal gold-and-blue tower that an Ottoman pasha had built for his dead daughter, and the ancient clay minaret of the Tomb of the Prophets. Luna, who had been walk-ing in stunned silence, abruptly said, "They are stupid. They destroyed their history." At the far end of the citadel, perched above the dead riverbed, was the abandoned house of the Turkoman woman who sold shoes and purses in the souk. Behind it, the orange ball of the sun was sinking. On one of the house's walls, someone had painted, "Long live the Turkomans—they are crowns on the heads of the Kurds." There was graffiti on other walls, too: "Kirkuk is the heart of Kurdistan," "The citadel of Kirkuk is the sign of the Kurds," and "The citadel of Kirkuk is a witness of its Turkomanness, whatever the conditions." On the courtyard wall of another half-ruined house, someone had painted, "The Turkoman people are brothers with the Kurdish people," but someone else had painted over the last two words.

"Ghosts are here," Luna murmured. "I can hear them in the night. Under the ground, my mother said when we were children, there's a road from Kirkuk to Baghdad. Underground, there's a door some-where—for people who wanted to escape Kirkuk."

Her disquiet grew as we approached the Tomb of the Prophets. "This isn't the citadel I know. I told you, I came once before. But there was a road, and people. I don't even know where that road was." She had come with three friends, one of them a Muslim, after she had a dream about the prophet Daniel.

We stood before the entrance, Down below, in the city, muezzins were beginning the evening call. I went inside the bare chamber and waited for Luna to follow, but at the doorway she recoiled with a muted cry. I followed her out.

"It was gold!" she exclaimed. When she visited the shrine after her dream, the tombs and walls had been covered in gold leaf; all of it had been scraped off. "Now I'm sad," Luna said. "Really, now I'm feeling depressed, because I can see the difference between that time and this visit. I can't feel the holy mystery of the place. That time when I prayed, I felt Daniel would give me my wishes. But now I don't feel it's holy. I'm even afraid to go inside."

It was getting dark, and we started back. Luna was silent again. Just before the opening to the alley that descended to the souk, there was a square hole in the ground. She stopped. "I remember the well we just saw. I remember there were trees. Now I'm remembering— I visited this place as a child."

Dusk had settled over the souk. The market stalls were closing up amid the last calls of prices, and the sweepers were cleaning up the day's trash. Luna spoke so quietly that she might have been a ghost herself. "What is a human being worth, if they steal such a place? It's better to be ignorant of all that's happening around us, because right now being human means nothing to me. I'm very sorry you brought me to this place. I shouldn't have come."

11

MEMORIAL DAY

ON THE EVENING OF NOVEMBER 8, 2003, at around 7:40 p.m., a two-Humvee convoy pulled out through the front gate of the American base at the Rashid military camp in south Baghdad. The mission was to pick up a sergeant attending a meeting at the combat support hospital inside the Green Zone. The convoy belonged to the scout platoon of Headquarters Company, 2-6 Infantry—John Prior's battalion. In the rear left seat of the lead vehicle sat a twenty-two-year-old private named Kurt Frosheiser.

There was nothing obvious to set Private Frosheiser apart from the tens of thousands of other young enlisted men who served in Iraq. He was from Des Moines, Iowa. He had a twin brother, a married older sister, and divorced parents. He had been an indifferent student and a bit of a rebel through high school, and by age twenty-one he was a community college dropout, living with his sister's family, delivering pizza, and partying heavily. He had a brash, boyish smile, with his father's full mouth and lidded eyes; he liked Lynyrd Skynyrd and the Chicago Cubs; and one day in January 2003, he flew through the door with the news that he had just enlisted in the Army.

His father, Chris, wasn't thrilled to hear it. There was a war on terror going on, and the strong possibility of a land war in Iraq. But he didn't try to argue with his son. In February, Kurt dropped by his father's apartment around two in the morning after a night out drinking and said, "I want to be part of something bigger than myself."

Kurt watched the invasion of Iraq on TV looking more serious than his sister Erin had ever seen him. He still had the option to get out of his obligation, but he left home on April 16 for Fort Knox, Kentucky, and basic training. In June the family drove down to see him at Family Day, and Chris Frosheiser was stunned by the transformation: his son, standing at perfect attention on Pershing Field for forty-five minutes in his dress uniform. It was the same in August, when they went back down for graduation: Private Frosheiser, marching, singing with his classmates, "Pick up your wounded, pick up your dead." The words sent a chill through Frosheiser, but the music, the sharpness and tightness of the formation, the bearing of his son, filled him with pride. Something new and important was happening in Kurt's life. After the ceremony, Kurt told his father, "You weren't hard-core enough for me." Chris always lingered in the gray areas, asking questions; Kurt wanted the clear light of an oath and an order.

They all drove back to Des Moines for their last two weeks together at the end of summer before Kurt would join the First Armored Division in Germany. He partied every night, but the departure hung over everyone, and on the last night, when Erin dropped him off at one final party and turned to look at him, he said, "I know," and ran off.

"Well, old man, I'm probably not going to see you for two years," Kurt told his father late that night. They both started to cry, and Frosheiser ran his hand through his son's crew-cut hair. "I know I'm going to be in some deep shit. But you know me, I'm a survivor." Frosheiser knew that the words were only meant to comfort him. His son said, "Live your life, old man."

In Germany, Kurt was bored out of his mind and eager to join the rest of his division in Iraq. On the phone with his father once, he mentioned that it looked like there were no weapons of mass destruction to be found in Iraq. "We're fucked, aren't we?" Not necessarily, his father said, there might be other reasons for the war, such as democracy in the Middle East, WMD might just have been the easiest to sell to the public. Kurt's officers at Baumholder prepared him and the others for what had become guerrilla warfare in Iraq, telling them not to pick up trash bags, not to take packages that kids would rush up to give them, and when Kurt repeated it all to Erin she couldn't begin to imagine herself in such a place, where a mother like her couldn't let her children outside the house for fear that something would explode.

Then suddenly Kurt was on a transport plane to Kuwait. By the end of October he was in Baghdad, just as the Ramadan Offensive was heating up.

On November 6 he managed to get online and e-mailed his sister: "Our sector that we patrol is a good one we don't get shot at that much nor do we find IED's (improvised explosive device) that's their main way of attacking us they usually put them in bags but now their putting them in dead animals or in concrete blocks to hide them better. It's kinda scary knowing their out there but like I said our secter is pretty secure so I'll be allright." Writing to his father about his first mission out in the city, an uneventful night drive, Kurt was more explicit: "I found myself thinking that I'm in a country where a lot of soldiers lost their lives but where we at it was so quiet except all friggin dogs barking the Iraqs hate dogs so they're all wild probably never had a bath their whole lives this country is a shit hole they dont have plumbing so they dig little canels and let all the shit and piss run into the streets it smells so fucking in some places and from what the other scouts who have been here from the beginning theyre places that smell so bad you almost throw up. From what I see its goin to take a lot longer then Rumsfeld and G.W. are saying to get this shit hole up and running." He spoke to his father once briefly on the phone. "IEDs, old man, IEDs," he said.

On the evening of the 8th, Kurt was sitting on his bunk, sorting and counting his ammunition, when word came of a mission to the combat support hospital. He was training for his license as a Humvee driver, and he jumped at the chance to experience driving through Baghdad by night. In his few days with the battalion he had already earned a reputation as a hard worker who was quick to volunteer. He and his best friend in the unit, Private Matt Plumley of Tennessee, raced each other to the vehicle. Because the right rear door was hard to open, they both headed for the left. Kurt got there first.

Five minutes out of the base, as the convoy was cruising north toward downtown Baghdad, on the left shoulder of the dark highway thirty feet ahead two 130-mm. artillery shells packed with Russian C-4 detonated in a tremendous blast—flash of light, black smoke, flying dirt, smell of explosives. The legs of the driver, Private First Class Matt Van Buren, were torn with hot chunks of shrapnel, but he accelerated another few hundred yards along the highway, thinking that he would try to make it to the Assassins' Gate, until the staff sergeant sitting next to him, Darrell Clay, told him to stop.

A muezzin somewhere began calling the faithful to prayer. In the back of the Humvee, Kurt was slumped in his seat. When Plumley checked his pulse, there was none. He had been looking out the window—which had no protective glass—his head turned to the left, and a piece of silvery metal 1¼" by ½" by ½" traveling upward had penetrated the right side of his skull just below the Kevlar helmet between the eye and ear and breached his brain. Private Kurt Frosheiser was airlifted by helicopter to the combat support hospital in the Green Zone, where he was pronounced dead at 8:17 p.m.

At six-thirty CST the next morning, a Sunday, the phone rang in Chris Frosheiser's cramped bachelor apartment in Des Moines. It was a lieutenant colonel in the Iowa National Guard, two blocks away and trying to find the address. "I have a message from the Army," he said tersely. Frosheiser knew then, because the week before he had asked an officer what to expect if something happened to Kurt, and the officer had said a phone call if wounded, a visit if killed. Frosheiser met the lieutenant colonel outside the building and invited him in, going through the motions in case it was all a mistake, and they briefly made small talk in the living room. Frosheiser went to the kitchen for a cup of coffee. When he returned, the lieutenant colonel suddenly stood at attention. "I regret to inform you that your son Kurt was killed as a result of action in Baghdad."

"Not Kurt! Not Kurt!"

Chris Frosheiser ran down the hall, and then he ran back into the living room. The lieutenant colonel asked if he could call someone, but Frosheiser was already calling Erin, and then a friend who drove him to the house of his other son, Kurt's twin, Joel. Frosheiser banged on the window, shouting, "It's Kurt, it's our Kurt!" and then he and Joel drove together to the suburb where Erin lived. The rest of the day and the following days were a blur of tears and friends and wine and exhaustion.

On November 11, Veterans Day, Kurt's battalion, the 2-6 Infantry, gathered in formation at the American base in south Baghdad for a memorial service. John Prior was there, and so was another captain, Robert Swope, who later wrote an account of the ceremony:

> In the background are voices of people talking, vehicles passing, and helicopters overhead. Some birds intermittently fly over us. A butter-fly goes by. I see one of the Iraqi translators who works in the TOC sitting in a chair reading a paper while the rest of the battalion stands in formation. At 1430 the ceremony is supposed to begin, but it doesn't start until 1448 because we have to wait for a couple generals to arrive.
>
> The memorial ceremony begins with an invocation by the chaplain, and then the battalion commander and the company commander both speak. Two privates who knew the soldier follow them. One of the privates chokes and starts tearing up while giving his tribute. I look around me out into a sea of sad faces and in the very back of the battalion formation I see that one of the female soldiers attached to our unit is crying.
>
> A bagpiper plays a crappy version of "Amazing Grace" and halfway through it doesn't even sound much like the song anymore. The soldier who plays "Taps" later on at the end of the ceremony does a much better job.
>
> After "Amazing Grace" but before "Taps" begins, the chaplain reads a few verses from the Bible, and then gives a memorial message and prayer. It's followed by a moment of silence. Then the acting First Sergeant for the company does roll call, yelling out the names of various soldiers in the unit. They all answer, one after another, that they are present. When he comes to the private who died, everything is quiet.
>
> He calls out his name again, and still there is no answer. He does it a final time, using his full name and rank:
>
> "Private First Class Kurt Russell Frosheiser!"
>
> Silence.
>
> And then the mournful melody of "Taps" begins. Midway through the bugler begins slowly walking away, letting the music softly fade

out in the distance. Jess walks over to where seven soldiers stand with seven rifles. He gives the order and they fire off three series of blanks, giving him a twenty-one-gun salute.

When they're finished the battalion commander walks up to the memorial, which is an M-16 with a bayonet attached and driven into a wooden stand. Resting on top of the butt stock is a helmet and hanging down are a pair of dog tags with his name, social security number, blood type, and religion on them. Directly in front of the M-16 and in the center of the memorial stand is a pair of tan combat boots. To the left and to the right of his boots are a bronze star and purple heart ensconced in their silk and velvet cases. A pair of sabers representing the scout unit he belonged to are crossed behind the rifle. Others follow the battalion commander who salutes the memorial representing Private Frosheiser, until all of the soldier's company has saluted, and the rest of those attending the ceremony can begin . . .

This is the second time I've had to go to a ceremony like this so far this year and I don't feel comfortable doing it. I walk up to the memorial the way I did last April for another soldier in my company, who we did this same ritual for in a field of dirt next to the tarmac at the Baghdad International Airport. I don't lower my head and pray or whisper anything as so many others do before me. I don't lean over and touch the tip of his boots like the sergeant major ahead of me just did. I just salute and then turn and walk away.

Chris Frosheiser wanted to escort his son's body back from Baghdad. He at least wanted to meet it at Dover Air Force Base in Delaware. In the end, it was enough to receive the coffin at the Des Moines airport with thirty family members and friends and see Kurt's face one more time. At the wake, Frosheiser tried to say that his son's courage filled him with awe, but he wasn't able to express himself well. Kurt received a military funeral after a Catholic service and was buried in Glendale Cemetery.

Frosheiser's ex-wife, Kurt's mother, Jeanie, told the local paper, "He loved this land and its principles. He loved Iowa. It's an honor to give my son to preserve our way of life." She had become an evangelical Christian, and she said that Kurt had volunteered to fight the forces of evil. This was too apocalyptic for Chris Frosheiser, suggesting some kind of religious war, and it wasn't how Kurt had talked. On the night of the terrible news, Governor Tom Vilsack had called to offer condolences and had said that he hoped the country's policies were as good as its people. Frosheiser was troubled by the thought that it might not be so. He kept comparing the president's oath of office to the oath Kurt had sworn when he became a soldier: Were they carried out with equal seriousness? In January, one of Kurt's friends from Fort Knox wrote in an e-mail, "I don't suppose he was in an up-armored HMMV, was he? Probably not, Uncle Sam wouldn't give us Joe's the good stuff." Frosheiser didn't know the answer, but thinking about it didn't help a bit with his grief.

The speed of it all, the historical vastness—his boy, in the Army, in Iraq, the Ramadan Offensive, hit in the head—was overwhelming. Frosheiser dreamed that he was in the Army with Kurt, though it was unclear whether they were father and son or friends, but both of them were sitting on the right side and when the explosion came they fell out of the Humvee together and everything was okay. The thought that he hadn't been with Kurt that night to protect him wouldn't leave Frosheiser alone, nor the thought that he hadn't had time to send Tolkien's *The Return of the King*, a book Kurt had requested. On his wrist he wore Kurt's watch, still set to Baghdad time, with an alarm that still went off every day at 6:30 a.m., 9:30 p.m. in Des Moines. For weeks and months he struggled with the meaning of his son's death, but he couldn't reach an answer.

Frosheiser was fifty-six years old. He was a salesman's son from Chicago, with a flat Midwestern accent, and he had worked most of his life in insurance before starting a new career as the Salvation Army's director of social services in Des Moines, trying to solve the problems of the hardship cases that came into his office, handing out food to men sleeping under bridges. He was a lifelong Democrat, and as a student in 1968 he had supported Robert Kennedy. He couldn't identify with the antiwar movement, though; he thought Vietnam was a terrible waste but not a reason to hate your country. Even the Gene McCarthy campaign struck him as too elite, too unconventional, and when McCarthy said that Kennedy was "running best among the less intelligent and less educated people," it touched the resentful nerve of a lower-middle-class kid attending Drake University. The Tom Haydens of the world were going to make it no matter how they spent their youth; the Chris Frosheisers had to be careful what they did with their time.

He was part of Middle America, but he didn't join the backlash of Nixon and Reagan; he remained a liberal, mostly on economic grounds. As the quality of the Democratic candidates deteriorated, he turned back to one of the academic interests of his college years, and the apartment he rented after his divorce in the mid-1990s filled up with books on Roosevelt, Truman, Acheson, the midcentury liberals who seemed wiser and tougher than the heirs of George McGovern. He read historical accounts of FDR's Four Freedoms and the Truman Doctrine, and when the report of the 9/11 Commission was published, he bought one of the first copies. Reading it, he concluded that the ideas of that earlier generation of Democrats, who had fought wars against fascism and communism while creating an alliance of democracies, should be brought back and applied to the war on terror and the conflict in Iraq. He was uneasy with his Democratic friends who thought that Iraq was another Vietnam, and he couldn't tolerate hearing that Kurt's life had been wasted. When a local Catholic peace group got in touch in April 2004 to offer condolences and let him know that Kurt's picture, along with those of the other fallen Iowans, would be on display at a weekly candlelight vigil, Frosheiser called and told them not to use Kurt's. Condolences, he thought, should have been offered much earlier, and the spirit of the vigil was about the politics of the war, not the soldiers. But when he bought a long-life candle at a Christian bookshop and told the cashier whose grave it was for, and she said, "Thank you for your sacrifice," that, too, sounded wrong. It had not been his choice.

In the Iowa caucuses that winter, Frosheiser supported Senator John Edwards. He had misgivings about John Kerry. When a friend called Kerry's vote against the eighty-seven-billion-dollar war appropriation a "protest vote," Frosheiser said, "Kind of a serious issue to be casting protest votes." He wondered if a President Kerry would hold steadfast in Iraq under pressure from the party's activist base. If not, what would Kurt's death mean then? When President Bush said in a speech, "We will hold this hard-won ground," he found the language inspiring. Kerry's language did not inspire. Frosheiser kept remembering Lincoln's 1862 message to Congress: "As our case is new, so we must think anew, and act anew. We must disenthrall ourselves, and then we shall save our country." He longed to hear words like these from a wartime leader; politics required the art of explanation. But Bush, who had made so many mistakes, was unable to admit or even see them; with the best education money could buy he seemed to know little about the world. The war was getting worse, with no sign that anyone in leadership could turn it around. Frosheiser wanted to see a government of national unity, composed of Thomas Kean and Lee Hamilton of the 9/11 Commission, and Senators Biden, Feinstein, Hagel, Lieberman, Lugar, and McCain. Iraq was too important to be left to the partisans.

While I was away in Iraq, a letter from Des Moines arrived. Chris Frosheiser had read something I'd written about John Prior, and he was looking for some way to comprehend Kurt's short life and death in Iraq. After I got back, we began a correspondence by e-mail. Frosheiser's were full of the restless questions, the constant return to the same inconclusive themes, of a man who has suffered a trauma and is determined to feel every contour of it, to avoid nothing.

April 1, 2004: Democrats need a foreign policy and a national security strategy to back it up. Now, I have gone too long and not answered your questions very well. It shows my ambivalence and the difficulty in talking beyond the personal. Sorry. May I write more later? I can't go on now. I have re-read Truman's "Truman Doctrine" speech and Marshall's Harvard Commencement speech of June 1947. I admired them and those policies. I must avoid bitterness. In honor of Kurt and the other soldiers, bitterness seems inappropriate. More later, if you don't mind.

April 1, 2004: What would Kurt want? He is my guide. Sometimes "force protection" and the job are in conflict, but all that is possible ought to be done to protect these brave people, our soldiers. I miss my son a lot! Tears flow everyday. What's it worth? A democratic Iraq? Our soldiers helping achieve a more free, democratic Iraq?

May 15, 2004: Sometimes I think about Kurt being in Baghdad, Iraq as part of something called "Operation Iraqi Freedom." Kurt said he wanted to be a part of something larger than himself. He was in the middle of something so huge it nearly defies understanding. There is more to be said about this, I just don't know what it is. My son died for something. And there is honor in simply enlisting, let alone serving in Iraq.

May 26, 2004: I want this to be a "success." For the Iraqis, the United States, and for the sacrifice made by Kurt and all the others. And for the pain of Kurt's not being among us anymore. Kurt; a son, a brother to Erin and Joel, and an uncle to Colin and Madelyn. Not trying to be overly dramatic, Mr. Packer, just trying to express how it "feels."

July 5, 2004 [In early July, the First Armored Division finally returned to Germany after more than a year in Iraq]: Now, I'm kind of lost with them leaving, and without Kurt. This probably makes no sense but Kurt's watch is on Baghdad time and his unit isn't there, though he was with them there. He is not with them now, back in Baumholder. This is why it takes so long to, what, carry on? Maybe I dwell on this kind of stuff too much. But that is me and I'll be alright.

August 28, 2004: Next Tuesday, George Bush will be campaigning near Des Moines, in a farm community called Alleman, Iowa. Apparently, the campaign invited us as Kurt's family to be there. Joel and I talked about it and Erin too. And we will attend. It is a tribute to Kurt, I think. It may or may not be construed as support for Bush. But, you know, I will put my Democratic loyalty up against anyone's. As a tribute to Kurt I am entitled to shake hands with the President. Besides, it is still a bit odd I think that very little was said to me, a loyal Democrat, by leading Democrats, about Kurt's service. I know a guy who was the State Party chair and who was an early Edwards supporter. I had expressed an interest in talking to Edwards about Kurt's service.

It was never arranged. I thought someone like Edwards should speak to someone who lost a child in combat. Is there a larger issue exposed here? About Democrats and the soldiers? Sometimes it feels like I don't have a Party. John Kerry did send a card to both Jeanie and me, but I really think there is an ill at ease sense among activist Democrats about the "warriors" because of opposition to the war.

September 5, 2004: In follow-up to my previous e-mail about meeting Dubya, it didn't happen. Out of a sense of obligation to honor Kurt, to receive his Commander in Chief's offer of tribute and condolences I went. We were just part of the crowd. The former wife who received the invite from the local Republican Party organization wasn't too happy either. We did get to hear the "stump speech," a longer version of which he gave to the Convention. He speaks of the "war against terror" as if it includes Iraq, no distinguishing between them. Is that a "lie," a "misimpression," is it misleading, is it true and he knows and isn't sharing all the information? What is a citizen to do? He received a lot of applause about lessening the tax burden and about his unwillingness to have our policy controlled by foreign governments or having our soldiers under the leadership of foreign governments. Someone made the point somewhere that Allawi exerted this control in Najaf and Fallujah. A fine point in a Presidential election I suppose, but where is John Kerry? Is it that he really can't talk about Iraq because the "base" of the Democratic Party wants to simply pull out? This talk of the "ownership society" sounds like a tearing of the New Deal/Great Society safety net/social compact. We are in trouble. I will be happy when the election is over. I can't take much more of the hyperbolic bullshit!

September 11, 2004: Grandson Colin spent the night last night. We ate popcorn, visited Borders, watched Star Wars, and this morning took a dip in the pool (a bit cool). Life goes on, ready or not. I have to say that Kurt is never out of my thoughts. Ever. That may not be healthy but it is the way it is. I am 57 years old, George, I may never fully recover from this. And maybe I shouldn't. The idea that Kurt left to "live your life, old man" and that Garrison Keillor included in his

Memorial Day Sonnet, "And may we live the good lives they would have lived." That hasn't been defined yet. One day at a time. I have two living children and two grandchildren. I don't know what to make of it all, yet.

October 4, 2004: What is best for America and Iraq now? That is the question. A better Iraq? Is it possible? Why did we go into Iraq? What justifies our remaining? American lives have been lost, precious lives, for what? Can something be achieved that is worthy of the sacrifice? Are there things not known to anyone other than the President and his advisers? No one in the Senate or any of the "attentive" and "informed" organizations? That would justify the sacrifice? And how much more sacrifice can be justified? For us to turn Iraq over to civil war would be hard to take. I don't have the right to advocate continued involvement because of my sacrifice that would lead to more, many more. What is best for America and Iraq? What is reality on the ground in Iraq? What is possible to achieve? Can Kerry and a team of his choosing do it? It is a great leap of faith.
And most of the time none of this matters to me. I want my son. My son.

THE HOME FRONT of the Iraq War was not like World War II, and it was not like Vietnam. It didn't unite Americans across party lines against an existential threat (September 11 did that, but not Iraq). There were no war bonds, no collection drives, no universal call-up, no national mobilization, no dollar-a-year men. We were not all in it together. Nor did it tear the country apart. As soon as the war began, the American antiwar movement quietly folded up its tent and went home. The first and second anniversaries of the invasion saw large demonstrations in Europe and parts of the Middle East and Asia, but in this country, organized opposition was muted by the imperative to support the troops in harm's way. Candlelight vigils like the one that displayed the pictures of fallen Iowans in Des Moines strove for a tone of respectful dissent.

This doesn't mean that the war wasn't controversial; no foreign venture has been more so since Vietnam. At a certain level—that of elite opinion, amplified in the media—Iraq generated words as bitter as any event in modern American history. But most American citizens didn't turn against other American citizens with a fury, any more than they joined together in a common cause. Iraq was a strangely distant war. It was always hard to picture the place; the war didn't enter the popular imagination in songs that everyone soon knew by heart in the manner of previous wars, including the good one and the bad one. It was unlikely that a novelist would spend six months in Baghdad and come back to update *From Here to Eternity* or *Dog Soldiers*. The one slender American novel that the war has produced so far, *Checkpoint* by Nicholson Baker, a dialogue over lunch in a Washington hotel room between two old friends, one of whom is preparing to assassinate George W. Bush, was a perfect emblem of a political culture in which hysteria took the place of thought. Baker's novel had nothing to do with Iraq and everything to do with the ugliness of politics in this country. Michael Moore, the left's answer to Rush Limbaugh, made a hugely successful movie in which Saddam's Iraq was portrayed as a happy place where children flew kites. Iraq provided a blank screen on which Americans were free to project anything they wanted, and because so few Americans had anything directly at stake there, many of them never saw more than the image of their own feelings. The exceptions, of course, were the soldiers and their families, who carried almost the entire weight of the war.

This state of affairs on the home front was, in one way, the natural outgrowth of a political atmosphere that had become increasingly poisonous for a decade. The culture wars produced Clinton hatred, which led to impeachment, followed by the contested election of 2000, followed by Bush hatred, which was just as intense and crazy making as its predecessor. Iraq provided another level on the downward spiral. Whereas the street fights of the late 1960s were the consequence of Vietnam, the word fights of the early 2000s were not the consequence of Iraq—if anything, the other way around.

It was the first bloggers' war, and the characteristic features of the form—instant response, ad hominem attack, remoteness from life, the echo chamber of friends and enemies—defined the quality of the debate about Iraq far better than the reasoned analyses and proposals that quickly disappeared from view in responsible newspapers and policy journals. One of the leading bloggers, Andrew Sullivan, who would later have honorable second thoughts about the Bush administration and Iraq, responded to the news of Saddam's capture in December 2003 by writing, "It was a day of joy. Nothing remains to be said right now. Joy." He had just handed out eleven mock awards to leftists who expressed insufficient happiness or open unhappiness at the news. In response to an Iraqi blogger's declaration of heartfelt thanks to the coalition forces, Sullivan, at his computer in Washington, wrote, "You're welcome . . . The men and women in our armed forces did the hardest work. They deserve our immeasurable thanks. But we all played our part." Sullivan's joy was vindictive and narcissistic glee, and he rubbed his opponents' faces in it. From the prewar period through the invasion into the occupation and insurgency, an ascendant, triumphalist right and a weakened, querulous left took more interest and pleasure in the other's defeats than in the condition of Iraq or Iraqis. In this country, Iraq was almost always about winning the argument.

This was never clearer than when I traveled from one place to the other. I would come back from Iraq with its swarm of contradictions as vivid in my mind as every individual face or voice: It was a liberation, it was an occupation; the Iraqis were hopeful, the Iraqis were furious; there was a chance for democracy, there was a reign of terror; the CPA was working hard, the CPA was getting nowhere; American soldiers were kindhearted, American soldiers were reckless. Then I would sit down to dinner with a group of progressive-minded people who all wanted to know what it was like over there, and before I could get halfway through one encounter with one Iraqi, the invective came at me with astonishing force, wind-aided by a change of subject to the sins of the Bush administration. The same was true, on the other side of the looking glass, in the columns and talk shows of right-wing commentators: Every shred of good news—the arrest of a top Baathist, the reopening of a museum—became definitive evidence that it was working. Everyone wanted to know whether or not it was working, and the question usually came loaded, and the answer had better be quick and simple. There were not many people in America who could stand the cognitive dissonance with which Iraqis live every day.

Actually going to Iraq didn't have to intrude on this mental self-sufficiency. Christopher Hitchens, who had just published a book titled *A Long Short War: The Postponed Liberation of Iraq*, flew in with the entourage of Paul Wolfowitz in the summer of 2003, spent a few days in the deputy secretary's wake, and came back to tell Fox News that the revolution from above was succeeding splendidly, with the Americans busy rebuilding the place, gathering intelligence, rolling up Baathists, and making friends with the people—none of which was appearing in press coverage. "I felt a sense of annoyance that I had to go there myself to find any of that out," Hitchens confessed to the Fox interviewer. The following March, with the long short war showing signs of turning into a short long war, Fred Barnes, an editor of the strenuously prowar *Weekly Standard*, parachuted into the Green Zone and discovered that the only thing wrong with Operation Iraqi Freedom was Iraqis. "They need an attitude adjustment," Barnes wrote. "Americans I talked to in 10 days here agree Iraqis are difficult to deal with. They're sullen and suspicious and conspiracy-minded." This wasn't the prewar judgment of hawks like Barnes, but something had to explain all the bumps in the road, which would lead to a successful democracy in Iraq only after "an outbreak of gratitude for the greatest act of benevolence one country has ever done for another." Naomi Klein, a columnist for the bitterly antiwar *Nation*, visited Baghdad at exactly the same time as Barnes and found that the insurgency was mushrooming because so many Iraqis shared her own antiglobalization views. In Iraq it was always possible to prove that you'd been right all along.

Because the Iraq War began in ideas, it always suffered from abstraction. But long after those ideas took actual shape in Kevlar and C-4 and shrapnel, the war's most conspicuous proponents and detractors continued to see it and speak of it in the French historian Marc Bloch's "large abstract terms." The key terms in Iraq were "imperialism," "democracy," "unilateralism," "internationalization," "weapons of mass destruction," "preemption," "terrorism," "totalitarianism," "neoconservatism," "appeasement." One month after he survived the bombing in Baghdad, I met Ghassan Salamé, the late Sergio Vieira de Mello's political adviser, in the lobby of UN headquarters in New York. Looking a little wan, Salamé said, "Iraq needs to be liberated—liberated from big plans. Every time people mentioned it in the last few years, it was to connect it to big ideas: the war against WMDs, solving the Arab-Israeli conflict, more recently the war against terrorism and a model of democracy. That's why all these mistakes are made. They're made because Iraq is always in someone's mind the first step to something else."

With their eyes turned to such lofty matters, few prowar ideologues allowed the bad news from Iraq to break their stride. Either they refused to credit it, blaming the media and the defeatists for hiding the truth, or they continued to take such a long view of history that a hundred Iraqis or a dozen Americans blown up in a suicide bombing hardly factored. But this was just as true on the antiwar side of the ledger. Experience taught me that the individual stories of Iraqis struggling against danger and the odds to create a better life for themselves and their country were impatiently flicked aside as soon as I tried to tell them. The retort was swift and sure: "This war is *illegal*, it's *immoral*. Nothing good can come of a lie." In spite of the enormous stakes and the terrible alternatives, most antiwar pundits and politicians showed no interest in success. When Iraqis risked their lives to vote, Arianna Huffington dismissed the elections as a "Kodak moment." It was Bush's war, and if it failed, it would be Bush's failure.

America in the early twenty-first century seemed politically too partisan, divided, and small to manage something as vast and difficult as Iraq. Condoleezza Rice and other leading officials were fond of comparing Iraq with postwar Germany. But there was a great gulf between the tremendous thought and effort of the best minds that had gone into defeating fascism and rebuilding Germany and Japan, and the peevish, self-serving attention paid to Iraq. One produced the Army's four-hundred-page manual on the occupation of Germany; the other produced talking points.

WHAT MADE THIS POLITICAL CULTURE particularly unfortunate for Iraqis was that the Bush administration, instead of forging the war into a truly national cause, conducted it from the beginning like the South Carolina primary.

In the aftermath of September 11, President Bush was granted what few presidents ever get: national unity and the goodwill of both parties. In the days that followed the terror attacks, we saw the early stages of something like a popular self-mobilization. The long lines of blood donors, the volunteers converging from around the country on Manhattan, the fumbling public efforts at understanding Islam: The response took on very personal tones. People spoke as if they wanted to change their lives. An unemployed young video producer waiting to give blood in Brooklyn said to me, "I volunteered so I could be part of something. All over the world people do something for an ideal. I've been at no point in my life when I could say something I've done has affected mankind." The feverish outbreak of public-spiritedness couldn't have lasted, but its intensity suggested that the country had snapped out of a collective daydream. A generation legendary for its self-centeredness seemed to grasp that here was a historic chance to aim for something greater.

It was much remarked at the time that President Bush did nothing to tap this palpable desire among ordinary people to join a larger effort. Americans were told to go shopping and watch out for suspicious activity. It was Pearl Harbor, and it was a bad day on the stock exchange; nothing would ever be the same, and everything was just the same. Joseph Biden wondered, "How urgent can this be if I tell you this is a great crisis and, at the time we're marching to war, I give the single largest tax cut in the history of the United States of America?" The tax cuts didn't just leave the country fiscally unsound during wartime; their inequity was bad for morale. But the president's failure to call for shared, equal sacrifice wasn't accidental. It followed directly from the governing spirit of the modern conservative movement that his presidency brought to full power. After years of a sustained assault on the idea of collective action, there was no ideological foundation left on which Bush could have stood up and asked what Americans could do for their country. We weren't urged to study Arabic, to join the foreign service or international aid groups, to develop alternative sources of energy, to form a national civil reserve for emergencies—or even to pay off the cost of the war in our own time. Its burdens would be borne by the next generation of Americans, and by a few hundred thousand volunteer soldiers in this one.

Perhaps it was a shrewd political read on Bush's part—a recognition that Americans, for all their passion after September 11, would inevitably slouch back to their sofas. It seemed fair to ask, though, how a body politic as out of shape as ours was likely to make it over the long, hard slog of wartime; how convincingly we could export democratic values when our own version showed so many signs of atrophy; how much solidarity we could expect to muster for Afghans and Iraqis when we were asked to feel so little for one another.

So the months after September 11 were a lost opportunity—to harness the surge of civic energy and to frame the new war against Islamist radicalism as a national struggle. It should have been the job not just of the experts in the intelligence agencies and Special Forces but also of ordinary American citizens to wage it. And it should have been waged on many fronts, with many tools—not just military, but also intellectual, diplomatic, economic, political, cultural. This had been the vision of the architects of the early Cold War, whom Chris Frosheiser read about in a college history course and whom he came to admire even more after September 11. But it wasn't the president's vision. Bush's rhetoric soared and inspired, but his actions showed that he had a narrow strategy for fighting the war, which amounted to finding and killing terrorists and their supporters. Other agendas, such as his tax cuts and energy policy and the bitter fights they stirred, disrupted the clarity and unity of September 11. Bush continued to govern from his ideological base. His message to the public was essentially, "Trust me," and the public slipped into a fearful passivity.

Whatever national cohesion remained by mid-2002 came undone in the buildup to the invasion of Iraq. The White House forced a congressional vote on a war resolution one month before the 2002 midterm elections, in an atmosphere of partisan invective. While Republicans on the floor of the House and Senate were accusing their Democratic colleagues of Chamberlain-like appeasement of Saddam, others on the campaign trail were charging their opponents with dereliction of duty in defending the country because of Democratic objections to a provision in the Homeland Security Bill designed to weaken civil service unions. (The White House, having rejected the notion of a Homeland Security Department at the outset, later wrote language into the bill that forced Democrats to choose between their own idea and their labor base.) Joseph Biden, working with his colleague Richard Lugar, the ranking Republican on the Senate Foreign Relations Committee, drafted a war resolution that placed a few constraints on the administration's ability to act, making it slightly less likely that America would go to war without international participation, but that stood a better chance of gaining bipartisan support. The White House maneuvered to block the Biden-Lugar bill and got its own passed on a more partisan vote. The strategy of Bush's political adviser, Karl Rove, paid off in November, when the Republicans regained the Senate and added to their majority in the House. But the administration left behind an embittered Democratic minority and an increasingly divided electorate, just as it was preparing to take the country into a major land war.

The president was pursuing two courses at once: to reshape American foreign policy, and to consolidate his party's hold on power. Perhaps it was old-fashioned to point out that these courses might eventually collide, at some risk to national interests. It wasn't impossible yet, in the fall of 2002, to imagine a policy that harnessed both parties and America's democratic allies in defeating tyranny in Iraq. Such a policy would have required the administration to operate with more flexibility and openness than it wanted to. The evidence on unconventional weapons would have had to be laid out without exaggeration or deception. Once the UN inspectors were back in Iraq, they would have had to be allowed to carry out their work rather than be undermined by a campaign of vilification. Testimony to Congress would have had to be candid, not slippery. Administration officials who offered dissenting views or pessimistic forecasts would have had to be heard rather than silenced or fired. Experts in nation building would have had to be welcomed, not shut out, even if they had things to say that the White House didn't want to hear. American citizens would have had to be treated like grown-ups, and not, as Bush's chief of staff Andrew Card once suggested, ten-year-olds.

After the invasion, European allies would have had to be coaxed into joining an effort that desperately needed their help. French, German, and Canadian companies would have had to be invited to bid on contracts, not barred by an order signed by Paul Wolfowitz (who once wrote that American leadership required "demonstrating that your friends will be protected and taken care of, that your enemies will be punished and that those who refuse to support you will live to regret having done so"). American contractors close to the Pentagon would have had to be subjected to extraordinary scrutiny—not just to make sure that billions of dollars weren't wasted in Iraq, but to avoid even the appearance of corruption. Congress would have had to be kept steadily and candidly informed of the situation on the ground. Tony Blair would have had to be given something in exchange for his steadfast support, such as a serious effort at resolving the Israeli-Palestinian problem. The UN would have had to be brought into Iraq as an equal partner, not a tool of American convenience. The top American civilian in Iraq might even have had to be a Democrat, or a moderate Republican such as the retired general Anthony Zinni, whom an administration official privately described as the best-qualified person for the job held by Paul Bremer. ("You've got to rise above politics," the official said. "You've got to pick the best team. You've got to be like Franklin Roosevelt.") Political appointees would have had to be screened out of the occupation authority as much as possible in favor of competent, nonpartisan experts with experience overseas. The occupation authority would have had to focus on Iraqi society rather than serving as an arm of the White House. Its media office's public statements would have had to pass the laugh test every single day.

And when no weapons of mass destruction were found in Iraq, the administration would have had to admit it to the world. President Bush would have had to give a nationally televised speech and, quoting his chief weapons inspector, David Kay, would have had to say, "We were almost all wrong." The president would have had to scratch evasive formulations like "weapons of mass destruction–related program activities" from his State of the Union address. Officials and generals who were responsible for scandal and failure would have had to be given the sack, not a pat on the back or the Medal of Freedom. When reporters asked the president to name one mistake he had made in Iraq, he would have had to name five, while assuring the country that they were being corrected *because* he had been able to identify them. He would have had to summon all his rhetorical skill to explain to the country why, in spite of the failure to find weapons, ending tyranny in Iraq and helping it to become a democracy as the start of change in the Middle East was morally the right thing to do, important for American security, and worthy of a generational effort. In fact, he would have had to explain this *before* the war, when the inspectors were turning up no sign of weapons, thus allowing the country to have a real debate about the real reason for the war, so that when the war came, it would not come amid rampant suspicions and surprises, and America would not be alone in Iraq.

Character is fate. What prevented any of this from happening was, above all, the character of the president. Bush's war, like his administration, like his political campaigns, was run with his own absence of curiosity and self-criticism, his projection of absolute confidence, the fierce loyalty he bestowed and demanded. He always conveyed the impression that Iraq and the war on terror were personal tests. Every time a suicide bomber detonated himself, he was trying to shake George W. Bush's will. If Bush remained steadfast, how could America fail? He liked to call himself a wartime president, and he kept a bust of his hero Winston Churchill in the Oval Office. But Churchill led a government of national unity and offered his countrymen nothing but blood, toil, tears, and sweat. Bush relentlessly pursued the partisan Republican agenda while fighting the war, and what he offered was optimistic forecasts, permanent tax cuts, and his own stirring resolve.

One of Bush's advisers once explained to the journalist Ron Suskind the worldview of the White House. Whereas the nation-building experts and the war critics and Ron Suskind lived "in what we call the reality-based community" where people "believe that solutions emerge from your judicious study of discernible reality," unfortunately "that's not the way the world really works anymore." The way the world now works amounted to a repudiation of reason, skeptical intelligence, the whole slate of liberal Enlightenment values. "We're an empire now, and when we act, we create our own reality. And while you're studying that reality—judiciously, as you will—we'll act again, creating other new realities, which you can study too, and that's how things will sort out. We're history's actors," the aide concluded, "and you, all of you, will be left to just study what we do."

This was the Bush presidency without the inspirational rhetoric, more Leninist than Christian in tone, determined not just to remake the world after its own unexplained will but to sweep away all opponents in the process. Philosophically as well as practically, there was a serious flaw in the project of such an administration becoming the bearer of democratic values to the world. Democracy was inherently self-critical. But because the president always prayed to be "as good a messenger of His will as possible," his Iraq policy would ultimately succeed. By believing so, by appearing to believe so, by forcing such discipline on his administration that no appearance to the contrary ever escaped the seal, he would create the reality that would follow. Faith, hubris, or both, it was a strategy for victory.

I asked Richard Perle whether the top Bush officials ever suffered doubts about Iraq. "We all have doubts all the time," Perle said. "We don't express them, certainly not in a public debate. That would be fatal." Expressing doubts in public would give opponents exactly what they were waiting for. In public, Perle himself essentially said, "I told you so." To a French documentary filmmaker he said, "Most people thought there would be tens of thousands of people killed, and it would be a long and very bloody war. I thought it would be over in three weeks, with very few people killed. Now, who was right?" That was early on. As the war became longer and bloodier, Perle was still right, but in a different way: If only five thousand INC members had gone in with the Americans as he had wanted, if only Ahmad Chalabi had been installed at the head of an interim government at the start, all these problems could have been avoided. Michael Rubin, one of Perle's young protégés, left the Office of Special Plans and then the CPA to start a second career as a writer, and his single subject was the stupidity of officials in the White House, the State Department, and the CIA in botching postwar Iraq by not listening to Michael Rubin and his neoconservative allies in the Pentagon—the agency that ran the occupation. Every key postwar decision was made by Rumsfeld, Wolfowitz, Feith, or Rumsfeld's appointee Bremer. None of them publicly uttered a single doubt, a syllable of self-scrutiny.

Leslie Gelb worked in the Pentagon during the last months of the Johnson presidency, and he directed the writing of the Pentagon Papers, the secret history of the Vietnam War that had been commissioned by Robert McNamara before leaving office. I expressed skepticism to Gelb that Donald Rumsfeld had commissioned anyone at the Pentagon to write a secret history of the Iraq War. "You can bet your bippy," Gelb said with a laugh. "Only liberals look back and say they were wrong." Neoconservatives, by contrast, "say they were stabbed in the back. It's not accidental that President Bush during the campaign couldn't answer the question whether he ever made a mistake. I've never seen those folks say they were wrong. Vietnam was a liberals' war. This is not. They're not dumb—they're very smart. And they're reckless." Comparing Bush to his own boss, Gelb went on, "Johnson was a tragic figure. He was driven by the imperative not to lose the war. He knew he couldn't win. Bush is Johnson squared, because he thinks he can win. Bush is the one true believer. We're talking about a guy essentially cut off from all information except the official line."

The theology of confidence served the president well in domestic politics. Steadfastness in wartime is an essential quality, and after the 2004 election no one could reasonably doubt his ability as a politician. For him, the result validated everything he had done and proved all his critics wrong. "We had an accountability moment," the president said, "and that's called the 2004 election." But in Iraq, which had a reality of its own, the approach didn't work as well.

When Bush spoke, as he did in his acceptance speech at the Republican Convention in September 2004 and again in his inaugural address in January 2005, about the power of freedom to change the world, he was sounding deep notes in the American psyche. His Democratic opponent came nowhere close to making such music. But when Iraq looked nothing like the president's soaring vision—when Iraq was visibly deteriorating, and no one in authority would admit it—the speeches produced either illusion or cynicism in the public. What would determine success or failure in the war was what happened in Iraq and how Iraqis perceived it. The president's relentless assertion that the war was succeeding forced the entire government to fall in line or risk the White House's wrath. So agencies sometimes issued reconstruction reports that prettified the truth, and officials here breathed easier for a while; but the total megawattage in Iraq hadn't changed. Covering up failures only widened the gap in perception between Washington and Baghdad—which, in turn, made Washington less capable of grasping and responding to Iraqi reality. Deception turned into self-deception, until it was hard to know where one ended and the other began. Eventually, the failures announced themselves anyway—in a series of suicide bombings, a slow attrition of Iraqi confidence, a sudden insurrection. War, unlike budget forecasts and presidential campaigns, is merciless with untruth. In refusing to look honestly at Iraq, Bush made defeat there more likely.

He wasn't pandering to the public, as most politicians would have. Unlike Clinton, he always operated from strength, not weakness. (Whether the Churchillian display of determination was in fact an extended case of overcompensation for crippling insecurity, one couldn't say without knowing him intimately.) No one ever seemed to believe the administration line more fervently than the president. But because the line didn't depend on facts, and because the distinction between policy and politics was erased, what Bush wanted Americans to believe often had damaging reverberations in Iraq. Sir Jeremy Greenstock, Tony Blair's envoy in Baghdad, watched governments in Washington and London try to bend Iraq to their own political needs and concluded that the CPA was hampered by its creators. "You have to make decisions on what you do judged against the criteria within and about Iraq, not within and about any other political context," Greenstock told me in his office at the palace just across from Bremer's. "If you want the American and British publics to be happy about the results in Iraq, you don't stare at them and say, 'What do they want next, or how should we judge this event?' You look at Iraq, and you produce the *substance* that will make them happy. You don't produce the presentation that might make them happy tomorrow. To some extent, both the U.S. and the U.K. underplayed the need to judge things by what was happening on the ground."

The advisers around the president understood his strengths and what he needed to know in order to make decisions. On the day before the election, I discussed the White House operation with a senior administration official, who said that the airtight bubble encasing Bush only exaggerated a recent tendency of American presidents. "They're *enshrouded* by yes-men and yes-women who tell them what they want to hear. George Tenet is at the top of the list. People who can smell the political angle and furnish the information that will give the president what the political angle is. No one ever walks into the Oval Office and tells them they've got no clothes on—and persists. You've got to persist. You can't just do it once." He went on, "I think it's dangerous that we have an environment where our principal leader cannot be well informed. It's part and parcel of the office." In this administration more than any other, the official said, the environment "is scary, because of the president and the atmosphere and the people there."

When a transport helicopter was shot down near Falluja in November 2003, killing fifteen soldiers who were flying out on leave, the public waited for the president to make a statement about the single worst combat incident of the war. But Bush said nothing for two days, until, pressed by reporters while he was touring wildfire damage in southern California, he put his hand over his heart and said, "I'm saddened any time someone dies. I'm *saddened*. Because I know a family hurts. And there's a deep pain inside somebody's heart. But I do want to remind the loved ones that their sons and daughters—or the sons, in this case—died for a cause greater than themselves, and a noble cause, which is the security of the United States." The president seemed not to know that two of the soldiers on the helicopter had been women. Another president—Reagan or Clinton—would not have missed such a detail. It wasn't indifference on Bush's part. It was a deliberate strategy of not being told too much, not getting bogged down in the day-to-day problems of the war, not waiting up past midnight like Lyndon Johnson in the Situation Room, the lines visibly deepening in his face, for the casualty figures to come in. Not knowing was part of the strategy for victory. It kept the news from overwhelming the message that the administration put out for each day's cycle, but it also kept the president himself from being distracted and discouraged. And, politically, it worked. Bush never seemed to be a president under siege. It went wrong only when he missed a detail like the postwar plan.

There was, for example, the question of what to do about the

.coffins arriving at Dover Air Force Base. Ever since the invasion of Panama in 1989, when a split screen showed the first President Bush giving a speech alongside the solemn spectacle of dead soldiers coming home, a picture that the White House didn't want, presidents recognized the unsettling power of the image and tried to avoid it. Rumsfeld's Pentagon made the policy official: There would be no photographs or film at Dover. Again, the move achieved a political success in keeping the steady death toll abstract for those Americans who were not personally affected. It played its part in making Iraq a remote war.

I asked Chris Frosheiser what he thought about the policy. He said, "We need to see the coffins, the flag-draped coffins. The hawks need to see it. They need to know there's a price to pay, there's a big price to pay. If they don't have skin in the game, they need to see it. And the doves need to see the dignity of the sacrifice. They don't always see that." He wanted to collect Kurt's posthumous medals, his folded funeral flag, his autopsy report, and a photo of the head wound, and take them on the road in fifteen-minute presentations around the country. He would tell the gung-ho, "Suit up and show up." He would tell the skeptical about the idea of soldier's duty. Or else he wouldn't say anything at all. He simply wanted people to see.

THE IDEA of diminishing the threat to America from ideologies originating in the Middle East by moving the politics of the region toward democracy, beginning in Iraq, had occurred to the Bush administration before the weapons turned out not to exist. Some officials had been thinking and writing about it for years, and the president had sketched it out in a speech at the American Enterprise Institute a month before the invasion. But this was not the casus belli that the American people signed on for, it was not the drumbeat of official statements before the war. So the way the administration shifted the argument later on without ever admitting it had every appearance of a bait and switch.

Still, despite the cynicism of its use, the idea was a serious one, and it deserved to be taken seriously by the political opposition at home and the allies around the world. Instead, the war's critics, including leaders of the Democratic Party, steadily refused to engage the debate. They turned the subject back to the missing weapons, or they scoffed at the administration's sincerity, or they muttered about the dangers of utopianism, or they said nothing. A few Democrats, like Biden, Ambassador Richard Holbrooke, and the editors of *The New Republic*, took up the idea without relenting in their criticism of the administration's conduct in Iraq. This was a difficult mental balancing act, but it was also important, because what Iraqis and democracy needed more than anything in this country was a thoughtful opposition that could hold the Bush administration to its own promises—not in a game of gotcha, but in a real effort to make Iraq a success. Without such an opposition, the negligent and reckless fathers of administration policy would be free to starve their newborn or force-feed it until it choked to death. And, in part because such an opposition never materialized, that's what they continued to do.

The administration had such a talent for polarization that the effects eventually turned inward. Though the public seal remained airtight for a full year after the invasion, internally the bitterness engendered by the ideological battles started to erode the effort in Iraq almost from the start. Colin Powell, the loser of almost every major policy fight, told a morning staff meeting, "We have one priority. That priority is Iraq. What Jerry Bremer asks for, Jerry Bremer gets, and he gets it today. Any questions?" And yet during the life of the CPA, the State Department didn't send all its best people to Iraq, even after the Pentagon's influence waned and Bremer began to use his back channel to Powell more and more. A department official said of the Bureau of Near Eastern Affairs, the archenemy of the neoconservatives, "We didn't do our best job to get things uncocked or to help. I watched NEA, for example, essentially say, 'Okay, you don't want us—fuck you.' And then from there on out it was, 'Let's see what impediments we can put in their way. Let's see how long we can be in delivering this particular commodity or individual or amount of expertise. Let's see how long we can stiff 'em.'"

It was easy to say that the White House, with its strategy of political annihilation, deserved no quarter from its opponents, least of all the Democrats. But the standoff brought out the destructive instincts of each party, and Iraq got the worst of it. Abdication also left the Democratic Party in a bad position, both morally and politically. The party's fortunes during the election year came to depend on Iraq turning into a disaster. When a journalist pointed this out to the antiwar candidate Howard Dean, who was then the front-runner for the nomination, Dean said, "I'm not betting on it, and I'm hoping against it, but there's no indication that I should be expecting anything else." An informed assessment leading to the conclusion that the American presence could only make matters worse, with no chance of a turnaround, deserved a hearing. But what the Democrats offered was something else: a detached and complacent negativism. The election year proved to be the year in which Iraq *did* turn into a disaster, and if the Democrats failed to benefit, it was partly because they had nothing to offer instead, and the public chose not to elect a party whose stance on the most important foreign-policy issue in a generation was arms folded across the chest. Chris Frosheiser ended up voting for Kerry by a hair, more out of party loyalty than anything else, but between Bush's attempts at Lincolnian rhetoric and Kerry's unconvincing multipoint plans, a slender majority of American voters went for jury-rigged hope. Yet the war continued to grow less and less popular.

The cynicism on both sides was bound to reach the troops and inform their political consciousness, which was already being shaped by what they heard and saw and did in Iraq. Especially among many enlisted men and women, the mission became harder over time to understand and justify. When I was in Mahmudiya, I looked up four of Kurt Frosheiser's platoon buddies, including Matt Plumley, who had been next to him in the Humvee the night of his death. We sat down together in a stifling trailer on the base. They were all privates, all but one in their early twenties, and they all expressed a tender and fatalistic affection for the young man they called Fro.

"That incident woke me up," said Marcus Murphy, a blond, soft-spoken Indianan. "These people are trying to kill us."

"It's amazing," Plumley said. "We're here trying to help."

Latrael Brigham, a black soldier from Texas, took Kurt's death as a failure of leadership. "I was pissed off, because we're riding around here with messed-up equipment. If you send men to war, you have to prepare them and equip them so they can fight. And have a vision of the aftermath of the war, have a plan about how you're going to finish it. And not just jump into it. And not put the whole burden on us Americans."

"Dealing with IEDs," said Patrick Weydemuller, a big, quiet Californian who was a few years older than the others. "That's what we're dealing with. We're not dealing with WMDs. We're protecting ourselves from insurgents."

"We got ourselves into something," Brigham said. "I wish I could have some real answers to why we're here, but I don't think I'll ever have them. Not anytime soon."

Plumley, Kurt's best friend in the unit, had a shy manner and a sweet Southern twang. He was less ready than Brigham to write the whole thing off. "If everyone here hated us, there'd be IEDs every five inches." He shook his head. "This urban guerrilla warfare—I joined the military, so I'm being sort of hypocritical, but I liked the isolationism that we had at one time." But when he compared his situation to that of Vietnam veterans, he said, "They had it a lot worse. Their morale was even worse than ours. Right next to Vietnam, this is the worst morale there's been."

"I don't see us changing hundreds of years of religion," Brigham said, "and I don't see us bringing democracy to the region. I just don't. We might be here ten years—depends on the casualties, the body bags coming home."

Weydemuller said, "We're really spreading ourselves thin. I don't think they anticipated any of this. Iraqis were thinking we were going to come here and put up homes and pick up the trash, and a year later the trash is everywhere and nothing's changed."

Murphy said, "I think that's what this country needs, is a big civil war. There's so many religions—we need to leave and let them work it out themselves."

"I think we might have did it too fast," Plumley said.

"I love our democracy," Brigham said, "but we can't impose it."

"I would hate if we did pull out," Plumley told him. "That would be very selfish for our country. We done messed it up."

Brigham said, "I don't think we're going to be here long enough.

The insurgency's going to get worse. We can't stop it. There's always going to be more of them."

I asked them about the meaning of Kurt's death. Plumley, who had missed sitting in Kurt's seat by the accident of losing the race to the Humvee, said that there was a reason why he was alive instead of Kurt, but he didn't know what it was.

Weydemuller, the older man, who had been in the second Humvee, said, "The more when I reflect on what happened—not only him, but a lot of people—was it worth it? Would you do something different? Some missions can wait till the next morning."

Brigham remembered Kurt arriving at basic out of shape and beating him by two minutes in the two mile. But Kurt had worked as hard as anyone to become a soldier.

"I never seen him in a bad mood," Plumley said.

"I think about Fro every day," Brigham said. "Once every day at least."

Plumley was smiling, remembering his friend. He had been the speaker at the Veterans Day memorial who couldn't hold back his tears, and for the first few days he had felt terribly down. "Then I thought: How would Fro want me to be if he could see me? Every time I don't want to do something, think it's stupid—would he think that? No. So he gives me a lot of drive."

They were all quiet. Then they asked how Kurt's family was doing.

FOR CHRIS FROSHEISER, Iraq was an unanswered question about his son and his country. He didn't need to be proved right; he needed to find out what was right, which he defined as honoring Kurt and the other soldiers. The war that had taken his son became one of his essential connections to his son, and he wanted to feel a connection to the soldiers with whom Kurt had served and the country where he had died, too. Nothing irritated Frosheiser more than when someone urged him to get on with his life. His search through poems, song fragments, magazines (he read not just *The New Republic* but the left-wing *In These Times* and the right-wing *American Enterprise*), Army documents, e-mails, the First Armored Division Web site, American history books, tomes on just-war theory, Kurt's belongings, and his own memories was obsessive and a little frantic. "What was my son involved in? Was it right?" he asked. "I'm looking for an account of it that can sit well in my mind and in my heart. I'm proud of Kurt's service. But the whole thing—were these guys misused? And for what?" He never made it easy for himself.

My correspondence with Frosheiser was rare and welcome. He wrote not just as a father but also as a citizen, as if he were cut from some older cloth that you didn't find much anymore. But e-mail didn't prepare me for the raw grief that was waiting in Des Moines when I went out to see him over Memorial Day weekend 2004. Within minutes of picking me up at the airport, Frosheiser was in tears, he was in tears when I left his apartment two days later, and in between there were tears, too. His narrow blue eyes were always red rimmed behind glasses, his fair skin raw with faint lines etched in his cheeks, his nose stuffed up. His voice was thick with Chicago roots and emotion; a sentence could erupt with a nervous laugh that broke into a sob and then came under control again to its end.

We drove a few miles east of Des Moines to the new development of Altoona, where there was a cookout in the driveway of his daughter's neighbors (it was the kind of place where they continued bringing over food and taking out her trash months after the funeral). Erin smiled when she saw her father's condition. "Not already, Dad." After dinner, we went to Erin and her husband Mike's house and sat around the dining room table, where there was a spread of Kurt's younger photos, his graduation portrait from Fort Knox standing in uniform in front of a Bradley, his combat patches, his "Killed in Action" banner framed in red, his Purple Heart and Bronze Star, and his tricornered funeral flag in a wooden frame.

Erin, a woman in her early thirties with a direct blue-eyed gaze, was having trouble explaining things to her small children. Her five-year-old son, Colin, kept asking, "Why didn't he shoot them? Why are they there?" Her younger child, Madelyn, wouldn't remember Kurt. Erin had been trying hard to picture Iraq, the lives of Iraqi mothers, the dangers they lived with. "I have trouble imagining anyone's life but mine. Does that sound selfish?" she said. "Sometimes I fear it's going to keep going until we blow up the world. And I wish we had a better plan." When she first saw the photos from Abu Ghraib, she said, "I thought: They blew up my brother—more power to them. Then more rational thoughts came up: We're trying to win them over, and this humiliation isn't helping our cause." She supported the war, but on a bad day in April when twelve Americans were killed, she thought: "We've got to get out. I don't want other families to go through what we went through. But what do you accomplish? Because we lost Kurt for *nothing* then."

For her father, the great challenge was simply to keep going. "This one-day-at-a-time thing works for me. I get in trouble when I start thinking: How am I going to get through these days and weeks and seasons?"

"Most days I just pretend like it didn't happen," Erin said.

"Me, too. Sometimes I think it didn't happen—just for a minute. Then I know it did."

The alarm on Kurt's watch went off.

"Tomorrow should be painless," Frosheiser said.

"I think they're just going to read off the names."

Frosheiser and I drove back to Des Moines. His apartment felt smaller than it was, because it lacked natural light and had become the cluttered repository for all of Kurt's things, his clothes and sports gear, his CDs stacked next to his father's old records and books, his memorial spurs, plaques, medals, flags. Frosheiser had been sleeping on the living room couch, as if keeping a vigil, since the day he left for basic training. I slept in Kurt's room. A dust-covered black U.S. Army shaving kit was on the toilet tank; in the closet, desert and jungle fatigues hung above desert combat boots, winter-weather boots, and a guitar. It was a long time before I fell asleep.

THE GRAVE WAS A PATCH of dark earth and green grass, surrounded by the graves of veterans of earlier wars, little Memorial Day flags planted in each of them and fluttering in the breeze of a beautiful Midwestern spring morning. Frosheiser, in nylon blue sweats, saluted. "Hey, buddy," he said, kneeling to run his hand over the stone marker, which was engraved with a cross and the words

KURT RUSSELL FROSHEISER
PV2 US ARMY
IRAQ
JUL 10 1981 NOV 8 2003
PURPLE HEART

"It was hard to keep the snow off it because it kind of built up all winter. When the dirt was soft, you could press it and leave your hand-prints. That was a good thing." He was talking to the grave now. "It's less painful trying to forget it, but you have to keep remembering. Random thing, just a random thing. Kurt said, 'Live your life, old man,' and that could mean I'd be a bitter son of a gun, and I don't want that. That could very easily happen." He was adjusting the long-life candle under blue glass. "We know that people live on in our hearts, but do they live on in another way? We just don't know the answer to that." He slowly got to his feet, and we walked back to the car. "What does it all mean? It means nothing. How we respond is what it means."

The ceremony in the park next to the state capitol was attended by a small crowd, including a number of old men in veterans' caps. The woman from the organizing committee recognized Frosheiser and escorted him over to a row of folding chairs, where he exchanged awkward greetings with his ex-wife. Jeanie was wearing a jacket with an image of the American flag and the words "These Colors Don't Run," but her face was crumpled with grief. A politician gave a short speech, and then the names of the fourteen Iowans killed in Iraq were read out. Frosheiser stood in line to place a rose beneath an M-16 stuck bayonet-first into the ground with a helmet perched on top, as at the service in Baghdad.

We drove across the state to his ex-wife's niece's high school grad-uation party in a small town toward the Illinois border (he wanted to keep family relationships as strong as possible, especially now). We passed lush rolling green hills, grain silos, seed factories, fields of early corn and baled hay, with the shadows of fleecy white clouds that raced across a blue sky. The dream landscape and the freedom of the road seemed to set Frosheiser's thoughts loose a little ways from the morn-ing's burdens. He was reading a book called *Paris 1919*, about the aftermath of the First World War, when Iraq was created at Versailles by T. E. Lawrence, Gertrude Bell, and others. Sir Arnold Wilson, the first colonial commissioner of Iraq, disagreed with his assistant Bell about a number of things, but he kept her on in Baghdad and valued her knowledge. "So when I hear this Tom Warrick was totally excluded from the process—*what?*" Frosheiser said. "Why? We need all the information we can get. When you're talking about sending Kurt Frosheiser to Iraq, a piece of metal goes through his head into his brain, and you've got his parents back here in Des Moines, Iowa—by God, you'd better go in with the best information you've got."

He began musing about the large ideas that had been nowhere near his mind during the memorial ceremony. "I wonder what Bush in private thinks about being against nation building, and now he's waist-deep in it. What is that—paradox or irony?" Since America was extending itself so deeply into other countries, he wanted us to be as shrewd and skillful as we were powerful, with a whole cadre of Gertrude Bells educated in the humanities and capable of working overseas. "I was thinking of that song the other day, 'Ain't Gonna Study War No More.' Maybe we should study it. Otherwise, we're going to screw it up. Because it's going to be our kids and grandkids doing it." He had heard the new Bush foreign policy described as Wilsonian, an inspiring term. "There's this phrase, 'America the great and the just.' Reagan used to talk about 'the city on the hill.' The first time I heard Condi Rice talking about democracy in Iraq, I got chills up my back. But then you ask, 'How do you do it? Is it necessary?' " Frosheiser drove in silence for a while, and when he spoke again his voice was quieter. "That's where I kind of run up against a wall with regard to Kurt."

I asked what he meant.

"Kurt's life—was he worth that? I'd say no. He was more important than that. So I pull back."

That night, back at his apartment in Des Moines, we were watching CNN—thirteen deaths in Iraq over the holiday weekend—when the phone rang. It was Matt Van Buren, the driver of Kurt's Humvee, calling from Germany, where he was still recovering from his shrapnel wounds. Frosheiser muted the TV sound and sat up in his rocking chair. The stress of the day had left him with a headache. "I'm not sure what I can ask you," he said. "Let me know if I go too far." On the other end, Van Buren was describing that night. "He got whacked on the head pretty good, he never had much of a chance," Frosheiser said. "I understand that. He got hit in the wrong place. He wasn't able to talk after he was hit, was he?" Listening, he broke into a sob. "But he was trying? Yeah, that sounds like him. He was a good guy. We're proud of him. They had nothing better to do so they went out? I believe it. Yeah, I believe it."

In the morning I would stop intruding, fly home, and leave Chris Frosheiser to get through another day of relics and memories and impossible questions. But just now, I was watching his muted television: terror attacks in Saudi Arabia, gun battles outside Najaf, Special Forces operations in Afghanistan, Memorial Day ceremonies in America. Without sound, these felt like scenes from a war that had already receded into history.

Frosheiser hung up the phone. "Van Buren says he tried to talk but couldn't. He fought hard to keep alive." Frosheiser had never heard this before, and he seemed unsure whether or not to believe it, whether or not to welcome it. He called Erin with the news, but she'd had enough emotion for one day and quickly got off the phone. Frosheiser sat back in his rocking chair. "I can't think about this too much," he said, "but if Kurt had made it through that night, he would be alive today."

12

SIMPLE CITIZENS

ALMOST A YEAR AFTER first meeting Dr. Baher Butti, the psychiatrist in Baghdad, I visited his tidy middle-class house in Dora, a neighborhood south of the Tigris that was dominated by the four smokestacks of a power plant and that had become an insurgent stronghold. We sat in the living room, and while their daughter watched Arabic monster cartoons on TV, Butti and his wife, Balsam, told me that they were thinking about leaving Iraq. Many people they knew, especially Christians like them, had taken their children abroad. Butti had a brother in the United Arab Emirates who could help them settle there. Kidnappings of professional people had grown into an epidemic, but the problem was also more basic, more quotidian, than that. Balsam had been told by the director of the primary health center where she worked as a doctor to stop wearing a tight red dress to work. Their neighbor, a Shiite music teacher, had been instructed by her boss to put on a veil. Butti had been obliged to ask a Shiite friend to mediate a dispute after Butti had cut the salary of a corrupt employee at the long-term-care hospital. The employee had threatened Butti, and Butti's friend, who was a tribal sheikh, had entered negotiations with a sheikh from the employee's tribe. Butti had no sheikh of his own—

he was a Christian—so he had to go to a Shiite for protection. These were things that foreigners seldom knew, but they were daily life for Iraqis like Dr. Butti and his wife.

In this atmosphere, Butti was turning for support to his own tribe, an organization of Iraqi Christians called the Chaldo-Assyrian Council. He had never before embraced his religious identity, but now he had nowhere else to go. Just to get a few cans of beer for our evening together, we had stopped by a Christian private club where he knew and trusted people, since most of the liquor stores in Baghdad had shut down after firebombings and shootings. His ideas for the Gilgamesh Center for Creative Thinking and other civic organizations had come to nothing. After a day of work and three hours in traffic, he was too exhausted to follow through on a notion of setting up a local block watch. "It's also a sort of selfishness that came in the last ten years of Saddam," he said. Everyone was focused on survival, on his own private struggle. New political parties and civic groups soon broke up over arguments and personal conflicts, or collapsed for lack of energy. Iraq's "technocrats," Butti said, were powerless, and the Americans, with bigger problems on their hands, had forgotten them.

Toward the end of 2004, it became almost impossible to work the way I always had in Iraq. Long meals in private houses were out; most home visits of any kind were out. Wandering around neighborhoods was out, as was any travel that wasn't carefully planned, targeted, and short. Conversations with strangers on the street or in a hospital or at a university were out. I was as dangerous to them as they were to me.

The media strategy of the insurgency eluded me. Like the CPA's Iraq Media Network, it failed at the level of understanding its audience. Since the ultimate arbiter of a guerrilla war was the public in both countries, and since the American public's willingness to tolerate the carnage in Iraq declined throughout the year 2004, why intimidate those best able to bring the story of that carnage back to the country of the occupier until they had no choice but to leave Iraq, as more and more journalists were doing? I once asked an Iraqi businessman with ties to the insurgency about this. He agreed that it was a bad policy to kidnap and behead journalists. "We are trying our best to moderate people, to keep them from extremes," he said, sounding like a man who had his hands full with unreliable business partners. Perhaps the insurgents wanted to maintain a siege mentality among the press corps in Baghdad, knowing that reporters tended to see the bigger picture in darker tones when their own security was threatened. (Paul Wolfowitz once criticized the press for being too scared to go out and find all the positive stories, the only statement about Iraq for which he ever apologized.) Or perhaps the intimidation was explained by the jihadis' sheer indiscriminate hatred of all infidels, and by the larger failure of the insurgency to arrive at a political strategy more coherent than fear.

The result was that foreigners were cut off from Iraqis. The bright light switched on by the fall of the regime seemed to be dimming by the day, with Iraq receding back into the shadows where Saddam had kept it for decades. If you were honest about it, you had to admit that you knew less and less about the thinking of Iraqis and the circumstances of their lives. "No foreigner really knows what is going on in Iraq," wrote Rory Stewart, a former British CPA official and Arabic speaker. "I certainly don't know what is going on in Iraq." Even the Iraqis on whom foreigners relied to explain the country to them—politicians, translators, those who could leave and come back—might have little idea about their compatriots living in the rural areas and slums, where the only security forces were insurgents or militias.

But this was exactly where the drama that mattered was being played out: in the minds of ordinary people. As the American faces in power gave way to Iraqi ones, how would the Iraqis respond? Would they begin to see the government as something that belonged to them and had to answer to them? Would they dare support it, even participate in it, or hang back out of their old instinct for survival?

These were abstract questions, but they led quite directly to the most interesting stories, the ones that kept me coming back to Iraq. The only justification for the war left standing, in my view, was the creation of a government that would give Iraqis the better lives they deserved. It would have to be democratic, but it would have to fill in the bare forms of democracy with substance. It would require more than the palace intrigues and backroom deals that were Iraqi politics under the CPA and the interim government. It would require the involvement of those ordinary people who had become so hard to know. If, by the end of 2004, with huge explosions and terrible casualties and the discovery of mass graves a daily occurrence, there was any will left at all to push ahead with the transformation of Iraq, the credit didn't belong to the Americans or the Iraqi political elite. It belonged to ordinary Iraqis, who, after so much suffering, were apparently capable of toughing out this, too.

The problem all along was that the strongest people in Iraq were the extremists with guns and militias. The most open-minded Iraqis were the weakest. From the start, Iraqi politics evolved in a way that was disfigured and illusory, though not all that unusual after totalitarianism. At the top were a handful of men in their sixties and seventies, mostly representatives of the former exile parties, who commanded backing along narrow ethnic and sectarian lines. (Ahmad Chalabi, who had almost no support of any kind inside Iraq, stopped talking about universal rights, attached himself to the Shiite bloc, became a champion of Moqtada al-Sadr, and revived his fortunes after the U.S. government dumped him and raided his house in Baghdad. Even Chalabi's harshest critics had to admire the man's shrewd opportunism.) These were the politicians whom the Americans dealt with—power brokers with armed militias—whatever the talk of liberal democracy might have been in the Pentagon, the White House, the think tanks, and the writings of Kanan Makiya. Bremer and his aide, Meghan O'Sullivan, put their time and energy into cultivating the leaders of the Shiite religious parties, Dawa and the Supreme Council for the Islamic Revolution in Iraq, which had thousands of men under arms. The American officials visited these leaders' houses and paid them special attention on the Governing Council, with the idea that, if the CPA could keep them inside the tent, it could have some influence over the outcome.

Instead, out in the streets, where the Americans had little control and little knowledge, the militias of the religious parties vied with Moqtada al-Sadr's followers for power. Mosques, hospitals, and schools were taken over by armed men chanting ominous slogans; women were threatened, and worse, for their un-Islamic appearance, or even for being out of the house. Inside the Green Zone, long hours of negotiation about the role of Islam and women's rights in the new state; outside the Green Zone, a harsh social code enforced by vigilante rule. Then there was the Sunni insurgency, which made sure that only the bravest, most dedicated citizens would dare show their faces at a public meeting.

In these circumstances, the growth of anything like normal civic life was impossible. The Iraqis one hoped would come to the fore—those with more democratic ideas but without powerful backers—remained off to the side, waiting to see which way things went. A tough old doctor named Mahmoud Othman, who was a Kurdish independent on the Governing Council, once said to me, "The country now is ruled by militias, mullahs, and warlords. The simple citizen is not allowed to have his own rights, to say freely what he wants." He put part of the blame on the Americans. "They are not caring much for a simple Iraqi citizen. They care for a chief of a tribe here, a mullah there, a religious man here, a militiaman here, head of a party there."

IT WAS POSSIBLE to find Iraqis who were already coming forward to lay claim to their country's political future. They were few in number, vastly outmatched in money and power by the parties and the militias, and they were, I thought, the toughest people on earth. Sometimes there were Americans ready to support them.

The National Democratic Institute was an organization funded largely by the U.S. government and affiliated with the Democratic Party; it operated with relative independence, under the direction of the National Endowment for Democracy. The institute's purpose was to find the "simple citizens" in a place like Iraq and help them to participate in democratic political life. This tended to be obscure, poorly funded work, but the Bush administration was trying to pour half a billion dollars into Iraq for "democracy-building" programs before the national elections. The escalation of violence made it hard to spend the money.

Early one morning, I drove to Hilla, ninety minutes south of Baghdad, with a group of Iraqis and Americans working for NDI. We traveled in unarmored vehicles, without guards. In the backseat of one of the sedans, wearing a navy blue suit, a salmon-colored tie, and glasses, was David Dettman, a pale, chain-smoking political consultant from Ohio. For years, Dettman, who was thirty-three and had the nervous, self-deprecating sense of humor of a Jack Lemmon character, had worked successfully as a campaign consultant. Then he ran for the Ohio state legislature as a Democrat, got creamed, and had an epiphany. "What got me charged up is that I really believed in the process," he said. He decided to leave the world of cold-blooded operatives and became one of NDI's democratization missionaries, posted in Ukraine (where, at the end of 2004, his work would bear fruit in the Orange Revolution that overthrew Ukraine's corrupt government). To the dismay of his wife, his mother, and his boss, Dettman had come to Iraq for two weeks to train groups of aspiring political party activists in Baghdad, Tikrit, and Hilla.

The workshop in Hilla took place in the city's former secret-police headquarters, which had become a human-rights center. Forty Iraqis—including a political science professor and an unemployed sports instructor—had traveled at some risk to attend the class. They listened intently and took careful notes as Dettman stood, shoulders hunched, before a flip chart and presented his ten-step program on message development and voter contact. Mayasa al-Naimy, an Iraqi staff member of NDI, gamely translated the exotic campaign terminology: "earned media," "communications strategy," "wedge and base issues." Dettman had told me earlier, "Politics is the art of getting people to vote for you. It's applicable all over the world. If it wasn't, I wouldn't have a job."

After two hours of discussion, an Iraqi raised his hand. "This shows me we're making a transition from dictatorship to democracy," he said. "That makes me feel good. But this is the question: Will the American administration leave it to us? Or just throw someone on us? Will all these efforts be lost?"

Outside, in the distance, there was an explosion—mortar fire—and then a second, closer one, followed by gunfire. Dettman glanced out the window and grinned with alarm.

"Does that answer your question?" someone asked.

"I'm not the government," Dettman said. "I'm NDI. We have to eat lunch. Can we talk about this later?"

After lunch, Dettman returned to the question. "My opinion is if America invaded Iraq for nothing other than to have a friendly dictator, then all of the American and Iraqi lives that were lost will have been wasted," he said. "I supported the invasion because I'm in the democratization business. I don't know anything about WMD—I don't know if anyone was telling the truth or not—but I do know the Iraqi people deserve freedom. I can't say the Americans won't do anything wrong, because they already have done many things wrong in this occupation. And I'm sorry. But there's a reason NDI is here now, and there's a reason we didn't bring a tank. We're the least armed Americans in Hilla. We're here trusting your hospitality. Because democracy is good and right." He went on, "And if this traumatic war was fought for anything other than that, I'm gonna be mad. Here's the problem: I can't do much. I'm just the arrogant American in a suit standing up in front of you. I haven't suffered as much as you have. Only you can build democracy here. But if I just thought America was going to steal the freedom we fought for, I would have stayed home with my wife and had a lovely time."

"Aren't you having a lovely time here?" someone asked.

"I am having a lovely time. But I miss my wife."

It was a heartfelt speech, and it was received with scattered applause. Then a man sitting near me muttered to himself, "A British guy named Hempher laid plans decades ago for presidents to take turns ruling Iraq."

The people in the room belonged to what Dr. Shaker, the forensic-medicine specialist at the Baghdad morgue, called "the middle level of mind." They were neither mullahs nor militiamen, and some of the parties they belonged to counted no more than several hundred members. They were hardly cast in the image of Western liberals; they wanted more religion in their government than the board members of the National Democratic Institute would likely have preferred. There were only three women present. The mention of Hempher, the supposed British spy blamed for so much trouble in the Muslim world, showed that these Iraqis were as prone to a sense of powerlessness and the conspiracy theories it gave rise to as most others. But what really mattered was that they had made the decision to take part in political life.

One of the participants was Jawdet al-Obeidi, a former army officer from Hilla. He fled Iraq after taking part in the Shiite uprising in 1991 and ended up in Portland, Oregon. He started a small limousine company there, and in 2003 he sold it and returned to Iraq, as a member of a militia aligned with the U.S. invasion force. In Iraq, Obeidi poured $150,000 of his savings into building a coalition of almost two hundred small political parties to challenge the larger parties in the national elections. The coalition's platform combined a moderate Muslim agenda with Iraqi nationalism and a respect for individual rights, a deliberately mild mixture that seemed designed to have broad support. Obeidi, a balding, middle-aged man with a salesman's cheerfulness, had received death threats, and his brother-in-law survived three bullets in the head.

Also at the meeting was a married couple from Mahawil, a village of dirt roads and salt marshes a few miles north of Hilla: Emad Dawood, who worked in a shop selling construction materials, and his wife, Saad, who had received a business degree in Baghdad but was unable to find work and was now raising their three children. Like the other women at the meeting, she covered her head.

Her husband explained to me, "We go everywhere together."

"Any educated couple would do this," Saad said.

"Of course, we have religion, and we go by the rules," Emad added. "The Islamic religion doesn't say women can't mix with other men, but everything has to do with limits."

Saad pointed out that Islam didn't deny women the right to participate in politics: "They should have a role in everything."

In Hilla, the repression of the 1991 Shiite uprising had been particularly brutal, and in 2003 mass graves containing thousands of victims were uncovered on the periphery of the town. Saad and Emad had each lost a brother and many friends. The couple had only the vaguest notion of what was in Iraq's interim constitution, but they knew very well what it was like to live under Saddam. "It's like a hammer on your head every day," Emad said, "and then they take it away."

The Dawoods had once seen the Americans as heroic liberators, but the feeling was short-lived. According to Emad, as the occupation ground on, with constant power outages and rampant crime, ordinary unhappiness was turning into a kind of insanity. "Things are just getting worse here," Saad added. "Of course, if there was democracy, things would change."

"But democracy needs a long period of time," Emad said, "because we've been living so long under Saddam."

"Most people do not get the idea of democracy," Saad said. "Ask anybody about democracy, and you'd find most people would say, 'What am I going to do with democracy? Give me security first.'"

Emad said, "I know a guy who shot two bullets at random. He said, 'Isn't this freedom?'"

As for Dettman's presentation, it clearly meant something to this couple that Americans had come to meet with them in Hilla. Dettman had given them a lot of helpful information, they felt. Their only complaint was that there was no exam at the end, to test how much they'd learned about democracy.

The chances of the people at the meeting in Hilla having any immediate success on the political stage were poor. Marina Ottoway, an expert with the Carnegie Endowment for International Peace in Washington, said that, after the fall of dictatorships, "You always have a lot of political parties forming, and they never get anywhere. For that reason," she added, NDI was "bravely doing something that is completely futile." But electoral success wasn't the only measure of its effect. In Hilla, it felt like an achievement simply to hold a discussion, amid gunfire, about democracy, in which there was a genuine give-and-take between Iraqis and foreigners. Les Campbell, NDI's Middle East director, said, "Even with all the problems in Iraq, there is already more civil society space and party organizing than in any other Arab country by orders of magnitude." He described how NDI's Iraqi staff members, such as Mayasa al-Naimy, had begun to blossom intellectually. "Even in the midst of the killings, which are terrible, and even though the planning and administration continue to be a joke, something interesting is going on here. And it makes me sort of sick to think it might not work."

I WENT BACK TO IRAQ one more time in January of 2005. The national elections that Ayatollah Sistani had been demanding ever since the fall of the regime were finally going to happen. The Bush administration, having resisted for the better part of a year and a half, had become their strongest advocate, and the date of January 30, 2005, was now set in stone.

There had been good reasons for delaying elections. The best-armed, best-organized groups, with funding from Iran, Syria, and Saudi Arabia, had all the advantage over the less sectarian or extreme ones, such as those I had seen in Hilla. There were examples in recent history—Bosnia was one—where precipitous postwar elections had simply enshrined the least democratic forces in power for years to come. UN experts had been as wary as American officials of early elections. But as with every other plan for Iraq, events ran out of control and overwhelmed the bright ideas of people in Washington and Baghdad. Former CPA officials began to say privately that the big mistake had been the failure to hold local elections at the start of the occupation. If Iraqis had been able to vote for their local councils soon after the fall of the regime, and then provincial councils, and finally a national government, they would have become participants in Iraq's politics in a way that never happened, and the occupation might have gone very differently. But it was much too late for alternative scenarios.

Instead, the country's first democratic vote would take place almost two years after the invasion, in less than ideal circumstances. Even after a Marine assault in November of 2004 pried Falluja out of jihadi control, the insurgents only seemed to gain strength as they expanded company-size operations from Anbar province to Mosul and took over large areas of Baghdad itself. In Washington there was a new conventional wisdom: Not only was there a full-blown guerrilla war in Iraq, but America was losing it (Colin Powell was reported to have said this to friends). Iraqis would have to vote under the direst threats. The Jordanian terrorist Abu Musab al-Zarqawi recorded a statement, posted on the Internet, that declared war on the Iraqi elections, calling democracy an evil form of polytheism that replaced God with politicians, a conspiracy of "crusader harlots" and Shiite "rejectionist pigs." Anonymous leaflets scattered around the capital threatened to "wash the streets of Baghdad with the voters' blood. To those of you who think you can vote and run away, we will shadow you and catch you, and we will cut off your heads and the heads of your children." In most parts of the country, the essential elements of an election campaign—public meetings, voter education, parades, door-to-door canvassing—were nearly impossible. The parliamentary lists kept the names of most candidates secret in order to protect their lives; voters would hardly know whom they were choosing to represent them. A team of international observers announced that it would monitor the Iraqi elections from Amman, hundreds of miles away in another country. The administration had defined its project for democracy in the Middle East so far downward that it seemed as if the elections would be a bloody exercise in going through the motions.

Amman was my point of entry and exit on trips to Iraq. It was a blessedly dull city where the stoplights worked and there were no police checkpoints. At the Four Seasons Hotel, the elevator music and turned-down bedspreads and buffet breakfasts were dreamlike luxuries. The desk clerks were trained to say, "Welcome back, Mr. Packer," and it always gave me a cheap pleasure to be personally welcomed to a place where I could let down my guard. Tame Amman, with its pleasant hilltop air and dyed-blond Arab women, was the closest thing the Iraq War had to Bangkok. In the plush lobby of the Four Seasons you always met journalists on their way in or out, international aid workers biding their time while they monitored the violence, Iraqi government officials holding meetings that would have been too dangerous in Baghdad, and Iraqi exiles sitting deep in armchairs, sipping Turkish coffee, glancing around with vaguely conspiratorial looks and all the time in the world on their hands.

By the beginning of 2005 there were at least three hundred thousand Iraqis in Jordan, and housing prices in Amman had skyrocketed. Some were escapees from the violence, usually with an unpleasant experience like burglary or kidnapping in their recent past. Others were just taking a breather, as if Jordan were a spa where fortunate Iraqis could go to have their nervous breakdowns. And still others were Sunnis unhappy with the new order of things in Iraq, where Shiite and Kurdish politicians seemed poised to take over their country. Some of these Sunnis had connections to the insurgency; a few were among its leaders.

I stayed in Amman for a few days this time before going on to Baghdad. I wanted to talk with the Sunnis, which had become difficult and risky inside Iraq. Most of their leaders—an assortment of party politicians and conservative imams—were boycotting the elections. Some candidates had withdrawn under threat, and others made the political calculation that boycott and violence would reduce their vote totals to humiliating levels. The hard-liners rejected the whole notion of an election held under occupation. But the insurgency had always been driven in part by the loss of Sunni group power, and as the elections drew near, its sectarian character became glaringly obvious. The Shiite south and Kurdish north were eager to vote. In the Sunni center, if people wanted to go to the polls, they kept their plans for election day to themselves. Real political leadership among the Sunnis, capable of persuading the alienated and armed that the political game was their only hope, did not yet exist. One evening in Amman, I had dinner with Ghassan Salamé, the late Sergio Vieira de Mello's political adviser. When I mentioned the underdeveloped state of Sunni politics in Iraq compared with that of the Shia and the Kurds, Salamé replied by asking me to name the Sunni faction leader in the Lebanese civil war. "You can't," he said. "Sunnis don't see themselves as one among many factions. They see themselves as power. They consider themselves the inheritors of the Ottoman Empire. This is not going to change."

Through the good graces of a former Baathist embassy official who had been close to Uday, I met a group of Sunnis from Anbar province who were vaguely connected to the insurgency. Two were tribal sheikhs from Ramadi; the third was a young businessman rumored to have been one of Saddam's bagmen. We met in the offices of his holding company on a quiet Amman street. The businessman, Talal al-Gaaod, had a master's in construction management from USC, wore jeans and suspenders, and was up on the latest op-eds from the American press. All of them presented themselves as anxious to build a democratic Iraq. They had nothing against Americans; they had long dreamed of the good things America could bring to Iraq, and they had welcomed the overthrow of the regime. "I am a believer in the Americans' good intentions," Gaaod said, "but something happened on the way from Washington to Baghdad." The whole guerrilla war was a terrible misfortune that needn't have happened if only the Americans had listened to people like them instead of invading their houses and dishonoring their women and compelling the Iraqis to seek revenge.

Gaaod admitted that some of the insurgents were living in the Middle Ages, extremists who gave the rest of them a bad name. But the legitimate resistance, as they called it, was an Iraqi resistance against occupation. It included two hundred thousand people, and if the elections went ahead, Gaaod said, it would increase tenfold. The civil war would become quite real. These were hardly the masked cutthroats of my imagination. They were recognizable Iraqis, the tribal sheikhs traditional, the businessman modern, and they had far more connections to my world than I had thought possible.

Then the underside began to emerge. One of the sheikhs, Zaydan Halef al-Awad, claimed that the Sunnis were the majority in Iraq—63 percent, in fact. "If Sunnis settled in America, they would rule America," the sheikh said. "We always carry the stick in the middle. We can move it any way—we control it." The politicians running for office in Iraq, Kurdish and Shiite, were illegitimate pawns of the Americans or the Iranians, and if they happened to be assassinated, too bad for them.

Gaaod distributed copies of boycott declarations issued by most of the major Sunni tribes.

"What if some people in the tribes want to vote?" I asked.

"They cannot."

"What would happen to them?"

"If anybody goes to vote, he will be killed."

THE IMMIGRATION OFFICER at the Amman airport looked at my passport, looked at me, and pointed to his temple. "Iraq. Iraq. Head—no head." There were several ways to interpret this, none of them reassuring. The charter flight to Baghdad, with its South African crew, was full nevertheless. There were always people ready to go to Iraq, most of them drawn by the money. In the seats around me I noted a group of grizzled construction contractors with Southern accents wearing baseball caps, and another group of beefy young security guys with iPods. Farther back there were South Asians and Iraqis. In the front row sat Hoshyar Zebari, Iraq's Kurdish foreign minister. The journalist next to me was chewing a piece of gum as if she was determined to destroy it. No one spoke. "We'll follow a zigzag course all the way to

Baghdad," the captain announced cheerfully. "Once we get overhead, we'll spiral down."

Baghdad was in a state of dread. There were more roadblocks than ever, more Apaches buzzing the city from low overhead. The last Humvee in the American convoys now displayed a sign that said, in English and Arabic, "Stay 100 meters back or you will be shot." Campaign posters of Prime Minister Allawi and of the coalition that Ayatollah Sistani had assembled covered the walls and hung from the streetlights, but all the election talk was of security measures and bloodbaths. I spent two nights at the Rashid Hotel, which meant that for the first time I slept inside the Green Zone, and being sealed off from Iraq only heightened the sense of anxiety. The Rashid was under the command of Lieutenant Colonel E. A. Strosky, of the Army Reserve and the Buffalo electrical utility. Strosky, a small, exasperated man with a big mustache, asked each new guest, "Do you want a room on the bullet side or the mortar side?" The house rules were: no communications equipment in the rooms, no visitors, no conversation with military personnel, stay off other floors and out of the canteen. "You are here to eat and live in a safe place," Strosky said. "If there's a mortar or rocket attack, go into the bathroom. A Gurkha will come to explain what is happening." For security reasons I was told to sign in under the name "Strosky #494." "Forget about logic here," he said. The war seemed to have entered the $M^*A^*S^*H$ phase—on my next trip, I would expect Lieutenant Colonel Strosky to be wearing a dress.

MY DESTINATION WAS BASRA, Iraq's largely Shiite second city, in the country's far southeastern corner. I wanted to see the elections where it would be possible to move around with some freedom, and where they would have more to do with politics than killing. I flew down in a British military transport plane. Basra was in the British sector. That interested me, too.

The flatness of the light told you that the Persian Gulf coast was only an hour away. The water table in this marshy region was so high that Basra depended on a system of canals for drainage. But the canals were blocked, and on one winter day a hard rain submerged whole neighborhoods under several feet of water and sewage; a week later, the flooding ebbed, turning the streets to mud and the city into a picture of soggy neglect. The poverty in Basra, surrounded by most of Iraq's oil reserves as well as export-crop plantations, was on an African or Asian scale. Clay houses that had proliferated illegally jostled for space amid the garbage heaps of the Shiite flats; they provided shelter to families that had been driven from the marshes drained by Saddam after 1991. The city center was choked with decaying shops and the ruins of concrete government buildings that were hit by American air strikes during the invasion. Near the Ashar mosque, an Islamic group had taken over a park with a derelict Ferris wheel and a sun-bleached tyrannosaurus. Looted buildings overlooked the banks of the Shatt al-Arab waterway, which emptied the waters of the Tigris and Euphrates into the Persian Gulf. Downstream, toward the gulf, was the domed palace complex that Saddam had built and allegedly visited only once. It was now occupied by the British and American regional embassies.

One mild, breezy evening, I visited the Corniche, the old street that ran along the waterway, and stood with my back to a row of concrete blast walls. Flocks of white egrets flew above the rusting smugglers' trawlers that floated alongside the wreckage of an Iraqi navy pilot boat. The moon was rising over the palm trees on the far bank, with Iran hidden a few miles beyond them, and it was almost possible to imagine the city at my back as the rich center of international trade that it once was. Basra's modern history was perhaps more tragic than any other city's, yet this same history had prepared Basra to be the testing ground for the future of political power in Iraq.

In 1982, in the second year of the twentieth century's longest conventional war, two young Iraqi army officers from Basra, Youssef al-Emara and Majid al-Sary, slipped separately across the border and defected to Iraq's enemy, Iran. Emara was a thirty-three-year-old major, Sary a twenty-year-old lieutenant. Like most people in southern Iraq, they were Shia; otherwise, they could not have been more different. Emara, bearded, stocky, and square headed, with the wary manner of a man long involved in underground politics, was a strict Muslim and bore a prayer bruise in the middle of his forehead. His intention in defecting was to fight to spread Iran's Islamic revolution to his own country. Sary, for his part, kept his cleft chin clean shaven; he was a dapper dresser who laughed and cried easily. As a young man, he liked to drink and chase women. Basra was then a cosmopolitan port with spice shops owned by South Asian merchants and nightclubs with Egyptian bartenders and Kuwaiti patrons; it had been a congenial place for him, until the war. Sary fled Iraq to escape the brutality of Saddam's regime and the pointless war it had launched.

Emara and Sary first met in an Iranian town east of Tehran, where they and other Iraqi defectors decided to form an opposition group. But they couldn't agree whether to call it the Free Officers Movement or, as Emara wanted, the Free Islamic Officers Movement. In the end, Emara's faction prevailed, and Sary was pushed out of the organization, which came under the control of Iran's Revolutionary Guard and was renamed the Badr Brigade, after a decisive battle in A.D. 624, when the Prophet and his faithful supporters, though vastly outnumbered, defeated the Meccan army.

Emara became Badr's artillery commander. The militia expanded with the recruitment of prisoners of war: Iran, which eventually held up to seventy thousand Iraqis, pressured the Shia whom they captured to join their Persian brothers against the apostate tyrant who was killing their religious leaders in the holy cities of Najaf and Karbala. Remarkably few Iraqi Shia were willing to place sectarian belief or self-interest ahead of national loyalty, even though those who refused faced years of squalid confinement. Those Iraqis who did reverse their allegiance were led into combat, in the marshes north of Basra, by Emara. The Badr Brigade earned a reputation for ferocity, and Emara felt no compunction about killing fellow Iraqis.

Sary quickly found that he liked revolutionary Iran no better than fascist Iraq, and he moved on to Pakistan. In 1985, the Pakistani intelligence service arrested him and turned him over to Iraq. Sary spent two years in Abu Ghraib and other prisons that were even worse. He was in solitary confinement for eighteen months; after being sentenced to death, he watched friends taken away for execution while he awaited the same fate. Instead, in 1987, Saddam, who was losing the war and was short of manpower, issued a general-release order, and Sary found himself once again a soldier in the Iraqi army. He served out the war back home in Basra with an air-defense unit. By then Basra was on the front lines; Iranian troops, just seven miles away, constantly shelled the city from across the Shatt al-Arab. Saddam had launched the war to seize the waterway and to prevent Ayatollah Khomeini from inspiring Iraq's oppressed Shiite majority to rise up and create the Islamic Republic of Iraq. But when the Iran-Iraq War ended in 1988, after eight years of human-wave and gas attacks, with missiles raining down on the two capitals and more than a million casualties, the border remained exactly where it had been in 1980: in the middle of the waterway. "Nobody won," Emara said when I met him at Sary's office in Basra just before the elections. "Ask Saddam what it was for."

The next war came to Basra in 1991, when the American-led coalition expelled Saddam's forces from Kuwait. Sary had been sitting in his house for three years, reading history and poetry; he was afraid to leave, and his record made him unemployable. When soldiers of the routed Iraqi army began to stream north on foot from Kuwait into the city, exhausted and hungry, some of them sold their weapons to Basrawin for a pack of cigarettes or just enough cash to reach their homes farther north. On the morning of March 2, Sary's cousin arrived at his house with news that, during the night, in al-Hayaniya, the vast slum west of downtown, young men trying to spring a group of friends from jail had taken over a police station and begun attacking Baath Party offices. Women were in the streets shouting, "Saddam is falling!" Sary was swept up in the spontaneous uprising. He had nothing to lose and, suddenly, nothing to fear. "It wasn't a decision," he said. "It was like a historical movement for me. I heard that the people started to move against the regime and I moved by myself. I attacked the intelligence building." Sary called the Iraqi intifada "ten days of happiness."

On the fourth day of the revolt, which had spread to other cities, two men in black suits appeared before a crowd outside a mosque in the Temimiya district. They had arrived in a Toyota Land Cruiser with license plates from Tehran. Speaking in accents of the Iranian border region, they urged local people to form checkpoints around the city and stop the advance of Republican Guard soldiers that Saddam had sent to quell the rebellion. They also instructed the women of Basra to wear full-length black *abayas*. Around the same time, an intelligence cell of the Badr Brigade was sent across the border by the Shiite exile opposition in Tehran, the Supreme Council for the Islamic Revolution in Iraq, or SCIRI, to organize the chaotic uprising in Basra and give it an ideological focus. Pictures of SCIRI's religious leader, Ayatollah Mohamed Baqr al-Hakim, appeared around Basra, along with images of Ayatollah Khomeini.

Seven days after the uprising began, as the Republican Guard approached the city center, Sary was navigating through pitched battles in the streets when he spotted a familiar face from a distance: that of Youssef al-Emara, who was on a reconnaissance mission to prepare for two hundred Badr fighters to attack Basra's main square and navy yard. Sary was suspicious of the Badr Brigade and worried that the intifada, which had begun as a popular movement without a sectarian cast—one of its first martyrs, he said, was a Sunni from Ramadi—would be overtaken by religious Shia under Iranian control. Still, the sight of Emara, after almost a decade, was welcome. "We were in a war," Sary said. "We needed any help." Emara was too far away for Sary to speak with him, but Sary was led to believe that Emara and other Badr members would supply the local fighters with Katyusha rocket launchers. They never materialized.

In fact, a Badr commander ordered Emara to withdraw his men from Basra and return to Tehran. He was told that Iraqi army helicopters were hitting the city with napalm. "I thought: Why should we come back if a few members were targeted? The situation was favorable," Emara recalled. "When I said that to my leader, I found that he didn't care, he was cold. I've never understood it until this day." Sary, however, saw the hand of Iran in Badr's retreat. The government in Tehran feared that Saddam was setting a trap for Iran's proxies.

On the tenth day, Emara and the Badr cell withdrew, and, according to a leader of the intifada, the Iranian army temporarily blocked Saddam's Iraqi opponents from crossing the border. A few hundred local Iraqis remained in Basra to resist the Republican Guard, in what amounted to a suicide mission. Men were hanged from the gun barrels of tanks; others were machine-gunned to death, their bodies bulldozed into mass graves. The cease-fire between the United States and Iraq had permitted Saddam to resume using helicopter gunships, and they strafed fleeing civilians. Tens of thousands of Iraqis across the south were slaughtered. Republican Guard tanks were painted with the mocking motto, "After today, no more Shia."

On March 17, Sary escaped into Kuwait and eventually arrived at an American prison camp in Saudi Arabia. From there he went into exile in Sweden, where he wrote a book about the intifada, *Death Coming from the West*. The title referred to western Iraq, the Sunni Arab heartland that was home to the Republican Guard leaders. But there was a larger implication. Like everyone in Basra who told me the story of the intifada, Sary felt betrayed by America as well as by Iran. Two weeks before the uprising, President George H. W. Bush had told Iraqis to overthrow Saddam; flyers dropped by American planes had urged the same thing. In the first days of the revolt, dissident Iraqis thought that the American military was on their side. U.S. soldiers positioned south of Basra had initially provided medical aid and food to people leaving Basra, and American planes had attacked Iraqi tanks. But the dissidents I spoke with said that the United States had suddenly stopped supporting them. "Bush told us to uprise," an Iraqi said at the time. "When we uprose, he went fishing." A Basrawi who had fled to the Kuwaiti border asked American officers there, "Can you help the people dying?" An officer answered, "We are military—there's nothing we can do. This is politics."

The no-fly zone that allowed the Kurds in the northern mountains to survive and create an autonomous region was of no use to the Shia in the relentlessly flat southern marshes and desert. "Saddam Hussein wasn't entering houses by plane, he was entering on foot, in cars," a leader of the uprising named Mufeed Abdul-Zahraa said. He ran a veterans' group whose certificate of membership asserts that the bearer "is one of the participants in the intifada, and he participated with all he owns and sacrificed his material goods and his soul to save our city, even to the last moment when the intifada ended, when the evil powers united, the Americans and the Baathists." Bitterness over the events of 1991 remained strong in Basra, and it helped to explain the wariness with which the Shia, more impoverished and disenfranchised than ever, greeted the American invasion in 2003. To many, the defeat of Saddam came twelve years too late.

Emara and Sary both returned home after Saddam's fall, but, just as they had tried to push the intifada in separate directions, they came back from Tehran and Stockholm with sharply different visions of a new Iraq—one Islamist, one secular. Emara and Sary, the former rebels, had become middle-aged men in pin-striped suits. The Badr Brigade, renamed the Badr Organization, now operated freely in Basra—the provincial governor was a member—and Emara was one of its top officials. A couple of weeks before election day, he was appointed to the local office of the national Defense Ministry, where Sary was also an official. One of Emara's first moves in his new job was to pay a visit, just three days before the elections, to Sary's office. He had some political business to discuss. They sat down under a wall plaque that commemorated the intifada after Sary's own persuasion: Its imagery emphasized the revolt's national character, with a Sumerian sun, an Arab sword, a Kurdish dagger, and symbols of workers and peasants. Emara didn't realize that he and the man behind the desk were old acquaintances, with a certain shared history, until Sary reminded him. Then they spent several hours talking over the unhappy past.

When the reminiscing was done, Emara got to the point. He wanted Sary to put a stop to the ministry's accusations of Iranian interference in the elections. The Iraqi Shiite religious parties were likely to come to power after the vote, Emara said, adding that if Sary wanted to keep his position it would be in his interest to cooperate. But Basra's experience since the fall of Saddam had left Sary deeply suspicious of the Islamist parties. "These are the realities," Sary said to Emara. "We're not making it up. Iran is interfering." And, as an Iraqi patriot, he was unwilling to forge alliances with people who served as proxies for Iran. "We're looking at the parties from Iran," he said after ushering Emara out of his office. "The good Iraqis we take. The others we leave."

AFTER THE 2003 invasion, more than a hundred thousand Iraqi Shia who, during Saddam's regime, had fled to Iran or were expelled returned to southern Iraq. With them came the Islamist political parties that had represented the Shiite opposition in exile: SCIRI and its armed wing, the Badr Organization; Dawa, the oldest Shiite party, whose cadres inside Iraq had been almost exterminated in the 1970s and '80s; and a host of smaller parties with names like Revenge of God—some of which were armed subsidiaries of Iranian intelligence.

The religious parties occupied government buildings in Basra, installed their militias, and organized faster than any of the local groups, except for the mostly poor and violent followers of Moqtada al-Sadr. The religious parties quickly established contact with the British military, filled the new police force with their cadres, and took control of the provincial government. "The Iran-backed parties had a strategic vision, which was more or less take over the south politically, cooperate with the coalition, enhance their religious position in Najaf, and then be in a position to get national power," a British official told me. "I think they've succeeded without wide support, which is why they've overstretched themselves. Not that many people in the south support the parties."

The religious parties imposed their strict ideology on Basra, alienating many residents who were already wary of militiamen who had sided with Iran during the war that inflicted so much suffering on the city. Armed militias assassinated Baathists, harassed women who dared to forgo the veil, and forcibly shut down Basra's DVD emporiums and Christian-owned liquor shops. Zealous university professors demanded that women and men sit apart from one another in classes, and a music school student told me that he could now study only theory, since playing instruments was considered immoral by some Islamists. This coercive social code sat uneasily on the worldly educated classes of Basra, though the city had grown increasingly conservative under the weight of war, sanctions, and the influence of Iran. The provincial government was widely viewed as incompetent and corrupt; oil products were reportedly being smuggled to floating markets in the Gulf. With vast oil reserves, date-palm plantations, and a strategically located port, Basra, long neglected by Baghdad, had the potential to become the engine of an economic boom in Iraq. In the governor's office, I met a representative of a Kuwaiti firm with plans for a sixty-eight-story office tower—to be called the World Trade Center—and a $5.5 billion investment. For now, violence and bad government stood in the way.

I spent several days with the British military in and around Basra. Most of them had been schooled in counterinsurgency tactics in Northern Ireland, and their posture in southern Iraq was a sharp contrast to that of the Americans up north. Their vehicles were smaller and less heavily armed, they wore soft hats on foot patrol, and in general they seemed far more at ease around Iraqis. Local cars could pass their convoys without fear of getting shot up. Some British soldiers were still shaking their heads over a recent incident on the highway near Nasiriya in which an American convoy traveling without lights had fired on British vehicles coming up on its rear. At the soldiers' bar out on the British air base (unlike the Americans, the Brits were allowed two off-duty beers per night, which seemed an essential part of good morale), a sergeant told me, "The Americans don't think. They react. When they come down here on exchanges we have to tell them. 'There's no danger yet. When there is, we'll tell you. Until then, just chill.' "

"I would be very disappointed to see a British soldier involved in a conversation or negotiation still wearing sunglasses," Major Alan Richmond of the Queen's Dragoon Guards told me on a trip south of Basra to the port of Umm Qasr. British training for Iraq included a bit of language instruction and some basic cultural sensitivity (don't show the soles of your shoes, don't reach with the left hand, don't look at the women). "You want to be approachable—softly, softly—you want to be able to speak to people because that's how you get things done."

"It also comes from fifty years of withdrawing from empire," Major Simon Johns said. "What we do down here has risks, but the longer-term benefit is considerable compared to the approach of an absolute standoff. At a certain point, you have to engage." He quickly added that the British might not have such success if they tried their tactics in more hostile cities like Baghdad or Mosul, where the Americans were under constant attack. When a unit of the Queen's Dragoon Guards was transferred to a sector near Falluja in advance of the American assault on the city, a suicide bomber killed three soldiers at a checkpoint, and the British immediately tightened up their rules of engagement.

It was clear that the scenario in Iraq—occupation, reconstruction, counterinsurgency—was easier for the British soldiers than the Americans. Several officers told me that these kinds of operations were at the core of British military doctrine and its role in the post–Cold War world. By contrast, American officers in Iraq either wanted to get back to the real business of the military, which was war training and war fighting, or else understood that Iraq *was* their real business but also acknowledged that the news hadn't entirely sunk in with senior leadership. Among junior officers—lieutenants, captains, lieutenant colonels—Iraq was having a profound effect, and many of the ones I met were essentially teaching themselves and one another how to do it well. But even John Prior returned from Iraq knowing that his long experience in Zafaraniya would bring him few career benefits.

As a result, there was much less friction between foreign soldiers and Iraqi civilians in Basra than in areas occupied by American forces. At the same time, some locals grumbled that the British were unwilling to impose order in Basra. In August of 2004, during a regionwide uprising of the Mahdi Army, the British military essentially ceded control of the city to Sadr's followers, who had the support of the police chief. Throughout southern Iraq, which had been under non-American control since 2003, government authority was extremely weak and the various Shiite militias had the run of the streets.

The question of Iran's role in Basra's political violence and religious repression was a murky one. To Majid al-Sary, the answer was simple. "There is no Iranian 'influence' in Basra," he said. "There is an indirect Iranian *occupation* of Basra." The Iraqi religious parties were agents of the occupation, Sary added, though even he drew distinctions between, for example, SCIRI and Dawa, which exerted a certain independence from Tehran, and the smaller parties that acted as hired guns. Iran, he said, wanted to prevent the establishment of a democratic and secular state next door; it also hoped "to put the American military forces inside the cloud of the Iraqi mess so they cannot hit Iran by military force." Several people in Basra claimed that the old colonial governor's residence on the Corniche was occupied by Iranian intelligence agents. According to one Western official, suitcases of cash were constantly ferried across what barely functioned as an international border. When Prime Minister Allawi visited Basra in November of 2004, he asked the governor, "Why aren't you flying the Iranian flag above your office?" Still, no one seemed to know who the

Iranians were. A farmer named Majid Moussa, who was attending a voter education meeting on the campus of Basra University, said, "They don't come here as Iranians holding a flag."

British officials took the view that Iran had a legitimate interest in Iraq: the establishment of a stable, friendly neighbor. Simon Collis, the British consul in Basra, said of the religious parties, "These organizations do have links with Iran. Are they Iranian owned? I don't think so. If you wanted to fight the tyranny in the eighties and nineties, Iran was the address. It's not obvious to me that these ties that they doubtless had and doubtless still have to Iran mean that there is some mullah in Qom who can jerk their chain and make them jump." Another British official, speaking anonymously, admitted, "I've come to the view that we cannot know as outsiders. Their communications systems are much faster and more accurate than ours. We're proud of our e-mail, our computers. But these are so much slower than word of mouth."

AT THE MATERNITY AND CHILDREN'S HOSPITAL in Basra's Jazaar district, Dr. Mohamed Nasir, the director, was fighting back against the religious parties that had taken over the city's other hospitals and its university campuses. Nasir had the tough, jowly face and slicked-back hair of Broderick Crawford as Willie Stark in *All the King's Men*; he looked more like a ward politician than a hospital director. There were no religious pictures in his hospital, only the uplifting get-out-the-vote posters of the election commission and quaint alpine-meadow scenes inside gold frames that had once contained portraits of Saddam Hussein. In 2004, a religious militia had demanded the use of a brick wall to cover with political propaganda. "Come back tomorrow morning," Nasir said. That day, he knocked down the wall with a sledgehammer. A few months later, one of his nurses was caught watching a pornographic DVD with her boyfriend, a receptionist. When Nasir ordered the receptionist transferred to another hospital, the man's friends went to the local Sadr office and reported Nasir for tearing down pictures of Mohamed Sadiq al-Sadr, Moqtada's martyred father. The militiamen confronted the doctor and demanded that he rescind the transfer order. "They said I need to be judged by a religious court in Najaf," he recalled with amusement. Nasir armed himself, hired his own hospital security force, and by sheer nerve faced down the intruders.

The hospital was now a model of order. "We need professional people who are expert at their work and they belong to Iraq only, not to any group, and they are brave people, they have brave heart," Nasir said as we walked the corridors and toured a new nutrition ward, built by Save the Children with money from the U.S. Agency for International Development. The doctor was counting on a democratic election and a strong new government to rescue Iraq from chaos. His brand of secularism was all about law and order: He wanted to practice medicine without religious interference. "We have no in-between solution," he said. "Either we will go ahead with freedom or the whole country will be destroyed. If you speak, I will speak. If you fight, I will fight. Because you have to protect yourself. And if you die, you must die with honor. You must not die a coward."

A half mile down the street, outside the modest headquarters of the Fadilah Party (the name meant Virtue, or Morals), someone had propped up a wide, vividly painted canvas: An old man with a white beard, standing against a flaming sky, was pushing a boatload of pilgrims across a desert-colored ocean toward the distant gold-domed shrine of Imam Ali, in Najaf. The old man was Moqtada al-Sadr's father. Fadilah's founder, Ayatollah Mohamed al-Yaqoubi, claimed that Moqtada's father, before his murder at the hands of Baathist agents, had chosen him as his successor—making Yaqoubi, not Moqtada, the genuine heir of hard-line Iraqi Shiism. Among the bewildering array of religious parties in Basra, Fadilah had the largest following among the pious educated classes, who wanted strict Islamic government but also independence from Iran.

Dr. Haider Mohsin, an earnest young internist, sat under a portrait of Ayatollah Yaqoubi and explained Fadilah's philosophy while, in the next room, bearded, leather-jacketed male campaign workers came and went in a flurry of preelection activity. "The Jean-Jacques Rousseau idea, the French Revolution ideas—we think that these ideas are typical ideas for the European society," Mohsin said. "But how far it is from Iraq to the European societies is the distance from Islam to the French Revolution." Cultural imperialism, he said, was the most dangerous kind of imperialism, and Iraq needed to resist the wave of low morals and rampant individualism emanating from the West. "One of the causes that made France fall down in the Second World War was the sexual freedom," Mohsin said. He was quick to add that the Islamization of Iraq should take place by entirely democratic, constitutional means that respected the rights of religious minorities. Mohsin was equally distrustful of Iranian and American designs on Iraq; no country except Iraq, he said, could have the interests of Iraqis at heart. In Mohsin's reasoning, the elections would allow Iraq to find the perfect balance of state and mosque, with the assent of the entire population.

The opposing view was expressed most forcefully by Majid al-Sary. "All the Islamic laws from the time of the Prophet until our day don't show acceptance of democracy," he said. "Show me any country where there is Islamic leadership that can accept democratic persons. Where could that happen? In Saudi Arabia? In Iran? I don't think so, no. The secular people, the communists—they accepted democracy. I don't think the Islamic parties will accept anyone who opposes them." Sary compared the prospect of monolithic Shiite rule in Iraq with the tyranny of the Baath Party. For this reason, he said, "religion is something between man and God and should be far away from politics." Sary, who was protected by at least half a dozen National Guardsmen, added, "I'm the only one who can talk like that in Basra, and I know that, at any time, I can be turned to smoke, because they can blow up my office."

THE ARABIC WORD FOR "secular" is a neologism, *almaany*, which comes from *aalam*, meaning "world." It wasn't often heard in public, for to many Iraqis *almaany* also meant "godless." As Hashim al-Jazairy, the dean of Basra University's law school, said, "This is not a good time for godlessness. God forgives, but the people don't forgive. I don't know if I'm going to hell or heaven, but there I can say, 'I'm sorry, God, please forgive me.' Here, the people don't forgive."

In Basra, the confrontation between doctors and militiamen, and between technocratic and religious parties, was not just a matter of guns and posters. In the days before the elections, Basra became the stage for a passionate political struggle between competing discourses and ideas. The idea of a society based on Islamic values and religious authority, which inevitably meant a sectarian Shiite vision, was embodied by List No. 169, which people called the Sistani list, because the grand ayatollah had overseen the formation of the Shiite coalition. The idea of a society based on civil law, in which Iraqiness would take precedence over ethnic and religious identity, in an effort to heal the country's deep divisions, was represented by List No. 285, headed by Iyad Allawi. Allawi himself inspired no great passion; people simply said that he was an educated man, a doctor, which seemed to embody a secular society. Sistani, however, was the most revered man in Iraq, even though he was an Iranian and not a candidate for anything. There were contradictions and illusions on both sides. Allawi supporters spoke of good government, though his administration was accused of being spectacularly corrupt; supporters of List No. 169 spoke of following the *marjayia*, the highest Shiite religious scholars, although Sistani, whose picture appeared on many 169 posters, had never formally endorsed the list he was so instrumental in forming. His fatwa said only that Muslim men and women had a religious duty to vote.

In a sense, Basra was ahead of the rest of the country. Elsewhere in Iraq, the question was whether or not to vote at all. In Basra, where the violence was at a comparatively manageable level—that is, two murders of secular candidates, three or four car bombs, a handful of attacks on polling stations, and rumors of jihadis heading south from the Sunni areas to create mayhem on election day—the question was whether to vote for Sistani or Allawi.

The religious parties had the best campaign song, chanted to a soundtrack, heavy on percussion and sweeping violins, that was blasted from loudspeakers on convoys of pickup trucks:

All the people should vote for 169
Because it contains those who were in the jails,
Those whose fathers and brothers were buried in mass graves,
The women who gave their sons,
Those who sacrificed for Iraq.
It's what the religious scholars want.

169 is like a garden for Iraqis
And Iraqis are the flowers
And these flowers grow because of the blood
Of those who gave their lives for Iraq.
God is great!
It's the day for the Shia to give their voice!

Allawi, in turn, was flooding the Arabic television channels with slick campaign ads paid out of official coffers, and his government had recently promised raises to civil servants and police officers. His ticket was gaining ground in the minority Sunni and Christian areas of Basra, as well as among professionals. In the days leading up to the elections, a number of Basrawin told me that they sensed a surge toward Allawi.

The day before the elections was a feast day called Ghadir al-Khumm. In 632, as Mohamed made his way back to Medina from his last pilgrimage to Mecca, he is believed to have stopped by a pool of stagnant water, or *ghadir*, in the desert and held up the hand of his cousin and son-in-law, Ali. "For whomever I am his *mawla*," the Prophet told the world, "Ali is his *mawla*." Those Muslims who took *mawla* to mean "master" and believed Ali to be the Prophet's chosen successor as caliph became the Shia, or the "partisans" of Ali and his son, Hussein, and all of the imams who descended from them, down to the twelfth and last, the hidden Mahdi, whose reappearance would usher in the apocalypse. Those who took *mawla* to mean "friend," and who believed in an entirely different account of who succeeded Mohamed, became the Sunnis. So Ghadir al-Khumm marked the beginning of the great fracture among Muslims, and the Arab Shia were its historical losers, living down the centuries under the religious authority of the Sunni caliphate, and, more recently, under the temporal power of Sunni politicians—even in Iraq, where the Shia were the majority. Shia had failed to join the first Iraqi government, under British occupation in the 1920s, because of a fatwa, and during Saddam's regime their leaders had been systematically murdered. For secular Iraqis, the country's first truly democratic elections meant that they could at last escape the nightmare of the Saddam years and join the civilized world. For religious Shia, after the martyrdom of Ali and of Hussein, after the centuries of penitence, quietism, and suffering, the elections would grant them their rightful share of power and correct a historic wrong going back more than a thousand years.

On the Friday before the elections, at the Hakemiya mosque, off a busy commercial street near the bombed intelligence building, Imam Mohamed al-Basry delivered prayers to the men packed into his small shrine. A loudspeaker blared his words to the surrounding neighborhood. He was just thirty-one, a former biologist with square-framed glasses, a missing front tooth, and an ill-at-ease manner. He made sure that his flock understood the significance of the fact that election day was the day after Ghadir al-Khumm. Ordinarily, Shia would travel to Najaf on Ghadir al-Khumm to visit the shrine of Ali, but this year, as part of the election security effort, there would be a nationwide ban on car travel beginning at dusk on the eve of the elections. The imam said, "There is something we can do that's maybe more important than this visit. We will make our rights clear. And that is much more important than visiting Najaf on the right day."

The imam's voice rose as he tried to galvanize the men kneeling before him. "The day after tomorrow is election day," he said. "It will be a great day, and we should prepare ourselves for this day as we prepare ourselves for any other Islamic feast, because this day will bring victory to the people who suffered from injustice. It will be the day when there will be no more suffering for the people. It will be the day when the victim will get rid of the person who abused him." On election day, the imam declared, Shia should follow their *marjayia*, their religious scholars, who were heirs to Ali and his family—the true heirs to the Prophet. The word of a *marja* was like the word of the Prophet, and following the *marjayia* meant accepting Ali as caliph: This was the doctrinal connection between Ghadir al-Khumm and election day. The imam had arrived at the point of the sermon. "The *marjayia* composed and support a list, the United Iraqi Alliance, which carries the number 169, which carries the candle symbol," he said. "Did anyone not hear me? I want this word to reach even to the outside loudspeakers, so no one will be able to say it is a lie. And I don't want to hear that the *marjayia* didn't support this list."

The imam was venturing onto controversial ground (and when I met with him afterward, he refused to discuss any of it). The other parties claimed that Sistani, who no one doubted had helped to compose No. 169, had blessed *all* the lists, and they cried foul when his picture started appearing on No. 169 campaign signs. Sistani himself said nothing to resolve the dispute. The clergy had previously kept out of it. Now Imam Basry wasn't content merely to clear up the doubt about Sistani's support for No. 169; he went on to imply that the Allawi government, by raising salaries, was trying to bribe voters. "I remind you that death is close to every person," the imam said. "No one knows when he will die—he might die at any moment. What will he say to our God? 'I voted for a certain list because they gave me money'? How can he face God with this answer?"

The imam then told his flock what time the polls would open and close, how many pieces of ID to bring, how to find List 169 on the ballot, and how to check the right square. Apparently satisfied that his instructions were clear, he offered his valediction: "God will be with you that day, so you should not fear anything, you should have no fear of terrorists. The Shia of Hussein should remember this saying: We refuse humiliation, and we should go to vote."

SUNDAY MORNING was strange and beautiful. The streets of Basra were so quiet that people later said it was like a feast day. Families, including small children and grandparents, were walking together along the wide avenues, everyone dressed in fine clothes. Many Basrawin I spoke with had discussed with their families what to do on election day—whether it would be safer to go out in the morning or afternoon, whether it would be better to lose only one or two members of the family or to die together. Policemen and National Guardsmen stood at intersections every couple of hundred yards, and snipers perched on the roof of the provincial government building. People on their way to vote were amazed to see men in uniform actually doing their jobs. By seven-thirty, at the schools that had been designated polling places, voters were already lining up; the queues were orderly and the faces a little solemn. People submitted without complaint to the frisks, and

they seemed to keep their voices down out of respect. Election workers—schoolteachers, housewives, unemployed college graduates—
wore badges on their shirts. They handed out ballots with the slightly
exaggerated seriousness of people performing a small but important
ritual, like professors distributing final exams. They guided each voters' right index finger down into the little glass half full of violet ink.
Ordinary Iraqis on any other day, the election workers were thanked as
if they were the heroes of 1991. The ballots themselves—beige for the
national elections, blue for the provincial—were large and crowded
with a bewildering array of party symbols. They looked cleaner and
newer than anything else I'd ever seen in Iraq.

At the Republican School, just off Independence Street, Shadha
Mohamed Ali, a fifty-year-old housewife in a stylish red-and-black
scarf, cast the day's first vote. "I spent thirty-five years of my life going
from war to war," she said. "Now my hopes are for my children. We
lost our future. We're looking for the future of our children." Mehsin
Richem Hashem, a teacher of Arabic at the school and the manager of
the polling station, said, "I've lived over fifty years, and I've never had
such a feeling. My skin had a strange feeling, like goose bumps. We've
had a great culture for six thousand years, and now I think our humanity is proved. We hope this democratic experiment brings this result, that the people are the real owners of the decisions in this
country." He wore a slightly tattered jacket and a floral tie, and his face
was taut, with a carefully clipped mustache. "There's a rumor they poi-
soned the water supply in as-Zubair this morning," he said, referring to
a Sunni suburb south of Basra. (The rumor proved false.) "We don't
care what the terrorists do. They have tried everything but they can't
do anything. Poisoning the waters shows they're desperate."

Around 8:20, the school shook slightly when a mortar round landed
a few hundred yards away. "*Yalla*," someone muttered. "No problem,
no problem," Laith Mahmood Shaker, a thirty-two-year-old traffic policeman who had brought his children, said. "What we are doing now
is a big thing against terrorism. It's like a challenge to them: We're voting—what can you do?"

A number of voters recalled the only elections they had known, the
farces that had certified Saddam's popularity. They had been offered a

choice between one box marked yes and one marked no; sometimes, the election workers simply cast their votes for them. This time, many people exercised their newfound right to keep their choices to themselves. Feisal Jassim, a retired oil-company employee—he had been among the worshippers who listened to Imam Basry's instructions—wouldn't reveal his choice. For him, the experience of voting freely for the first time, at age seventy, was what mattered. "Most Iraqis don't know what democracy means," he said. "Is it sweet, is it bitter? Does it have a taste or a smell? We don't know. After the elections, we'll find out."

In one polling place, I met Abdul-Khadem Hussein Abood, a uniformed National Guard colonel with a fragile physique, a hollow face, and piercing black eyes. Fifty-six years old, he had been a prisoner of war in Iran for seventeen years, during the prime of his life; he was released and came back to Basra two days before the start of the war in 2003 and was overjoyed to find that his small children had grown up to become engineers and a doctor. Colonel Abood held up four fingers, one for each child: His index finger was stained.

My translator in Basra was an overweight, pleasantly melancholy young doctor from Baghdad named Omar. After the first bombs fell on the city in March of 2003, Omar stayed at his hospital for three weeks to treat the wounded and then, when order collapsed, to stave off the looters; by the end he was one of only five doctors still on duty. He was easily bored, even during the occupation, when the endless explosions and high body counts meant that every young doctor became a hardened trauma specialist. Election day, said Omar, a secular Sunni without strong political views, was "just another day." So he felt—until, as we were about to leave a polling station after talking with a dozen voters, he suddenly exclaimed, "Please wait!" He went back inside and begged the election workers to let him vote, even though he was registered in Baghdad. Phlegmatic Omar came out beaming. "I feel great!"

His family lived in Amariya, a western Baghdad neighborhood off the dangerous airport highway that was a notorious hotbed of the insurgency. No one in the family knew that Omar worked with Westerners for a living. All morning, he kept calling home to see whether his family had voted, and around noon he was stunned to hear that his mother and brothers, having looked out the front door to find their neighbors trickling into the street, had made a dash to the polls themselves. They returned home safely, and before nightfall even his father, a retired army officer who was becoming a Sunni extremist in his later years, was envious enough of their purple fingertips, of the tremendous excitement spreading through Baghdad and most of Iraq, to go down and vote as well. Omar's best friend, Ali, who also lived in Amariya, made three attempts to vote. On the first try, Ali got halfway down the street when a friend known to be a sympathizer with the insurgency greeted him suspiciously. "Where are you going?" he asked. "To get some bread," Ali said. "I'll go with you," the friend said, and Ali proceeded to the bakery for a loaf of bread he didn't need. A few hours later he tried again, and some men coming out of the mosque cornered him. "Where are you going?" they asked. "To the pharmacy, for my aunt's prescription," Ali said. "We'll go with you," the men said, and when they reached the pharmacy Ali had to pretend that he'd forgotten the prescription at home. As the afternoon grew late and the polls prepared to close, Ali, who had been watching scenes of people lining up to vote on television all day, panicked and called Omar in Basra. Patiently, Omar talked Ali through a two-mile detour around the back streets of Amariya. Ali reached the polling station only to find out that it wasn't his: He was supposed to vote in the school just behind his house. And so Ali did, and as soon as he made it home his mother frantically scrubbed the purple dye off his finger with chlorine.

I returned to the Republican School in Basra just before the polls closed, at dusk. The last person in line was Abid Hamid, a policeman who had been so busy all day that he'd almost forgotten to vote. "It's not important whom I choose," he said. "I just want to participate." The outer gate was locked, and I was allowed to stay and watch the count. The ballots were collected in bundles of twenty-five, and then laid out, one after another, on a wooden table in the middle of a sixth-grade math classroom. The right hand of the counter, a math teacher named Salih Younis Mahdi, was deformed; he had only the three middle fingers, and they were webbed together. He ran his hand rapidly down the ballots like a ruler, slapping the paper when he came to the checked box, then calling out the number. Ahmad Salih Mahdi, an elderly first-grade teacher, stood silently at the chalkboard and recorded the votes in groups of five. Monitors from the parties and the election commission stood by, and when, predictably, the power failed, hurricane lamps were produced, and the classroom became a chiaroscuro study of long shadows and illuminated faces.

The final count at the Republican School was 721 for the Allawi list, 595 for the Sistani list, and a handful of votes scattered among the others. The total number of ballots distributed was two greater than the number of votes counted, and so the men stood around the table in the middle of the room for half an hour more, their faces lit from below, going over the tallies again and again, until they realized that two ballots had been left blank. Everything had come out right.

THE ARRIVAL of the Americans and the British in 2003 freed Iraqis from Saddam but not from their own suspicions and grievances and fears. It was a victory of foreigners, and the occupiers wondered why they were greeted with prickliness instead of mere gratitude. Liberation was, in a way, humiliating, and the almost two years that followed brought new calamities. On election day, the foreign troops were nowhere to be seen, and when Iraqis went to vote, the achievement was finally their own.

Two days after the election, I went back to see Majid al-Sary and found him elated. After the fall of the regime, with all the looting and violence, he had been too ashamed of his country to bring his family to Basra, and he had been thinking of going back to Sweden if the election results meant the loss of his job in the Defense Ministry. Now, he was determined to stay: Iraqis, he had learned, were worth fighting for. "The elections showed the strength of religious ideas here. I will stay and fight those bad ideas. It's changing from a fight against violence and explosions to a new category—thoughts."

After a few days, the euphoria from the elections began to wear off, along with the ink on index fingers. Nationwide, the Sistani list won nearly half the vote, and in Basra it took 70 percent. The Allawi list won less than 15 percent nationally, 20 percent in Basra. In the provincial election, the local Shiite coalition won a third of the vote, with the Fadilah Party a strong second and the Allawi list a distant third. The coalition of small parties put together by Jawdet al-Obeidi, the former limousine company owner from Portland who had attended the workshop in Hilla, didn't even register in the national results. The success of the religious parties left the supporters of Allawi and other secular candidates stunned, and some of them attributed the result to the misuse of Sistani's name and face. Some Iraqis said that Mohaméd Rida, Sistani's son and spokesman, had panicked on the eve of the elections and ordered the imams to hand down an official endorsement of List No. 169. (Sistani's office denied this.) It was the Ghadir al-Khumm Surprise. In this first chance to "give their voice," most Shia had obeyed their religious leaders.

In Basra, at least, there had been a contest. Iraq as a whole emerged from its first democratic election profoundly split between those who voted and those who did not. The national turnout was 58 percent, but the voters were overwhelmingly Shia and Kurds. The Sunni turnout was estimated to be 15 percent; in Anbar province, it was 2 percent. The party of Ghazi al-Yawer, the interim president and a tribal sheikh from Mosul, won two seats in the new national assembly. Adnan Pachachi, a former foreign minister and elder statesman of Arab politics, could not even win a seat for himself.

I visited Pachachi in Baghdad to find out how Iraq could move forward from such a divisive event, in which the country's historical losers had become winners and its winners losers. The transformation would be felt beyond Iraq: The country's Arab neighbors were already alarmed by the specter of Iranian and Shiite influence rising in the Middle East, disturbing the old Sunni order. Pachachi, a man of liberal views, told me, "I hope there will never be Sunni politics in Iraq. I don't think there should be Shiite politics, either. We don't want to be like Lebanon. I think this is a temporary thing, this ascendancy of Shiism. Eventually, the majority of the Shia will turn away from the religious parties. It's an aberration," he said. "You will see. I think probably sooner rather than later Iraqis will go back to their secular roots."

Pachachi was busy holding meetings with Sunni politicians and religious leaders to find out what it would take to bring them and their constituents into the political game. "They said they were eager to rectify this mistake" of sitting out the elections, he said, chuckling—"without admitting it, of course." Pachachi was acting as a broker between the

marginalized groups and the new centers of power, trying to find a for-
mula by which Sunni leaders could join in the writing of a new Iraqi
constitution despite their lack of representation in the assembly. This
would both act as a brake on Shiite sectarianism and provide a way for
Sunnis who were weary of fighting to rejoin politics. The vote magni-
fied ethnic and religious divisions, and it moved the Americans farther
from the center of Iraq's political life. The contest was more and more
among Iraqis themselves. At a meeting of tribal leaders in Baghdad
several weeks after the elections, a Sunni Arab from Kirkuk said; "The
Americans aren't the problem. We're living under an occupation of
Kurds and Shia. It's time to fight back." Kirkuk once again became
ground zero for the dreaded, threatened, desired civil war. Another
tribal leader at the gathering declared, "The Kurds are asking for
Kirkuk. Later on they will start asking for Baghdad. It was Saddam
Hussein who gave the Kurds too much, more than they deserved." The
Arabs would soon rise up, he said. "The last remedy is burning."

Dr. Baher Butti didn't vote; Dora, the violent Baghdad neighborhood
where he lived, was too dangerous. But when I met him after the elections, Butti had some news: His old idea for the Gilgamesh Center for
Creative Thinking would take the form of a new psychiatric clinic that
was about to open, with Iraqi and American funding, near the Olympic
Stadium in a former social club of Uday's. The al-Janna Center, with
twenty inpatient beds and fifty outpatients, would allow Butti to teach
advanced techniques to the dozen psychologists and social workers on
his staff, and to provide good care for the ailments of Iraqis' minds.

After almost two years, Butti still harbored suspicions about the
Americans. Before we said goodbye, he asked me for the fifth or tenth
time whether there had been some plan behind the chaos that the occupiers had allowed to overtake his country. "I'm not being paranoid,"
he said, "but it's a question." I agreed that it was a question, and I said
that, as far as I knew, the chaos was worse than a crime, it was a blun-
der. But the Americans were a fact in Iraq, and Butti was now counting on them to prevent the religious Shia from taking too much power
and to protect American interests, which had converged with his.
Meanwhile, for better or worse, he and his wife would stay.

"It's Russian roulette," he said. "Every morning we leave, and we don't know if we will come home. We are habituated to this Russian roulette. So we go on."

Aseel voted. She and her parents walked six hours across the city to Adhamiya, their former neighborhood, where their food-ration cards were registered, and back. Aseel wore a full-length black *abaya* and training shoes, and in the pro-Saddam streets of Adhamiya the family walked under the unfriendly gaze of local young men. Aseel was frightened but defiant, and when they finally reached their polling station, she cast her vote for the Sistani list only because it included Ahmad Chalabi, whom she was counting on to finish off the Baathists once and for all.

When I saw her after the elections, Aseel had exchanged the *abaya* for a resplendent royal blue tailored suit with a knee-length skirt and a jacket with padded shoulders, a cream-colored turtleneck, stockings, and high heels with ankle straps. She was also wearing lipstick, mascara, and plenty of jewelry. We sat together in the garden of the Palestine Hotel, enjoying the mild winter sun, and she undid her braid and let her hair down in the golden light. There was something different about Aseel, as if she had cast off a burden. She was working as a secretary at a ministry in the Green Zone (there had been no follow-up to her interview with Kanan Makiya), and a man in her office had proposed marriage. He was good-looking but dull; she knew that she couldn't love him and told him so, but she consented to let him and his family visit hers. They sat in the living room of her family's newly constructed house, and as the two sets of parents discussed a dowry, Aseel imagined a life with this man: As soon as they were married, he would break all his promises to respect her independence of spirit and start crushing it into that of an Iraqi housewife. Tears came to her eyes, and the prospect filled her with such dread that she imagined it would be just like living under Saddam again. For the first time in months, she remembered exactly what that had felt like. She could never let it happen. She said nothing that day, but she knew that she would refuse the offer.

"I want to travel," she said as we walked out of the hotel to say goodbye on the street. "My mind doesn't match this society. I need more freedom."

EPILOGUE

IN THE FIRST DAYS of 2005, Drew Erdmann packed up his desk at the National Security Council, left government service, and joined his wife and their baby daughter in St. Louis, where he planned to take a job in the private sector. Erdmann had been working on Iraq, in Baghdad and in Washington, for the better part of three years. It had been challenging and fulfilling work, and, as for his own part in it, he could sleep at night. But he was still going home with the sense that he hadn't contributed enough. The cost in human lives weighed heavily. He had lost friends, both American and Iraqi, and he considered himself lucky, but if he'd been single, he would have stayed on in Iraq.

In St. Louis, Erdmann tried not to follow the news from that part of the world. Though he would never again be a professional historian, he wanted to achieve enough distance to consider the war historically, which would probably take years. The biggest questions—Would it succeed? How could it have been done better? If it couldn't be done right, should it have been done at all?—were out there waiting for him, and for others like him, but Erdmann was not yet ready to answer them.

But he did read a book—from cover to cover, for the first time in a while—that had some relevance. It was *Bureaucracy Does Its Thing* by "Blowtorch" Bob Komer, who had run the pacification program in Vietnam under Johnson. Copies had been circulating in Baghdad, and a few people there had said, "You want to understand what's going on out here? Read this report." A copy landed on his desk in Washington. Erdmann had always rejected crude Vietnam analogies, and he still did: Iraq was strategically far more central, the nature of the insurgencies was different, and the chances for success in Iraq were better. The constant remained the U.S. government: the ongoing effort to put its civilian and military branches to work in concert, the institutional constraints that made it so hard, the halting efforts to adapt imaginatively to new kinds of war, the sheer organizational difficulty of pulling off something on the scale of Iraq. All of this had been the theme of his dissertation, and when Komer's book sent Erdmann back to it, he discovered that he had foreseen much of his own experience. "There are many things about Iraq that fit right into the pattern of the kind of stuff I was thinking about and working on before," Erdmann said. In 1917, for instance, with the American Expeditionary Force readying to sail to Europe, General John "Blackjack" Pershing looked around for a plan and found none. "So it doesn't come as a surprise to me, and only now that I have a little time can I piece things together in the mosaic and see more clearly some of the continuities."

His dissertation had focused on the elusiveness of victory. The defeat of Japanese militarism did not come with the surrender in August 1945 on board the battleship USS *Missouri*, but six years later, with the end of the American occupation and the birth of a democratic Japan. Because victory is a process, not an event, with fundamentally political rather than military goals, victory in Iraq, including the transformation of Iraqi politics, lay beyond the reach of American power alone. "Ultimately, it is always about the Iraqis," Erdmann said. "The ultimate objectives can only be achieved by the Iraqis. Maybe these are peculiarly American objectives. We can help. But we are in a position where victory will only be achieved through the efforts of others. That's a paradoxical situation. We may have the power, but precisely because of the nature of our objectives, we can't use our power to force a specific outcome. Ultimately, our fate is tied to theirs."

IN THE SAME WEEK of early January that Erdmann left Washington, Colin Powell was summoned to the White House for his farewell conversation with the president. All along, Powell had been the dutifully quiet dissenter on Iraq, concerned about the damage to alliances, skeptical (but not enough) of the administration's more fevered claims about weapons and terrorism, realistic about the difficulties of the postwar. But his prestige was badly tarnished when his prewar speech to the UN about Iraqi weapons was proved mostly false. Though Iraq became more and more the responsibility of his agency, Powell had lost almost every major fight back when the crucial decisions were made. His tenure as secretary of state was a great disappointment. In his final months at the State Department, an aide quoted to Powell Churchill's answer to someone's comment on the ingratitude of the British public for voting him out before the Second World War was even won. "Neither look for nor expect gratitude," Churchill said, "but rather get whatever comfort you can out of the belief that your effort is constructive in purpose." Powell, the aide believed, had served some constructive purpose. This was probably a lower standard than the one to which Powell held himself. Now, sooner than he wanted, he was being replaced by Condoleezza Rice, a shrewder bureaucratic survivor.

After a few awkward minutes in the Oval Office, Powell realized that Bush had no idea what his secretary of state was doing there. The White House chief of staff, Andrew Card, was summoned, but he, too, was clueless. Who had called for the meeting? It began to seem entirely possible that the phantom vice president had arranged one more parting humiliation for his old colleague and more recent nemesis. Powell drew himself up and informed the president that he had come not for their weekly meeting but to say goodbye. Finding himself alone with Bush for perhaps the last time, Powell decided to speak his mind without constraint. The Defense Department had too much power in shaping foreign policy, he argued, and when Bush asked for an example, Powell offered not Rumsfeld, the secretary who had mastered him bureaucratically, not Wolfowitz, the point man on Iraq, but the department's number three official, Douglas Feith, whom Powell called a card-carrying member of the Likud Party. Warming to his talk, Powell moved on to negotiations with North Korea, and then homed in on Iraq: If, by April 1, the situation there had not improved significantly, the president would need a new strategy and new people to implement it. Bush looked taken aback: No one ever spoke this way in the Oval Office. But because it was the last time, Powell ignored every cue of displeasure and kept going until he had said what he had to say, what he perhaps should have said long before.

The following weeks seemed to prove Powell wrong about Iraq. The elections were the most decisive event since the overthrow of the regime, and Bush's insistence that they not be postponed turned out to be one of his best decisions. Voting gave Iraqis a new confidence in themselves and even, to a degree, in their institutions. In the wake of elections, the insurgency seemed to lose force. Iraq's first elected government, with the first Kurdish president in the country's history, still faced the most daunting tasks: building up its security forces so that the fragile democracy could defend itself, winning public trust, writing a constitution, and sorting out the hardest problems, such as the place of former Baathists in government and the military, the role of Islam in society and the law, and the status of Kirkuk. Drew Erdmann liked to say that it all came down to whether Iraq's new leaders were capable of drawing lines on a map.

Beyond Iraq, a new historical wind was starting to blow through the Middle East. Lebanese gathered in massive numbers in Beirut to demand the withdrawal of Syrian troops; Egypt's Hosni Mubarak reluctantly agreed to a contested presidential election; the opposition in Syria was growing bolder; and the stalled Israeli-Palestinian negotiations lurched into motion for the thousandth time. How much credit went to Iraq, how much to the internal dynamics of each country, and how much to luck depended on whom you asked and what position he or she wanted to justify. The administration's neoconservatives had learned their lesson back in 2003; only in private were some of them ready to declare victory again, even as violence in Iraq returned stronger than ever.

Kalev Sepp, the retired Special Forces officer who had trained soldiers in El Salvador, went back to Iraq in November 2004 after a meeting in which General George Casey, Sanchez's successor as commander, asked for his counterinsurgency expert and was met with dead silence: there was none. In Baghdad again, Sepp found that the U.S. military still didn't have a viable campaign plan that addressed the insurgency in a serious way. With a team of American, British, and other officers, he helped design a new strategy that for the first time put the focus on Iraqi security forces, with thousands of American advisers working intensively with the new battalions. In February 2005, an unnamed official was quoted as saying that "it's dawning on [senior leaders] what they're dealing with now" is the need for an overarching counterinsurgency campaign plan. Almost two years after the fall of the regime, the military had finally come to terms with the fact that the Iraq War never ended. But Sepp was under no illusions about an easy victory. "This is going to be a long war. Americans are going to be shot in the streets of Baghdad five years from now."

Most of the war's architects remained in power: Bush and Cheney, Rumsfeld and Rice. They spoke of Iraq so rarely now that one could almost think that Americans were no longer dying there, that the mission was at last accomplished. In the middle of 2005, with Iraq once again consumed in violence that was killing dozens or scores of people every day, Cheney broke his silence to announce that the insurgency was in its "last throes." He had said the same thing after Saddam was captured, a year and a half before. The administration's policy on Iraq was completely adrift; it amounted to saying such things, in the hope of making them so.

The Pentagon announced that Douglas Feith would be leaving to spend more time with his family. Shortly before his departure, Feith described himself to a journalist as a follower of Edmund Burke, the conservative eighteenth-century British philosopher of stability and tradition. He said that the Bush administration had never wanted to impose American values in Iraq, where "Shiite democracy" was a perfectly acceptable substitute. As philosophy this had the sound of an excuse, turning the chaos and violence for which Feith bore much responsibility into an example of American wisdom and restraint in allowing the Iraqis to do things their way. But it was also likely that

Feith, and others in the administration, had never intended from the start to do anything more than remove the tyrant and then walk away.

Paul Wolfowitz became president of the World Bank, the job in which Robert McNamara had sought refuge after leaving the Pentagon at the height of the Vietnam War. But Vietnam, as Leslie Gelb pointed out, had been a liberals' war. Wolfowitz took the job as vindication, not atonement. "Of all the people in this administration who have a hard time sleeping at night," a former senior official said, "Paul's probably at the peak, because he has a conscience. I'm not sure some of these others do." When I asked who else had trouble sleeping, the former official said, "That's a good question," and then he repeated it. But whatever soul-searching Wolfowitz might be doing, he would always believe in the necessity of the war, and in fifty years he might be proved right—"and if some blood is shed and some people die, that's part of life." Did Wolfowitz feel the shedding of blood? "I think so," the former official said. "I'd like to think so, anyway. I don't think I would like him very much if I didn't."

Since America's fate is now tied to Iraq's, it might be years or even decades before the wisdom of the war can finally be judged. When Mao's number two, Chou En-lai, was asked in 1972 what he thought had been the impact of the French revolution, he replied, "It's too early to tell." Paul Wolfowitz and the war's other grand theorists also took the long view of history; if they hadn't, there never would have been an American invasion of Iraq, or, at least, not nearly so soon. Pragmatic officials who asked hard questions about allies, evidence, timing, and plans—especially those, like Powell, who'd been tempered in combat—were not likely to doom flesh to metal on behalf of an idea, even one as compelling as the transformation of the Middle East from an incubator of mass killing to a collection of ordinary, semidemocratic states. There was no immediate threat from Iraq, no grave and gathering danger. The war could have waited.

Who has the right to say whether it was worth it? Chris Frosheiser, who lost so much in Iraq, asks himself the question every day, but he never comes closer to an answer than pride in his son's service and grief at his death. He would not have chosen to give up Kurt for democracy in the Middle East; now he wants Kurt's death to be part of some historical good. Yet Frosheiser always has to pull back, he said, whenever the vision grows too grand, the language too abstract, or else what matters most will be lost: one life, one death.

Daily existence in Iraq remains a nightmare. In the world's newest democracy, most people aren't free to speak their minds, belong to a certain group, wear what they want, or even walk down the street without risking their lives. During the worst of the violence, some Iraqis said that they had been better off under Saddam, that America should never have overthrown him if the result was going to be so much more bloodshed. Few Iraqis I knew ever said it, though. Experts in suffering, they are better qualified than people in Cairo, Rome, London, or Washington to balance their costs against their gains. When I told Aseel that, after the weapons turned out not to exist, some Americans felt betrayed by the Bush administration and Ahmad Chalabi, she exclaimed, "We are more important than missiles!" What the war gave people like her is hope.

The long view of history made the war possible, and the long view of history made the war costly. Out of government, Drew Erdmann dwelled on the institutional character of the administration's mistakes, but in Baghdad in the summer of 2003 he had said that success or failure would largely depend on the judgment of individuals. I came to believe that those in positions of highest responsibility for Iraq showed a carelessness about human life that amounted to criminal negligence. Swaddled in abstract ideas, convinced of their own righteousness, incapable of self-criticism, indifferent to accountability, they turned a difficult undertaking into a needlessly deadly one. When things went wrong, they found other people to blame. The Iraq War was always winnable; it still is. For this very reason, the recklessness of its authors is all the harder to forgive.

ONE DAY IN JANUARY, I met three Iraqi men who were having lunch in the lobby of the Four Seasons Hotel in Amman: a Shiite, a Sunni, and a Kurd. They were in Jordan on business, but they had all lived in Baghdad throughout the rule of Saddam. Wearing jackets and ties, they had the gentle manners of an older Iraqi generation, and they invited me to join their table. The Kurd, a financier named Mahmood, and the Sunni, an architectural engineer named Hisham, were friends of the father of Kanan Makiya. Hisham, the oldest of the three, mentioned with a slight smile that he had made an appearance in Makiya's book *The Monument*. He had been the consulting engineer on a memorial to the Iraqi dead in the war with Iran, the Martyrs' Monument, and had written a fawning tribute to the "Leader-President" for the unveiling in 1983, which Makiya quoted at length.

Mahmood said, "Kanan Makiya was too idealistic, too detached from reality. He came to Baghdad and saw that everything was different."

"Everyone living on the outside thought Iraq was different," Hisham said.

"From the first day, there was a distinct difference between how the internals thought and how the expatriates thought," Mahmood said. "You could see it. Those from outside, the liberal idealists, wanted to put in power believers in Jefferson. That was a good thing. But on the ground, you have people who are still living in the Middle Ages, the tribes, the deprived, the criminal, the religious. And all these will have to be either appeased or won. They couldn't just be swept aside. We knew these people, we were living among them."

During Saddam's time, whenever Hisham traveled from Baghdad to London, the exiles there assumed that he was an agent of the regime. Hisham, who had been imprisoned and sentenced to death after the concrete paving slabs of the Martyrs' Monument began unaccountably to curl up at the edges, would say to them, "After you have your revolution and get rid of Saddam, there will be one million Baathists. What are you going to do with them? Are they all enemies, to be set aside?" The exiles had no answer, or else they answered with a single word—debaathification. "They weren't ready for what they are facing now," Hisham said. "They did not think of a solution for a million Baathists." After the fall of the regime, he added, Kanan Makiya was given too large a role in Iraqi politics.

"I disagree," Mahmood said. "We need him in Iraq. We need his ideas."

"I agree with you," Hisham said. "But that attitude should not be made a ruler of the country. I need such a person to argue with, to hear his ideas, to learn from. But I cannot take him as a legislator."

Mahmood said, "When people are being beheaded and there is so much cruelty in the country, you are glad there's someone like Kanan Makiya, because he is so idealistic. His ideas are so good that we need him. Even if he is a dreamer."

Two months later, in March, I went to see Makiya at his clapboard house on a side street in Cambridge. This wasn't the same place where we'd had so many conversations before the war: After his divorce he had bought this house and filled it with his books. When I arrived, workmen were putting the last coat of paint on the woodwork before sanding the floors.

Makiya wasn't alone in his new house. Wallada al-Sarraf was with him now. Just six weeks before, she had packed two small bags, left her husband and everything else, and come to America to join Makiya. It was an extraordinary act for an Iraqi woman; her friends couldn't understand why she didn't do the normal thing, which was to keep the affair an open secret and go on living as a respectable woman in Iraqi society. Now the gossip was flying around Baghdad, her two older sons refused to talk to her, and Wallada was miserable. Yet she had an air of decision and relief about her.

"I was tired of the lies," she said. "I couldn't stand the pretending." Makiya was still traveling back and forth to Baghdad, but she wanted him to stop going, for her sake and his own. "They are hypocrites. They use him," she said. "They aren't worth someone as naïve and good as Kanan. I know Arab culture—he doesn't."

We went around the corner for lunch. It was snowing, the big wet flakes of a New England nor'easter turning the sidewalks to ponds of slush. I thought back to the snowy Cambridge night in late 2002 when Makiya and I had spent hours discussing the future of Iraq after Saddam, back when everything still lay ahead. He was a dreamer, and his words that night had the purity of untested thoughts, which, more than two years later, I still associated with the white snowfall outside his window. Too much had happened since then for any thought to stay pure. I had seen Makiya many times, in Cambridge, New York, Washington, London, and Baghdad, but I had never been able to sort out my feelings. He was my friend and I loved him. He had devoted his life to an idea of Iraq that I embraced. He had attached that idea to the machinery of war, and a lot of people had gotten killed. No idea remains intact once it's been bloodied by history, and history had not followed Makiya's blueprint. At times, his vision of Iraq had been so at odds with what I saw and heard there that dreaming began to seem irresponsible and dangerous. I wanted to know what the past two years had done to him.

Makiya seemed to guess my thoughts. As we ate our lentil soup, he mentioned his friend Mustafa al-Kadhimi, the exile I'd met in London who went back to Baghdad and was now working for Makiya's Memory Foundation. Mustafa had never been an intellectual, but he had been one of the few exiles who showed real wisdom as he negotiated the realities on the ground in Iraq. What mattered was the elusive human factor. "The single biggest test Iraqi exile politicians coming back faced was not one of ideas," Makiya said, and I sensed that he was speaking of himself. "The ideas were fundamentally all there and sound. Ideas are important, yes. But the test was one of character. And here they virtually all failed." The world of exile politics was dominated by programs and statements, including many that Makiya himself had written or signed. "But in the actual playing out of this since April of 2003, suddenly human character, individual character traits, become very important. People fall flat on their face or shine not because of their great ideas, but because of certain traits of character which suddenly acquire great importance in the actual practice of politics in these extremely tumultuous times."

Ideas like debaathification and demilitarization, Makiya said, weren't wrong. He still believed in them. But he had been living in Iraq now for the better part of two years, and the staff of the Memory Foundation at his house in Baghdad was scanning fifty or a hundred thousand Baath Party documents a month. Those two years and all those documents had shown Makiya the complexity of Iraq both under Saddam and since. Ideas required this deep human knowledge. Culpability was often gray and vague. People did things for the most complicated reasons, and politics was too narrow to explain and judge them all; true understanding required Makiya's real love, literature.

He realized that he wasn't suited to politics, and he had pulled away from Iraq's, away from his old friend Ahmad Chalabi. Makiya was putting his energy into the Memory Foundation, to which the city of Baghdad had leased the one square kilometer at its heart where the crossed swords and parade ground displayed Saddam's vision in all its brutality. Makiya wanted in effect to turn the monument's meaning upside down, making it a memorial to Saddam's victims.

As we talked, Wallada laid her head on Makiya's shoulder. She was exhausted, and we walked back through the snow to their house. The plumbers had the water on in the new bathroom, and Makiya insisted with his characteristic excitement that Wallada and I watch as he turned on the shower. The shower head was sitting at an angle, and when the water came, it sprayed half the bathroom. Wallada laughed, saying, "Just like Kanan."

She went to take a nap, and Makiya made a pot of Turkish coffee. Shortly, he would go pick up his young daughter for the weekend. As we stood in the kitchen, he was still thinking about his project for the crossed swords monument. He hoped that a new generation of Iraqis would visit the memorial when it was finished and learn what had been done in their country. He wanted them not to point the finger of blame, but to draw a human lesson and say, "My God, what happened here? Anybody in certain circumstances can do terrible things to other people. We should never let those circumstances happen in our country again." Out of such recognitions, such self-scrutiny, a new Iraqi identity might be born.

The Turkish coffee was boiling over on the stove.

Makiya said, "I think it was Ahmad who once said of me that I embody the triumph of hope over experience."

In January 2006, near the end of the third year of the Iraq War, I arrived in Baghdad during Eid al-Adha, the feast that concludes the pilgrimage to Mecca. The city's streets were empty, except for long lines of cars at gas stations; Baghdad was in the grip of a fuel crisis, mainly due to attacks on refineries and pipelines, which in turn had worsened the electricity shortage that now cut power for eighteen or twenty hours a day across the capital. At night, whole neighborhoods went dark. There were fewer American patrols than I was used to seeing, and more Iraqi police and soldiers manning checkpoints. The Palestine Hotel, where, in the first year after the regime's fall, journalists and contractors had trouble getting rooms, was vacant except for four of its eighteen floors. In early December, a suicide bomber driving a cement truck packed with explosives had nearly brought the tower down, and a month later the lobby's blown-out windows were still covered in plastic, the wiring hanging down from blasted ceiling tiles. Most of the foreign press corps had gone home. A lonely manager sat behind his desk in the lobby as if expecting the clientele to return any moment. Outside, at a concession stand, a vendor announced to no one, "Jack Daniel's, beer, vodka, everything." A boy of around ten walked past and asked me, in an aggressive Southern accent that would be some American soldier's lasting contribution to the transformation of Iraq, "You lookin' for somethin'?"

It felt as if the Americans had already abandoned Iraq to its underemployed hotel managers, its street kids, and its armed militiamen. One could almost imagine that, after three years of occupation, after tens of billions of dollars and thousands of lives and the feverish efforts of foreigners and Iraqis to lift the country out of its own history, the interlude of grand visions was over and Iraq was returning to its true nature, sectarian and sinister.

In fact, the Americans were still here—most of them now hidden away in high-walled compounds or out in the desert on remote bases that were like small cities. And Iraq was not becoming more like itself. It was entering a period that Iraqis had never known and deeply feared. Their leaders, elected in December 2005 in a nationwide vote that amounted to a census of the country's three major groups, were trying to form the first representative government in the country's history; meanwhile, street by street and village by village, Iraqis were killing Iraqis in terrible numbers.

The Sunni insurgency was as relentlessly brutal as ever. And now Shiite militias, some of them working under the guise of the official security forces that they had infiltrated, were raiding Sunni neighborhoods and rounding up young Sunni men, who disappeared into secret prisons or turned up bound, blindfolded, and dead on the street or in shallow graves, the corpses burned, full of drill holes, mutilated, shot in the head. After years of suicide bombings and mass killings of Shiite civilians by Sunni insurgents, Shiite militiamen had begun to ignore Ayatollah Sistani's counsel of restraint and were retaliating, creating widespread fear among Sunnis for the first time. In the cycle of revenge, Shia were being driven from the heavily Sunni neighborhoods of western Baghdad and the mixed towns surrounding the capital, while their longtime neighbors stood by and said nothing. The same was happening to Sunnis in the Shiite areas. Thousands of displaced families were gathering in camps and shelters around Baghdad. It amounted to a campaign of ethnic cleansing in a low-grade civil war.

Iraqis had always avoided the words "civil war" as if simply uttering them might release a malignant spirit into the air. Ethnic and sectarian identities, they insisted, were brought to Iraq after the invasion by the Americans and their allies, the exiles. Iraqis had been living together, in mixed marriages and mixed neighborhoods, for decades and centuries. To start a civil war would mean turning a single household, a single marriage chamber, against itself. It couldn't happen here, they said, meaning, "We don't want it to happen here," and the subject was so unwelcome that even mentioning the words "Sunni" and "Shiite" was taken as the rudeness of a clumsy outsider. But after three years of politics and violence carried out along sectarian lines, the labels were now used openly, with fear and hatred.

Dora, a middle-class neighborhood of Sunnis, Shia, and Christians in southern Baghdad, had become ground zero of sectarian violence. It began with the killing of barbers, a businessman from Dora told me: Sunni extremists decided that shaving beards was against Islam, and then extended the ban to Western-style haircuts. "After the barbers, they went on to the real estate agents," the businessman said. A fatwa was issued declaring that in the time of the Prophet there was no buying or selling of property. Then an ice vendor was shot dead on the street because ice wasn't sold in the seventh century. The targets became grocery shop owners, exchange shop owners, clothing shop owners. "At that time they were giving reasons, but then things developed and they started killing for no reason," the businessman said. Every day in the heart of the district, around the Assyrian Market, a list of names of the next batch of intended victims—mostly merchants, and always Shia—circulated by word of mouth. Within a few days, those who didn't take precautions were shot to death in broad daylight by gunmen from outside Dora. Police at the local stations didn't get involved, and American soldiers rarely entered the district, though the businessman said that he went to sleep at night to the sound of gunfire, helicopters overhead, and bombs dropping, as if he lived on the front line of a battle. "Dora is out of the government's control," the businessman said, and there were hardly any Shia left.

A senior Iraqi official with access to classified intelligence said that the campaign of killings in Dora was part of a strategic effort by Sunni insurgents to "shape the battlefield," to clear the district of potential enemies and use it as a staging area for attacks in Baghdad. Dora had key infrastructure facilities—an oil refinery and a power plant—and it lay along the route from the Sunni-dominated tribal areas south of Baghdad into the heart of the city. The killings there were part of a trend, the official said, away from attacks on American and Iraqi units, which exposed insurgents to great risk, toward killings of individual officials and ordinary citizens, intended to undermine the public's confidence that the government could protect it. In January, he said, there were seven hundred of these cold-blooded murders, the highest number of the war up until that month. "So 2006 maybe will be the year of assassinations and infrastructure attacks," the official said.

Whatever the strategic reasons for the killings, they created an atmosphere of sectarian hysteria that residents of Baghdad had never known before.

I met a butcher named Mohamed Kareem Jassim, who owned a small shop on a busy thoroughfare, the doorway obstructed by the hanging carcasses of skinned lambs. His brother was also a butcher, with a shop in Dora. One morning in January, the brother was cutting meat for two women customers when a man walked into the shop, asked the women to excuse him, came up to the counter, and said, "Good morning." The brother looked up, said, "Good morning," and was shot in the nose. His grown son rushed into the room, shouting, "Daddy, Daddy!" and he, too, was shot dead. A second brother, also a butcher, came running from an adjacent shop with a carving knife in his hand; he was also killed.

When I sat down ten days later to talk with the surviving brother, a stout, bearded man in his fifties, he was hyperventilating with rage. "Dirty fuckers, sons of bitches. They have no faith, no religious leaders, since the time of Omar and Abu Bakr until now," he said, going straight back to the seventh century. "The only reason for this is because we are Shia and we love Imam Ali." He expressed great bitterness that Sunni religious and political leaders rarely condemn the killings of Shia, and he despaired at being protected by American or Iraqi security forces. The butcher's shoulders heaved and he said, "If our religious leaders gave a fatwa, there would be no more Sunnis in Iraq anymore. The one who stayed would be killed—everyone else would have to leave. Because everybody now has a broken heart. I wish I could catch them with my hands and slaughter them. I could do it—I'm a butcher."

Each group had its own story of victimhood, in fierce competition with the other. One day, I visited the headquarters in western Baghdad of the Iraqi Islamic Party, the country's largest Sunni party, with roots in the Muslim Brotherhood. On the walls of its human rights office hung pictures of corpses bearing marks of torture, inflicted, according to a party official, by Interior Ministry forces. While I was in the office, an elderly couple arrived in a state of panic. A week before, at six in the morning, fifteen police commandos in black masks had broken into their house and taken their son from his conjugal bed. Since then the parents had been unable to get any information about him. The old woman described the commandos as members of the Badr Organization, the largest Shiite militia in Iraq. One of its leaders, Bayan Jabr, had been the minister of interior for the past year and was accused of allowing Shiite militias to infiltrate key offices of the ministry, creating rogue units within the police forces. Sunnis now routinely called Shiite politicians like Jabr Iranians; the mother used a Persian name for him. "Fifty-five years I'm alive and I never saw something like this," she cried. "They are bringing it from Iran, from the Persian people—Iran, which is now trying to get the nuclear bomb to destroy the world."

The party official, Omar Hechel al-Jabouri, told the old couple that he would contact the Interior Ministry about the case, to prevent their son from being killed during interrogation and torture. Every day, he said, a hundred people came to his office with complaints, so many that he had taken to sleeping on a cot in the corner of the room. "The main problem is our brothers the Shia are very smart in crying about their suffering," he said. "We others are not as smart."

Iraq was breaking apart—not cleanly into the three autonomous regions of some politicians' dreams, but neighborhood by neighborhood, in thousands of pieces. This was not true just of Baghdad and the areas around it, or of mixed cities like Mosul and Kirkuk, but of the south as well. The elections of January 2005, which had made Iraqis citizens for one triumphant day, brought to power Shiite groups that governed more like mafia organizations than national parties. A year later, Basra was full of militias—fragments of the Sadr and Badr organizations, along with shadowy Iranian-run gangs, each led by its own mullah. They amounted to death squads and had the run of the streets. An official I had met during the elections in Basra reported that, in one ten-day period, fifty people—doctors, teachers, officials, university students—were assassinated around the city. The death squads moved in pairs of cars known as Bata, or, in Arabic, "swan." "The story of this car is horrible and anybody must avoid this kind of car—black window glass, four armed people, and always another car following and some invisible ghosts sit inside," he wrote. One morning, as he drove to work, the official found himself trapped between two Batas, and when armed men calmly got out and approached, he thought that the death squads had come for him—only to witness the execution of a man in the car next to his. "Thousands of people are like me," he wrote, "our hearts in Iraq are made of wood, our eyes full of sand, and we are like sheep under the shepherd's order, waiting for the knife of the butcher."

The disintegration of the country had been underway for a long time; in a sense, it had begun years before the Americans crossed the Kuwaiti border in March 2003. But by 2006 it was happening with alarming speed, and with all the signs of being irreversible. Iraqis who had once said that Iraq would need one or two years to emerge from violence now spoke in terms of a decade or more: a generation of chaos following generations of tyranny.

Iraq never ceased to offer paradoxes. American policies and military tactics had contributed a great deal to the strength of the insurgency and the spiral of sectarian violence that followed. And yet, in the same month when I saw how far Baghdad had descended, I also saw evidence that the American military was finally learning to fight the insurgency in an effective way. In the northwestern town of Tal Afar, which had repeatedly fallen into the hands of Sunni extremists after the Americans failed to hold it, an armored cavalry regiment under a brilliant colonel named H. R. McMaster spent the better part of 2005 living in the city, developing relationships with local people, training counterparts in the Iraqi army, and practicing the classic counter-insurgency strategy of separating the civilian population from insurgents, providing security, and setting up institutions of government that could win popular support. All of this required a large, long-term American presence in the city and a willingness to take risks and suffer casualties. McMaster and his young officers had trained for this approach in Colorado and undertaken it in Tal Afar on their own initiative, as rebels against the intellectual failures of their senior civilian and military leaders. In Tal Afar, which had been the Falluja of the north, American and Iraqi forces managed to achieve a fragile peace. I saw what might have been possible had such things been done at the outset.

It was too little and too late. After the years of mistakes and incoherent strategy from the Pentagon and the White House, America's leverage in Iraq has greatly diminished. The tens of thousands of American soldiers who are still there, and who continued to die by ones and twos, are placeholders, buffers, trying to hold the structure of a national government together until it can exist as facts on the ground, while suppressing even worse violence—the nightmare specter of a full-scale civil war and a regional war that could consume the whole Middle East and leave the carcass of Iraq to be picked over by militias, terrorists, and predatory neighbors. America might still be able to avert the worst in Iraq, but there is no prospect of a stable, decent country for years to come. That chance was already slipping away when I first went there in the hopeful, troubled summer of 2003; it is now long gone.

The failure of American policy in Iraq raises the biggest, hardest questions about the war. Was the insurgency inevitable? Could such a damaged and divided society ever have been expected to stay in one piece, let alone find its way to democracy? Could the administration of President George W. Bush ever have succeeded at a project as difficult as this, undertaken with such arrogance and blindness, with so few friends and so much international scorn? The stated cause for war—weapons of mass destruction and links to international terrorism—proved to be exaggerated or false. Could any other cause—the rescue of a country with which America has for years been historically entangled, the end of a tyranny, the beginning of Arab reform—have justified it?

It's still possible that the fondest hopes of the war's architects will be realized in a generation or two, that regime change in Iraq will advance democracy and reduce extremism across the Middle East. But policy makers are accountable within the parameters of their own watch. For now, and into the foreseeable future, American and liberal, Western interests have been badly damaged by the fighting in Iraq. The war has been a disaster for our military, which has suffered grievous death and injury, lost a measure of its honor at Abu Ghraib, and in the deaths of far too many Iraqi civilians, and been overextended to the point where withdrawal might become necessary simply for want of available troops. The vast majority of soldiers did all that was asked of them, but many of the best—including John Prior—have decided to leave an institution they love. Failure in Iraq has been marked by a complete lack of accountability in Washington, which finally drove a handful of normally reticent retired generals to do something almost unprecedented in American military history: speak out publicly and point the finger of blame at their former boss, Donald Rumsfeld.

The direct costs to national treasure are easy to measure, now well over $300 billion; the fraying of alliances, the loss of American power and prestige, the draining of attention and resources from other crises, especially the struggle against the twin dangers of worldwide jihad and nuclear proliferation, are harder to quantify but no less real. The war's outcome has proved it to have been a mistake—a huge one, such as only happens once every few generations.

The Iraq War brought to an end the age of humanitarian intervention, which had helped to make it thinkable. The war revealed what was already obvious to experienced soldiers and should have been to civilian idealists: moral purpose combined with force, without knowledge and wisdom, can be more dangerous than indifference. The consequences of any war are unknowable, other than inevitable death, and the ground in Iraq was always inhospitable to building anything durable and good. A war to end tyranny there—even one as monstrous as Saddam Hussein's, for which the United States had a historical responsibility, first by arming him against Iran, then by leaving him in power in 1991, and finally by imposing sanctions that ruined the lives of millions of Iraqis—such a war should not have been undertaken as it was against such long odds, with so little legitimacy in the eyes of the world. Nothing is inevitable; human beings, organized by activities called politics and war, make things happen as they do, and Iraq might have turned out otherwise if the human beings involved had been and done otherwise. But war is too blunt an instrument to be used when the chance for success is so slight.

The war has given rise to a deeply skeptical view in this country: that Iraqis have proven that they were always incapable of living together, of forming a nation, of creating a democracy; that they have the wrong culture. It's true that, once the lid was lifted, Iraq turned out to be more religious, more tribal, more suspicious, and more violent than most outsiders had imagined. This had less to do with something hereditary and permanent called "Iraqi culture" than with a history of government by force, from Iraq's origins in boundaries drawn by Europeans to the damage inflicted by thirty-five years of Baathist rule. If the best armed and least tolerant factions came to dominate post-Saddam Iraq, this hardly reflected the free will of the Iraqi people. The cardinal sin of the Americans was to create the conditions for chaos. From the moment of the old regime's fall, no one in Iraq was safe from violent intimidation, and it was only a matter of time before insurgents and militias became powerful. Ordinary Iraqis, whatever society they might have wanted to live in—and many of them could not yet have known—were never allowed to practice the art of citizenship. The three elections of 2005 showed that Iraqis were capable of political courage and maturity, but the elections also ratified what had already become reality in the streets: sectarian violence led to sectarian votes. The rule of the tyrant was followed by the rule of the gunmen. By failing to secure the country, the Americans failed to give Iraqis the true freedom to decide their future for themselves.

For better or worse, our fate is now tied to theirs. There can be no phased withdrawal from the future of Iraq. Some significant withdrawal of American troops in 2006 and 2007 seems inevitable. Whether it happens according to a timetable determined by American politicians, through a plan negotiated between the American and Iraqi governments, or according to the advice of military commanders under great pressure to show success on the ground, the withdrawal will have far more to do with American politics than with the war in Iraq. The debate in Washington is so shrouded in partisanship and illusion as to be almost meaningless. For Iraq to have any real chance of stability, large numbers of foreign troops will need to remain in Iraq, heavily involved in security and reconstruction, for years to come. Perhaps the U.S. government will decide that the large-scale American commitment has achieved all it can in Iraq, and that our national interests require moving troops to Kuwait or Qatar, where they will try to secure oil supplies, deter neighboring countries from encroaching, and act as a last-resort intervention force in case the insurgency makes dramatic gains and the Iraqi government is about to fall. If that day comes, it will have nothing to do with success in Iraq. The administration will declare victory, the opposition will declare vindication, but Iraqis will know that they are being left to sort it out among themselves. And although the American presence in Iraq has thrown the Middle East into turmoil, an American departure will only enhance the position of the regional powers—Iran, Saudi Arabia, Turkey—and tempt them to fill the vacuum left behind. There is also a good chance that western Iraq will be under the control of no government, Iraqi or foreign, and will become a base of operations for regional jihad. The effort to create representative government and hold the country together against forces of violence and fragmentation will have lasting consequences for Americans, far greater than Vietnam ever did. The notion that we can withdraw our forces and be done with it, leaving the Iraqis to sort things out, is a fantasy.

Throughout the new nightmare into which they awoke from the nightmare of Saddam, Iraqis have shown a patience and a resilience, born of many years of suffering, which is one of the very few sources of hope I can find in Iraq today. The ordinary people I know there who long for a decent life, without suicide bombs, electrical outages, or the secret police, make it difficult for me to write it all off as an irredeemable disaster. It took me a long time even to be able to consider the biggest historical questions about the war; they required a distance from the hope and suffering in Iraq that I couldn't achieve. Once the regime fell and I began traveling there, all the old arguments about the merits of the war fell away with it. What mattered was the drama being played out across the country, and I had no doubt where my sympathies lay: I wanted Iraqis to have the chance at the decent life they'd been denied for so long. I wanted what the American invasion had unleashed to succeed. I also wanted to understand why it was failing, but my feelings made the detachment that truly objective analysis needs impossible.

For all the horrors of daily life in Baghdad, I always wanted to return there, and while I was there I didn't want to leave. There was something strangely compelling about the place even after the worst violence began. Human encounters were more intense; relationships formed quickly, conversations got straight to the point; the Iraqis I knew felt no shame about expressing strong emotions, and this was also true of Americans, including soldiers. People of very short acquaintance were sometimes prepared to risk their lives for each other. The news in Iraq was full of unspeakable brutality, but my experiences were marked far more by generosity and kindness, and I always found it hard to leave behind friends who have to go on living there, whose lives grow more precarious every day.

I came to feel that the most appropriate response to the events of the past few years was neither justification nor reproach, but simple grief for the hopes and sacrifices of Iraqis and Americans alike. The Iraq War is not an argument to be won or lost; it's a tragedy.

On a quiet street in eastern Baghdad, behind a garden with lawn chairs arranged in rows, there is a small, unremarkable two-story building. The sign in front, which says "Al-Janna Center," is barely visible from the street, for reasons of safety. Al-Janna means "Paradise," and Dr. Baher Butti, who directs the clinic, had been warned by anonymous fundamentalists that paradise cannot be found on Earth.

In the three years that I had known him, Dr. Butti had been perpetually, and increasingly, skeptical about the motives of the Americans, Iraqi politicians, religious leaders, and the country's neighbors; and yet he pursued with great persistence the idea that had first come to him after the fall of the old regime: he wanted to open a "psycho-social rehabilitation clinic" that would rebuild the humanity of his countrymen. Dr. Butti believed that, after decades of dictatorship, wars, sanctions, and occupation, Iraqis need to learn to talk, to think, to tolerate. He had registered his proposal for the clinic with the occupation authority and successive Iraqi ministries, but none of them had given him support. In 2005, a Baghdad newspaper owner donated funds, and in January 2006, just before I visited, the al-Janna Center finally opened.

In the waiting room, brightly colored abstract paintings by patients hung on the walls. Up a narrow flight of stairs, there were several small meeting rooms where Dr. Butti planned to hold lectures, poetry readings, computer-training courses, and women's mental-health group meetings. The center was humble and barely furnished, but, amid the grinding ugliness and violence of Baghdad, it felt like an oasis of calm. "If we gain humanitarian care for our patients, then the rebound will be a humanitarian movement in all of the society," Dr. Butti said. "This place is not just a scientific institute. It's also a place for literature and arts. We are trying to educate people about communication."

Dr. Butti lived in Dora, the mixed neighborhood in south Baghdad that had been particularly violent. "There are no direct clashes in the streets, but when every day you have one or two of your acquaintances killed, this is civil war." Most of his friends and colleagues were leaving Iraq, along with much of the country's professional class.

When we sat down in his office, with cups of tea, he said, "Let me tell you about my own conflict." His conflict was simple: to stay or to leave. In May 2005, his young daughter was badly injured when her school bus was hit by a suicide car bomb. After that, his wife insisted that the family move to Abu Dhabi. Yet Dr. Butti had finally achieved something tangible in Iraq, and to leave now would be like abandoning a child. "I feel like someone who's been cut from the roots," he said.

Dr. Butti's decision depended on what would happen in the next few months, and on the formation of a new government. He didn't have much hope for improvement any time soon, but he was looking for some sign of stability. "Or it will go into a civil war, and all will be lost, and there will be nothing to be done here anymore. It's either this year or none." He added, "Not one of the Iraqis believes that you should leave tomorrow. Believe me. Even the Sunni leaders—they announce it in the media, but that's for, let's say, public use. They know that we can't have the American army leaving the country right now, because, excuse me to say, George Bush did a mess, he must clean it." He shrugged and smiled, in his pained way. "We are attached in a Catholic marriage with our occupiers. It's not able to have a divorce."

He walked me outside into the sunlit garden. On the street a car passed slowly by. For an hour, I had forgotten to be afraid, and now that we were saying goodbye I was reluctant to go. In the past we had always shaken hands, but on this occasion Dr. Butti kissed my cheeks, in the Iraqi way. Perhaps he felt, as I did, that we might not meet again for a long time.

May 2006

NOTE ON SOURCES

This is mainly a book of reporting. Dozens of Americans, Iraqis, and others allowed me to interview them, follow them around, and learn from them. Some people gave me many hours or even days of their time. They are too many to be named here, and a few wouldn't want to be, so at least the published version of my thanks will have to remain collective and anonymous.

In addition to interviews, I depended for information and insight on the Iraq coverage in the world press, especially *The New York Times, The Washington Post, Los Angeles Times, The Boston Globe, Newsweek, Time, The New Yorker, The Atlantic Monthly,* Knight-Ridder, the Associated Press, Reuters, *The Telegraph, The Guardian* and *The Observer, Le Monde, Corriere della Sera, The Daily Star* of Beirut, the Stanhope Centre's *Iraqi Media Developments Newsletter,* and the Institute for War and Peace Reporting's *Iraqi Press Monitor.* I was also helped by the publications and Web sites of the Center for Strategic and International Studies, the Council on Foreign Relations, the United States Institute of Peace, the Brookings Institution, the Royal Institute for International Affairs, and the Middle East Media Research Institute. I regularly read a number of Iraqi blogs, especially www.healingiraq.blogspot .com, and I also benefited from information and links on www.andrewsullivan.com, www.juancole.com, www.warandpiece.com, and the "Iraq'd" blog of *The New Republic.*

The following books and articles were also useful:

Fouad Ajami, *The Dream Palace of the Arabs: A Generation's Odyssey.* New York: Pantheon, 1998.

Hanna Batatu, *The Old Social Classes and the Revolutionary Movements of Iraq.* London: Saqi Books, 2004 (3rd ed.).

Gertrude Bell, *The Letters of Gertrude Bell: Vols. I and II.* London: Ernest Benn, 1927.

Paul Berman, *Terror and Liberalism.* New York: Norton, 2003.

Richard A. Clarke, *Against All Enemies: Inside America's War on Terror.* New York: Free Press, 2004.

Ivo H. Daalder and James M. Lindsay, *America Unbound: The Bush Revolution in Foreign Policy.* Washington, D.C.: Brookings Institution Press, 2003.

Larry Diamond, *Squandered Victory: The American Occupation and the Bungled Effort to Bring Democracy to Iraq.* New York: Times Books, 2005.

David Dudley, "Paul's Choice," *Cornell Alumni Magazine,* July/August 2004.

James Fallows, "Blind into Baghdad," *The Atlantic Monthly,* January/February 2004.

Franklin Foer and Spencer Ackerman, "The Radical," *The New Republic,* December 1, 2003.

David Fromkin, *A Peace to End All Peace: The Fall of the Ottoman Empire and the Creation of the Modern Middle East.* New York: Henry Holt, 1989.

Thomas X. Hammes, *The Sling and the Stone: On War in the 21st Century.* Osceola, WI: Zenith Press, 2004.

Seymour M. Hersh, *Chain of Command: The Road from 9/11 to Abu Ghraib.* New York: HarperCollins, 2004.

Robert Kagan, *Of Paradise and Power: America and Europe in the New World Order.* New York: Knopf, 2003.

Robert Kagan and William Kristol (eds.), *Present Dangers: Crisis and Opportunity in American Foreign and Defense Policy.* San Francisco: Encounter Books, 2000.

Mark Lilla, "Leo Strauss: The European" and "The Closing of the Straussian Mind," *The New York Review of Books,* October 21 and November 4, 2004.

Kanan Makiya, *Cruelty and Silence: War, Tyranny, Uprising, and the Arab World.* New York: W. W. Norton, 1993.

———, *Republic of Fear: The Politics of Modern Iraq.* Berkeley: University of California Press, 1991 (rev. ed.).

James Mann, *Rise of the Vulcans: The History of Bush's War Cabinet.* New York: Viking Books, 2004.

Jane Mayer, "The Manipulator," *The New Yorker,* June 7, 2004.

Yitzhak Nakash, *The Shi'is of Iraq.* Princeton, NJ: Princeton University Press, 1994.

David Rieff, "Blueprint for a Mess," *The New York Times Magazine,* November 1, 2003.

Micah L. Sifry and Christopher Cerf (eds.), *The Iraq War Reader: History, Documents, Opinions*. New York: Touchstone, 2003.

Sam Tanenhaus, "Bush's Brain Trust," *Vanity Fair*, July 2003.

Charles Tripp, *A History of Iraq*. Cambridge, MA: Cambridge University Press, 2002 (2nd ed.).

Lawrence Weschler, *Calamities of Exile: Three Nonfiction Novellas*. Chicago: University of Chicago Press, 1996.

Bob Woodward, *Plan of Attack*. New York: Simon & Schuster, 2004.

David Wurmser, *Tyranny's Ally: America's Failure to Defeat Saddam Hussein*. Washington, D.C.: American Enterprise Institute Press, 1999.

ACKNOWLEDGMENTS

I AM ABOVE ALL GRATEFUL to the Iraqis who worked with me, in extenuating circumstances, in Iraq. Those who can be named here are Omar Abdelkhader, Ali Fadhil, Ali Hussein, Qais al-Jalili, Dhia al-Lamy, Omar Salih, and "Serwan." They kept me alive and allowed me to get to know their country, for which they have my deep thanks. I am also grateful for the hospitality of my friends at the Baghdad bureau of National Public Radio and of The New York Times. I also thank Tom Rhodes and Tamam Zeidan of USAID for their hospitality in Basra. Ranya Kadri of Amman always got me in and out of Iraq safely.

The editors of The New York Times Magazine first put me on the Iraq story, and for that I thank Katherine Bouton, Megan Liberman, Gerry Marzorati, and Adam Moss. For my four trips to Iraq and the chance to write about the subject at length and in depth, I owe a great debt to The New Yorker and especially to its editor, David Remnick, to Dorothy Wickenden, and to my editor at the magazine, Daniel Zalewski. I also thank Virginia Cannon, Bruce Diones, Pam McCarthy, Lauren Porcaro, and the fact-checking department, especially Nana Asfour, Gita Daneshjoo, Allison Hoffman, Raffi Khatchadourian, Nandi Rodrigo, and Andy Young.

Kathy Anderson, my agent, has provided consistent support. Douglas Gillison did conscientious work as a research assistant. At Farrar, Straus and Giroux, I am grateful for the work of Wah-Ming Chang, Cary Goldstein, Debra Helfand, Cynthia Merman, Jeff Seroy, Annie Wedekind, and above all Jonathan Galassi, who is a great friend as well as editor.

ACKNOWLEDGMENTS

Thanks to these friends for sharing and enriching my Iraq obsession: Deb Amos, Jon Lee Anderson, Dan Bergner, Paul Berman, Robyn Creswell, Dexter Filkins, Bill Finnegan, Annie Garrels, Marcela Gaviria, Jeff Goldberg, Philip Gourevitch, Feisal Istrabadi, Mustafa al-Kadhimi, Fred Kaplan, Kanan Makiya, Scott Malcomson, and Ammar al-Shahbander. I thank my mother and sister for their love and support through nerve-racking absences and their unfailing interest in my work. Laura Secor gave this book and its author the full measure of her love and intelligence. For that I owe her my greatest thanks.

INDEX

INDEX

Cheney, Richard, 25, 27, 38, 51, 53, 104, 107, 113, 124, 136, 145–46, 446; background of, 42–44, 64; Chalabi and, 77, 147; DPG and, 13, 14, 43; on liberation of Iraq, 97–98; Makiya and, 74, 96; military deferment of, 26; 9/11 and, 43; on WMD, 61–62

Chomsky, Noam, 57

Chou En-lai, 447

Christians, 338, 341, 348, 405–406, 432, 455

Churchill, Winston, 334, 390, 393, 444

Clark, William, 105

Clarke, Richard, 39–40

Clay, Darrell, 373

Cleveland, Robin, 143

Clinton, Bill, 265, 382, 393, 394; foreign policy of, 14–15, 20, 40, 117; Iraq policy of, 10, 23–24, 36, 78, 119

Coalition Provisional Authority (CPA), 3, 146, 180–218, 240, 304–305, 313–25, 327; collapse of credibility of, 325; end of, 332; understaffing of, 184; *see also* Bremer

Cohn-Bendit, Daniel, 56

Collis, Simon, 428

Communist Party, Iraqi, 335

constitution, Iraqi, 321, 356; interim, 262–63, 316, 317, 351, 356, 363

Conway, James, 323

Cordesman, Anthony, 307

Crocker, Ryan, 67

Dafir, 275–76

Daniels, Mitchell, 143

Dawa Party, 93, 151, 408, 425, 427

Dawood, Emad, 412–13

Dawood, Luna, 337–42, 347, 349, 367–69

Dawood, Saad, 412–13

Dean, Howard, 397

Dearlove, Sir Richard, 61

Defense Planning Guidance (DPG), 13–14, 21, 24, 43, 63, 90

democracy: compared to well-functioning army, 67; ethnic warfare as strategy against, 310; in Iraq, 27, 46, 58, 67–68, 74–75, 78–83, 96, 99, 136–37, 166, 184, 398, 403, 407–13, 443, 446, 459, 460, 461; Islam and, 208, 272, 330, 430; in Middle East, 22, 60–61, 395–96, 445; neoconservatives and,

17–21, 37, 53; Zarqawi's denunciation of, 414; *see also* elections

DeMuth, Chris, 111–12

Dettman, David, 409–13

Diamond, Larry, 315–16

Di Rita, Larry, 129, 133

Diwaniya, 198–200

Dodd, Christopher, 127

Dole, Robert, 22

Dora, 455–56, 464

Dostoyevsky, Fyodor, 31, 50

Duelfer, Charles, 298–99

Dwitch, Abdul-Jabbar, 172, 229–30, 250

Edwards, John, 377, 380

elections, 413–39, 457, 461; in Basra, 434–39, 458; Bush's insistence on, 413–14, 445; nationwide results of, 438–39; Saddam's, 435–36; Sistani on, 213, 316–17, 413, 431, 434

al-Emara, Youssef, 419–22, 424

Emerson, Ralph Waldo, 85

Erbil, 285–86, 343, 347, 353

Erdmann, Andrew P. N. (Drew), 100–104, 113, 129–30, 133, 134, 139, 141, 143, 146, 187–89, 192–93, 202, 208–12, 304, 442–43, 448

Ezekiel, shrine of, 288

Fadhel, Gha'ab, 348

Fairbanks, Charles, 55

Falluja, 221–24, 277, 281, 282, 297, 310, 323, 331, 334, 394, 414

Fedayeen Saddam, 179, 224, 231, 233, 298

Feinstein, Dianne, 378

Feith, Douglas, 29–32, 38, 62, 79, 105–107, 109, 114, 115, 138, 193–94, 299, 304, 391, 444, 447; Chalabi and, 127–28; on debaathification, 192; postwar planning and, 121–23, 125–30, 133, 147

Feldman, Noah, 77, 138, 144

Fenton, James, 186

Fleischer, Ari, 318

Fleischer, Michael, 318, 320

Ford, Gerald, 17, 26, 42

foreign jihadis, 310–11

Forrest, Charles, 88–89

Franks, Tommy, 45, 118–20, 134, 137, 138, 139, 142, 147, 244, 298

Fromkin, David, 189, 334

INDEX

origin of, 257–58, 432; parties of, 431; pleasure marriage in, 272–73, 279; restoration of monarchy and, 30; retaliation against Sunnis, 454; theocracy in Iraq and, 314
Shinseki, Eric K., 114–17, 147, 246
Shulsky, Abram, 13, 38, 105–106, 107, 108, 122
Shultz, George, 18
Silverman, Jerry, 243–44
al-Sistani, Ayatollah Ali, 213, 264, 271, 312, 313, 316–17, 321, 322, 324, 332, 413, 434, 439, 454; election coalition of, 418, 438, 441
Sky, Emma, 358–60
Slocombe, Walter, 194, 306
Soane, E. B., 342
Solzhenitsyn, Alexander, 12, 48, 70
South African mercenaries, 240–41
Spanish troops, 315, 323
Special Plans, Office of, 105–109, 122, 127, 128, 134, 141, 391
Stalin, Joseph, 49, 57, 153
Stewart, Rory, 407
Strauss, Leo, 26, 31, 44, 54–55, 56, 105–106
Strosky, E. A., 418
suicide bombers, 298, 327, 393, 426, 453, 462
Suleimaniya, 283–87, 353, 362
Sullivan, Andrew, 383
Sumaidaie, Samir Shakir, 365
Sunnis: alliance of Shia and, 324; election boycott by, 415–17; in elections, 439–40; insurgency of, 312, 323–24, 409, 416–17, 454–457, 458; as modernizers, 308; origin of, 257, 452; traditional rule of Iraq by, 333–35, 465; United Nations and, 213
Sunni Triangle, 300, 327
Suskind, Ron, 390
Swanson, Brad, 186–87, 318–20
Swope, Robert, 374
Sykes-Picot agreement (1916), 126, 333

Talabani, Hawry, 346
Talabani, Jalal, 92, 140, 285, 359
Tal Afar, 458–59
Talib, Ali, 270–74, 277, 288
Talib, Tariq, 166
Taylor, Glade, 118–20
Tenet, George, 394
al-Tikriti, Barzan, 338

torture: hunger as protection against, 284; Washington's responsibility for, 326
Trotsky, Leon, 67, 68, 74
Truman, Harry, 19, 377, 378
Turkomans, 339, 342, 344, 345, 348–49, 352–53, 356, 368

Ukrainian troops, 315, 323
United Nations, 389; asked to return to Iraq, 317; in Baghdad, and its bombing, 212–18, 255, 310; CPA endorsed by, 146; DPG's failure to mention, 13; Human Rights Commission, 33; inspectors in Iraq from, 10–11, 24, 82, 130, 388; sanctions on Iraq by, 10–11, 24, 28
United States Armed Forces, 219–50, 296–97, 327–32, 370–74, 397–99; alcohol use in Iraq by, 247, 248; Commanders Fund of, 241, 250, 297; redeployment of, 327; strength needed for Iraq War, 111, 113–16, 118, 244–46, 316, 327
United States Marines, 134, 315–16, 324
universities: debaathification in, 193, 209, 251–52; Iraqi presidents elected by, 187–89

Van Buren, Matt, 373, 403–404
Vidal, Gore, 59
Vieira de Mello, Sergio, 212–18, 384
Vietnam War, 19–20, 26, 32, 87, 103, 233, 243–44, 299, 301, 304, 376, 377, 381, 392, 398, 443, 462; Bush on, 323; neoconservative attitude to, 15
Vilsack, Tom, 376

Wahhabis, 267–69
Wallace, William, 298
Walzer, Michael, 82–83
Ward, George, 131
Warrick, Thomas, 67, 79, 91, 124, 125, 403
Weinberger, Caspar, 53
Wershow, Jeffrey, 101, 210
Westmoreland, William, 120
Wetherington, Karl, 330, 331
Weydemuller, Patrick, 398–99
White, Thomas E., 113, 114, 117
Wieseltier, Leon, 59–60, 87
Wilson, Sir Arnold, 333, 334, 403

THE
ASSASSINS'
GATE

AMERICA IN IRAQ

GEORGE PACKER

About This Guide

The questions and discussion topics that follow are designed to enhance your reading of George Packer's *The Assassins' Gate: America in Iraq*. We hope they will enrich your experience of the history and frontline reporting presented in this unsettling portrait of war.

Introduction

Providing unprecedented insight into America's most controversial foreign-policy decision since Vietnam, *The Assassins' Gate* recounts how the Bush administration set about changing the history of the Middle East and became mired in brutal guerrilla warfare in Iraq. During four tours on assignment for *The New Yorker*, award-winning reporter George Packer observed firsthand the complex struggles of soldiers and civilians from myriad backgrounds. Bringing to life the people, ideas, and history that led America to the Assassins' Gate—the main point of entry into the American zone in Baghdad—Packer reveals the gritty realities of nation-building and insurgency in a war that followed none of the preconceived scripts. The result is a masterwork of journalism, providing answers on a subject seldom addressed with clarity while raising important new questions about the future.

Questions for Discussion

1. What wisdom is revealed in the book's epigraph, written by a Syrian diplomat and poet?

2. The book's prologue describes the crowds that gather at the Assassins' Gate and gives the history of the gate itself (built by Saddam Hussein as an imitation of antiquity). In what way is the gate a metaphor for the current situation in Iraq, and America's role in the world?

3. George Packer offers a history of not only the creation of Iraq but also of American foreign policy in the twentieth century, including portraits of the original neoconservatives. Which aspects of this history were most surprising to you? What should world leaders have learned from this history?

4.   Discuss the men who advocated invading Iraq early on, such as Robert Kagan and Paul Wolfowitz. Is there a common denominator (idealism about democracy, flexing a military muscle) in their rationales? According to Packer's account, why was George W. Bush so determined to topple Saddam's regime?

5.   Chapter three begins with Kanan Makiya's decision not to participate in the State Department's Future of Iraq Project. Were his views about the war misguided? What does his story say about the opinions of exiles?

6.   What did you discover about the Coalition Provisional Authority by reading about administrators such as Drew Erdmann, whose story opens chapter four? What drives Drew, Meghan O'Sullivan, and the numerous other men and women like them who hoped to build representative government in Iraq?

7.   Chapter six describes the transition of authority from Jay Garner to Paul Bremer, who soon issued the uncompromising Debaathification Order. Do you believe that the flourishing insurgency is the result of Paul Bremer's inexperience, or would the situation have decayed just as much under Jay Garner?

8.   How does the rebuilding of Iraq compare to the rebuilding of Japan, Germany, Bosnia, and other postwar scenarios in history? To what degree should the current turmoil in Iraq be attributed to the era of T. E. Lawrence ("Lawrence of Arabia") and British colonialism? What did you make of the Iraqis who told George Packer they thought the British were better than Americans at being occupiers?

9.   Packer observes the problem of unproven accusations, paired with a thirst for vengeance, permeating many of Iraq's factions. What does it take to overcome such deep-seated cultural attitudes?

10. Are looting, sabotage, and the general chaos of Iraq purely a result of too few American troops being sent to move the country from Phase III to Phase IV (combat to stability operations)?

11. Chapter eight introduces Aseel, a progressive Iraqi woman who asks, "Do you think my dreams will come true?" How would you respond to her question?

12. *The Assassins' Gate* provides considerable insight into Iraqi attitudes toward sexuality. What accounts for the obsession with the virginity tests for women? In what way do these attitudes exemplify other aspects of Iraqi culture? Will these attitudes ultimately undermine any hope for peace or human rights in the region?

13. Discuss the experience of journalists as described in *The Assassins' Gate*. What did you discover about the process by which Packer gathered his facts, and the variety of backgrounds among his translators? How has the prevalence of journalists from around the globe, combined with technologies that allow soldiers and civilians to e-mail personal observations to their friends back home, changed the face of war? How has coverage of this war, in which journalists have become targets, compared to the Gulf War, and to Vietnam?

14. In what way does the story of Private Kurt Frosheiser speak to the schism between those who support and those who decry the war? What did you make of the vast differences between the way Kurt's mother and father reacted to his death?

15. In the long run, what will the social repercussions of the invasion be, for both Americans and Iraqis? What might the various figures mentioned in the book say if Packer were to interview them again in twenty years?

16. Do you think American troops will ever leave Iraq altogether? If so, when and how?

Further Reading

A Pretext for War: 9/11, Iraq, and the Abuse of America's Intelligence Agencies, by James Bamford; My Year in Iraq: The Struggle to Build a Future of Hope, by L. Paul Bremer III; Squandered Victory: The American Occupation and the Bungled Effort to Bring Democracy to Iraq, by Larry Diamond; Cobra II: The Inside Story of the Invasion and Occupation of Iraq, by Michael R. Gordon and General Bernard E. Trainor; Cruelty and Silence: War, Tyranny, Uprising, and the Arab World, by Kanan Makiya; Republic of Fear: The Politics of Modern Iraq, by Kanan Makiya; American Theocracy: The Peril and Politics of Radical Religion, Oil, and Borrowed Money in the 21st Century, by Kevin Phillips; Understanding Iraq: The Whole Sweep of Iraqi History, from Genghis Khan's Mongols to the Ottoman Turks to the British Mandate to the American Occupation, by William R. Polk; The Prince of the Marshes: And Other Occupational Hazards of a Year in Iraq, by Rory Stewart